The Pandora Guide to Women Composers

The Pandora Guide to Women Composers
Britain and the United States 1629–Present

Sophie Fuller

Pandora
An Imprint of HarperCollins*Publishers*

Pandora
An Imprint of HarperCollins*Publishers*
77–85 Fulham Palace Road,
Hammersmith, London W6 8JB
1160 Battery Street,
San Francisco, California 94111–1213

Published by Pandora 1994
10 9 8 7 6 5 4 3 2 1

A catalogue record for this book is
available from the British Library

ISBN 0 04 440897 8 (hardback)
       0 04 440936 2 (paperback)

Printed in Great Britain by
Woolnough Bookbinding Limited,
Irthlingborough, Northamptonshire

Contents

Acknowledgements

Many thanks to the following:

All the people who have helped me over the years with memories of friends and relatives, or have shared their own work with me, including Michael Baker, David Bedford, Sarah Burn, Lionel Carley, Sir Edward Compton, Liane Curtis, Paula Gillett, Daphne Henghes, Michael Hurd, Cara Lancaster, Iris Lemare, Anne Macnaghten, Kathleen McCrone, Derek Scott, Rosamund Strode and Elizabeth Wood.

June Gardner at the American Music Center, Tom Morgan and Matthew Greenall at the British Music Information Centre, Nicola Murphy at the Contemporary Music Centre in Ireland and Paul Collen at the Department of Portraits at the Royal College of Music for their invaluable help.

The staff at the British Library, Royal College of Music and Royal Academy of Music Libraries, University of London Library, National Sound Archive, Westminster Music Library, Fawcett Library, Corporation of London Records Office, City of Gloucester Library and Chertsey Museum.

Clare Scherbaum at Boosey and Hawkes, Samuel Roberts at Carl Fischer, Fiona Southey at Novello, Helen Thomas at OUP, Kathleen Kilbane at Peer-Southern, Ed Matthew at Schirmer, Sally Groves at Schott, Christopher Saward at UMP and Elizabeth Webb at the Society for the Promotion of New Music for supplying all sorts of information and to Ladi Odeku and Fred Scott at Composers Recordings, Inc. for their help.

All the composers who supplied me with tapes, scores, details of their lives and cups of tea.

My colleagues and friends at Women in Music and King's College.

Sara Dunn at Pandora without whom this book would not exist, Nicola

LeFanu for many years of support and Jennifer Doctor who has been endlessly generous and inspiring.

John, Prue, Louisa and Emily for all their love and encouragement, Nick for all his help and Elaine, last but never least, for everything.

Preface

I knew when I first heard Maude Valérie White's song 'so we'll go no more a roving' and read her compelling memoirs that the music history I had been taught was missing something vital and exciting. My work with the music of women composers involves a curious combination of deep anger and sadness that so much music has been lost or forgotten and excitement at the power and beauty of the music that has survived.

The history of women as composers of music in the Western classical tradition is not by any means one of doom, gloom and lost opportunities but rather a history of determination and triumph. I am fascinated by the many different ways in which women have expressed themselves through music during the centuries. If I can convey any of the sense of excitement and inspiration that I have found in the work and lives of these women, then this book will have achieved one of its main aims.

It is inevitably a very personal book. Deciding who to include was an extremely difficult task. I set certain basic limits. During the significant part of their careers, the composers lived and worked in Britain, Ireland or the United States. They are women who worked within the tradition of what is usually called classical music, although some of them stretched its boundaries. Even with these limits, the 100 or so women I have written about are just a few of the many hundreds who have written or are writing this kind of music in these countries. I have had to decide to leave out many composers whom other writers might well have included. My selection was not made on any basis of quality. If anything, I simply wanted to present as wide a picture as possible of women from different backgrounds with different career patterns writing different kinds of music.

I am aware that it may at first seem somewhat odd that, given the relative sizes of their countries, there are more British than North-American women in the book. The main reason is that much less has been written on British women composers than their North-American counterparts. There is, for example, no British equivalent to the pioneering books by Christine Ammer and Judith Tick. I felt that it was time to redress the balance. There were also many more women composers working in Britain than in the United States in the earlier periods that this book covers.

One interesting problem I came up against was what to call many of these women. Some of them were known during their lifetimes under several different names, depending on whom they were married to or which pseudonym they were using. I have ended up choosing what I felt to be the name most commonly used in each woman's musical career. In most cases this is the name under which they published their music. So I have used the pseudonym Claribel rather than that composer's married name Charlotte Barnard or even her maiden name Charlotte Alington, although she published some music under this name. But I have used the name Amanda Aldridge, rather than the pseudonym Montague Ring, as this composer was better known by the name under which she taught than that under which she composed.

This is an introductory book, designed to whet readers' appetites and send them off in search of recordings, sheet music and more information. I have not included work lists – for many composers these can be found in the *New Grove Dictionary of Women Composers*. There is a chronological list of the composers (see page 351) and I have given some useful addresses and contacts for those who want to discover more about the growing body of recordings and scores of music by women (see page 365). I have also included suggestions for further reading (see page 354), and these books and articles will themselves point to further sources.

Introduction

The countries we now know as Britain, Ireland and the United States have many rich musical traditions, from the folk music of the Celts and Native Americans to blues, jazz, rock and the other forms of music that have grown from African-American roots. Although women have played important roles in all these traditions, this book is a guide to their work as composers of just one kind of music, usually described as 'classical', 'art' or even 'serious'. It is a music coming from a European tradition and one whose history has usually been presented as a series of 'great composers' – almost without exclusion white men.

When thinking about women's contribution to music, perhaps first of all we need to recognize the many differences between women. Women from different classes and races, different places and periods of history have equally different experiences when it comes to expressing themselves through music. Yet women are linked by the way in which society constructs an identity for them because of their gender and by the boundaries and expectations that society creates for their participation in musical life.

There are many ways in which women have contributed to the classical-music tradition. They have been performers, conductors, teachers, patrons and organizers as well as composers. The history of women composers and other musicians is inextricably caught up with that of the mainstream of music history. Although women have often been regarded as essentially different from men, and in many ways their contributions have been different, they have worked with and alongside their male contemporaries. But all too often their involvement has been forgotten. Remembering and acknowledging their many achievements can only enrich our understanding and bring us a clearer picture of the past.

Some of the earliest music in the

Western classical tradition to have been written down rather than transmitted orally, and therefore to have survived, is the music of Christian worship in the Middle Ages. The daily lives of monks and nuns revolved around a succession of services in which music played a central role. Both monks and nuns wrote and sang the music for these services, and for many centuries the convent was one of the best places for a woman to receive a musical education. Manuscripts from several convents in Germany have preserved the music of some of the earliest-known women composers such as the extraordinary Hildegard of Bingen. In Britain, nuns would also have provided the music for the services in their nunneries although the names of individual composers have not yet been unearthed. A late example of a manuscript from a British nunnery is the 15th-century hymnal from Barking Abbey, which contains music not found in other sources and therefore was probably written by the nuns themselves.

Outside the monasteries and convents in the Middle Ages, secular music was being made both by travelling minstrels and by members of the nobility. The very fact that there is a Middle-English word for a female minstrel – *gliewméden* – shows that such women existed, travelling with their male companions from town to town to perform their music. The poetry and music in celebration of

courtly love that was written by the male troubadour and the female trobaritz flourished in Provence in southern France. In the north of the country these aristocratic musicians were known as *trouvères*. An important patron of such artists was Eleanor of Aquitaine whose second marriage in 1154 was to Henry II of England. One of the female *trouvères* of this time, Marie de France, is thought to have worked at their English court. The words of her works survive but her accompanying music has been lost.

The Middle Ages saw the growth of complicated polyphonic styles of music, and women were excluded from most of the places, such as the cathedrals or universities, where men received the education needed to write such music. Nevertheless, as can be seen from the records of guilds and other organizations, women continued to work as performers throughout Europe during the 15th and 16th centuries, the period known as the Renaissance. The Musicians' Company of London was established in 1472 and included women as well as men.

Throughout the Renaissance, English noblewomen learned to sing and to play instruments such as the lute or the harpsichord within the home, in spite of the views of writers such as Philip Stubbes who warned his readers in 1583, 'if you would have your daughter whoorish, bawdie, and uncleane ... bring her up in musick and daucing'.

Some of these women wrote music as well as playing it. Anne Boleyn (1507–30), the ill-fated wife of Henry VIII, was renowned for her skill as a musician and is thought to have written the mournful song 'O Death Rock Me Asleepe'. Women in positions of power, such as Elizabeth I (1533–1603), were often influential patrons of music. Elizabeth's reign was a time when English music flourished, with the madrigals, motets, songs and viol music of composers such as Thomas Tallis, William Byrd, Thomas Morley and John Dowland.

Music continued to flourish in England in the early years of the 17th century until the Commonwealth ban on much of musical life in the 1640s and 50s which was lifted in 1660 with the restoration of Charles II. Aristocratic women continued to be taught to sing and play music as some of the ladylike accomplishments with which they were expected to grace the home. They appear to have played a range of instruments. In his diary for June 1661, Samuel Pepys wrote of 'two young gentlewomen' and that 'one of them could play pretty well upon the viallin'. More common instruments for women to play were the various keyboard instruments or the lute. The three songs composed by Mary Dering that have survived show that women also wrote music although most noblewomen would not think of exposing themselves to such public attention by publishing their work. Women were not supposed to be anything more than objects for display. In the words of the contemporary poet Anne Finch, Countess of Winchilsea:

Alas! a woman that attempts the pen,
Such an intruder on the rights of
    men ...
They tell us we mistake our sex and
    way;
Good breeding, fashion, dancing,
    dressing, play
Are the accomplishments we should
    desire ...

Women took part in the masques and other entertainments by composers such as Henry Purcell and John Blow. Two of the best known of these works, Purcell's *Dido and Aeneas* and Blow's *Venus and Adonis*, were performed at girls' schools. The earliest public concerts in Britain, organized by Thomas Britton from 1678, involved women performers.

With the beginning of the 18th century came the introduction of Italian opera into Britain and the opportunity for women to work as opera singers. One of the earliest British prima donnas was Katharine Tofts (c. 1685–1756) who demanded and received huge payments for her performances and had, according to Colley Cibber, an 'exquisitely sweet, silvery tone of voice'. The 18th century was a period when many aspects of British musical life were dominated by musicians and composers from Europe. George Frederic

Handel settled in Britain in 1712, followed in 1762 by Johann Christoph Bach. British singers faced competition on the London stage from Italian rivals, not only from women such as Francesca Cuzzoni (1698–1770) and Faustina Bordoni (1700–1781), who both sang for Handel in the 1720s and 30s, but also from male castrati such as the hugely popular Farinelli (1705–82).

The triumphant careers of the early prima donnas were tempered by their reputations as demanding, extravagant and immoral, all stereotypes of the female opera singer that existed into the 20th century. One of the most successful British singers, Elizabeth Billington (1768–1818), whose parents were both musicians, started her career as a keyboard soloist and published two sets of keyboard sonatas at the age of twelve. She was just one of a growing number of women who started to publish their music during the later 18th century and into the early 19th century. Almost all these women were professional musicians, either singers, pianists or harpists. They usually came from musical families, were taught music as the family trade and married other musicians. The music they wrote included sonatas, songs and other pieces for the amateur market as well as more complex works that they would have played or sung themselves.

Meanwhile, upper-class women continued to be taught music as one of the skills that, along with drawing and embroidery, would enhance their marriage prospects. In many scenes of her novels Jane Austen paints scathing pictures of these women and their musical accomplishments. In *Sense and Sensibility* (1798), Marianne Dashwood, having been asked to play, 'went through the chief of the songs which Lady Middleton had brought into the family on her marriage, and which perhaps had lain ever since in the same position on the pianoforte; for her ladyship had celebrated that event by giving up music, although by her mother's account she had played extremely well, and by her own was very fond of it'.

Nevertheless, many women did become very skilful musicians, singing and playing the harpsichord, pianoforte, harp and guitar, instruments that were regarded as sufficiently ladylike. They did not usually play violins and flutes, instruments thought suitable only for men. The early 19th-century diaries of the landowner Anne Lister, an unconventional woman in many ways, show that she played the flute. But even a woman such as Mary Granville (Mrs Delany, 1700–1788), a celebrated harpsichord player and friend of Handel, never played outside her circle of friends and relatives. In the middle of the 18th century one woman, Ann Ford, was arrested on the orders of her own father to prevent her performing music in public.

The history of Western classical music in the United States is in many ways very different from that of Britain. Even more than Britain, North America was a country where the classical musical world was dominated by foreign musicians. This may have led to a general willingness to embrace any native composers, whether they were men or women, and it does seem that certain women throughout the 19th and 20th centuries may have found it easier to work as composers in the United States than their contemporaries did in Britain. Yet many of the factors that affected women's involvement in music, such as questions of propriety or capability, were remarkably similar in both countries.

The musical life of the early settlers in North America revolved around sacred vocal music. No women appear to have contributed to the hymn books and psalm collections of the 18th century. By the end of the century, European musicians were beginning to visit North America and some stayed and settled there. These musicians were often from Britain and included women singers such as Mary Ann Pownall (Mrs Wighton, 1751–96), who wrote and published a few songs while she was in North America during the last four years of her life. In the early 19th century choral societies were established in some of the larger cities and one of these, the Handel and Haydn Society, was unusual in employing a woman, Sophia Hewitt

(1799–1845), as its organist and accompanist for several years.

Throughout the 19th century a middle- or upper-class woman's place was still firmly within the home, whether in Britain or North America. Music was regarded as a particularly feminine art form and women from these classes were expected to be able to play and sing but always as amateurs. Appearing on the public stage was still something that no 'respectable' woman would do, unless perhaps for a charitable occasion. Professional musicians belonged to a lower class. Clara Kathleen Rogers remembered a holiday in south Wales in the 1850s when the parents of a family she met on a beach would not allow their children to play with her because her father was a musician. George Eliot's novel *Daniel Deronda*, first published in 1876, contains fascinating pictures of contemporary attitudes towards music and musicians. The well-to-do Arrowsmiths disown their daughter when she decides to marry the composer Herr Klesmer; and the penniless, aspiring singer Mirah Lapidoth shows her innate gentility when told that her voice is only suitable for private drawing-rooms by replying, 'I would rather get my bread that way than by anything more public'.

Women from middle- or upper-class backgrounds performed in public only under financial pressure or with much trepidation. In the late 1850s Clara Louise Kellogg (1842–1916), one of the earliest American-born opera singers, explained to her friends that she was about to make her debut as a singer and that she would quite understand if they wanted nothing more to do with her. Nevertheless, increasing numbers of middle-class women did enter the professional musical world during the 19th century, mostly as teachers but also as performers and composers.

Women from musical backgrounds or those who ignored the social pressures of respectability were becoming more and more visible as celebrated performers. One of the best known pianists of her day was Clara Schumann (1819–96), who often played in Britain. Arabella Goddard (1836–1922) and Teresa Carreño (1853–1917) were among the well-known pianists who were born or grew up in Britain or the United States. Many British performers received their training at the Royal Academy of Music which had opened in London in 1823. Girls were taught harmony and counterpoint, piano, singing, harp, Italian language, dancing and 'writing music'. Boys were taught the same subjects, with the exception of dancing, and also learned the violin, cello and oboe. Respectability was an issue in the Academy's early days. A report to one of the founders shows that one of the first students, a Miss Jay, was removed from the Academy by her father 'merely because she was to have gone to the London Tavern to perform amongst the other students'.

In spite of women's obvious achievements and abilities as performers, it was often asked whether they had the stamina and strength for playing certain instruments. Although women had been working as organists since the early years of the century, as late as 1893 the *Girl's Own Paper* was advising a reader, 'Organ-playing is not considered advisable for women. Strong, unmarried, middle-aged women may play the foot-keys without suffering from the unsuitable strain on the back and loins ...'. The violin gradually became an accepted instrument for women. A writer in *Etude* in 1901 remarked that 25 years previously 'the mere thought of a refined young gentlewoman playing the violin, either in private or in public, was indeed intolerable'. Although the occasional professional woman musician had played the violin at public concerts in Britain since the 18th century it was not until the careers of Wilma Normann-Neruda (Lady Hallé, 1840–1911) and Camilla Urso (1842–1902) that women established international reputations as violinists.

This was also the age of the 'diva', the enormously popular female opera singer who was adored but at the same time often seen as little more than a glorified prostitute. The Swedish singer Jenny Lind (1820–87), hugely popular in Britain and the United States, did much to change public attitudes. She maintained a spotless image, always wearing plain white dresses, doing frequent charitable work and emphasizing her devout protestant Christianity. The public identification of opera singers with fallen women doubtless had much to do with the roles they had to perform. The American singer Emma Abbott (1850–91) refused to sing the role of Violetta in Giuseppe Verdi's *La Traviata* on moral grounds but by doing so ruined any chance of a successful European career. Many women, such as the British contralto Clara Butt (1872–1936), established themselves exclusively as singers of concert music which enabled them to avoid appearing in theatres. African-American and British black singers had no choice. It was not until the middle of the 20th century that African-American singers such as Marian Anderson (1897–1993) were allowed to perform in the major opera houses of the United States. Earlier African-American singers such as Elizabeth Taylor Greenfield (c. 1817–76) or Sissieretta Jones (1869–1933) had to be content with singing extracts from opera in the concert hall.

Continuing in the tradition of the 18th-century women composers, many of these successful performers, such as the pianist Kate Loder or the singer Charlotte Sainton-Dolby, also wrote music and established careers as composers. Loder studied at the Royal Academy of Music where women were always able to study composition. A report from 1824 claims that 'Some of our present pupils are making rapid strides in composition ... two of the girls shew great talent in this line ...'. Loder later taught harmony herself at the Academy, one of the very few women during the 19th century to teach anything there other than singing or piano. Other women who wrote music, such as Augusta Browne or Oliveria Prescott, also worked as music teachers or journalists.

By the 1860s there had been a large increase in the number of women of various classes writing and publishing music, especially ballads and songs. For upper-class women at this time, publishing their own compositions could be seen as entering into the public, commercial world, something a well-bred woman was taught she should avoid. This led to many women in both the United States and Britain publishing music under pseudonyms such as 'A Lady', 'Dolores' (pseudonym of Ellen Dickson, 1819–78) or 'Claribel' (pseudonym of Charlotte Alington Barnard). But whether they wrote under a pseudonym or not, some of the best-known and best-selling song-writers of the time were women. In fact, songs and ballads in a popular style became so identified as a women's genre that men started writing under female pseudonyms.

Florence Fare, a composer listed in Aaron Cohen's *International Encyclopedia of Women Composers*, was actually the pseudonym of Alfred William Rawlings. The American composer Septimus Winner published songs under the pseudonym Alice Hawthorne.

Women's particular identification with songwriting was to last well into the 20th century. As society began to accept the idea of large numbers of women composing and publishing music, it was still expected that they would write in a style and genre that mirrored the Victorian image of woman as pretty, delicate and undemanding. There were, of course, women in the middle of the century who ignored these expectations, such as Kate Loder who wrote an opera, an orchestral overture and much chamber music, or Alice Mary Smith whose orchestral music was often heard in London in the 1860s. But there were many reasons for women to concentrate on writing songs. Songwriting could be extremely profitable and was one of the few ways for any composer to make large amounts of money. There was a great demand for sheet music from the amateur market and sales could be huge. Publishers did all they could to promote their songs, including the introduction by Boosey in 1867 of highly successful ballad concerts.

For women, earning money from sheet-music sales and performance royalties was, along with teaching, one of the few ways in which they could make a living from music. Other professional jobs in the musical world were closed to them. They were excluded from most careers in the church, although some women did work as organists, and they were not allowed to play in professional orchestras or even study at the universities, let alone teach at them. This exclusion from many musical careers also limited women's experience of music-making. Unlike many other genres, songs could be performed within the home, which was seen as woman's natural sphere, and by the composer herself or with friends without the involvement of large groups of other musicians.

Although composition classes were generally open to them in Britain and the United States, women were not often encouraged to study composition at the conservatories and so frequently lacked the education needed for the composition of large-scale works. Clara Kathleen Rogers, who had studied at the Leipzig Conservatory in the late 1850s when women were not admitted to composition classes, wrote in her memoirs: 'Had I acquired early in life a good technique in writing for instruments I really think I might have accomplished something worth while in orchestral composition'. Liza Lehmann also had regrets about her early education: '... I often wish I had given to the study of composition the years I devoted to the assiduous study of singing ... but in those days women-composers were not thought of at all seriously'. Added to insufficient education for women was a widespread belief that they were simply not capable of writing in genres of any greater complexity than the song, being unable to cope with the necessary logical creative thought. It must be remembered that this was also an age that believed that women's reproductive organs would shrivel up if they went into higher education! A lack of belief in their own abilities was often internalized by women themselves.

The importance of the pioneering work of these songwriters and other composers of the mid-19th century should not be underestimated, and nor should the music that many of them wrote. Their achievements paved the way for the explosion of music by women that was heard in both Britain and the United States in the 1880s and 90s. This was the time of composers such as Hubert Parry, Charles Villiers Stanford and Arthur Sullivan and the so-called Renaissance in British music history. In the United States it was the time of the New England School of composers such as Edward MacDowell, George Chadwick and Horatio Parker. It was also the age of the 'new woman', a time when women were fighting for legal equality, for the right to education and for the vote. They were taking up bicycling and other sports and challenging many of the assumptions about what they

could and could not do with a new ferocity and determination. In the mid–1890s the composer Hope Temple (pseudonym of Dotie Davies, 1859–1938) gave an interview to *The Young Woman* in which she declared, 'I am fond of pretty well all sports – riding, rowing, shooting, mountaineering. And for my own part I don't see why women should be debarred from any of these things ... Let all spheres of action, all professions be thrown open to women ... if a woman qualifies herself for the Bar, why should she not be a barrister?'

This growing refusal to conform to expectations led to more and more women in both Britain and the United States writing music in all styles and genres, even though this often led to accusations that they were being unwomanly or simply imitating men. Women such as Amy Beach, Dora Bright, Rosalind Ellicott, Margaret Ruthven Lang, Ethel Smyth and many others showed great determination in their attempts to get their large-scale orchestral works performed by a musical establishment that still felt women were not capable of writing anything other than songs or piano music. Some women, such as Maude Valérie White, Liza Lehmann or Frances Allitsen, continued to concentrate on songwriting, still the most profitable and accessible genre for women. Whatever they wrote, those women who did not come from musical backgrounds still had to fight their parents' objections to the idea of music as a suitable career for a respectable woman. Maude Valérie White, for example, wrote of having to overcome her mother's 'prejudice against even the shadow of public life'.

Many of the women composers of the 1880s and 90s also worked as professional performers. This gave them many opportunities to promote their own music. Ethel Barns, for example, was also a violinist and frequently included her own chamber works in her recitals. As celebrated concert pianists, Dora Bright and Amy Beach both gave performances of their own piano works before their marriages. Many women gave up performing on marriage. For a woman to continue to appear in public implied that her husband was unable to support her. Clara Kathleen Rogers, who had established a very successful career as a singer and a teacher, married at the age of 34 and remembered wondering: '... would it be proper for me to keep up my musical activities after marriage ... I felt, without any prompting, that it would be right for me to retire from public life ...'. But she was not attracted by the idea of doing nothing other than housework and socializing: 'It even seemed wicked to let the strivings and attainments of a lifetime go for naught ...'. With the support of her husband, she compromised and gave up performing but continued to teach.

For several women, including Rogers as well as Liza Lehmann and Amy Beach, giving up performing after they were married enabled them to concentrate on composition and devote time and energy to it that they would otherwise have spent in touring and rehearsing. Not all women stopped working as performers after they were married. Those who married other musicians, or for whom the income was necessary, usually continued to appear in public. Many women, such as Rosalind Ellicott, Margaret Ruthven Lang, Oliveria Prescott, Ethel Smyth or Emma Steiner never married at all, either because they were attracted to women rather than men or because they found it difficult to reconcile the demands of a career with duties as wife or mother.

Several married women, such as Ethel Barns or Helen Hopekirk, kept their maiden names for professional purposes. Others, such as Carrie Jacobs-Bond or Charlotte Sainton-Dolby, hyphenated their new names to their old ones. Some composers continued to use pseudonyms. Mary Frances Bumpus, whose parents were much opposed to her taking up a musical career, wrote under the name Frances Allitsen. A few women used male pseudonyms, such as Helen Rhodes (1858–1936), the composer of extremely popular songs who wrote as Guy d'Hardelot, a name taken from her maiden name and the place of her birth. In an interview with *The Musical Leader* she explained that 'this name had led to many mistakes as to my sex, for everyone thinks I am a man ...'.

Several composers, particularly at the start of their careers, published works using just their initials and surname and thereby remaining sexually ambiguous. This, combined with society's expectations of the kind of music that women were capable of writing, led to some surprises. George Bernard Shaw described a perfor-mance of one of Smyth's orchestral works in 1890: 'when E.M. Smyth's heroically brassy overture to Antony and Cleopatra was finished, and the composer called to the platform, it was observed with stupefaction that all that tremendous noise had been made by a lady'.

The increasing prominence of large-scale compositions by women led to much discussion about women's capabilities as composers and whether they could write 'great music' or not. In 1880 the American music critic George Upton published a book on *Woman in Music* in which he claimed, 'It does not seem that women will ever originate music in its fullest and grandest harmonic forms. She will always be the recipient and interpreter but there is little hope that she will be the creator.' This was expanded on by the British *Musical Times* of 1887, in an article written by a woman:

... that no woman has ever been a great composer is an accepted fact; that she is never likely to become so, more than a probability ... To obtain music of the highest order the composer must have an imagination touched to the finest issues and the true mathematical instinct. Rare such a union must always be, and with the relatively smaller area to choose from, for we suppose no one would deny that the average capacity of women is enormously less than the average capacity of men, such a case is most unlikely to occur among women.

In 1901 Landon Ronald was still explaining to readers of *The Lady's Realm* that '... to compose there must exist an innate creative instinct – a faculty to invent; and since the world began, man has always proved himself superior to woman as inventor and creator'.

Many people, both women and men, argued against these views, usually pointing to women's lack of opportu-nity, education and encouragement. Stephen Stratton in his paper 'Woman in Relation to Musical Art', given to the Royal Musical Association in 1883, explained that '... woman's genius has been developed in exact proportion to the educational advantages at her command ...' In a 1910 article on 'Women and Music' in *The Musical Times* Ernest Newman pointed out that 'till social and economic conditions enable women to make composition their life-work, as men can do, it is idle to dogmatise upon what the natural limitations of the feminine brain may or may not be'. Most of those who believed in women's capabilities still felt strongly that women and men were essentially different and that once women had been given more opportunities to learn to compose, the music that they would produce would be a new kind of music, expressing female or feminine qualities. An anonymous article on 'The Feminine in Music' in *The Musical Times* in 1882 urged:

> The woman artist should always regard her art from a woman's point of view. Were this done distinctiveness would follow. The result may not compare with the works of men for strength and comprehensiveness, but that is neither necessary nor desired. What we regard as both necessary and desirable is the emancipation of woman within her own musical domain ... It will be of good augury for the sex and for music when some pioneer woman arises, who, having mastered the power of musical expression, consults her own nature and not the productions of men, when determining what to say and how to speak.

In his 1883 paper, Stephen Stratton disagreed:

Women have received much advice to cultivate art from the feminine stand-point. What is feminine? Is working at the forge, driving barge horses, ruling a great empire? All these we allow women to do in this country. If a woman has what we call a masculine mind, is it not, she being a woman, really feminine?

The composer Ethel Smyth, in her 1928 essay 'A Final Burning of Boats', felt that the qualities that distinguished women's art were energy and directness and added:

> ... I fancy that even an average woman has more inward freedom than men; is less conventional, and on the other hand less haunted by the dread, if an artist or a writer, of being commonplace. None of the few women composers who have contrived to get their songs printed are afraid of melody. I think men are.

Women's exclusion from much of the machinery of the musical establishment and from male societies and networking prompted them to set up their own organizations and develop their own support systems. The Royal Society of Musicians, an organization founded in 1738 for the welfare of professional musicians, did not let women become members and, although it gave support to its members' widows, female musicians who fell on hard times were left to their own devices. In 1839 a group of women, including Charlotte Sainton-Dolby and Ann Mounsey Bartholomew, established the Royal Society of Female Musicians 'for the relief of its distressed members'. In 1866 the Royal Society of Musicians finally admitted women and the two organizations merged.

The support and encouragement that friendships between women composers provided was very important. In her memoirs Liza Lehmann remembered that when she was young, 'I simply worshipped at the shrine of any woman who wrote music. Maude Valérie White, Marie Wurm, Chaminade – they seemed to me goddesses!' Lehmann and White later became friends and played each other their works. Many of the women composers working in late 19th-century Boston, such as Amy Beach, Margaret Ruthven Lang, Helen Hopekirk and the young Mabel Daniels, were close friends.

In the early years of the 20th century more formal organizations were set up to encourage the work of women as composers. In Britain the Society of Women Musicians was formed in 1911 with Liza Lehmann as its first president. The founders aimed to provide a centre where women musicians and composers could meet for informal concerts, lectures and discussions, bring composers and players together so that composers would have opportunities of hearing their works, promote public concerts and advise women on professional and business matters. Many composers, including Maude Valérie White, Rebecca Clarke and Ethel Smyth, were early members, and the Society's work was supported by several men, such as W.W. Cobbett who established the Society's library of chamber music. An organization specifically for composers, the Society of American Women Composers, was founded in the 1920s with Amy Beach as its first president. Among the early members were Marion Bauer, Gena Branscombe, Mabel Daniels and Mary Howe.

From the late 1860s onwards, women's music clubs in the United States provided a focus for many women's mainly amateur musical activities. Part of the women's study club movement, they provided opportunities for women to learn about music (with frequent lectures on women composers) and to listen to concerts given by other members or by visiting professionals. By 1919 there were more than 600 clubs throughout the country.

Performances in semi-private, semi-public spheres are a much neglected aspect of music-making in both Britain and the United States. In Britain from the 19th century until well into the 20th century the private concerts of music patrons such as the Gladstone family, Sir Edward and Lady Speyer or Frankie Schuster provided invaluable opportunities for the performance of a wide range of music involving a variety of composers and musicians, both amateur and professional. Many new works, such as Liza Lehmann's *In a Persian Garden*, were heard at such occasions which often involved women as performers, composers and hosts.

Women's work as patrons and organizers was of considerable significance in the late 19th and early 20th century. Many women founded or took major roles in organizing the music festivals that were an important part of musical life in both Britain and the United States. They included Mary Wakefield (1853–1910), who founded the Westmoreland Musical Festival in the north of England during the 1880s, and Elizabeth Sprague Coolidge (1864–1953), who established the Berkshire Festival of Chamber Music in Massachusetts in the early years of the 20th century, and encouraged chamber music through competitions and commissions. In 1908, after her husband composer Edward MacDowell's death and on his wishes, Marian MacDowell (1857–1956) founded the MacDowell Colony in New Hampshire, a place where composers and other artists could spend time away from everyday life concentrating on their creative work. The Colony was always notably supportive of women composers and provided a vital haven for many women throughout the century.

Women's orchestras were one of the most visible results of women coming together to form alternative organizations to the male institutions from which they were excluded. In 1880 *The Musical Times*, reporting on an 'Orchestra of Ladies' playing at Newbury in Berkshire, remarked that 'twenty years ago the idea ... would have been received with derision ...' and wondered whether 'with a band of such powerful attraction, we can hope to secure perfectly independent critics'.

Like most musical activities the early women's orchestras and ensembles can be divided into amateur and professional groups. The amateur musicians seem to have played a strictly classical repertoire. Parry wrote his *Lady Radnor's Suite* (1894) for Lady Radnor (Viscountess Folkestone) and her women's orchestra which performed in England during the 1880s and 90s. Professional women musicians played in orchestras and bands such as the British Anglo-Saxon Ladies' Band, Caroline Nichol's Boston Fadette Lady Orchestra or the Vienna Damen Orchestra which toured the United States in the early 1870s. These orchestras played in theatres as vaudeville acts and at the seaside as well as being hired for weddings and garden parties. Their repertoire seems to have consisted of 'light' classics and arrangements of popular songs and ballads.

In England during the first world war many women from these orchestras played in the major symphony orchestras while the male musicians were away fighting. When the war was over a fierce campaign was waged to establish women musicians in these orchestras on a permanent basis. But few conductors would allow women (other than harpists) in their orchestras, with the exception of Henry Wood who had been employing women in his Queen's Hall Orchestra since before the war. When Hamilton Harty was appointed conductor of Manchester's Hallé Orchestra in 1920 he actually sacked all the women players and, despite vigorous attacks from Ethel Smyth, refused to employ any women (again, other than harpists) during his 13 years with the orchestra.

Women's continued exclusion from the major orchestras led to the formation of several professional women's symphony orchestras in the 1920s and 30s. These seem to have been more successful in the United States than in Britain. One of the earliest was the Philadelphia Women's Symphony Orchestra, founded in 1921 by the trumpet player Mabel Swint Ewer. The following year Gwynne Kimpton founded the British Women's Symphony Orchestra. In 1923 the London Women's Symphony Orchestra was formed by Elizabeth Kuyper who moved to the United States when it failed and tried again, equally unsuc-cessfully, with the New York American Women's Symphony Orchestra in 1924. More successful orchestras that played an important part in the musical life of their respective cities were the Women's Symphony Orchestra of Chicago, formed in 1924, and the Boston Women's Symphony Orchestra, formed in 1926. The pioneering conductor, Ethel Leginska (pseudonym of Ethel Liggins from Hull, 1886–1970) worked with both these orchestras. Other notable conductors were Frédérique Petrides (1903–83) who founded the Orchestrette Classique in 1932 and Antonia Brico (1902–89) who founded the New York Women's Symphony Orchestra in 1934. Leginska and Brico also worked with male orchestras, as did women conductors such as Iris Lemare (b. 1902) in Britain. After women had taken the places of men again during the second world war, most orchestras stopped refusing to employ women although some held out for many years. It was not until 1980 that the London Symphony Orchestra employed a woman musician who was not a harpist.

During the 1930s, years when the music of composers such as Igor Stravinsky, Claude Debussy and Arnold Schoenberg was becoming more widely known, many women were establishing careers as composers. By this time it was generally accepted that there was no stigma attached to women of any class appearing as public figures or making careers as musicians although there were still certain assumptions about the kind of music that women would write. A group of extremely talented women studied at the Royal College of Music in London during the late 1920s and early 1930s. These women, including Dorothy Gow, Imogen Holst, Elizabeth Maconchy and Grace Williams, remained close and supportive of each other throughout their lives. They all had their early work performed at the Macnaghten–Lemare concerts during the 1930s. This series of chamber and orchestral concerts promoting the work of unknown British composers had been the idea of Elisabeth Lutyens and was put into action by violinist Anne Macnaghten (b. 1904) and conductor Iris Lemare. Works by women featured heavily in all the programmes, not so much as a conscious gesture but simply because Macnaghten and Lemare were programming the works of their friends.

The critics found that much of this music was not what they were expecting from composers who were women. One particular concert in 1935 at which new works by Lutyens, Maconchy and Williams were played, prompted the reviewer for the *Glasgow Herald* to wonder 'when a woman composer is going to write some music reminiscent of the sex as it used to be'. William McNaught in the *The Evening News* saw the concert as 'an interesting study of the young female mind of

today. This organ, when it takes up composition works in mysterious ways. No lipstick, silk stocking or saucily tilted hat adorns the music evolved from its recesses ... On the whole these three ladies were too formidably clever, or tried to be'. In the United States, Ruth Crawford was writing in an even more radical musical language but, probably because she was not associated with any other women composers, does not seem to have been perceived as such a threat.

During the first half of the 20th century women were able to move into many areas of life that had previously been closed to them. But even so there were many restrictions still in place. A backlash against the feminism of the late 19th and early 20th century and the economic effects of the depression denied women many opportunities in the 1940s and 50s. For some women the pressures to marry and then devote their lives to looking after house, husband and children, rather than to a career, were overwhelming. Many found themselves returning to composition only after their children had grown up. Some women, such as Nancy Van de Vate, knowing that they wanted to bring up children, chose composition as a career because they knew they could work from home. There were women who had supportive husbands or were strong enough to demand the time and space to compose. Other women remained single. Many women still lacked confidence in their own abilities. Both Dorothy Gow and Ina Boyle, for example, suffered from extreme shyness and were incapable of promoting their own work, despite endless support and encouragement. Even some women composers themselves found the idea of women working throughout their lives as professional composers somehow hard to take seriously. In 1949, when she was 42 and working as a freelance composer, Grace Williams wrote a letter to a friend in which she described the idea of a symphony by a woman of 50 as 'something revolting – and perhaps a bit pathetic'. She was later to complete her Second Symphony at the age of 50.

Most women continued to fight throughout the 20th century against stereotypes and continued to compose, even through years when their work was ignored by the musical establish-ment. For women as well as men, per-formances of their music often depended on the prevailing musical trends within influential organizations such as the BBC. In a world where vig-orous self-promotion is vital, women's socialization as compliant and accommodating was of little help in furthering their careers. Expected to be gentle and nurturing, women found, and still find, that assertiveness was interpreted as aggression. Several women composers, such as Daphne Oram, Margaret Lucy Wilkins, Daria Semegen and Jean Eichelberger Ivey,

have found that working with sound in an electronic studio frees them from reliance on the male-dominated machinery necessary for achieving acoustic performances, especially of larger works.

The growth of the women's movement in the late 1960s brought about a new wave of organizations that aimed to promote the work of women composers and musicians. The League of Women Composers (later the International League of Women Composers) was founded in the United States in 1975 by Nancy Van de Vate. The following year Tommie Ewart Carl founded American Women Composers. In 1987 in Britain the organization Women in Music was formed with aims remarkably similar to those of the Society of Women Musicians in 1911. The Society of Women Musicians had folded in 1972, having modified its aims over the years to focus almost exclusively on getting women orchestral players accepted into the major orchestras.

Several new women's orchestras were founded, such as the Bay Area Women's Orchestra in the United States and the European Women's Orchestra in Britain. These differed from the earlier women's orchestras in that they were formed specifically to play repertoire, both old and new, by women com-posers. Conducting, a very visible position of power, continued to be a difficult area for women to break into. Most women conductors work with

ensembles that they have formed themselves, making very occasional guest
appearances with other orchestras.

The development of mass communication and information technology has
enabled many women to exploit new
ways of ensuring that their work
reaches as wide an audience as
possible. The pioneering recording
company Leonarda was established in
the United States by Marnie Hall in
1977 and focuses on producing both
historical and contemporary music by
women. Getting compositions into
print and thereby available both for
wider performance and for posterity
has always been important for any
composer. The relationship that
publisher Arthur Schmidt built up with
many of the Boston women composers
in the late 19th and early 20th centuries has ensured that many of their
works have survived. Many women
today, such as Julia Usher or Margaret
Lucy Wilkins, have set up their own
publishing companies to distribute
their work while others have been
taken on by the major publishing
houses. In a burst of feminist scholarship since the early 1980s, musicolo-
gists, analysts, cultural historians and
critical theorists have produced a
growing body of work examining
women's involvement in music and
developing various feminist critical
approaches to the study of music.

The debate over whether women's
music is somehow different from that
written by men is still continuing
today, often repeating the arguments
of the 1890s. There are still people who
believe that women are physically
incapable of writing certain kinds of
music. In the 1970s Libby Larsen was
told by a colleague in graduate school
that, as a woman, she would not, of
course, be able to write large-scale
works. Various studies of the brain
have concluded that women are not
'naturally' suited to studying mathe-
matics, playing chess or writing music.

There are many women composers
working today who refuse to be
categorized as such, seeing their
gender as totally irrelevant to their
work. Others are less sure. In her
answer to a questionnaire sent to
women composers by Ellen Barkin in
1981, Marga Richter said that she
believed that her music was different
from that of men, 'After all, I am a
woman and I express what I am.'
Miriam Gideon felt that 'women are
freer and more generous about
expressing emotion than men (wow!)
and this often seems to carry over into
their music'. In 1987, in her article
'Master Musician: An Impregnable
Taboo?', Nicola LeFanu argued:

> Most people believe that music
> transcends gender, that you can't tell
> if a composition is by a man or a
> woman. I know, however, that my
> music is written out of the whole-
> ness of myself, and I happen to be a
> woman. I'm not bothered by whether

I compose better or worse than a man, because I take both possibilities for granted; but I am interested in what I can do that is different. In my thoughts and actions there is much that is similar to those of a man, and much more that is different. Can it really be otherwise in my music?

The history of women's work as composers of classical music is largely one of spirit and persistence in the face of a widespread belief that writing music was simply not something that women should or could do. The position of women as composers has been enormously varied. In some ways women had more access to opportunities for writing music and getting it heard in the 12th century than they did in the 15th century, or in the 1890s than in the 1950s. To work as composers women need confidence and belief in themselves, as well as access to education and performance opportunities. The contributions that women from the past have made are often forgotten, only to be remembered and then forgotten again. The music of Fanny Mendelssohn Hensel (1805–47) was being performed and written about in Britain in the 1890s only to be forgotten and then 'rediscovered' in the 1980s. During her lifetime Maude Valérie White was regarded as one of Britain's foremost songwriters yet she is not mentioned in any of the major textbooks on the British musical Renaissance that have been written in the last 20 years. Do we remember her now only to find that future generations will have to 'rediscover' her?

Part of the problem is that many women composers worked in ways that fall outside the main concerns of musicology. Our music history is primarily that of complex, large-scale works played in a public forum by professional performers and written by composers who devote themselves as exclusively as possible to composition. By ignoring everything else, the work of many people, not just that of women, is lost. We need to accept the challenge presented by the work of women to the way in which we understand the past, the present and the possibilities of the future. Above all, there is a lot of music out there waiting to be heard.

... if something of the immense
savour of life that hope deferred has
been powerless to mar; if the sense
of freedom, detachment and serenity
that floods the heart when suddenly,
mysteriously, the wretched back-
water of a personal fate is swept out
of the shadows and becomes part of
the main current of human experience; if even a modicum of this gets
into an artist's work, that work was
worth doing. And should the ears of
others, whether now or after my
death, catch a faint echo of some
such spirit in my music, then all is
well ... and more than well.

Ethel Smyth,
A Final Burning of Boats (1928)

Harriet Abrams
1760–1822

Harriet Abrams was unusual among 18th-century women musicians in not having parents who were musicians, although most of her many brothers and sisters also made musical careers. Her father and mother, John and Esther Abrams (or Abrahams), were probably servants.

A pupil of Thomas Arne, Abrams made her debut as a soprano at the age of 15 at Drury Lane in October 1775 in an afterpiece *May Day* written for her by David Garrick with music by Arne. The prompter William Hopkins wrote in his diary: 'She is very small, a swarthy complexion, has a very sweet voice and a fine shake, but not quite power enough yet – both the piece and the young lady were receiv'd with great applause.' Later that season she appeared in Charles Dibdin's *The Padlock*. During the following season (1776–7) she was paid £2 10s a week for a variety of roles.

Abrams continued to sing at Drury Lane until 1780. In 1776 she had appeared with her sister Theodosia at the Concerts of Ancient Music, and gradually moved away from the opera house to concentrate on singing for types of entertainment, such as oratorio performances or private concerts, that were seen as more respectable than those that took place in the theatre. She sang at the Handel Memorial Concerts in 1784 and at many of the concerts of the Academy of Ancient Music. For the 12-concert Academy season of 1787–8 she and Theodosia were paid 60 guineas, a fee considerably higher than that of any of the other singers.

Abrams also organized many concerts herself, including a series of 'Ladies' Concerts' that took place at Lord Vernon's house in the winter of 1791–2 and many benefit concerts for herself and her sisters. When he was in London in the 1790s, Joseph Haydn performed at several of her benefits. A collection of letters from Abrams to Lord Hardwicke written in the mid–1780s show how important patrons and benefactors were to musicians. On behalf of herself and her sisters Theodosia and Eliza, Abrams expresses grovelling thanks to his Lordship as well as continuously asking for his support for her benefit concerts. She also gave private performances at his house in Richmond. The King was another benefactor, as the sisters remind him in a petition sent shortly before Abrams' death, seeking an official appointment for Theodosia's husband Mr Garrow which will provide support for all of them as they live together 'in the utmost harmony'.

Abrams started publishing her own music in the 1780s and doubtless sang it at her concerts. Her first works were two sets of Italian and English canzonets for one or two voices with harpsichord or pianoforte and occasionally violin accompaniment. The duet 'And must we part' from the second set became particularly popular, with several reprintings during her lifetime. All Abrams' surviving music is vocal, including glees and duets as well as songs. A collection of 12 of her songs dedicated to Queen Charlotte was published in 1803 by Lavenu and Mitchell. As in many of her songs, the texts she sets, although mostly by male authors, tend to express a woman's point of view. The vocal parts are often elaborate and decorative and the music frequently mirrors the text, as in 'The Gamester' to words by Miles Peter Andrews, in which a wife sits waiting for her errant husband, and in which the words 'the clock struck one ... two ... four ...' in succeeding verses are preceded by one, two and then four single, ominous notes in the accompaniment. In 'A Ballad of the Eighteenth Century', with words by Mrs Hunter about 'a hapless maniac', Abrams makes extensive use of mad-sounding semitones; and in 'The Eolian Harp', to words by Joseph Atkinson, she uses intricate vocal melismas to depict the sound of a harp. One of Abrams' most popular songs was 'Crazy Jane', a setting of verses by Matthew Lewis, first published in about 1800 and still being printed and arranged long after her death in 1822.

Eleanor Alberga
b. 1949

Eleanor Alberga's music has an immediate appeal, with vital rhythms and luxurious harmonies always within a clearly defined structure. She was born in Jamaica and begged to be allowed to learn to play the piano after hearing the music lessons at the school run by her mother. She had piano lessons from the age of five and later studied singing as well as teaching herself to play the guitar. She started making up piano pieces and songs when she was about 10 years old but did not think of herself as a composer until much later. While still at her Catholic convent school she began playing the guitar with the highly successful Jamaican Folksingers.

In 1970 Alberga came to England on a scholarship to the Royal Academy of Music where she studied piano and voice. After leaving the Academy she began to establish a career as a concert pianist as well as working as a dancer with the semi-professional African dance company Fontom From. In 1978 she joined the London Contemporary Dance Theatre as a pianist and started composing for them in about 1980. The music she was writing at this time was mostly for piano but she also produced scores such as *Mobile I* (1983) for string orchestra, written for the Midland Dance Company. The title of this work reflects the way in which Alberga saw the parts relating to each other, each moving in their own differing but interrelated ways. She used the same procedure in *Mobile II* (1988) for clarinets, saxophones, piano and string quartet. Her piano works written for dance often included electronics or tape, used to stretch the sound world available using one performer as in *Stone Dream* (1986) for prepared piano and tape or *Whose Own* (1988) for prepared piano and sound processor.

Alberga left the London Contemporary Dance Theatre in 1988 to concentrate on a freelance career as a pianist and composer. She played with Graeme Fitkin's Nanquidno (four players on two pianos) for several years and wrote

Eleanor Alberga

Music in 1990. The first movement, 'Red Dawn', uses syncopated rhythmic patterns in the woodwind over slow-moving string chords with the strings taking up the dance-like motifs. The calm and meditative slow movement, 'Mirrors of Blue', is followed by 'Golden Palace', a joyful finale that again uses repeated rhythmic patterns.

Another work from 1990, *Dancing with the Shadow* for flute, clarinet, violin, cello, piano and percussion, shows a change in Alberga's music away from the straightforward tonality of her earlier works towards a more complex and dissonant language. The work was commissioned by contemporary music group Lontano as a dance piece choreographed by Sue MacLennan. It also stands as a concert piece and any of the five movements can be played separately. A suite using the first, fourth and fifth movements has been frequently performed. A dramatic duo for clarinet and piano is followed by a quintet with fluid, sensuous melodic lines underpinned by rich harmonies before the catchy rhythms of the energetic final sextet.

music for the group including *Hill and Gully Ride* (1990), a five-movement musical evocation of the Jamaican landscape. Like most of her early music, this work uses a language based on tonal harmonies and exciting, driving rhythms. Alberga's orchestral work *Sun Warrior* was premiered by the European Women's Orchestra conducted by Odaline de la Martinez at the first Chard Festival of Women in

In 1991 Alberga wrote the music for the film *Escape from Kampala*, which was nominated for a BAFTA award (British Academy of Film and Television Arts) in 1992, and composed *The Edge* for flute, cello, sitar and keyboards for Priti Paintal's group Shiva Nova. In the same year she wrote another orchestral work, the overture *Jupiter's*

Fairground, for the European Women's Orchestra.

Alberga's musical language continues to change. *Nightscape: The Horniman Serenade* (1993) for two oboes, two clarinets, two basset horns, four horns, two bassoons and double bass incorporates elements of jazz. Her String Quartet no. 1 (1993) uses much more dissonance than any of her previous works. Alberga was a featured composer at the Glamorgan Festival in 1993, alongside John Adams and Steve Reich, a composer she has always admired. 1994 saw several important commissions. 'One Cezanne Apple' is a lament for voice written for singer Kate Westbrook's music-theatre project *Even/Uneven*. Other works included String Quartet no. 2, premiered by the Smith Quartet at the Greenwich Festival in London, and *Snow White*, a work for narrator and orchestra with words by Roald Dahl, written for the London Philharmonic Orchestra.

Amanda Aldridge
(Montague Ring)
1866–1956

Amanda Aldridge was the daughter of the famous tragic actor Ira Aldridge and his second wife, Swedish opera singer Amanda Pauline von Brandt. Ira Aldridge was an African–American who had emigrated to England in the 1820s. He died on tour in Poland in August 1867, only 18 months after his youngest daughter Amanda had been born at the family home in Upper Norwood, London.

Aldridge's mother made sure that her two daughters and son were brought up with a sense of pride in their African heritage. Aldridge later added her father's name Ira to her own. As children, Aldridge and her elder sister Luranah were sent to a convent school in Belgium. One of Aldridge's earliest appearances as a singer was at a Crystal Palace concert in 1881. Two years later, at the age of 17, she won a scholarship to the newly founded Royal College of Music where she studied singing with Jenny Lind and George Henschel. She also took harmony and counterpoint lessons with Frederick Bridge and Frances Edward Gladstone.

Aldridge made a successful career as a contralto, often appearing with her brother Ira Frederick Aldridge as accompanist until his early death in 1886 at the age of 25. Her sister Luranah also became a singer. She lived for many years in Paris, appeared at the Bayreuth Festival of 1896 and was a close friend of George Sand and Richard Wagner's daughter, Eva. Aldridge's own singing career ended after an attack of laryngitis which damaged her voice.

In the early years of the 20th century Aldridge often appeared as accompanist to Luranah in concerts at the Queen's Small Hall and other well-known London venues. She also concentrated on teaching and composing, playing an important part in the musical life of London's black community and the many visiting African–American musicians. In the early 1920s she helped tenor Roland

Hayes and his accompanist Lawrence Brown when they first arrived in London from the United States. Hayes went on to sing her songs throughout England and Europe and Aldridge remained in contact with Brown for the rest of her life, leaving him £10 and a portrait of Pushkin in her will. Her singing pupils included the daughter of African nationalist Herbert Macaulay, contralto Ida Shepley and Marian Anderson. She also taught members of the white upper-classes. In 1930 she gave elocution lessons to Paul Robeson before his first appearance as Othello.

Aldridge started composing in the early years of the 20th century, when she was in her 30s. She always published under the name Montague Ring, claiming that this was in order to keep her work as singer and teacher separate from her work as a composer. Most of her music is in a popular style, often using syncopated dance rhythms. Her best-known work is *Three African Dances* (1913), originally written for piano but endlessly arranged for various combinations of instruments. The slow, central movement, 'Luleta's Dance', uses themes reminiscent of music from West Africa. Other piano dance suites included *Three Arabian Dances* (1919) and *Carnival* (1924). Aldridge also published over 25 songs. These were often followed by a dance

for the piano. She wrote her own words for many of her earliest songs such as 'My Dreamy, Creamy Colored Girl' and 'When the Colored Lady Saunters Down the Street'. Another early song 'Where the Paw-Paw Grows', subtitled 'African Serenade', set words by Henry Downing, an African–American writer living in London. Her last two published songs 'Summah is de Lovin' Time' and 'Tis Morning' (1925) are settings of the famous African–American poet Paul Laurence Dunbar. 'Summah' is dedicated to the Robesons and is more complex than any of her earlier songs. Other poets whose work she set include the popular writers of song lyrics F.E. Weatherly, Frederick G. Bowles and P.J. O'Reilly.

Although Aldridge appears to have stopped writing (or at least publishing) music by the end of the 1920s, she continued to teach and play an important part in musical life, broadcasting on radio and appearing on television into her 80s. She never married, claiming that as well as her teaching work and composition she had for much of her life the added responsibility of looking after her elderly mother and her sister. Luranah had developed severe rheumatism and spent the last 20 years of her life in a wheelchair, killing herself in 1932. Aldridge died the day before her 90th birthday in 1956.

Frances Allitsen

(Mary Frances Bumpus)
1848–1912

Frances Allitsen was the pseudonym of Mary Frances Bumpus, best known for her fiery patriotic and religious songs. She came from a family of London booksellers who objected strongly to the idea of musical careers for women. Allitsen described her early life as one where '... the chief talk was on the subject of garments, and the most extravagant excitement consisted of sandwich parties'.

As a young woman Allitsen concentrated on writing, producing a novel and several short stories which do not appear to have been published. Eventually, in the early 1880s when she was in her 30s, she wore down her parents' opposition. With the encouragement of principal Weist Hill, she began studying at the Guildhall School of Music, paying for her tuition by giving music lessons. During her time as a student she had many works performed at student concerts, usually to enthusiastic reviews. In 1884 she won the Lady Mayoress's prize for her *Slavonic Overture*. Allitsen's first public appearance had been in 1881, when she sang in several concerts with the Kilburn Musical Association. She did not make a career as a singer although she became well-known as a teacher and occasionally performed in public as an accompanist.

Allitsen kept a detailed record of financial transactions with her various publishers from 1885 to 1896. At first she tended to sell her songs outright for about five guineas, sometimes with a further lump sum if sales reached 2,000 copies. Towards the end of the 1880s, as her songs were reaching a wider public, she was able to negotiate a royalty of anywhere between 2d and 6d a copy. Her *Album of Six Songs*, published by Ascherberg in 1889, brought in over £18 in six years on a royalty of 6d a copy after the first 500 sold. By the end of the century many of her songs had achieved great popularity, especially after the famous singer Clara Butt took up the jingoistic 'There's a Land, a dear Land' (a setting of words by Charles Mackay) during the Boer War. Allitsen's sacred songs, such as 'Song of Thanksgiving' and 'The Lord is my Life', were equally well known and widely sung.

Towards the end of her life, Allitsen suffered from bad health and general despondency, as can be seen from a short diary that she kept for a few months in 1911. A typical entry reads: 'As usual – health delicate, people unkind, remiss and neglectful – professional anxieties and indecisions. Awful mental depression.' The professional anxieties included attempts to get her opera *Bindra the Minstrel* put on in Berlin and legal wrangles with Boosey over the publication of her dramatic cantata *For the Queen*. The projected production of *Bindra* never took place and 18 months later, on 2 October 1912, Allitsen died of pleurisy at the age of 63, leaving the copyrights of her most famous songs to the Salvation Army and the Gordon Boys' Home.

None of Allitsen's orchestral music appears to have survived although there are records of several short works having been performed at London concerts. She does not seem to have written much chamber music and wrote only a few piano pieces, including a *Caprice* (1886) played by Vladimir de Pachman and a lost sonata. The majority of her music was vocal. She published nearly 150 songs in a variety of styles. The forthright strength and stirring rhythms and

harmonies of many of her patriotic and religious songs, together with her slightly ambiguous first name, led many people to assume that her music was the work of a man. Other songs were slightly more subtle, such as her moving setting of Alfred Tennyson's 'Come not when I am dead'. In several songs she adds to the already rich harmonic texture of her piano part with an accompaniment for violin or cello.

Her songs use texts from a range of poets and include several German settings. In 1893 Robert Cocks issued her *Eight Songs from Poems by Heine* in their 'Series of Artistic Songs'. More experimental and typically dramatic writing can be heard in her song cycle *Moods and Tenses* (1905), subtitled Phases in a Love Drama, to texts by various poets. In *Four Songs from 'A Lute of Jade'* (1910), settings of translations of old Chinese texts, she used a sparer harmonic texture to bring an eastern atmosphere to the music.

Allitsen wrote several large-scale vocal works with orchestral accompaniment. Her 'scena' *Cleopatra* was composed for Clara Butt who sang it several times at various venues including a Crystal Palace Saturday concert in 1900 and one of her own orchestral concerts at the Royal Albert Hall. Setting text largely from Shakespeare's *Anthony and Cleopatra* with the words for the central aria by Thomas Collier, this dramatic work explores the wide range of Butt's deep and rich voice and was published by Boosey in 1904.

Another large-scale work was the cantata *For the Queen*, to a libretto by Frank Hyde, for baritone, mezzo-soprano, bass, chorus and orchestra which was first heard at the Crystal Palace in 1911. It tells the story of a defeated king in 12th-century eastern Europe who is stung into action by his queen singing him war-like songs and offering herself to go back and stir up the people to rebel against the usurper. Elements of this story, in particular the power of song to move and inspire, are also found in *Bindra the Minstrel*, Allitsen's only opera. This two-act work for which she wrote her own libretto is set in 10th-century western Asia. It is about a king whose throne is usurped but who is saved by his trusty minstrel, Bindra, who rekindles the love and devotion of King Ita's people through his songs. Central to this fiercely passionate and declamatory work is a theme called the 'Song of the Sword', the national song of the defeated country. This is at first heard in an orchestral prelude and then again in the orchestra as Bindra begs King Ita to be strong. Bindra also plays a fragment of the theme as he is winning over the people, and it is heard again as he explains to a messenger that it is the signal for attack. Finally the song is heard in its full majesty, sung by Bindra and his minstrels before armed men rush in and kill the usurper. *Bindra* has still never been performed although it was published by Weekes & Co. in 1912, the year that Allitsen died.

Beth Anderson
b. 1950

Beth Anderson grew up in Kentucky. She had piano lessons as a child and was encouraged by her piano teacher to compose. Some of her pieces were performed by her high-school band, and in her last years at school she discovered serialism.

From 1966 for two years she studied at the conservative University of Kentucky as a piano major. Already fascinated with the music and ideas of John Cage, she organized a chaotic 'Happening' – complete with dogs and confetti – at Kentucky before moving to California and finishing her degree at the University of California where she studied with Cage. After graduating in 1971, Anderson supported herself by teaching voice and piano and performing. At the same time she was studying for master's degrees in piano and composition at Mills College with various teachers including Terry Riley. Anderson soon established a reputation as one of the more avant-garde composers on the West Coast and began to express some of the concerns of the growing feminist movement in her works.

A significant year for Anderson was 1973, when she became co-editor and publisher of the avant-garde musical and literary magazine *Ear*, and wrote several important works. These included her first 'sound environment' piece, *Hallophone* for two saxophones, steel guitar, voice, tape, slides and dancers, and two 'string quartets', *I Am Uh Am I* and *Music for Charlemagne Palestine* (actually for two string players and two lighting technicians). In the same year, Hysteria, a group of women composers and performers of which Anderson was a member, gave the first performance of *Peachy Keen-O* for organ, electric guitar, vibraphone, percussion, voices, tape, dancers and light.

At the end of the year, Anderson's opera *Queen Christina* was performed at Mills. Loosely based on the life of the 17th-century Swedish queen, this work opens with a recording of a woman talking about the women's movement over a recording of a woman singing a Schubert song played at half speed. It uses an intriguing mixture of music, dance, audience participation and visuals including erotic gay movies and Bay Area women's groups processing on stage for Christina's coronation. The following year Anderson wrote another work based on the life of a strong historical woman, her oratorio *Joan*, to her own text for four singers, dancer, orchestra, tape and live electronics which was commissioned by and premiered at the Cabrillo Music Festival.

In 1975 Anderson moved to New York where she continued to publish an East Coast edition of *Ear* and to write for other magazines as well as teaching music in various colleges and accompanying dance classes. Finding herself short of the money needed to put on concerts of her music using other performers she concentrated on working with text-sound pieces which she could perform herself. Her earliest text-sound work, in which words are used to make music, a genre Anderson has described as 'avant-garde rap', was *Torero Piece* of 1973. This work was first performed by Anderson and her mother and explores their particular relationship as well as that between all mothers and daughters.

Throughout the 1970s and into the early 80s Anderson produced a series of short text-sound pieces, such as *If I*

Were A Poet (1975) for a fast-moving voice playing with the words from the line 'If I were a poet, what would I say?' or *The People Rumble Louder* (1975) which uses the same technique with the line 'The people rumble louder than the poet speaks' and in which the voice is gradually drowned out by a rumbling tape. Several of the pieces use drumming accompaniments such as the insistently frantic *I Can't Stand It* (1976) and the more funky *Ocean Motion Mildew Mind* (1979). *Country Time* (1981), somewhat reminiscent of Edith Sitwell and William Walton in *Façade*, creates an evocation of the countryside with lists of clover, daisies, bumble bees, alfafa and peachtrees over drums and bird song. In 1981 Anderson put together a series of 18 radio programmes in a series entitled 'Poetry is Music' which presented text-sound works by herself and other composers and poets.

Anderson continued to teach, working at the College of New Rochelle for eight years between 1978 and 1986. She also wrote music for plays and film and played the piano for dance classes at the Martha Graham and Alvin Ailey dance schools. Being asked to produce music for dance that was easy to follow and that had regular rhythmic patterns was one of the factors that led to a gradual but radical change in Anderson's musical language. In works such as *Skate Suite* (1979) for violin, cello, electric bass and voice and *The Praying Mantis and the Bluebird*

(1979–80) for flute (or other treble instrument) and keyboard or harp, she introduced a much simpler way of writing, using straightforward rhythms and tonal or modal harmonies and often quoting from or imitating folk music.

In 1981 Anderson published an article, entitled 'Beauty Is Revolution', in *Ear* magazine explaining that the idea of writing music that was simply aiming to be beautiful was a revelation to her. She began to work by using cut-ups of such music (either newly composed or taken from an existing source) that she then put together to make 'a harmonious whole'. This is the way that the orchestral piece *Revelation* (1981) and its shortened version *Revel* (1984), were constructed. The title refers to the *Ear* article and the work presents a joyfully rich pattern of sounds and rhythms.

Anderson had always used elements of popular music in her work and the progression to writing musicals was an easy one. *Nirvana Manor* (1981) with lyrics by Judith Morley and *Elizabeth Rex; or the Well-Bred Mother Goes to Camp* (1983) with lyrics by Jo-Ann Krestan were followed by *The Fat Opera* (1993), again with lyrics by Krestan for a story written jointly with Anderson. A work building directly on a popular musical form, *Belgian Tango* (1984), written for piano and later arranged for instrumental ensemble, is a lush and slightly peculiar dance which Anderson has described as 'Satie in South America'.

In the mid-1980s Anderson started using 'swale' as a title for many of her works. A swale is a patch of marshy land, especially in the middle of the prairie, where wild plants grow. Anderson finds the image particularly resonant for her collages of different musical swatches. The first works to use the title were two one-movement string quartets commissoned by the Soldier String Quartet, *Pennyroyal Swale* (1985) and *Rosemary Swale* (1986). Like many of the swales, *Pennyroyal Swale* creates a vividly American sound-world with repeated fragments of fiddle tunes and other folk-like material. Later swales include two brass pieces *Brass Swale* (1991) for brass quartet and *Saturday/Sunday Swale* (1992) for brass quintet. *August Swale* (1992) is for flute, oboe, horn, bassoon, violin and viola and *Guitar Swale* (1993) is for two guitars. Anderson's first orchestral swale was *Minnesota Swale* (1994), commissioned by the Minnesota Sinfonia. This piece reworks material from *German Swale* (1990) for DX7 synthesizer and piano on tape which had been written for a group of German galleries and museums. Anderson uses and reuses a variety of material, including the opening succession of bare fourths, a repeated semiquaver pattern, a jaunty folk-like tune, a more plaintively lyrical theme and a percussion cadenza, to create an instantly appealing and enjoyable work.

Ethel Barns
1874–1948

Ethel Barns was born in 1874, although a date of 1880 has often mistakenly been given. In January 1887, at the age of 13, she entered the Royal Academy of Music. Her principal study was the violin, still a fairly unusual choice of instrument for a girl student although both Wilma Normann-Neruda (Lady Hallé) and Camilla Urso had been regarded as leading violinists in Europe and the United States since the 1870s.

Barns studied with Emile Sauret and was soon winning prizes in violin and piano playing and in harmony. One of her earliest public appearances as a violinist was at an Academy concert in St James's Hall in 1890 where she played two movements from a violin concerto by Louis Spohr. The following year she sang and played the violin at a concert in Cadogan Gardens and published a tuneful *Romance*, one of her earliest works for violin and piano.

In 1892, at 18, she became a sub-professor at the Academy, giving her services in return for continuing her lessons with Sauret. A versatile musician, Barns appeared as a pianist at an Academy concert in January of that year, playing a Beethoven piano concerto. A few months later she played the violin part of her own *Polonaise* for violin and piano at an Academy concert in St James's Hall. In the same year, two of her songs, 'A Fancy' and 'Waiting for Thee', were published by Stanley Lucas. While she was at the Academy, Barns also wrote the first movement of a violin concerto. She remained at the Academy until 1895, by which time she was appearing regularly as a violinist in London's concert halls, including the Crystal Palace. In 1894 she was heard at the Steinway Hall playing violin pieces by Martin Sarasate, Gabriel Fauré and a *Mazurka* of her own.

Barns had met the singer Charles Phillips as early as 1891 when she performed at one of his concerts. They married in 1899 and, like many women who married other musicians, Barns did not give up performing. She even kept her own name for her work as a performer and composer. Together the couple instituted the very successful series of Barns-Phillips Chamber Concerts at the Bechstein Hall, a series which provided an important platform for Barns' chamber music and songs. She also played her music at other concerts such as one at the Steinway Hall in 1900 at which she performed her Violin Sonata no. 1 in D minor. A reviewer for *The Musical Times* described this work as 'terse and deft' and compared it to the work of Edvard Grieg, Anton Rubinstein and Johannes Brahms. This first sonata remained unpublished but her Violin Sonata no. 2 in A major, op. 9, was published by Schott in 1904, the year that Barns played it at a Barns-Phillips concert. A typically tempestuous and lyrical work with rich, sonorous piano harmonies and a difficult but always violinistic solo part, it was also performed by Joseph Joachim.

In 1904 Barns' Piano Trio in F minor was played at a Barns-Phillips concert, and two years later she performed her third violin sonata at her first public performance after a serious illness. Neither of these works appears to have survived. In 1907 her *Concertstück* for violin and orchestra in D minor, op. 19, was premiered at the Proms. The reviewer for *The Musical Times* gave this work a characteristically back-handed review, 'Though not strong the work is graceful, and may be termed

Ethel Barns

feminine in the best sense of the word.' The following year it was published by Schott with the orchestral parts arranged for piano.

Barns seems to have established a contract with Schott, who between 1907 and 1928 published an elegant series of at least 35 of her works for violin and piano. These include the richly romantic *Chant Élégiaque* (1907), *Hindoo Lament* (1907) with open fifths and repeated grace notes, the complex *Idylle Pastorale* (1909) with no key signature and the simple teaching pieces *Eight Pièces* (1910). Schott did not publish Barns' intense and difficult Suite for violin and piano, op. 21, which was played, along with four of her piano pieces, at a Barns-Phillips concert in 1908.

Barns' Violin Sonata no. 4 in G minor, op. 24, performed at a Barns–Phillips concert in 1910 and published by Schott the following year, is another difficult work which shows a distinct change in her writing towards a more impressionistic musical language. The slow second movement, 'Elégie', opens with an atmospheric, chromatic progression of fourths and fifths in the piano which leads into a beautifully languid violin melody. This kind of writing can also be seen in *Crepescule*

(1913), a short piece for violin and piano.

In 1911 W.W. Cobbett commissioned a work from Barns for the Musician's Company. Barns often performed the resulting *Fantasie Trio* for two violins and piano with her old teacher Sauret. Although Barns concentrated on writing for the violin, she also produced some rather unadventurous songs and a few other instrumental works including an *Idylle* (1913) for cello and piano and several dramatic piano pieces such as the exciting *Cri du Coeur* (1916). Barns continued writing into the 1920s, performing her fifth violin sonata in 1927 and publishing three pieces for violin and piano in 1928. Little seems to be known about the final years of her life. She died in Maidenhead on the last day of 1948.

Maria Barthelemon
c. 1749–1799

Maria Barthelemon, born Mary (Polly) Young, was the daughter of organist and treasury clerk Charles Young and part of a large musical family. Two of her sisters and three of her aunts worked as singers. Barthelemon appears to have been brought up by her aunt Cecilia who had married the composer Thomas Arne in 1737.

In 1755 Barthelemon went with the Arnes and several other singers, including her sister Elizabeth, to Dublin where she made her stage debut singing in Arne's opera *Eliza*. *Faulkner's Dublin Journal* reported that 'Miss Polly Young, a Child of Six Years of Age, pleased and astonished the whole Company, having a sweet melodious Voice, accenting her Words with great Propriety, and Singing perfectly in Time and Tune'. A year later Thomas Arne abandoned his wife and returned to England. Barthelemon remained with her aunt in Dublin and continued to perform at the theatres and the pleasure gardens. The Arnes were eventually reconciled in the 1770s

with Barthelemon acting as intermediary.

Barthelemon returned to England in 1762 and made her London debut singing and playing the harpsichord at Drury Lane in *The Conscious Lovers*. In 1766, at the age of about 17, she married the French violinist and composer François Hippolyte Barthelemon who had arrived in England the previous year and was working as principal violinist of the orchestra at the opera. The Barthelemons often worked together. In the early 1770s they were both working at the Marylebone Gardens in London. They gave a joint benefit concert in 1774 and in 1776–7 toured Germany, Italy and France where they performed to Marie Antoinette.

By the 1780s it seems to have become difficult for Barthelemon to secure work, not having the support of the necessary benefactors and patrons. In November 1784 a complaint by her was published in the *Morning Post* in which she details refusals to employ her from the opera houses, the theatres, public and private concert series and the pleasure gardens and 'humbly begs to know in what manner she should act in this unfortunate situation, having not the least misconduct or indecorum to charge herself with knowingly!'. Maybe the answer lay in an unwitting arrogance. Earlier that year she and her husband had performed in Dublin from where the singer and actor Mrs Billington had written to a friend, 'the Barthelemons are as much detested here as they are everywhere else'. Nevertheless, the Barthelemons were close friends of Joseph Haydn who spent much time with them when he was in England.

Barthelemon died in September 1799. Her only surviving instrumental works are a set of six sonatas for harpsichord or pianoforte with a violin accompaniment, published in about 1776 and dedicated to Queen Charlotte. They are all fluent, two-movement works that could be performed by amateurs. Barthelemon's other surviving music is all vocal. Her set of *Six English and Italian Songs,* op. 2, was probably published in the early 1780s and was dedicated to the Countess of Salisbury. The long list of subscribers to this publication included members of the aristocracy and well-known members of the musical establishment such as Dr Burney and Dr Hayes, the music professor at Oxford University. These songs were doubtless performed by

Barthelemon herself. They are elaborate, operatic settings with some dramatic writing and long, taxing melismas. The voice, which covers a wide range, is accompanied by strings.

In 1795 one of Barthelemon's anthems was performed in Brighton at a benefit concert for the School of Industry and the Sunday School of the New Chapel. This may have been one of the *Three Hymns and Three Anthems*, op. 3, that were published sometime in the early 1790s. These works were composed 'for the Asylum, and Magdalen Chapels' and were dedicated 'to the governors of those charities'. The subscribers included Harriet and Theodosia Abrams, Jane Guest and Joseph Haydn. They are short works setting either verses from psalms or words by James Merrick and using a mixture of solos, duets and choral writing.

Barthelemon's last surviving work was *An Ode on the late providential preservation of our Most Gracious Sovereign*, op. 5, to words by Baroness Nolcken. The published score of this work suggests an instrumental accompaniment that included horns, suitable for the fanfare-like opening. The piece consists of a 'maestoso' accompanied recitative followed by a solo aria, ending with a duet, repeated as a chorus.

The Barthelemons had one child, Cecilia Maria Barthelemon, born in

1770, who was also a musician. As well as playing the harpsichord and harp and singing, she published several accompanied sonatas in the 1790s as well as writing a memoir of her father which appeared as the preface to his oratorio *Jefte in Masfa*. She married twice and the date of her death is unknown.

Ann Mounsey Bartholomew
1811–1891

Ann Mounsey Bartholomew was a prolific composer. Her published music for the piano is mostly in dance forms such as waltzes, mazurkas, polkas, quadrilles and marches although she also wrote sets of variations and songs without words. Writing in *The Englishwoman's Review* in 1887, André de Ternant found her piano works 'worthy to be classed among the brightest examples in the Mendelssohn school'. But most of Bartholomew's output was vocal, ranging from oratorio, cantata and part-song through hymns and liturgical works to duets and songs with English and German texts.

She was born Ann Sheppard Mounsey in London in 1811. Although neither of her parents were professional musicians, she was sent at an early age to study music at Johann Logier's Academy in London. When the German composer Louis Spohr visited this establishment in 1820 he singled out the nine-year-old girl for praise and published her harmonization of a melody in his memoirs. She later studied with Samuel Wesley and Thomas Attwood.

In 1828, at the age of 17, Bartholomew became the organist of a church at Clapton and the following year took a post as organist at St Michael's in Wood Street. She also taught the piano, with aristocratic pupils such as the daughters of Count Munster, the Minister of State for the Kingdom of Hanover. One of her earliest compositions to be published was a song 'The Frost King' to words by William Bartholomew, issued in 1830. This highly descriptive work was subtitled 'A Fantasia' and makes much use of icy semitones. Other early publications included the canzonet 'Love' which appeared in *The Musical Keepsake* in 1834 and the Italianate cantata *The Farewell* to words by 'L.E.L.' which was sung at the City Amateur Concerts sometime in the early 1830s. Her songs were also heard at the 'Nobilities and Public Concerts'.

Several of Bartholomew's early works were written for dancing, such as *The Brunswick Quadrilles,* for piano or harp, dedicated to the Duchess of Gloucester and giving instructions for the steps to be danced. She also wrote more elaborate piano pieces such as the 'rondo varié', *Le Départ pour Munich,* a long, virtuosic piece dedicated to Johann Baptist Cramer. Other early instrumental works include the lively *Six Polonaises* for piano and violin.

In 1834 Bartholomew became a member of the Philharmonic Society, and in 1837 she was elected to the post of organist at St Vedast in Foster Lane after an open competition. She retained this post for nearly 50 years. At some time in the late 1830s she used the pseudonym Phaeton to publish a rather uncharacteristic work, a topical, comic song 'The Daguerreotype', dedicated to Louis Daguerre, one of the pioneers of photography who invented the daguerreotype in 1838.

Bartholomew was one of the founder members of the Royal Society of Female Musicians in 1839. This was an organization that distributed funds 'for the relief of its distressed members' and one which she supported for many years, writing a collection of *Six Songs* for its benefit. In 1843 Bartholomew established a series of Classical Concerts at Crosby Hall in London. The aim of this critically acclaimed series was to provide choral and solo sacred music at a reasonable price. She herself played the organ at these concerts, sometimes including her own music. Works by her friend Felix Mendelssohn were also heard at the concerts, including the hymn *Hear My Prayer* (1844), which he wrote specifically for the concerts, at the request of William Bartholomew.

In 1853, at the age of 42, Bartholomew finally married this writer, whom she may have known as early as 1830 when she set his poem 'The Frost King'. They certainly had known each other for some time before they married, as they collaborated on *The Child's Vocal Album* in the early 1840s. William Bartholomew was best known as translator, adapter and librettist for many of Mendelssohn's works and also provided the texts for many of Bartholomew's vocal works. Bartholomew published a wide variety of music in the 1850s, including two sets of six four-part songs, opp. 30 and 37; two collections of three-part songs and glees entitled *Polyhymnia*, opp. 32 and 33; and several piano pieces such as the complex *Variations for the Pianoforte on the Portugese Hymn Adeste Fideles*, op. 34.

In 1855 Bartholomew's long oratorio *The Nativity*, op. 29, to words by her husband was first heard at St Martin's Hall in a performance conducted by John Hullah. The same year her short

Ann Mounsey Bartholomew

after many years of illness. Bartholomew spent the rest of her life living with her younger sister Elizabeth Mounsey in the house in Brunswick Place, London, to which they had moved with their parents when they were children. Elizabeth Mounsey was also an organist and a composer who published works for piano, organ and guitar. Together, the sisters had published a collection of psalms and hymn tunes entitled *Sacred Harmony*, sometime in the early 1860s. This was followed by another collaboration, *Hymns of Prayer and Praise*, published in 1868. In 1875 Bartholomew published her sacred cantata *Supplication and Thanksgiving* with words that had been selected from the Psalms by her husband. She continued to compose and publish piano pieces and songs for several years, winning great praise from *The Musical Times* for her

eight-part choral piece, *A Choral Ode*, op. 31, also to words by her husband, was performed at Birmingham for the laying by Prince Albert of the foundation stone of the Midland Institute.

William Bartholomew died in 1867

Six Songs to words by Shakespeare, Edgar Allen Poe, Thomas Hood and others, published in 1882, when she was in her 70s. By the end of her life Bartholomew described herself as 'a great invalid' and she died in 1891 at the age of 80.

Marion Bauer
1887–1955

The youngest of seven children, Marion Bauer was born in Walla Walla, Washington where her French parents ran a shop. Her father, who had been an enthusiastic amateur musican, died when she was three and the family moved to Portland, Oregon. Bauer had her first piano lessons from her eldest sister Emilie Frances who went on to study music at the Paris Conservatory and moved to New York where she worked as music critic. Emilie was an important influence on Bauer and continually supportive of her career, often providing the money for her studies. After leaving school at 16, Bauer joined her sister in New York where she started to write songs and continued her piano and harmony studies with Emilie and other teachers.

In the spring of 1906, when she was 18, Bauer went to France to stay with violinist Raoul Pugno and his family whom she had met and taught English when they were in the United States the previous year. Pugno gave her piano lessons and introduced her to

Nadia Boulanger, who was exactly her age. Bauer gave Boulanger English lessons in exchange for harmony lessons, becoming the first of Boulanger's many American pupils. Bauer stayed in France until early 1907. On her return to New York she began teaching theory and piano and getting her impressionistic songs published and performed as well as continuing her own studies.

In 1910, at the suggestion of conductor Walter Henry Rothwell, Bauer went to Berlin for a year to study counterpoint and form. She continued to write songs, and on her return to New York in 1911 arranged a seven-year contract with publisher Arthur Schmidt. She began to write piano pieces and chamber music as well as songs, producing works such as *Up the Ocklawaha* (1913), for violin and piano, written for her friend, the well-known violinist Maud Powell.

Towards the end of the decade Bauer made her first visit to the MacDowell

Colony. Like many other composers she was to spend much time composing and writing there. The surroundings of the Colony provided the inspiration for one of her best-known piano works, the suite *From New Hampshire Woods* (1923). Bauer continued to study and returned to Paris in the spring of 1923 where she spent nearly three years taking lessons in fugue with André Gédalge and making important contacts with French musicians and composers. During her time in France she wrote several chamber works including *Fantasia Quasi una Sonata*, op. 18, for violin and piano and a String Quartet, op. 20. She returned to the States in January 1926 when Emilie became seriously ill.

After Emilie's death a few months later, Bauer took over her job as New York music critic for *The Musical Leader*. Writing about music played an important part in Bauer's musical career. She worked as a critic all her life and wrote articles for journals such as the *Musical Quarterly* as well as several books about music. Three of these, *How Music Grew* (1925), *Music Through the Ages* (1932) and *How Opera Grew* (1956), were written in collaboration with Ethel Peyser. Two others, the popular *Twentieth Century Music* (1933) and *Musical Questions and Quizzes: a Digest of Information about Music* (1941), were written on her own.

In 1926 Bauer joined the teaching staff in the music department of New York University where she was to teach composition, form and analysis as well as aesthetics and music history for the next 25 years. She provided an inspiring role model for many of her women students such as composers Julia Smith and Nettie Simmons. She also taught at the Juilliard School of Music and at a variety of summer schools.

Bauer was always supportive of American music in general and contemporary music in particular. In 1921 she had been the only woman founder member of the American Music Guild and in 1926 joined the executive board of the League of Composers. Although after the 1920s her own music was no longer regarded as particularly modern or radical, she always helped to promote those whose music was, through her work as a teacher and lecturer and with organizations such as the American Composers' Alliance and the Society for the Publication of American Music. One of the ultra-modern composers whose work and career she was always keen to support was Ruth Crawford whom she met at the MacDowell Colony in 1929.

Bauer's own music continued to show the influence of her years spent in France, remaining basically tonal and impressionistic although becoming increasingly dissonant. She sometimes used elements of music from other cultures in works such as *Indian Pipes* (1927) for orchestra or *A Lament on African Themes* (1928) for chamber orchestra. Performances of her music were not frequent. In 1936 her Sonata for viola and piano, op. 22, was first performed at a League of Composers concert, and in 1940 her Concertino for oboe, clarinet and string quartet, a work commissioned by the League of Composers, was broadcast.

The 1940s saw Bauer composing an increasing number of orchestral works including the *Symphonic Suite* (1940), op. 34, for strings, and *American Youth* (1943), op. 36, a concerto for piano and orchestra written for and first performed at the High School of Music and Art in New York. She also arranged several earlier works such as *Up the Ocklawaha* and *Sun Splendor* for orchestra. Other works from the later 1940s included several choral pieces and a symphony. In 1951 a concert of her music, initiated by her pupil Julia Smith, was given at Town Hall in New York with first performances of her Trio Sonata no. 2 (1951) for flute, cello and piano and *Moods for Dance Interpretation* (1950), op. 46, for dancer and piano. That year she retired from her teaching post at New York University and died four years later, a few days before her 68th birthday.

Amy Beach
1867–1944

Amy Beach is one of the few women composers to have found a place in mainstream histories of music, as part of the New England school of classicist composers that also included Horatio Parker, Arthur Foote and George Chadwick. But unlike most of her contemporaries she did not study in Europe and was almost entirely self-taught as a composer.

She was born Amy Cheney in New Hampshire in 1867, and by the age of four was composing little piano pieces and playing music by ear. Her mother, who had performed as a pianist and singer before her marriage, encouraged her precocious daughter and gave her piano lessons three times a week. Beach first appeared in public in 1875, aged seven, at a church concert where she played one of her own pieces as an encore.

In the mid–1870s the family moved to Boston where Beach went to a private school and took piano lessons and a few harmony lessons, the only music theory teaching she was to have. To learn orchestration she translated treatises on the subject, and wrote down music she heard then compared her version with the original. In 1883, at the age of 16, she made her debut as a pianist with a Boston orchestra and the same year her first song was published, a setting of Henry Wadsworth Longfellow's 'The Rainy Day' that she had written three years previously. In 1885 she gave her first performance with the Boston Symphony Orchestra and started her long professional relationship with the publisher Arthur Schmidt when he published her song 'With Violets'. Schmidt was to publish most of the music that she wrote, including orchestral music as well as the more profitable songs and piano pieces.

Later in 1885, at the age of 18, she married the successful physician Dr Henry Harris Aubrey Beach who was slightly older than her own father. In spite of the brilliant start she had made to her career as a pianist, after her marriage, like most women of her class, Beach stopped performing in public except for occasional appearances at charity concerts. But she did continue to compose, always under the name Mrs H.H.A. Beach, and was encouraged by her husband who was a keen amateur musician. Music always remained central to her life. She once said, 'Music means my inner soul.'

With all her attention concentrated on composition, Beach started producing large-scale works as well as continuing to write songs and piano pieces. During the 1890s she wrote some of her most accomplished works, music with expansive melodies and rich, luxuriant harmonies. Her *Mass in E♭*, op. 5, for four soloists, chorus, organ and orchestra, written in 1890, was premiered in 1892 by the Handel and Haydn Society in Boston. This youthfully joyous work combines dramatic, operatic writing for the soloists with a variety of choral writing that manages to incorporate both strict fugue and a waltz. In the same year her scene and aria *Eilende Wolken, Segler die Lufte*, op. 18, setting a text from Johann Schiller's *Maria Stuart* for alto and orchestra and which she had written at the request of Madame Carl Aves, was premiered by the New York Symphony Orchestra. This is one of Beach's first works to quote a Scottish tune.

During the 1890s she produced some of her most popular songs including 'Ecstasy' (1892), op. 19, to her own words. It was later said that she had bought her summer house on Cape Cod with the royalties of this song alone. The following year she wrote her op. 21 songs which included 'Elle et Moi' to words by Felix Bovet, another popular song but one in the German lied tradition rather than the more sentimental vein of 'Ecstasy'.

In 1892 Beach had been asked by the president of the board of lady managers, Bertha Palmer, to write a work for the dedication ceremonies of the World's Columbian Exposition in Chicago. But the members of the Bureau of Music, all men, overruled Palmer's decision and refused to programme Beach's *Festival Jubilate*, op. 17, for soloists, chorus and orchestra. It was finally played in the concert of women's music at the opening of the Women's Building at the Exposition in 1893.

The following year Beach started work on her 'Gaelic' Symphony in E minor, op. 32, which was premiered by the Boston Symphony Orchestra in 1896. This was the first symphony to be written by an American woman and the critics were generally encouraging. The 'Gaelic' Symphony is in four movements and incorporates themes from Beach's own song 'Dark is the Night' (1890) as well as several Irish folk tunes.

In 1893, Anton Dvorák, director of the National Conservatory of Music in

Amy Beach

New York from 1892 to 1895, had suggested that a national American music should be based on the music of African-Americans. In a response published in the *Boston Herald*, Beach pointed out that there were many immigrant groups whose music could form the basis of a national American music, and suggested that the use of English, Scottish or Irish folk music was more appropriate for many composers in the north of the United States. Beach's settings of poems by Robert Burns, *Five Songs* (1899), op. 43, use various elements of Scottish folk music such as snap rhythms and modally inflected harmonies. The following year she wrote her popular Robert Browning settings, op. 44, including the well-known 'Ah, Love but a Day!'.

In the same year her Piano Concerto in C♯minor, op. 45, was first performed by the Boston Symphony Orchestra with Beach playing the piano part herself. This was the last large-scale orchestral work she would write and was a great success, with frequent performances in the United States and Europe. In four movements, it has a virtuosic piano part with passionate melodies and richly chromatic harmonies.

In the summer of 1910 Beach's husband died. The following year she took up her performing career again and embarked on a hugely successful tour of Europe playing works such as the Piano Concerto, the Sonata for violin and piano (1897), op. 34, and the Piano Quintet in F♯ minor (1908), op. 67. Her stay in Europe lasted until 1914. On her return to the United States she settled in New York and established a routine whereby she performed during the winter and composed during the summer. By the 1920s her music was so popular that Amy Beach clubs were appearing all over the States.

Beach was a close friend of Marian MacDowell and first stayed at the MacDowell Colony for artists in 1921. It was at the Colony that she met and became friends with women composers such as Mabel Daniels and Mary Howe. In 1924 she became the first president of the Society of American Women Composers. During the 1920s and 30s, Beach wrote a considerable amount of church music including anthems, a motet and a Service in A major, op. 63, as well as other choral music such as *Canticle of the Sun* (1928), op. 123, for chorus and orchestra, performed at the Worcester Festival in 1931.

Her later works show stylistic changes away from the late romantic language of her earlier works. Beach was always interested in bird song, producing a whole volume of bird calls that she had written down in the field. In two piano pieces of 1922, *The Hermit Thrush at Eve* and *The Hermit Thrush at Morn*, she used exact transcriptions of the hermit thrush's song in its original key. Some of her later works used a more impressionistic language, as in piano pieces such as *By the Still Waters* (1925) or *A Hummingbird* (1932). The *Theme and Variations* (1920), op. 80, for flute and strings, incorporates an unusual amount of dissonance and the lost String Quartet (1929) apparently also had a high degree of dissonant writing as well as using Inuit folk melodies. Another work to incorporate Inuit music was the Piano Trio in A minor (1938), op. 150. Beach's widening search for folk material included the use of Creole folk melodies in her one-act chamber opera *Cabildo* (1932), a work not performed until after her death in 1944 at the age of 77.

Janet Beat
b. 1937

As a child Janet Beat was intently aware of sound, spending hours listening to the natural sounds of the country around her as well as having vivid sound dreams. She was born near Birmingham in the West Midlands and was not encouraged to take up music by her parents who would have preferred her to work in the family engineering business. But she had piano lessons from the age of nine and, inspired by the music of Béla Bartók and Alban Berg, started composing music in secret, teaching herself harmony and orchestration.

When she was in the sixth form, Beat was finally allowed to study music at school and also took up the French horn. In 1956 she went to Birmingham University where she studied music, graduating in 1960. She then took her postgraduate certificate in education and started part-time musicological research while also working as a freelance horn player and school teacher. She continued to compose and took a few composition lessons

with Alexander Goehr.

In 1963 she spent time in Venice and Naples doing research into early Italian opera and listening to as much contemporary music as possible at the Venice Biennale. In the later 1960s Beat lectured in music at teacher-training colleges while writing up her thesis. In 1972 she joined the staff at the Royal Scottish Academy of Music and Drama in Glasgow where she has taught ever since, working part-time from 1991 in order to spend more time on composition. Beat has worked as music critic for *The Scotsman* and was one of the founder members of the Scottish Society of Composers in 1980.

Beat became interested in electronics in the late 1950s. Largely self-taught, she began making *musique concrète* with a tape recorder and then took a correspondence course in basic electronics. She established the electronic music and recording studios at the Royal Scottish Academy and gradually built up her own private studio with analogue, digital and computer music systems. The earliest electronic work that she still acknowledges is *Apollo and Marsyas* (1972) for clarinet and tape.

Beat also continued to write for acoustic instruments and in *Le Tombeau de Claude* (1973) for flute, oboe and harp she pays homage to Claude Debussy, using letters from his name to create chords and melodic shapes. She uses this technique in several of her works including *Landscapes* (1976–7) for tenor and oboe which includes a wordless lament based on pitches representing the name of Beat's mother who died during the composition of the work. *Mitylene Mosaics* (1983–4) sets fragments by Sappho for soprano and three clarinets, using pitches from her name, while *Scherzo Notturno* (1992) for string quartet uses Beat's own name together with those of her parents. She has also worked with number concepts, as in her Sonata for piano (1985–7) in which durations and phrase lengths were built from the Fibonacci series. This is a virtuosic work in four movements which passes through a central bell-like stillness to the furious energy of the last movement.

Ever since she was a teenager, Beat has been fascinated by ancient civilizations and different cultures from all over the world but particularly by the art and music of Asia, where she has travelled extensively. Although her musical language is always firmly rooted in the harmonic and rhythmic procedures of the West, she frequently draws inspiration from the cultures of Indonesia, India, Tibet and Japan and brings elements from the music of these countries into her own. The influence of Indonesian music can be clearly heard in a work such as *Piangam* (1978–9) for piano and tape. The title is an amalgam of the words piano and gamelan and the music is built on a twelve-tone row which incorporates the Javanese pelog scale (used in gamelan music). In *Echoes from Bali* (1987) for computer and DX7 synthesizer, Beat creates hypnotic patterns of repeated rhythms and in *Puspawarna* (1988–9) she adds a mezzo-soprano voice and a low gong to the gamelan-influenced computer-controlled synthesizer. *Ongaku* (1981) for harpsichord and tape takes inspiration from a Japanese shakuhachi melody as well as from baroque harpsichord suites.

Beat's fascination with sound and timbre can be heard in all her works but perhaps most clearly in her works for solo instruments, with or without tape. *Hunting Horns are Memories* (1977) for horn and tape uses an extraordinary range of sounds made using the horn, including water bubbling inside the instrument. In many of her works, Beat uses quarter tones and developed a set of fingerings for producing quarter tones on the horn. *Mestra* (1980–81) for flute player on four different flutes uses quarter tones as well as a wide range of other sounds that can be produced from the instrument such as singing while playing or clicking the keys. The work is based on the idea of transformation (the title is taken from one of the stories in Ovid's *Metamorphoses*), both of the pitch material and in the transition through the four movements from bass flute to piccolo.

Beat's works are often constructed with great flexibility, enabling performers to use whatever resources are available. *Cross Currents and Reflections* (1981–2) for piano, electric piano, mono synthesizer and tape can be played as a three-movement suite for piano alone but the full version also includes two 'Reflections' for the other instruments and tape which are to be inserted between the movements of the suite. The 1988 work *A Vision of the Unseen*, a series of creation dances inspired by ancient Greek and Hindu visions of creation, can be performed in two versions. *A Vision of the Unseen no. 1* is for tape and improvising trio while *A Vision of the Unseen no. 2* is for tape alone.

Beat has always been fascinated by the interaction of live performers with music created electronically or by computer. In 1989 she founded Soundstrata, a group that performs music using acoustic instruments together with music technology. Soundstrata has performed works by Beat such as *Mandala* (1990) for flute, WX7 saxophone synthesizer and computer-controlled synthesizer which has elements of improvization for all the performers who also ring Tibetan hand bells to signal a change in pattern from the computer, which has its own improvization. Nearly 20 years after she wrote *Le Tombeau de Claude*, Beat again paid homage to Debussy in *Fêtes pour Claude* (1992), written for Soundstrata, in which her music for tape, voice and flute weaves a continuous web around performances of three of Debussy's works.

Margaret Bonds
1913–1972

Born in Chicago in 1913, Margaret Bonds grew up in a house visited by some of the leading African–American artists, writers and musicians of the early 20th century. Musicians, such as soprano Abbie Mitchell and composers Florence Price and Will Marion Cook, were particularly welcomed by Bonds' mother, church organist Estella Bonds.

Throughout her life Margaret Bonds was an indefatigable promoter of African–American music and musicians. The works of Harry T. Burleigh were a strong influence on her early music but she quickly developed her own individual musical style using a blend of jazz and blues rhythms and harmonies, a lyrical sense drawn from the African–American spiritual and elements of the European classical tradition in which she was trained. Known primarily for her vocal music, Bonds made many arrangements of spirituals, several of which were commissioned and recorded by Leontyne Price.

Bonds had her first piano lessons from her mother. She started composing young, writing her first piece, *Marquette Street Blues*, at the age of five. While still at school she had private composition lessons with William Dawson and Florence Price. She also worked as an accompanist for various singers and dancers in supper clubs and shows, copied music parts for other composers and became involved with the National Association of Negro Musicans.

After graduating from high school, Bonds became one of the few African–American students at Northwestern University in Evaston, Illinois. In 1932 she won a Wanamaker Award for her song 'Sea Ghost'. Two years later, at the age of 21, she left university with bachelor's and master's music degrees and opened the Allied Arts Academy, a short-lived school for ballet, art and music. As a pianist she performed with the major symphony orchestras in Chicago, appearing with the Chicago Symphony Orchestra in 1933 and the following year performing Florence Price's Piano Concerto with the Women's Symphony Orchestra of Chicago. In 1939 Bonds moved to New York where she worked as a music editor and collaborated on the writing of several popular songs, such as 'Peach Tree Street' and 'Spring will be so sad'. She married probation officer Lawrence Richardson in 1940 and later had a daughter.

In New York, Bonds embarked on further piano and composition study at the Juilliard School of Music. She also studied composition privately with Roy Harris and Emerson Harper and tried to study with Nadia Boulanger. Although Boulanger admired the music that Bonds showed her, she rather unhelpfully refused to teach her and told her that she did not need to take further lessons from anyone. The piece that Bonds showed Boulanger was one of her best-known works, *The Negro Speaks of Rivers* for voice and piano, written sometime in the 1930s and first published in 1942. A passionate setting of an early Langston Hughes poem, *The Negro Speaks of Rivers* demonstrates Bonds' assimilation of spiritual and blues styles into her music. She had been told by one of her teachers to take out the 'jazzy augmented chords' but refused. Bonds had discovered the poetry of Langston Hughes while still at school. He became a close friend and she was to set much of his poetry to music.

After her marriage and while studying, Bonds continued to teach the piano, compose and perform, working as a soloist with major symphony orchestras and in a two-piano duo with Gerald Cook. She also formed the Margaret Bonds Chamber Society, a group that put on concerts of music by African-American composers played by African–American musicians. Bonds lived in Harlem and worked on many local music projects. She was the minister of music at a local church and helped to establish a Cultural Community Centre.

Bonds' works from the 1950s include *The Ballad of the Brown King* to a libretto commissioned from Hughes. Originally written for voice and piano and later revised for chorus, soloists and orchestra, this work was first performed in December 1954 in New York. It tells the story of the three kings who visited the new-born Jesus, focusing on the 'brown king' Balthazar. A big piece in nine movements, it uses elements of African–American idioms such as spirituals, jazz and blues and calypso. Another setting of poetry by Hughes, the deeply moving *Three Dream Portraits* for voice and piano, were published in 1959. Her Mass in D minor for chorus and organ was performed in the same year.

Expanding on her many vocal works, Bonds started working in the theatre. As well as becoming involved as music director for many productions she also wrote two ballets and several music-theatre works including *Shakespeare in Harlem* to a libretto by Hughes, first performed in Westport, Connecticut in 1959. In 1965, at the time of the march on Montgomery, capital of Alabama, Bonds wrote *Montgomery Variations* for orchestra, dedicated to Martin Luther King. Two years later she moved to Los Angeles where she taught music at the Los Angeles Inner City Institute and at the Inner City Cultural Center. In 1972 Zubin Mehta and the Los Angeles Symphony Orchestra gave the first performance of her *Credo* for chorus and orchestra. A few months later she unexpectedly died, shortly after her 59th birthday.

Ina Boyle
1889–1967

Ina Boyle's music was greatly admired by those who knew it, including Ralph Vaughan Williams and Elizabeth Maconchy who described it as 'predominantly quiet and serious'. That it is not better known is perhaps not surprising, given that Boyle chose to live and work in almost total isolation. She spent all her life at the family home at Bushey Park near Enniskerry in Ireland where she was born and spent her childhood. Her father, Rev. William Boyle, was a clerk in holy orders, and much of Boyle's music consisted of sacred vocal works.

As a child, Boyle had violin and cello lessons and also studied harmony and counterpoint. Later she studied composition with Dr Hewson and Dr Kitson in nearby Dublin and also sent her work to her cousin, Charles Wood. Her earliest published works appear to be the two anthems *He will swallow up Death in Victory* and *Wilt not Thou, O God, go forth with our Hosts?* issued by Novello in 1915 when she was 26. Two years later they also published

Soldiers at Peace for chorus and orchestra, a setting of words by Herbert Asquith. When this work was given an amateur performance at Woodbrooke in 1920, Boyle described the occasion as 'the happiest evening of my life'.

Boyle first sprang to public attention in that same year when her orchestral rhapsody of 1919, *The Magic Harp*, received a Carnegie Trust award. Under the publishing scheme of the Trust, the work was published by Stainer and Bell in 1921 as part of the Carnegie Collection of British Music. This seems to have been the only time that Boyle published a piece of music under her full name, usually preferring to appear as 'I. Boyle'. *The Magic Harp* was inspired by the idea of the Durd-Alba, the magic harp of the ancient Irish gods which was said to have an iron string of sleep, a bronze string of laughter and a silver string that caused all people to weep. It is an impressionistic and atmospheric work with a prominent harp part and effective writing for the woodwind and horns. Boyle followed it with other orchestral works such as *Colin Clout* (1921) and a symphony entitled *Glencree (in the Wicklow hills)* (1924–7). She also continued to write sacred music such as *The Transfiguration* (1921), an anthem for the festival of the transfiguration dedicated to the Rev. H. Kingsmill Moore D.D., and her *Gaelic Hymns* (1923–4). These were settings of 15 of the hymns from Alexander Carmichael's *Carmina Gadelica* for unaccompanied chorus. Five of them were published by Chester in 1930 and performed the following year by the Oriana Madrigal Society.

In the spring of 1928 Boyle came to London for a brief period of study with Vaughan Williams. She continued to have occasional composition lessons from him until the late 1930s, when the outbreak of war doubtless put a stop to her visits to London. Possibly under the influence of Vaughan Williams, she turned to writing music for dance in the early 1930s. Her *Virgilian Suite* (1930–1), a ballet based on Virgil's *Ecologues*, was to have been performed by the Carmargo Society in 1933. The Society folded before they were able to perform the work but not before Boyle had designed the costumes and the set. Her next dance work was *The Dance of Death* (1935–6), a set of variations

inspired by Hans Holbein's woodcuts. Her final ballet was *The Vision of Er* (1938–9) based on the tenth book of Plato's *Republic* and scored for orchestra and three solo voices.

Boyle also continued to write chamber music and orchestral works as well as the solo songs, song cycles and other vocal music that were central to her output. In 1938 Boyle followed her string quartet of 1934 with a setting of John Donne, *Thinke then my soule* for tenor and string quartet, published by Oxford University Press in 1939. In 1948 she set Edith Sitwell's *Still falls the rain* for contralto and string quartet, while in the middle of another Sitwell setting, *From the darkness,* a symphony for contralto and orchestra which she worked on from 1946 to 1951. Another work for voice and orchestra was a setting of Emily Brontë, *No coward soul is mine* for soprano and string orchestra, written in 1953.

Words were always a very important point of inspiration for Boyle, even for her instrumental music. One of her last works was an opera, *Maudlin of Paplewick* (1964–6), for which she wrote her own libretto based on Ben Jonson's *The Sad Shepherd* and which she finished in 1966, the year before her death from cancer at the age of 78.

Gena Branscombe
1881–1977

Gena Branscombe is best known for her pioneering work as a choral conductor, for her work with the Branscombe Choral Society, her own chorus of women's voices, and for the many richly romantic choral works she wrote for them and other performers. She was born in Picton, near Lake Ontario in Canada, just over the border from the United States, and began to write piano pieces and accompany her older brother in public from an early age. After graduating from High School in 1897, at the age of 15, she won a scholarship to Chicago Musical College where she studied composition with Felix Borowski for seven years. She won two gold medals for composition during her time there and also studied the piano with several different teachers. Two of her earliest songs, 'In Blossom Time' and 'Eskimo Cradle Song', to words by Sara Branscombe, were published in 1901 while she was still a student.

After her graduation in 1903 Branscombe herself taught the piano at the college for four years. In the year of her graduation several of her works were published; these included four piano pieces *Chansonette in the form of a Valse, Impromptu, Valse-Caprice* and *Cavalcade* and two songs 'A Dirge' to words by Alfred Tennyson and 'I love you' to words by Sara Branscombe. In 1907 she moved for a short while to Washington State where she taught the piano at Whitman College Conservatory of Music and continued to publish her songs, including the cycle *Love in a Life* (1907) with words from Elizabeth Barrett Browning's *Sonnets from the Portuguese*.

In 1909 Branscombe went to Berlin for a year where she studied composition with Englebert Humperdinck, the composer regarded as the best composition teacher in Berlin. She also gave several recitals of her own works. On returning to the States in 1910 at the age of 29 she married lawyer John Ferguson Tenney and settled in New York. The couple had four daughters, one of whom died at an early age. Their eldest daughter Gena was to study music at the Royal College of Music in England. Although Branscombe spent much time looking after and bringing up her family she was determined to continue to compose.

In the years after her marriage Branscombe published many songs and song cycles including *The Sun Dial*, subtitled 'A Cycle of Love Songs of the Open Road' (1913), to words by K. Banning, and *A Lute of Jade* (1913), settings of translations of old Chinese texts. She also wrote and arranged several choral works and part-songs and became increasingly interested in conducting. She enrolled in the conducting class at New York University and also had private lessons from various conductors including Albert Stoessel and Frank Damrosch. Branscombe was to conduct many different choirs and orchestras over her long career. Always active in women's organizations and supportive of women musicians, she was one of the early members of the Society of American Women Composers and was its president from 1929 to 1931. It was doubtless through the society that she developed her friendships with composers Amy Beach, Mary Howe and Mabel Daniels. She also spent five years (1930–35) as chair of music and folk song in the General Federation of Women's Clubs.

It was not until the late 1920s that

Branscombe began to achieve more frequent performances of her large-scale works such as the suite *Quebec*. This work for tenor and orchestra to her own text about sixteenth-century French settlers in Canada was taken from her unfinished opera *The Bells of Circumstance*, and Branscombe herself conducted the first performance with the Chicago Women's Symphony Orchestra in 1928. The following year saw the first complete performance of a choral work she had been writing since 1919. This was *Pilgrims of Destiny* for soloists, chorus and orchestra, a setting of her own libretto about the first English settlers sailing to America on board the *Mayflower*. A *New York Times* reviewer described it as 'bubbling with tunefulness'.

In 1933 her popular choral work *Youth of the World*, completed the year before, was first performed in New York. This was also the year in which Branscombe formed the Branscombe Choral Society of New York, the group she was to work with for the next 21 years. They gave regular concerts at Town Hall in New York and many broadcasts. Branscombe wrote many of her works for them as well as making arrangements of works by a variety of composers.

In July 1935, Branscombe visited the Society of Women Musicians in London, presumably at the time of one of the London performances of *Youth of the World*. In 1941 she conducted a huge choir of a thousand voices for the golden jubilee of the General Federation of Women's Clubs in Atlantic City, New Jersey, in a programme that included several pieces by women. During the war the Branscombe Choral Society gave many performances in military hospitals, and the Nazi bombing of Coventry Cathedral in England inspired *Coventry's Choir* (1943), a setting of a poem by Violet Alvarez for soprano solo and women's choir. Branscombe's favourite among her own works, it was first performed by the Branscombe Choral Society in May 1944 at New York Town Hall. Branscombe continued to write choral music and songs into her 90s. Her last music was commissioned for a service at Riverside Church in New York in 1973, four years before her death at the age of 95.

Dora Bright
1863–1951

Dora Estella Bright was born in Sheffield in 1863. She entered the Royal Academy of Music as a pianist in 1881 at the age of 17 and remained there until 1888. She studied the piano with Walter Macfarren and also took composition lessons with Ebenezer Prout, winning prizes and scholarships in both subjects. In 1888 she became the first woman to win the Charles Lucas medal for composition with an *Air and Variations* for string quartet. While at the Academy, Bright became part of a group of students calling themselves 'The Party' who attended public concerts together and played and criticized each other's works. Members of the group included Edward German and Bright's close friend Ethel Boyce.

In 1888 Bright, Boyce and their friend John Greenaway travelled in Germany and Switzerland. Boyce wrote home that '... Dora is very trying. I believe she would like to do nothing better than to get up late – dawdle about all day – and go to the opera at night'.

Bright and Boyce remained friends, playing each other's works in public and collaborating on a collection of children's songs, *The Orchard Rhymes*, published in 1917.

Bright's first public appearance as a pianist was at the Covent Garden Proms in 1882, not long after she arrived in London. In the same year her first piece of music appeared in print, the simple but effective song 'Whither?' to words by Henry Wadsworth Longfellow. *Two Sketches for Pianoforte*, dedicated to her teacher Walter Macfarren, were published by Stanley Lucas in 1884. Bright was a frequent performer of her own and other composers' works at Academy concerts during the 1880s. In 1885 she played her own *Concertstück* in C♯ minor for piano and orchestra, and the following year her Suite for piano. In February 1888, Bright and Boyce first performed Bright's *Variations for two pianos on an original theme of G.A. Macfarren*, a substantial and difficult work they were often to perform together and which was published some years later. In the summer of 1888 Bright's Piano Concerto was performed at an Academy concert in St James's Hall and repeated at the Proms to very good reviews.

After leaving the Academy and returning from Germany, Bright gave a series of piano recitals at the Prince's Hall in London in 1889. The recitals featured her own works and pieces by British composers such as George and Walter Macfarren, Edward German, Ethel Boyce and Alexander Mackenzie, and were well received. In the same year her *Romanza and Scherzetto* for piano (dedicated to Boyce) and a collection of 12 songs were published. The song collection consists of four settings of Robert Herrick and three of William Shakespeare with various other writers such as Henry Wadsworth Longfellow and Charles Kingsley. They are all short, lieder-like songs that are quite demanding and obviously not intended for the profitable amateur market.

For the next few years Bright performed to great acclaim throughout Britain and Germany, playing with orchestras and organizing her own recitals and chamber concerts. In 1892 she gave the first performance of her *Fantasia in G minor* for piano and orchestra at a Philharmonic Society Concert. This was the first orchestral work by a British woman to be heard at these notoriously conservative concerts. The following year she included her own Piano Quartet at a concert of chamber music that she put on at Prince's Hall. *The Musical Times* described this work as 'vigorous, melodious and interesting'. Other chamber works from the early 1890s included a *Suite of Five Pieces* for violin and piano and a *Romance and Seguidilla* for flute and piano.

Sometime in the 1890s Bright married the landowner and Crimean-War veteran Colonel Wyndham Knatchbull, and began to divide her time between a London house in Eaton Place and an estate at Babington near Bath in Somerset. She more or less stopped performing in public although she continued to compose. In 1897 her *Liebeslied* for orchestra was performed at the Proms. Works published in the early years of the century included the dramatic cycle *Six Songs from the Jungle Book* and various other vocal works. She continued to enjoy entertaining and giving parties, including one in Bath where she appeared as Carmen. Boyce thought her dress '... a bright cherry colour and short skirts, rather too daring ...'.

In the late 1890s Bright formed a local amateur operatic group called the Babington Strollers and organized many performances and charity concerts. She became interested in ballet and wrote a short work called *The Dryad*. This tells the story of a dryad imprisoned in a tree by a jealous

Aphrodite. Allowed out once every 10 years, the dryad will only be set free when she can find someone who will remain faithful for 10 years. The ballet was given a charity performance organized by the Duchess of Somerset in 1907; the famous dancer Adeline Genée danced the part of the dryad. Genée took the work into her repertoire at the Empire, Leicester Square and the two women embarked on a fruitful professional relationship. After going to Paris for further composition lessons from Moritz Moszkowski, Bright wrote the music for some of Genée's best-known ballets, including *La Camargo* (1912) and *The Dancer's Adventure* (1915), as well as compiling the music from scores in the British Museum by Jean Baptiste Lully, Luigi Boccherini, Léo Delibes and others for *La Danse* (1912). She also continued to produce orchestral music. A *Concertstück* for six drums and orchestra was performed in Nottingham in 1915 and a *Suite Bretonne* for flute and orchestra was premiered at the Proms in 1917. Bright's last collaboration with Genée took place in 1932 when she put together a collection of old-fashioned dances for *The Love Song*, given as a benefit performance at Drury Lane.

None of Bright's many orchestral works was published and none appears to have survived. Her surviving songs, chamber works and piano works (including arrangements from some of her ballets) show her ability to write flowing, well-constructed melodies. Reviews commend her orchestration. Her music remained resolutely old-fashioned, unaffected by the many developments of the early 20th century. In the 1940s she wrote a regular column 'Radio in Retrospect' for *Musical Opinion* where she gave vent to her hatred of most modern music from Benjamin Britten and Michael Tippett to Igor Stravinsky and Arnold Schoenberg, finding it all ugly and noisy. The music Bright admired the most was that of Romantic composers such as Felix Mendelssohn and Robert Schumann, although she found some works by Claude Debussy and Maurice Ravel to be bearable. She died at her home in 1951 at the age of 88.

Radie Britain
b. 1899

Radie Britain's music is often inspired by the nature and culture of the places in which she has lived, particularly by the deserts and plains of her native Texas and the cowboy and hoedown music that is found there. She is a prolific composer, best known for her many orchestral works.

Britain grew up on a ranch near Amarillo in Texas. Her father, Edgar Charles Britain, who worked as a horse wrangler and cow hand, used to play square-dance tunes on the fiddle and sing cowboy songs; her mother, Katie Ford Britain, played religious songs on their pump organ. They both encouraged Britain's own interest in music and she took piano lessons at the conservatory attached to the Methodist Clarendon College from the age of seven. After graduating from the college in 1918, she spent the next year at a girls' finishing school in Arkansas where she studied piano and organ.

In the autumn of 1919 Britain entered the American Conservatory in Chicago where she gained a teacher's certificate and a bachelor's degree, majoring in piano, in two years. She also began composing and became gradually less interested in performing, especially after she developed neuritis in her arms. Returning to Texas in 1921 she taught piano and music history at Clarendon College for a year and set up as a private piano teacher in Amarillo in order to earn enough money to achieve her long-held ambition of studying in Europe.

In 1923 she was able to make a brief trip to Paris where she took organ lessons with Marcel Dupré. The following year she went to Munich where she embarked on her long relationship with the teacher of composition and theory, Albert Noelte, who encouraged her to use the cowboy songs and Native American music of her home state in her music. Britain stayed in Munich for two years and had her early works published and performed while she was there.

In 1926 Britain's sister died and she had to return to the United States. The devoted Noelte followed her and settled in Chicago where Britain came for further study with him. She herself was teaching at the Girven Institute of Music and Allied Arts, and her music was beginning to be performed. In 1927 her first orchestral work, *Symphonic Intermezzo*, was premiered and then toured by Ethel Leginska and the Chicago Women's Symphony Orchestra. One of Leginska's conditions for taking on the work was that Britain toured with the orchestra as a percussionist!

Britain wrote one of her most popular orchestral works, *Prelude to a Drama*, in 1928, and the following year completed *Heroic Poem*, an orchestral work dedicated 'to an American aviator' and written after Charles Lindbergh's historic flight accross the Atlantic. *Heroic Poem* won several prizes although it was not performed until 1932. Britain was unable to attend the premiere and the conductor Howard Hanson, confused by her unusual first name, was astounded when he discovered, many years later, that the composer of this work was a woman.

In 1930 Britain married Leslie Moeher and had a daughter, Lerae, two years later. Sometime in the early 1930s she first met sculptor Edgardo Simone. She eventually divorced Moeher and married Simone in 1939 after a period of juggling the attentions of both men. On one occasion, when she had rented a secluded cabin in Upper Michigan in order to complete a large orchestral work, they both turned up to visit her at the same time.

Simone's suggestion that Britain compose a fiery, Bacchic orchestral work prompted her *Saturnale* (1933). This uncharacteristically passionate piece brought about a final split with her teacher Noelte who strongly disapproved of it. In 1934 Britain joined the faculty of the American Conservatory in Chicago where she taught until 1938. The 1930s were a very productive time for Britain. Her symphonic poem *Light*, written in 1935, was first performed by the Boston Women's Symphony Orchestra. She had several works programmed by the Federal Music Project that was working to encourage music during the Depression. Her *Southern Symphony* (1935) was premiered in 1940 by the Illinois Symphony Orchestra under an FMP scheme. Other orchestral works of this period included *Ontonagon Sketches* (1939) and *Drouth* (1939). Britain also wrote several chamber and choral works including her String Quartet no. 2 (1935).

In 1939 Britain and Simone moved to San Diego in California, and two years later settled in Los Angeles. Britain established herself as a private teacher of piano and composition. The Spanish–American culture in

California and trips into nearby Mexico inspired pieces such as *Serenada del Coronado* (1940) and *Serenata Sorentina* (1946). But Britain also continued to write music inspired by her native Texas with works such as *Red Clay* (1946), celebrating the open spaces of Texas cattle country, or *Paint Horse and Saddle* (1947).

Simone had a stroke and died in 1949. Britain met aviator Theodore Morton in 1955 and married him four years later. While continuing to write descriptive orchestral music such as *Chicken in the Rough* (1951) and *Cactus Rhapsody* (1953), Britain began to explore opera and ballet with works such as *Carillon*, a three-act opera to a libretto by Rupert Hughes (1952), her chamber opera *Kuthara* (1960) and *The Dark Lady Within* (1962), a ballet based on William Shakespeare's sonnets.

Britain never moved away from her essentially conservative tonal style of music although from the 1960s her music became rather more impressionistic, as can be seen in her *Cosmic Mist Symphony* (1962) with three movements entitled 'In the Beginning', 'Nebula' and 'Nuclear Fission'. In one work, *Les Fameux Douze* (1965) for orchestra, she experimented with using a 12-tone row. Although the piece won a prize, Britain claimed she hated it and refused to have it performed.

She continued to compose throughout the 1970s and 80s with orchestral works such as *Pyramids of Giza* (1973) and *Texas* (1987). In the late 1970s she wrote a book based on her relationship with Simone who was undoubtedly the most important of the many men in her life. The articles she had written as musical editor of *The Penwoman* were published as *Composer's Corner* in 1978. She has also written her autobiography, entitled 'Ridin' Herd to Writing Symphonies'.

Augusta Browne
1821–1882

Augusta Browne was born in Ireland in 1821 but her family emigrated to the United States by the time she was nine years old. Nothing seems to be known about her family background or her musical education but she spent her early career in New York, working as the organist of the First Presbyterian Church in Brooklyn. She also taught music and music theory and worked as a journalist, writing articles on music for various popular magazines such as *The Musical World and New York Musical Times* as well as writing short stories and two books. In 1863 she wrote an article entitled 'A Woman on Women' for *Knickerbocker Magazine* in which she showed how ridiculous it was to think that a musical training would stop women from carrying out their other duties:

> Why should concocting a sonnet hinder a woman from concocting a pudding ... working out a harmonic fugue from working a pan of dough, or manipulating a magnificent symphony of Beethoven from deftly handling a broom?

Most of Browne's surviving music is for voice or keyboard. Published in the 1840s and 50s, these works are strictly classical in style. Browne was particularly insistent on resisting the influence of more popular music-hall styles. Her most successful song was the dramatic 'The Warlike Dead in Mexico' (1848), a setting of words by Mrs Balmanno. Many of her piano works are sets of variations, often using folk themes. She called several of her piano variations 'Bouquets', including *The Caledonian Bouquet* (1841), *The French Bouquet* (1841), *The American Bouquet* (1844) and *The Hiberian Bouquet* (n.d.), which used themes from Thomas Moore's *A Selection of Irish Melodies*. Other piano pieces include fantasies, waltzes and other dances. Browne also wrote two sacred choral works for four-part mixed chorus and organ, *Grand Vesper Chorus* and *Hear Therefore O Israel*.

In her mid-30s, Browne married a man
called Garret but he did not
survive long after the wedding. She
continued to support herself by
writing, performing and teaching. By
1875 she had moved to Washington,
DC, where she died in 1882, at the age
of 61.

Diana Burrell
b. 1948

Diana Burrell has written of her love for 'rough-edged things' and for brave, imperfect sounds, distrusting the 'tasteful nice-ness' of much contemporary culture. In her short career as a composer she has created a powerful collection of works that project her personal vision with passion and energy through a strikingly individual language full of the shrieking of birds and strange sounds from other worlds. Her works are built on clear, strong structures and always communicate directly with her audience.

Burrell was born in Norwich where her schoolteacher father was assistant organist at the cathedral. She began composing during her last year at school and decided to study music at Cambridge, where she concentrated on performing rather than composing, although a composition portfolio formed part of her final exams. After leaving Cambridge, she taught for four years at Sutton High School for Girls where she provided music for school plays as well as an opera for the pupils

to perform. Burrell then spent several years as a freelance viola player, touring and playing with many different orchestras including the City of London Sinfonia and the orchestras for Sadler's Wells Ballet and London Festival Ballet. During this time she married and had two children, always sharing the responsibility of bringing them up with her husband, a freelance singer.

Burrell's first composition to attract critical attention was her *Missa Sancte Endeliente,* written in 1980 for conductor Richard Hickox to perform at the St Endellion Festival in Cornwall. Composed in many different places throughout England while she was on tour, the *Missa* is a huge work for soprano, alto, countertenor, tenor and baritone soloists, choir and orchestra, setting the liturgy in Cornish and Latin and including a prayer to Saint Endelienta. Another remarkable choral work was *Io Evoe!* (1984). Scored for chorus, three trumpets, three trombones and

Diana Burrell

strings, this series of dramatic settings of ancient Gallic and Native-American chants celebrates the rituals of birth, initiation and death, and was one of her first works to be broadcast by the BBC.

As she began to receive more and more commissions for works, Burrell gradually cut down on her performing to concentrate on composition. In 1986 she attended the International Dance Course for Professional Choreographers and Composers at Surrey University where she worked with Swedish choreographer Bengt Jorgen on a piece, *Dalliance of Eagles*, for viola, percussion, tape and two dancers. Burrell later reworked the score, recording the viola part herself so that it could be performed from tape in Toronto, Canada. In 1987 Burrell was the featured composer at the Greenwich Festival in London for which she wrote *Archangel* for woodwind and brass. During the same year she wrote an uncommissioned two-act opera, *The Albatross*, to her own libretto based on a short story by Susan Hill. Despite interest from various opera companies, the work has yet to be staged.

One of Burrell's most frequently performed works has been *Landscape* for orchestra, commissioned by the Piccadilly Festival in 1988. From the opening bird-like keening calls of the bassoon and cor anglais the listener is transported to a wild, primeval landscape which, with a percussion section including steel pans and pieces of metal from a scrap-yard, is also strangely urban. The work uses various instruments in unusual and unexpected ways. The steel pans have moved far from the calypso style with which they are usually associated, and in one of the most extraordinary moments of the work, two tenor recorders emerge as the first stirrings of life from the bowels of the earth to which the music has sunk.

A very particular world is also conjured up by *Barrow*, written in 1991 for a chamber ensemble of horn, bassoon, piano, cello and electric guitar, with cellist and guitarist also playing drums. This work grew from a vivid dream in which Burrell found herself being led through ancient woodland in the cold, misty moonlight of very early morning towards an ancient barrow or burial mound. Banging on the barrow with the wooden stick she was carrying produced a frenzy of drumming after which the mound opened, giving birth to a pale boy-child in a cradle of twigs. The clear, open textures of the work with its passages of haunting drumming perfectly conjure up the eerie world of Burrell's imagination.

Another work reflecting the world of ancient religious rites was written in 1989 when Burrell was commissioned by BBC television to contribute to 'The Cry', a series of Easter programmes of music with visual images. The images for Burrell's orchestral work *Landscape with Procession* (or *The Cry of the Cosmos* as it was called for the series) included a Wicker Priestess celebrating Mass with an Anglican Priest in a bleak northern landscape. Recent commissions for church music have produced music with less pagan imagery and include an anthem for the Three Choirs Festival, *Come Holy Ghost, our Souls Inspire* (1993) for chorus and organ.

Burrell has frequently been asked to compose works for young players, and has been involved in various educational projects in schools in London and Bradford. She has also written music for and taught on COMA (Contemporary Music Making for Amateurs) summer courses. In her works for children and amateurs, Burrell is always concerned to provide music written in the same idiom as her music for professionals and thereby introduce the sounds and structures of contemporary music to a wider audience. Burrell's many commissions from a wide variety of performing groups, festivals and other organizations have included chamber, vocal and keyboard music. Her string quartet *Gulls and Angels* (1994) juxtaposes the harsh screeching of gulls with the richly sonorous music of the angels.

But Burrell has perhaps become best known for her vital and original orchestral music, including two works from 1992: the string orchestra prelude and fugue *Das Meer, das so gross und weit ist, da wimmelt's ohne Zahl, grosse und kleine Tiere* written for the Orchestra of St John's, Smith Square; and the chamber orchestra work *Resurrection*, written for the Bournemouth Sinfonietta, in which the rest of the orchestra attack and silence the outsider cor anglais who by the end of the work has been joyfully resurrected. Burrell's Viola Concerto (1994) was written for Jane Atkins, and the BBC Symphony Orchestra have commissioned a symphony for their 1995–6 season.

Mary Carmichael
1851–1935

Mary Grant Carmichael was born in Birkenhead near Liverpool. As a girl she was educated in France and Switzerland and persuaded to learn the piano by her older sister. She later studied music in Munich where she took harmony lessons from Heinrich Porges and attended the National Academy for the Higher Development of Pianoforte Playing, studying with Oscar Beringer and Walter Bache. She also studied at the Royal Academy of Music in London where she took harmony and counterpoint lessons with Ebenezer Prout.

Carmichael became a much sought-after accompanist, working with artists such as violinists Joseph Joachim and Wilma Normann-Neruda (Lady Hallé), cellist Alfredo Piatti and many singers including Liza Lehmann and Gervase Elwes. She made many appearances at the important Monday and Saturday Popular Concerts at St James's Hall. Her earliest published work appears to be the dance-like *Idylle* for piano, dedicated to Ebenezer

Prout and published by Stanley Lucas, Weber and Co. in about 1874. The composer appeared on the title page of this and other early piano works, such as the *Two Sketches* dedicated to Hans von Bülow, as M.G. Carmichael. Most of Carmichael's piano pieces, which she published throughout her life, are in dance forms and often highly rhythmic. They are not showy pieces but clearly demonstrate her feeling for her own instrument and her technical ability. She is said to have described her fingers as like pincushions!

Carmichael's earliest vocal works were published in the late 1870s and included two William Blake settings and two sets of lyrics from Heinrich Heine's *Book of Songs*. She wrote and published many songs and they were performed by some of the leading singers of her day including Louise Phillips, to whom several were dedicated. Her songs are written in a straightforward classical lieder style, and the poets she set included Emanuel Geibel, William Shakespeare,

Robert Herrick, William Blake and Ben Jonson as well as contemporary lyricists such as F.E. Weatherly, Robert Hichens and W.E. Henley. She also wrote many duets and part-songs.

In November 1887, *Songs of the Stream*, Carmichael's song cycle for four voices and piano, a setting of poems by Hichens, was sung at the Lyric Club in London and was given a public performance in December 1888 at the Steinway Hall. The song cycle with several voices was not a common form in England at this time. *The Musical World* described *Songs of the Stream* as 'the first attempt at a work of its kind in England' and *The Musical Times* bestowed 'unreserved praise'. But although it received several performances, the work does not appear to have been published and no manuscript has survived.

Carmichael started writing sacred music in the 1890s, and produced a *Stabat Mater* which has not survived and a Mass in E♭ which was published by Houghton in 1900. This work for four-part chorus and organ in a simple chordal style was obviously intended for liturgical use. In 1897 publishers Joseph Williams issued her operetta *The Frozen Hand, or the Snow Queen* with a libretto adapted from Hans Christian Andersen by May Gillington. This three-act work uses children as choruses of flowers and snowflakes and was performed twice in Brighton. Carmichael also became involved in the revival of English music of the past and published several arrangements of old English songs by composers such as William Boyce, William Shield, Thomas Arne and James Hook. Towards the end of her life her music was broadcast on the radio, to her great pleasure. She died in 1935 at the age of 84.

Claribel
(Charlotte Alington Barnard)
1830–1869

Charlotte Alington Barnard, writing under the pseudonym Claribel, was the most popular and commercially successful song and ballad composer of the 1860s. Building on the achievements of women ballad composers such as Dolores (the pseudonym of Ellen Dickson), Maria Lindsay, Caroline Norton and Virginia Gabriel, Claribel showed that women songwriters were capable of earning large sums of money and of becoming household names.

Born on 23 December 1830, she was the only child of Henry Alington Pye, a solicitor in Louth, Lincolnshire, and his first wife Charlotte. Claribel's early education took place at a Ladies' Academy in Louth. Showing an interest in music, she also had piano lessons from the organist of the local church, and from an early age composed piano pieces and songs, usually to her own poems. Her mother died in 1847 and a few years later, at the age of 20, Claribel became engaged to barrister John Holloway. Her father disapproved

of Holloway, the engagement was dissolved and Claribel was sent away on a European tour. On her return she wrote two piano pieces, *March de la Vivandière* and *Die Alpen-Rosen Wältzer*, which her father had published in 1853 for the benefit of the Louth Mechanics' Institute and which seem to be the only works to appear in print under her own name.

In 1854 Claribel married Rev. Charles Cary Barnard, and in 1857 the couple moved to London. Here Claribel was not only able to enter London society but also to take further music lessons and start to find a wider audience for her compositions than her friends and relatives. The first of her songs to be published, at her own expense in 1859, was a setting of Alfred Tennyson's 'The Brook'. Like most women of her class she was unwilling to have her name exposed to the public and adopted the pseudonym Claribel. She was also to publish some poetry under the ambiguous pseudonym 'Condor'. Her next song was also initially issued at her own expense. The costs of engraving, printing and proof-reading amounted to £2 13s and the bill was sent to her husband. This work was 'Janet's Choice', a lively, ballad that became one of her best-known and loved songs, doubtless to the annoyance of the publishers who refused it. By 1865 it had reached a 20th edition.

Early in 1860 Claribel sent some of her songs to Charlotte Sainton-Dolby, the famous ballad-singer. Sainton-Dolby, who was to become the singer most associated with Claribel's songs and to earn much money for singing them, wrote back saying that the songs were 'very clever' but suggested further study. Claribel took her advice and had lessons from Bernard Althaus and William Henry Holmes, a teacher at the Royal Academy of Music, as well as joining Sainton-Dolby's singing class 'for ladies only'. She also took singing lessons with well-known singers such as Guiseppi Mario and Euphrosyne Parepa.

Claribel soon had a contract with the publishers Boosey and Sons, negotiated for her by her father and husband. Her songs started to be introduced by singers such as Sainton-Dolby, Parepa and John Sims Reeves. In 1863 an exclusive contract was signed with Boosey giving her an annual £300 retaining fee. In this year the Barnards moved back to Lincolnshire, primarily so that Charles Barnard could concentrate on his work as a clergy-

man. Claribel started writing sacred songs and hymns as well as continuing to produce ballads. The popularity of her work grew steadily throughout the mid-1860s and can be clearly seen in the prominence given to her songs in Boosey advertisements as well as in the many arrangements made of her work. These included the *Claribel Lancers* for piano of 1866 arranged by Charles Coote from five of her songs and the *Claribel Galop* and *Claribel Polka* arranged by E. Audibert. In 1867 Boosey published *A Guide to Claribel's Songs,* a booklet containing all the words of her works with the opening phrases of the music.

By 1866 there were increased attacks in the press on the royalty system of payment for songs, seen as encouraging singers to include songs and ballads of dubious quality in their programmes because they were being paid by the publisher to sing them. Sainton-Dolby's performances of Claribel's songs were often singled out for criticism. In May 1866 *The Orchestra* published a parody of 'I cannot sing the old songs', one of Claribel's most popular ballads:

I cannot sing the old songs
Because they do not pay
There is no royalty attached
So they're not in the way.
I much prefer some rubbish written
  by Dowzibel
For everyone can sing them,
And oh my! Don't they sell.

Boosey ignored these attacks and in 1867 instituted their famous ballad concerts at which singers such as Sainton-Dolby promoted songs and ballads from the Boosey catalogue. John Boosey himself defended Claribel in an article in *The Musical World* in 1868: 'It has been the fashion to sneer at Claribel, and talk of her being forced upon the public by singers. I can only answer that many other writers have enjoyed the same chances of popularity as Claribel, but with a very different result!'

Later that year disaster struck the Barnards when Claribel's father filed for bankruptcy and disappeared leaving a trail of debt and fraud behind him. Such financial disgrace was total. Claribel, who had herself lost a substantial amount of money, fled England with her husband and her father and his second wife and child. They all settled in Belgium where

Claribel started to take composition lessons from teachers at the Brussels Conservatoire, realizing that her music was now the family's only financial support. She even started writing songs with French texts, such as 'Vous voulez que je chante'.

Returning to England for a clandestine visit in early 1869 she was taken seriously ill and died at Dover on January 30. The popularity of Claribel's music survived her death and her financial disgrace. Arrangements of her songs were still being issued as late as 1920. She preferred to use her own sentimental texts, although she also set several poems by her cousin, the poet Jean Ingelow. Her songs are characterized by an undemanding simplicity of melody, harmony and texture but always with an appealing tunefulness, or as *The Press* put it in 1861, 'the gift of pure and expressive melody'.

Rebecca Clarke
1886–1979

Rebecca Clarke was born in Harrow, near London, in 1886. Her difficult and often abusive American father, Joseph Clarke, was an enthusiastic amateur cellist who loved chamber music and made sure that his family learnt to play the instruments that would enable them to play string quartets. Clarke's German mother, Agnes, took up the viola and Clarke herself learnt the violin from the age of eight. In 1902 she entered the Royal Academy of Music where she studied the violin with Hans Wesseley and harmony with Percy Miles. But after she had been at the Academy for two years, Miles proposed marriage and her father insisted that she leave.

Back at home, Clarke started writing songs, mostly to German texts by Dehmel, finding composition 'a refuge, an outlet and finally a passion'. In 1907 she became the first female student of Charles Stanford at the Royal College of Music. She also studied counterpoint and fugue with Frederick Bridge and, on Stanford's suggestion, took up the viola. She was later to have a few lessons with Lionel Tertis, the leading viola player of the time who was doing so much to popularize the instrument.

At the College, Clarke concentrated on writing vocal and chamber music. Her earliest instrumental works date from 1909, the year she finished a large three-movement violin and piano sonata that she had been writing for Stanford and that won her a scholarship. In her vocal music she moved away from setting German texts. Her first songs to reach a wider public were her two W.B. Yeats settings, 'Shy One' and 'Cloths of Heaven', both dedicated to and often performed by the famous tenor Gervase Elwes. Written around 1912, the two songs were not published until 1920 and even then their dissonance was found to be too modern by some reviewers.

Clarke's father had thrown her out of the house in 1910. Finding herself with just £12 in savings and forced to make her own living, Clarke became a professional viola player. In 1912 she became one of the first women to be employed by Henry Wood in his Queen's Hall orchestra. But she was primarily known as a chamber music performer and played with some of the leading musicians of the early 20th century including Pablo Casals, Artur Rubinstein, Jacques Thibaud, Jascha Heifetz and Myra Hess, a friend from her Academy days. She also played in a string quartet with the famous d'Aranyi sisters, Adila and Jelly, and cellist Guilhermina Suggia and founded the English Ensemble, a pianoforte quartet with Marjorie Hayward, May Muckle and Kathleen Long.

Clarke's work involved much travel. From 1916 to 1923 she appears to have been based in the United States and in 1923 undertook a world tour with Muckle, visiting countries such as China, India and Japan. In the spring of 1918 Clarke's *Morpheus* for viola and piano was given its first performance at Carnegie Hall in New York. This work was one of her first public successes and also one of the few pieces for which she used a pseudonym, Anthony Trent. The following year she entered her Viola Sonata into the anonymous competition at Elizabeth Sprague Coolidge's Berkshire Festival. Clarke's piece tied for first place with Ernest Bloch's Suite for viola and piano, and Coolidge gave her casting vote to Bloch's work. Clarke and Coolidge were to become

close friends and Coolidge later described to Clarke the astonishment of the jury when they discovered that her work had been written by a woman. The Viola Sonata was published by Chester in 1921 and given many performances throughout Europe in the next few years. It is a fiery yet lyrical work, headed with a quotation from Alfred de Musset, 'Poet, take up your lute; tonight the wine of youth is fermenting in the veins of God'.

Two years later, in 1921, Clarke's remarkable Trio for violin, cello and piano won second prize at the Berkshire Festival. It was first performed in Britain in November 1922 at the Wigmore Hall (by Hess, Hayward and Muckle) when *The Musical Times* remarked that there was 'passionate feeling in every section and even had it been the work of a man, it would be called a virile effort'. Like so much of Clarke's music, the Trio belongs to the European world of Bloch and Maurice Ravel (and English composers such as Frank Bridge or Arthur Bliss). It opens with a commanding motif, first heard in the piano in sevenths, which is used throughout the work. From the restless first movement through the sensuous slow movement to the wild country dance of the finale, this is an urgent and powerful work.

Other instrumental works of the 1920s developed Clarke's feel for sophisticated rhythms, instrumental colour and individual, often modal, harmonies. They include the evocative *Chinese Puzzle* (1921) for violin and piano, the large-scale *Rhapsody* for cello and piano which was commissioned by Elizabeth Sprague Coolidge (for $1,000) and first performed by Muckle and Hess at the Berkshire Festival in 1923 and *Midsummer Moon* (1924) for violin and piano, dedicated to and first performed by Adila d'Aranyi. Clarke also wrote many songs in the 1920s, all displaying a strong talent for word setting. One of the most striking is 'The Seal Man' (1922), her haunting setting of words by John Masefield with an almost recitative-like vocal line accompanied by a shimmering piano part evoking the lure of the sea. Other songs included another Masefield setting, the exquisite 'June Twilight' (1925), a beautifully lyrical setting of Anna Wickham's 'The Cherry-Blossom Wand' (1927) as well as the dramatically disturbing setting of A.E. Housman's 'Eight O'Clock' (1927) and the ironically comic 'The Aspidistra' (1929) to words by Claude Flight.

Clarke continued to perform throughout the 1920s and 30s, and in 1925 a concert of her works was given at the Wigmore Hall. She also wrote several articles on chamber music for the journal *Music and Letters* and contributed to her friend W.W. Cobbett's *Cyclopedia of Chamber Music*. Clarke was very aware of the position of women who wanted to make their living as musicians, and had been present at the inaugural meeting of the Society of Women Musicians in 1911. She had several works performed at concerts given by the Society in the 1920s and 30s, and in 1926 gave a talk at the Society's Composers' Conference on 'Some American Aspects of Music' in which she pointed to the significant part that women played in founding and running American music clubs and the importance of the work that Coolidge was doing in commissioning and promoting chamber music.

Clarke seems to have written virtually no music during the 1930s. She later suggested that this was because she was having an affair with a married man which took all her energies away from composition, something that she found always demanded her total absorption and concentration. When the second world war broke out Clarke was in the United States and, unable to return to England, took a job as a governess in Connecticut. She also started writing again, although most of her later music remained unpublished. Her *Passacaglia on an Old English Tune* (1941) for viola and piano was published by Schirmer in New York, and in 1942 her fascinating *Prelude, Allegro and Pastorale* (1941) for clarinet and viola was performed at the International Society of Contemporary Music Festival in San Francisco. In the same year she wrote one of her last songs, a powerful setting of G.K.

Chesterton's poem 'The Donkey'.

Two years later, in 1944 at the age of 58, Clarke married James Friskin, a piano teacher at the Juilliard School of Music who had been one of her contemporaries at the Royal College of Music. After her marriage, for no apparent reason, Clarke stopped composing and performing. She settled in New York City where she occasionally lectured or broadcast on music and wrote her fascinating, and as-yet-unpublished, account of her early life, 'I had a Father Too: or The Mustard Spoon'. Shortly before her death in 1979 she admitted that she very much missed composing, saying that there was almost nothing in the world that she found more thrilling.

Ruth Crawford
1901–1953

Ruth Crawford composed some of the most experimental and innovative American music of the late 1920s and early 1930s. Her small but fascinating output of concert music is all the more impressive for the fact that she virtually stopped composing such works while she was in her early 30s and became far better known during the remainder of her short life for arrangements and transcriptions of American folk songs.

Crawford was born in East Liverpool, Ohio. Her father was a Methodist minister who died while she was a teenager and her mother, an independent woman, was one of the first female stenographers. The family moved around frequently and were living in Jacksonville, Florida at the time of Clark Crawford's death. Crawford had piano lessons from an early age. After graduating from high school in 1918 she taught at the Jacksonville School of Musical Art, as well as continuing to study the piano and beginning to compose.

In 1921 an anonymous gift of money together with the money she had managed to save enabled Crawford to move to Chicago and enrol at the American Conservatory where she studied piano and composition. She had originally intended to become a professional pianist but a combination of muscular problems in her arms and the encouragement of her theory and composition teachers John Palmer and Adolf Weidig led to her gradual concentration on composition.

Crawford studied at the American Conservatory until 1927 when she gained her master's degree. For the next two years she studied privately on a Juilliard scholarship with Weidig, earning money to live by giving music lessons. From 1924 Crawford had been studying the piano with Djane Lavoie Herz, a former pupil of the experimental Russian composer Alexander Scriabin. Crawford was fascinated by both Scriabin's philosophy and his music and became part of Herz's radical musical circle, which included the avant-garde composers Henry Cowell, Dane Rudhyar and Edgar Varèse.

The use of dissonance in Crawford's music is apparent from one of her earliest works to survive, the *Five Piano Preludes* (1924–5) which were first performed at a League of Composers in New York in 1925. She followed these with four more piano preludes (1927–8), one of which she claimed represented a human laugh. As well as instrumental chamber works, such as the recently revived *Two Movements for Chamber Orchestra* (1926), Crawford was also writing teaching pieces and more popular works (under the pseudonym Fred Karkan) which were never published. During this period she got to know the poet Carl Sandburg who introduced her to American folk song, and for whose collection *The American Songbag* (1928) she provided several piano accompaniments.

Ruth Crawford

In 1929 Crawford spent the summer at the MacDowell Colony where she completed her *Five Songs* for voice and piano to poems by Sandburg and first met composer and critic Marion Bauer who became a staunch supporter of her work. In the autumn she moved to New York where Cowell had arranged for her to live with Blanche Walton, a wealthy patron of many composers. Cowell also managed to persuade one of the leading 'ultra-modern' theorists, Charles Seeger, to give Crawford composition lessons despite Seeger's initial reluctance to believe that there was any point in teaching a woman.

Seeger and Crawford soon realized that the lessons would be successful. She was fascinated by his theories of 'dissonant counterpoint' and he was impressed by her work. They studied the music of serialist composers such as Schoenberg together but rejected a strict 12-tone method of working as too rigid. Dissonant counterpoint treated dissonance as the norm with consonant intervals working in the same way that dissonant ones work in tonal music. Seeger's ideas also stressed the importance of musical elements other than the harmonic or melodic, such as rhythm, dynamic and timbre. Crawford's music from her period of study with Seeger, such as *Piano Study in Mixed Accents* (1930) and the four *Diaphonic Suites* (1930) for one and two instruments can be clearly seen as exercises in this way of composing.

During the summer of 1930 Crawford and Seeger worked together on his book about dissonant counterpoint, *Tradition and Experiment in the New Music,* a work that was never published. They also realized that they had fallen in love with each other shortly before Crawford left for Europe on a Guggenheim Fellowship, the first awarded to a woman. She took no further lessons while she was in Europe but concentrated on writing music and meeting other composers such as Alban Berg, Egon Wellesz, Maurice Ravel and Béla Bartók. She spent the first few months in Berlin where 'Rat Riddles', a Sandburg setting that she had written in March 1930, was performed. She also worked on a set of chants for women's voices (to meaningless syllables and humming) and began to compose a string quartet. Crawford's complex String Quartet is one of her best-known works. It uses various innovative compositional devices such as the 'dynamic counterpoint' of the intense second movement in which all the instruments play a different dynamic pattern so that, for instance, they never reach a loud climax together. The last movement is structured round a 10-note set. The work was eventually published in 1941 by Cowell in his magazine *New Music* which was a forum for many radical works, including several by Crawford.

Crawford spent the last few months of her European stay in Paris where she learned to her great disappointment that her fellowship would not be renewed for a further year. In November 1931 she returned to New York and moved in with Seeger. They were married in October 1932 when Seeger's first wife finally agreed to a divorce. Seeger had a very traditional view of marriage and of women's position, feeling that a woman should put her primary energy into bringing up children. At the time of their marriage he was involved in setting up the New York Musicological Society, an organization that excluded women although Crawford was later allowed to attend meetings. Nevertheless, in the early days of her married life, Crawford continued to teach the piano and to compose, using her maiden name for her professional work.

In 1932 she finished her fascinatingly radical Sandburg settings, *Three Songs* ('Rat Riddles', 'Prayers of Steel' and 'In Tall Grass') for voice, oboe, percussion, piano and orchestra. In the same year she wrote *Two Ricercari* for voice and piano. These were setting of two texts by H.T. Tsiang, 'Sacco, Vanzetti' about the unjust execution of two Italian Americans and 'Chinaman, Laundry-man' about the exploitation of Chinese immigrant workers. This work doubt-less grew out of her involvement with the Composers' Collective of New York, a socialist group of composers who responded to the problems of the Depression by exploring the relation-ship between music, society and politics and aiming to use music as a part of the class struggle. Both *Three Songs* and *Two Ricercari* were performed in 1933, the *Three Songs* representing the United States at the International Society for Contemporary Music Festival in Amsterdam.

These works were the last she was to write for several years, turning instead to, as she later put it, 'composing babies'. Her first child, Michael, was

born in 1933 and her second, Peggy, in 1935. Later that year Seeger took a job with the Resettlement Administration and the family moved to Silver Spring, Maryland, near Washington. The following year Crawford started to work at the excellent arrangements and transcriptions from field record-ings of folk song that were to occupy so much of her time for the rest of her life. Her work in this area included transcriptions for Alan Lomax's *Our Singing Country* (1941) and work with Seeger on John and Alan Lomax's *Folksong USA* (1948) as well as compil-ing and editing her own collections such as *American Folksongs for Children* (1948) and *Animal Folksongs for Children* (1950).

There has been much speculation as to why Crawford stopped composing concert music after such a promising and successful start to her career. There are many factors involved. One of the most important was lack of time. As well as her work with folk song, Crawford continued to teach the piano privately and also taught in several schools and nurseries. The family was never particularly affluent and Crawford's work as a teacher was undoubtedly far more lucrative than the composition of avant-garde concert music could ever have been. She had two more children, Barbara and Penny, in 1937 and 1943, and as well as looking after her own four children appears to have been involved in bringing up Seeger's three children from his first marriage. Her children were very important to her and yet she also seems to have longed for the time and space to compose her own music again.

Her works were still being heard. In 1938 a selection of her music, including the String Quartet, was performed in a concert given by the Composer's Forum Laboratory in New York. The following year CBS radio commissioned *Rissolty Rissolty*, an orchestral piece based on three folk songs, which was broadcast in the early 1940s. In 1952 Crawford completed her Wind Quintet which shows a return to her radical language of the 1930s while absorbing the rhythms and patterns of folk materials. The work won first prize in a competition organised by the local branch of the National Association of American Composers and Conductors and was premiered in December 1952. Although it seemed that Crawford might be moving back to composing concert music again, she was diagnosed with cancer in the summer of 1953 and died a few months later at the age of 52.

Melanie Daiken
b. 1945

Melanie Daiken's mother was a Canadian actor and her father was a writer of Russian Jewish origin from Ireland. Much of Daiken's music is inspired by images and ideas of different countries, particularly those relating to her family and her family history. Born in London, as a young child Daiken lived briefly in Israel and Canada before returning to England. She played the violin and piano, and when she was 10 became a Junior Exhibitioner at the Trinity College of Music where she started composing.

In 1963, Daiken went to the Royal Academy of Music to study the piano, but composition, which she initially took as a second study with Hugh Wood, gradually became more important. In 1964 Daiken spent a short time at the University of Ghana where she studied the structures and rhythms of traditional West-African music with J.H. Kwabena Nketia. Strong rhythmic patterns are very important in her work, although they are drawn more from the music of

Russian and East-European composers than from the traditional and popular music of West Africa.

During her time at the Academy, Daiken heard a performance of Olivier Messiaen's *L'Ascension* for organ and decided she wanted to study with him. Having won a French Government Scholarship, she spent two years, from 1966 to 1968, at the Paris Conservatoire studying with both Messiaen and Yvonne Loriod. Her first important works date from this time. *Les Petits Justes* (1967), a song cycle to poems by Paul Eluard, was first performed at the Wigmore Hall early in 1968 and then played at the Cheltenham Festival and broadcast by the BBC. Daiken's love of Robert Schumann's music led to two works, the piano duet *Four Pieces on a theme of Robert Schumann* (1967), using a theme from *Dichterliebe*, and her first dramatic work, the chamber opera *Eusebius* (1968). For this work, based on Schumann and his writings as Eusebius and Florestan, Daiken wrote her own libretto with help from Samuel Beckett. The first act was performed in Paris in 1968. *Eusebius* is still in progress and will eventually incorporate electronics, which Daiken studied on a course with Peter Zinoviev in London in 1970. In her early works Daiken was already focusing on the technique that has remained important in many of her works, that of transforming themes from folk tunes or works by other composers, in her own music. The idea of building music on the transformation of basic material is central to Messiaen's work. His emphasis on rich textures has also found resonance in Daiken's music.

On her return to London, Daiken started teaching at Goldsmiths' College, London University and at the adult education centre, Morley College. Teaching has remained her central occupation and means of earning a living. She taught harmony and composition at Morley until 1985 and still works at Goldsmiths', but the main focus of her teaching is at the Royal Academy of Music where she has worked since 1971, from 1985 to 1990 as deputy head of composition and contemporary music.

An interest in early Soviet culture led to Daiken's music-theatre piece *Mayakovsky and the Sun* for which she put together a text about Mayakovsky and his life using his own poetry. Commissioned by the Edinburgh Festival, it was first performed by the Music Theatre Ensemble under Alexander Goehr in 1971. In the mid–1970s Daiken wrote several pieces inspired by the work of Federico Lorca, including settings of his poems for two singers and piano and a work for solo baryton, *Cielo Vivo*, written for Riki Gerardy. Through Gerardy, Daiken met Hungarian viola player Csaba Erdelyi for whom she wrote her powerful Sonata for viola and piano in 1978. The strongly rhythmic first movement is influenced by the music of Franz Liszt and Béla Bartók, and the more lyrical second movement is built on a theme from Ambroise Thomas's opera *Mignon*. The following year Daiken continued using Hungarian influences in her *Eight Songs of Attila Jozsef* for mezzo-soprano, viola and piano and she is now working on more settings of Jozsef, *O Zordan Szepseg* for choir, string quartet, harp, wind and percussion.

Daiken married Patrick Cuming in 1980 and although she has no children has been involved in looking after his three daughters from a previous marriage. She works slowly, partly due to the amount of time she spends teaching and partly due to periods of illness which prevent her from composing. Her works have become increasingly tonal, although she will still sometimes use small, three- or five-note rows to construct her music. Each of her works creates its own individual sound world and style, and she builds

her music on a variety of initial inspirations. The striking piano work *Requiem*
(1985), written for her mother, grew
from memories of Canada.

Words and poetry are extremely
important in the structure and genesis
of Daiken's music, even when they are
not actually heard. *Gems of Erin* (1980)
for wind and brass ensemble, piano,
percussion and double bass actually
sets the rhythmic patterns of the
words of Samuel Beckett's *Poems in
English* as well as using the imagery
suggested by the poems. Daiken used
this technique again in *Der Gartner*
(1988) for 13 solo strings and piano.

This work is built round a theme from
Hugo Wolf's song of the same name as
well as wordlessly setting poems from
Rabindranath Tagore's *The Garden*.
Words and pictures played a part in
the genesis of *Spectres Classiques*
(1989), a work commissioned by the
ensemble Gemini for flute, clarinet,
trumpet and string trio. Described by
Daiken as 'a nightmare of sketches of
Paris in the past', it was inspired by
the paintings of Jean-Antoine
Watteau, Louis David, Eugène
Delacroix and Jean-Baptiste-Camille
Corot and the poetry of Paul Verlaine,
Charles Baudelaire, Arthur Rimbaud
and Guillaume Apollinaire.

Mabel Daniels
1879–1971

Mabel Daniels came from a wealthy New England family with a strong interest in music and particular associations with the Handel and Haydn Society of Boston for which her grandfather had acted as organist and her father as president. She was born in Swampscott, Massachusetts in 1879 (a date of 1878 is also given) and had piano lessons from an early age. As a child she wrote stories and poems as well as piano pieces. Daniels studied at the newly founded Radcliffe College, where she was director of the glee club for which she wrote and conducted two operettas in 1900, the year she graduated. She was to retain a close connection with the college for the rest of her life, directing the glee club again when she was in her 30s, writing music for important anniversaries, becoming a trustee and endowing a loan fund for music students.

After leaving Radcliffe Daniels studied composition privately with George Chadwick, one of the leading composers of the New England School.

During this time she also collaborated on the composition of another operetta, *The Show Girl* (1902). In the autumn of 1902, at Chadwick's suggestion, she went to Munich for further composition study with Ludwig Thuille. When Daniels arrived in Munich, women had only been permitted to attend counterpoint classes at the Conservatory for five years and she caused consternation by becoming the first woman to take part in the score-reading class. As well as studying composition, she also took singing lessons and went frequently to the opera. She spent two winters in Germany and on her return to the States published an account of her time there, *An American Girl in Munich: Impressions of a Music Student*.

Although Daniels sang with the Cecilia Society, a chorus that performed much modern music and from which she undoubtedly learnt much about contemporary repertoire as well as gaining the experience of working with an orchestra, her early works have been described as essentially conservative. In 1908 the Boston Pops under Gustav Strube performed her first orchestral work *In the Greenwood.* In 1911 she won a prize from the National Federation of Music Clubs for her part-songs *Eastern Song* and *The Voice of My Beloved*, for women's voices with the rather unusual accompaniment of two violins and piano. At this time she was working with the Radcliffe Glee Club and spent the three years from 1911 to 1913 as music director for Bradford Academy.

In 1913 Daniels became the director of music at Simmonds College in Boston for five years, the only other music post she was to hold, although she did later serve on the advisory committee on music for Boston public schools. Also in 1913, Daniels was asked to conduct her cantata *The Desolate City* for baritone, chorus and orchestra at the MacDowell Colony summer festival in New Hampshire. Daniels was to spend much time at the colony, wrote many of her works there and in 1931 was awarded a MacDowell Fellowship.

Daniels also developed important friendships with other New-England women composers such as Amy Beach, Margaret Ruthven Lang and Helen Hopekirk. Continuing in the crusading spirit with which she had tackled the Munich Conservatory, Daniels demonstrated for women's right to vote and was a member of the Society of American Women Composers, founded in 1924. She believed that women needed talent, strong constitutions, perseverance, ingenuity and courage in order to compose, feeling that they were naturally rather too weak for the hard work involved in composing large-scale works. This obviously did not apply to herself, as she composed many large-scale works including several orchestral pieces.

One of Daniels' best-known works was *Exultate Deo*, op. 33, a cantata for chorus and orchestra written for Radcliffe College's 50th anniversary in 1929. Another frequently performed work was the prelude *Deep Forest*, op. 34 no. 1, originally written for chamber orchestra in 1931, first performed in New York in 1932 and then revised for full orchestra in 1934. This was also the year of her comical orchestral piece *Pirate's Island*, op. 34 no. 2, later choreographed and performed as a ballet, as was another satirical work, the *Three Observations for Three Wooodwinds* (1943).

In 1940 Daniels' cantata *Song of Jael*, op. 37, for soprano solo, chorus and orchestra, was first performed at the Worcester Festival. She based the work on a poem *Sisera* by her friend Edward Arlington Robinson who had died five years previously. It tells the story of Jael, a woman who kills the tyrant Sisera and becomes a heroine. With a strongly dramatic part for the soprano as Jael and some striking writing for the chorus, *Song of Jael* indicated a move away from Daniels' early conservative style to a more contemporary idiom. She produced many other works in a variety of genres in the 1940s including a *Pastoral Ode* (1940), op. 40, for flute and strings, *Four Observations for Four Strings* (1945) and *Digressions* (1947), op. 41 no. 2, for string orchestra.

Endlessly generous to other musicians, Daniels gave several anonymous composition prizes and established a scholarship at the New England Conservatory of Music, of which she was also a trustee. She continued writing into her 80s, producing *A Psalm of Praise*, op. 46, for chorus, three trumpets, percussion and strings for Radcliffe College's 75th anniversary in 1954 when she was 75, and completing her last work, the choral piece *Piper, Play On!*, op. 49, in 1961, 10 years before her death in 1971.

Mary Dering
1629–1704

Mary Dering's father was Daniel Harvey, a well-to-do Croydon merchant and brother of the Dr William Harvey who discovered the circulation of the blood. As a child she was sent to school at a Mrs Salmon's establishment in Hackney where one of her closest friends was Katherine Philips (1632–1664), later to be known as 'the matchless Orinda', one of Britain's leading women poets. Girls' schools flourished in the 17th century. Pupils were taught the various skills that they would need as young ladies in society, and one of the most important of these accomplishments was music. The extent of music performed or practised at Mrs Salmon's is not known, but later in the century Josiah Priest's girls' school in Chelsea saw early performances of important works such as Henry Purcell's *Dido and Aeneas* and John Blow's *Venus and Adonis*.

Around 1645 when Mary Harvey was about 16 she married her cousin and father's apprentice William Hawke.

Accounts of this marriage vary. According to some the marriage was never consummated, while others claimed that the couple lived together for a year. Whatever the truth, the marriage was dissolved in the ecclesiastical courts in time for her second marriage in 1648 to Sir Edward Dering, a Kent landowner and holder of various political posts. In 1649 Dering had her first child and over the next 23 years produced 17 children, 10 of whom lived to adulthood. After she was married, Dering continued to study music, taking lessons from composer Henry Lawes. Edward Dering's account books record a payment of 30 shillings to Lawes 'for a month's teaching of my wife' in May 1649.

Dering's friendship with Katherine Philips continued during her married life. Although neither of the Derings appear to have been members of Philips' closest circle – 'the Official Order of Friendship in the Kingdom of feminine sensibility' – they were recipients of her poems. Edward, who wrote poetry himself, was given the pseudonym 'the noble Sylvander' and Mary was probably known as 'Philoclea' or 'Ardelia'. Henry Lawes, 'gentle Thirsis', was also a member of Philips' circle. He had been a court musician during Charles I's reign and turned to teaching at the outbreak of civil war. Many of his pupils were society ladies and several were members of Philips' circle.

Dering's lessons were probably in singing and playing the keyboard but Lawes obviously encouraged her to write music as well. In dedicating his *Second Book of Select Ayres and Dialogues* (1655) to her, he wrote '... you are not only excellent for the time you spent in the practise of what I set, but are yourself so good a composer, that few of any sex have arriv'd to such perfection'. He took the unprecedented step of including in the collection three songs written by Dering herself to lyrics by her husband. These appear to be the first surviving published compositions by a British woman. Publishing her work was obviously not something that Dering would have attempted on her own. Lawes admits that he included her music 'although your Ladiship resolved to keep it private'. The three songs, 'When first I saw fair Doris's eyes', 'And is this all? What one poor Kisse?' and 'In vain fair Chloris, you designe' are typical of their time, short, tuneful pieces for solo voice and accompaniment. Dering was doubtless not the only woman of her time to write music. That these three songs were published and have survived probably reflects the appreciation of female creativity which was central to the circle around Katherine Philips in which Lawes and Dering moved.

Lucia Dlugoszewski
b. 1934

Lucia Dlugoszewski has always been fascinated by exploring the boundaries of sound and creating music that evokes a sense of wonder and involves the listener in hearing as if for the first time. Unlike many other experimental composers, she is concerned to retain the spirit, immediacy and spontaneity of live performance rather than use electronic composition. Early in her career she invented instruments in order to create new timbres and textures for her music. In later years she explored a variety of techniques to expand the sound possibilities of traditional instruments.

Certain concepts are central to Dlugoszewski's ideas about her composition and are often reflected in the titles of her works. These concepts include the 'suchness' (*tathata*) of Zen Buddhism (or the 'quidditas' of James Joyce). The suchness of a thing is what makes it what it is, and involves an immediate experience of the 'thing in itself'. Another important concept for Dlugoszewski is 'otherness' or 'strangeness', the shattering of 'ordinary reality'.

For many years Dlugoszewski's work was largely ignored by other musicians and most appreciated by visual artists and writers. She herself has written poetry since she was a teenager and published a book of poems, *A New Folder*, in 1969. She has also written an article on aesthetics, 'What is sound to music?' with the philosopher F.S.C. Northrop, published in *Main Currents in Modern Thought* in 1971.

Dlugoszewski's mother was a painter and her father was an engineer. She was born in Detroit and showed a very early interest in music, composing at the age of three and studying the piano at the Detroit Conservatory from the age of six. She continued to take both piano and composition lessons at the Conservatory and also studied as a pre-medical student at Wayne State University from 1949 to 1952, graduating with a degree in chemistry at the age of 15. Her first acknowledged compositions date from 1949 and include *Moving Space Theater Piece For Everyday Sounds* which was performed in Detroit in that year. In 1951 she built her timbre piano, a customized instrument with the strings sounded by various beaters, picks and bows.

Having abandoned her plans to become a doctor, Dlugoszewski moved to New York in 1952. Here she continued her musical studies, taking piano lessons with Grete Sultan and studying musical analysis at Mannes College. A few years later she also took composition lessons with Edgar Varèse. In 1952, soon after arriving in New York, Dlugoszewski gave another performance of a work using everyday sounds, *Everyday Sounds for e.e. cummings With Transparencies*. A third everyday sounds piece, *The Structure For The Poetry Of Everyday Sounds*, was written for a production of Alfred Jarry's *Ubu Roi* given by the Living Theatre in the same year. Dlugoszewski was also writing works using her timbre piano, such as the theatre score *Desire Trapped By The Tail* (1952) for voice and timbre piano, and *Archaic Timbre Piano Music* (1954–7). She continued to use the instrument in many of her later works, including *Skylark Cicada* (1964) for violin and timbre piano, *Velocity Shells* (1970) for timbre piano, trumpet and percussion and *Duende Newfallen* (1982–3) for bass trombone and timbre piano.

In 1952 Dlugoszewski first met choreographer Erick Hawkins and began her long musical association with the Erick Hawkins Dance Company for which she has worked as musical director and written many dance scores. This provided her with an invaluable outlet for her music especially in the 1950s and early 1960s when her work was not taken seriously by the musical establishment. In 1958 Hawkins asked her to write the music for *Eight Clear Places*, a dance that was a meditation on nature. Dlugoszewski wanted to use percussion instruments for the piece but disliked the 'aggressive' quality of traditional percussion and felt that they did not achieve the 'suchness' dimension of sound that she wanted. So she created a large collection of new percussion instruments, including elegant ladder harps and various rattles, which were made for her by sculptor Ralph Dorazio. Her work for Hawkins' dance, *Suchness Concert* (1958–60), used an ensemble of 100 of these instruments, and she continued to use this ensemble in other works such as *Geography of Noon* (1964), another dance score for Hawkins, and *Percussion Airplane Hetero* (1965). She also incorporated the instruments into other works such as *Delicate Accidents in Space* (1959) for five unsheltered rattles, or the theatre score *Concert Of Many Rooms And Moving Space* (1960) for flute, clarinet, timbre piano and four unsheltered rattles.

Lucia Dlugoszewski playing her invented percussion instruments

From 1960 Dlugoszewski worked as a teacher and composer at the Foundation for Modern Dance. She has also taught at New York University and the New School for Social Research. Much of her music continued to be written for Hawkins with works such as *The Suchness of Nine Concerts* (1969–70) for clarinet, violin, two percussion and timbre piano for Hawkins' dance *Black Lake*, and *Tender Theatre Flight Nageire* (1971) for brass sextet and percussion for Hawkins' dance *Of Love*. Dlugoszewski's interest in the sound possibilities of brass instruments led to the composition of one of her best-known works, the dazzlingly virtuosic *Space is a Diamond* (1970) for trumpet. In the same year she wrote an opera, *The Heidi Songs*, setting John Ashbery's *Animals of all Countries*.

In the mid-1960s Dlugoszewski began to write music which centred around the concept of 'leaping', using elements of surprise and extreme speed to create the sense of immediacy that is so important in her music. The first of these works was *Balance Naked Flung* (1966) for clarinet, trumpet, bass trombone, violin and percussion, written for Hawkins' *Lords of Persia*. *Fire Fragile Flight* (1974) for 17 instruments explores a continual leaping of new sounds and ideas. In 1977 this piece became the first work by a woman to win the Koussevitsky International Recording Award.

Dlugoszewski received her first major commission in 1975, from the New York Philharmonic Orchestra. Her work for the commission, *Abyss and Caress* (1975) for trumpet and small orchestra, again explores unusual sounds, asking the string players to play their instruments with bows made of different materials and using the timbre piano. At this time she began work on several pieces for large ensembles, such as two works that are still in progress, *Strange Tenderness of Naked Leaping* (1977–) and *Wilderness Elegant Tilt* (1981–).

In the early 1980s, Dlugoszewski's mother became very ill and Dlugoszewski spent most of the decade looking after her, with little time to concentrate on composition. After her mother's death in 1988, Dlugoszewski was able to return to her music. In the early 1990s she produced a series of chamber works including two pieces for flute, clarinet, trumpet, trombone, violin and bass, *Radical Otherness Concert* (1991) and *Radical Suchness Concert* (1991), and a piece exploring subtlety, *Radical Narrowness Concert* (1992) for the same instrumentation. Her percussion work *Radical Quidditas For An Unborn Baby* (1991) uses a large ensemble of traditional percussion instruments together with her own invented instruments, all played by one performer, to create music that is both tender and reckless.

Sophia Dussek
1775–c. 1830

Sophia Dussek was born in Edinburgh into a family of musicians of Italian origin. Her father Domenico Corri was a composer and music publisher and her mother had been one of his singing pupils. As with so many women musicians of the 18th century, Dussek's first teacher was her father. She went on to have further music lessons from men such as singer Luigi Marchesi and composer and teacher Giambattista Cimador.

Dussek first played the piano in public in Edinburgh at the age of four. In 1788 she moved with her family to London and made her first public appearance there at a Salomon concert at Hanover Square in April 1791. *The Gazetteer* was complimentary: 'Her voice is pleasing and flexible, and it has con-siderable compass. Her ear is admirably correct, and ... she evinced much skill as a musician. Upon the whole Miss Corri promises to become a very distinguished ornament of the profession'. Later that year she sang and played the piano at her own benefit concert at which Joseph Haydn also performed. She sang in many of the concerts organized by Salomon to promote Haydn.

In September 1792 Dussek married the virtuoso Czech pianist Jan Ladislav Dussek who had performed a piano sonata at her debut concert in London. This was presumably after he had finished his affair with the German composer and harpist Anne-Marie Krumpholtz (1755–1824) who eloped with him to London in the late 1780s leaving behind a devastated husband who drowned himself in the Seine. It is interesting to see that both Jan Ladislav and Sophia performed at Krumpholtz's benefit in May 1792. Jan Ladislav Dussek was himself from a musical family, his sister Veronica Dussek came to London in the mid-1790s where she established a career for herself as performer, published several works for the piano and married the composer and teacher Francesco Cianchettini.

After their marriage, Sophia and Jan Ladislav Dussek lived at her father's house and frequently performed together. But theirs was not a very successful relationship. In 1800 Jan Ladislav appears to have deserted his wife by leaving the country when his music-publishing business collapsed. Dussek retired from performing and concentrated on teaching and publishing her compositions. After Jan Ladislav died in 1812, Dussek married the viola player John Avis Moralt and lived with him in Paddington where they established a piano school. Dussek's daughter by Jan Ladislav, Olivia Dussek (1799–1847), was also a musician who worked as organist of Kensington parish church for the last seven years of her life and who published several compositions including piano and harp works, songs and teaching pieces.

Sophia Dussek was a prolific composer and arranger. She always published as S. Dussek, an early example of a woman using a name with ambiguous gender under which to publish her music. Her surviving works are dedicated to a wide variety of women, probably her pupils, and are written for piano, harp or piano and harp duet. The works for harp include many arrangements of popular (or 'favourite') airs with sets of variations and there are also piano and harp sonatas. Dussek wrote in a simple, tuneful style suitable for the amateur performers at whom her music was aimed. She also made many arrangements for the harp of works by other composers such as Ignace Pleyel and Gioachino Rossini. She is thought to have died in about 1830.

Rosalind Ellicott
1857–1924

In the last two decades of the 19th century Rosalind Ellicott's choral and orchestral music was often heard at the prestigious but conservative Three Choirs Festival, held in rotation at Gloucester, Worcester or Hereford. Although Alice Mary Smith's *Ode to the Passions* was performed at Hereford in 1882, it was not until the 1920s that any other woman was to have orchestral work programmed at the festival. It may have helped Ellicott that her father had been appointed Bishop of Bristol and Gloucester in 1863, although John Ellicott was notoriously uninterested in music.

Ellicott was born in Cambridge on 14 November 1857. Her mother was a keen singer who was involved in forming the Gloucester Philharmonic Society and the Handel Society in London. Reputed to have started composing at the age of six, in 1874 at 16 Ellicott entered the Royal Academy of Music where she studied the piano for two years. She then took composition lessons from Thomas Wingham until

the early 1880s by which time her music was being heard at a variety of concerts.

In 1883 her song 'To the Immortals' was sung (and encored) at the Gloucester Festival. The following year a string quartet in B♭ was performed at the Steinway Hall in London by the Society of Musical Artists. In 1886 there were two performances of orchestral works by the 29-year-old composer. Her *Overture to Spring* was played by The Strolling Players in February, and in September her *Dramatic Overture* was performed at the Gloucester Festival. Her mother wrote to an acquaintance:

> She is bringing out an Overture (her second Orchestral work) at the Tuesday Evening Concert and to judge from its reception by the band at the rehearsal on Wednesday morning I think it is likely to produce a sensation. She calls it 'dramatic' because one of its leading features are recits for celli.

Rosalind Ellicott

This work was played in London at the Crystal Palace in 1891 and in the United States at the grand opening of the Woman's Building at the Chicago World's Columbian Exposition in May 1893.

Meanwhile Ellicott had had two large cantatas performed at the Gloucester Festival. *Elysium*, for soprano, chorus and orchestra to a libretto by Felicia Hemans, was first heard in 1889 and thought by the critic of *The Musical Times* to be 'expressive of the sentiments of the poetry, technically good, and aesthetically attractive'. In 1892 *The Birth of Song*, a setting of a poem by Lewis Morris for soprano, tenor, chorus and orchestra, was performed. *The Musical Times* found that 'it challenges comparison with masculine work. There is certainly strength in the orchestration, and occasionally a display of vigour in construction and expression, such as would warrant the qualification "manly"'. This was a constant theme in reviews of her work. A reviewer of her *Album of Six Pieces* (1892) for violin and piano thought that 'in qualities usually regarded as peculiarly masculine her compositions are vastly superior to those of many male writers who have the public ear'. Reviewers also tended to refer to her as an amateur. Her mother, however, described her as '... in all respects a member of the musical profession and not an amateur. You may be amused by my emphatic underlining but she is always annoyed at being spoken of as a "talented amateur"'.

It was, of course, hardly proper for a Bishop's daughter to be seen to follow a career. An article in *The Lady's Realm* of 1897 stressed that Ellicott '... has already won wide recognition as a musical composer, but she has never allowed her musical studies to interfere in any way with her home duties'. Ellicott must have been gratified when she was elected to membership of the Incorporated Society of Musicians, following a successful performance of her part-song 'Bring the Bright Garland' at the Bristol Madrigal Society in 1890. Novelist Robert Hichens described her as 'very ambitious' and she worked hard at trying to obtain performances of her music. In 1886 she sent her *Dramatic Overture* to the prestigious Philharmonic Society in London, asking them to accept it for performance, and although the work was rejected she applied again in 1891, and was again rejected.

In 1894 *King Henry of Navarre*, a choral ballad for men's voices setting verses by Thomas Babington Macaulay was performed at Queen's College, Oxford. The next year a *Fantaisie* in A minor for piano and orchestra was premiered at the Gloucester Festival and repeated at the Crystal Palace in 1896 and by the Westminster Orchestral Society in 1897. These repeat performances were very important. All too often large works were only ever given a single performance and then left to gather dust on the composer's shelves. *King Henry of Navarre* was performed again at the Gloucester Festival in 1898 although the organizers had asked her for a new work. This performance prompted the reviewer of *The Musical Times* to claim that 'the fire of Macaulay's verses is not shared by the music and, after all, who can wonder at it? Such a theme needs to be handled by a strong man, not by a woman...'.

Although *Elysium* and *The Birth of Song* were published by Novello, no other orchestral or choral works and very little chamber music by Ellicott was ever published, and the manuscripts do not appear to have survived. The eloquently lyrical violin and piano piece, *A Sketch*, was published by Schott in 1883, and Novello issued a *Reverie* for cello and piano in 1888 and six pieces for violin and piano in 1891. Neither the early String Quartet in B♭ nor any of the later chamber works (two Piano Trios, a Sonata for violin and piano and a Piano Quartet) have survived, although all these works were performed, many of them several times, at concerts given by well-known musicians such as David Bispham, Alfredo Piatti, Sybil Palliser and Lionel Tertis, at series organized by the Society of Musical Artists or at the Ernest Fowles British Chamber Music Series. The works that do survive bear a strong resemblance to the early music of her exact contemporary Edward Elgar.

From the mid–1890s onwards Ellicott seems to have concentrated on producing chamber music, probably because it was comparatively easy to obtain performances of music not involving large orchestral forces. In 1896 she gave a highly successful concert of her own chamber music and songs in the Small Queen's Hall in London. In the early years of the century she established her own series of chamber music concerts in Gloucester with a Miss Hirschfeld.

There is no surviving record of Ellicott's activities during the last years of her life. Her father died in 1905, and although she was living in London during the first world war she had moved to a seaside village in Kent by the early 1920s. Here she died in 1924 and was buried with her parents in the local churchyard.

Eibhlis Farrell
b. 1953

Eibhlis Farrell was born and grew up in Rostrevor in County Down, Ireland. As a child she had piano lessons at the local convent and played the Irish fiddle. The changes to music in the Roman Catholic Church decreed by the Vatican Council in 1962 did not take effect in rural Ireland until the 1970s, and Farrell grew up singing rigorous plainchant in her local church. She also became fascinated with bells, and in particular with the ninth-century bronze bell that had come from a nearby monastery and was reputed to have magical powers.

Farrell began writing music while she was still at school and knew she wanted to be a composer by the time she left. At Queen's University in Belfast where she studied music there was no formal composition teaching, but the students were encouraged to write and Farrell heard much of her music performed. After studying for a master's degree in composition at Bristol University with Raymond Warren, Farrell returned to Ireland in 1983 to take up a position as Deputy Principal at the Dublin College of Music. The pressures of a full-time job which involves a lot of administration means using her ingenuity to find the time to compose. Nevertheless she has written a series of intensely lyrical works in a variety of genres which are being heard with increasing frequency throughout Europe and in the United States.

In 1988 Farrell took two years' leave from the college to take up a fellowship in composition at Rutgers University in New Jersey where she studied with Charles Wuorinen. While at Rutgers she took her doctoral exams and received her doctorate in 1991, having returned to her post in Dublin. Her examination work was *Exultet* (1991) for soloists, choir and orchestra. Setting liturgy from the Easter Exultet and parts of Boethius' *The Consolation of Philosophy*, this 40-minute work draws on her childhood experiences of plainchant and of bells. Other works that explore the world of sacred choral music include *A Garland for the President: Sancta Maria* (1990), a moving lament for soprano and chorus, and the richly textured *Exaudi Voces* (1991) for four soloists and chorus.

Another composition from 1991 is *Canson* for violin and piano, a one-movement work commissioned by the Irish broadcasting company RTE, in which Farrell evokes the sound world of the baroque violin sonata. It opens with a long, lyrical line from the violin high in its register accompanied by a starker supporting line from the piano. The music moves through a tense and dramatic section with agitated rhythms before recalling the opening and then dying away.

The music of the Baroque period, and particularly the vocal music of composers such as Monteverdi, holds a particular fascination for Farrell. Her dramatic *Concerto Grosso* (1988) for two violins, cello and string orchestra echoes the Baroque love of contrast in its juxtaposition of a lyrical solo group with the more rhythmic tutti strings. *Orpheus Sings* (1992), for violin and guitar, uses the violin to represent Orpheus, accompanied by the guitar in a recitative-like manner. In

Soundshock (1993), a vigorous work for concert band, Farrell explores the tone colours of the different woodwind, brass and percussion instruments as well as looking back to the Baroque again in her use of rhythmic patterns.

In recent years, Farrell has become increasingly interested in writing solo vocal music. In her haunting *Windfalls* (1990), setting text by Seamus Heaney, the soprano is accompanied by Irish harp, bodhrán (frame drum), violin, flute and clarinet. *The Love-Song of Isabella and Elias Cairel* (1993), a chamber concerto for mezzo-soprano, oboe, viola and glockenspiel setting 12th-century troubadour poetry, was commissioned for the International Congress of Women in Music in Alaska. *The Silken Bed* (1994) for cello, violin, harpsichord and mezzo-soprano, is a setting of a poem by Nuala ni Domhnaill in the original Gaelic and in English and Italian translations. Farrell believes strongly in the central importance of sonority and texture in her music and this work, with vocal writing drawing on both Baroque arioso recitative and traditional Irish *sean nos* singing, creates a gloriously rich and sensuous sound world.

Vivian Fine
b. 1913

Vivian Fine was born in Chicago, the daughter of Russian-Jewish immigrants. She started playing the piano at five and had lessons with Djane Lavoie Herz from the age of 11. Herz was impressed with Fine's musical abilities and arranged for her to study theory and harmony with another of her piano pupils, composer Ruth Crawford. Fine studied with Crawford for four years and started composing at the age of 13 when Crawford asked her to write a piece of music, something that it had never occurred to her to do before. From that point on, composition became extremely important to her. She left school at 14 and concentrated on her studies with Crawford, whose influence both stylistically and as a role model was enormous.

In 1929, when Fine was 16, a New York concert of the Pan-American Association of Composers organized by Henry Cowell, provided the first public performance of one of her works, *Solo for Oboe*. Like all her early works, such as *Four Pieces for Two Flutes* (1930), this was a highly dissonant piece. When Crawford moved to New York in 1929, Fine studied with Crawford's old teacher, Adolf Weidig of the American Conservatory, for a year.

Fine herself moved to New York in 1931. To earn a living, she worked as a dance accompanist, playing complex scores such as Igor Stravinsky's *Petrushka* and Richard Strauss' *Salome* on the piano, and began to gain a reputation as a performer of contemporary music. She also continued to compose, and became the only female member of Aaron Copland's Young Composers Group, as well as taking further composition lessons with Roger Sessions. *Four Songs* (1933) for voice and string quartet (1933) were the first of her works to be published when they appeared in Henry Cowell's *New Music Edition*. Like most of her music at this time, they use dissonant counterpoint, the technique developed by Crawford and Charles Seeger.

At the age of 21, Fine married the sculptor Benjamin Karp and later had two daughters. She continued to work as a pianist, performing a great deal of new music for organizations such as the League of Composers and the Pan-American Association of Composers. She also continued to play as a dance accompanist, and her work for choreographers such as Doris Humphrey and Charles Weidman led to the composition of several ballets in a more accessible, tonal idiom. These included *The Race of Life* (1937) for Doris Humphrey, a humorous piece based on drawings by James Thurber about a middle-class American family and their search for wealth.

In 1938 she wrote *Opus 51* for Charles Weidman's company, and the same year arranged the concert piece *Dance Suite* (1938), using material from both *The Race of Life* and *Opus 51*. The following year she wrote two ballets, *Tragic Exodus* and *They Too Are Exiles* for choreographer Hanya Holm. Fine's concert music during this period included her two-movement *Concertante for Piano and Orchestra* (1943–4), a tightly constructed and appealingly lyrical work with a strongly neo-classic texture and rhythmic energy.

From 1945 Fine took on various teaching jobs at New York University, the Juilliard School of Music and the State University of New York at Potsdam. As she moved away from concentrating on music for dance, her style became more dissonant and experimental again, although it was never to return to the radical atonality of her early works. In 1956 she wrote one of her best-known works, *A Guide to the Life Expectancy of a Rose*. This is a comic setting of an article from the gardening column of the *New York Times* for soprano, tenor, flute, violin, clarinet, cello and harp. It was commissioned by the Rothschild Foundation, for whom she worked as music director for six years in the late 1950s, and was staged by the choreographer Martha Graham. A few years later Graham commissioned a ballet and Fine wrote *Alcestis,* based on the legend of the woman prepared to sacrifice herself in return for her husband's immortality, but was saved by Hercules who wrestles with death and wins. Fine's music was scored for double winds, piano, harp, percussion and strings and arranged as a frequently performed orchestral suite the same year.

From 1961 to 1965 Fine was the vice-president of the American Composers' Alliance, an organization she had helped to found in 1937. She continued to teach, taking a post at Bennington College, Vermont in 1964 that left her with little time for composing but that she was to hold for the next 23 years. Nevertheless, she continued to produce an impressive series of works, each seeming to develop its own individual style and often creating unusual and original sound worlds. The dramatic cantata *Paean* (1969) for brass ensemble of trumpets and trombones, women's chorus and tenor soloist uses extracts from John Keats' *Ode to Apollo* as its text. Fine uses the voices in a variety of conventional and unconventional ways, from talking through screaming, whispering, crying and hissing to singing and creates a strangely disturbing piece.

One of Fine's most intense and moving works is the *Missa Brevis* (1972) for four cellos and a four-track recording of a mezzo-soprano voice. It sets parts of the liturgy in Latin and Hebrew and creates a dark sound world which moves through laments and anger to a certain feeling of peace. In 1976 Fine wrote her large work for narrator, soloists, chorus and orchestra, *Meeting for Equal Rights 1866*, putting the text together from various 19th-century writings and speeches about women's suffrage. It is a complex work needing three conductors but displaying Fine's sense of humour in many of its touches, such as the musical suggestion of Johannes Brahms' famous lullaby when the text is presenting the argument that a woman's place is in the home.

Two years later Fine wrote her first opera, *The Women in the Garden* (1978), a fascinating chamber work for five singers and nine instruments. Using Emily Dickinson, Isadora Duncan, Gertrude Stein and Virginia Woolf as the central characters, Fine created a plotless text out of their various writings. The fifth part is for a tenor who plays all the necessary male roles. But this is an opera about women and their attitudes towards their creativity, towards their lives and experiences and towards each other.

During the 1980s Fine wrote several orchestral works including *Drama for Orchestra* (1982), commissioned by the San Francisco Symphony Orchestra, and *Poetic Fires* (1984) for piano and orchestra, premiered in 1985 with Fine herself playing the piano part. In 1988 as a celebration of her 75th birthday, the Bay Area Women's Philharmonic commissioned and premiered *After the Tradition*, a work with its roots in Fine's Jewish background. One of her most recent projects is the chamber opera *Juliana Rooney*, about a Russian woman composer with seven husbands, which Fine has described as 'opera in the form of a newsreel'.

Jennifer Fowler
b. 1939

Jennifer Fowler was born and grew up in Bunbury, a town about 100 miles south of Perth in Western Australia. Her mother had been a piano teacher and Fowler started reading and playing music at an early age although she was not allowed formal piano lessons until she was about nine. It was at this age that she started making up her own music and attempting to write it down. In 1957, at the age of 18, she went to the University of Western Australia in Perth where a music department was in the process of being established. She graduated in 1960, one of the first students to gain an arts degree specializing in music.

After a year's teacher-training course in 1961, Fowler spent a couple of years teaching in secondary schools in the country. She then returned to Perth where she taught full time as well as studying for the new composition-based B.Mus degree from the University of Western Australia which she received in 1967. During her early student years in Australia, Fowler had many of her works performed in Perth and broadcast by the ABC, although most of this music has now been withdrawn.

In 1968, at the age of 29, Fowler received a scholarship from the Dutch Government Scholarship which enabled her to study at the Studio of Electronic Music in Utrecht for a year. This year free from teaching commitments was a turning point in Fowler's career. She was fascinated by the musical developments that were taking place in Europe at this time, although she decided that the complex serial techniques that many composers were using were too rigid for her own music. She has not since had the access to an electronic studio that would allow her to use electronics in her work, but certain approaches to writing music that had been suggested to her by working with electronics, such as the use of wave-like shapes or the exploration of new sounds, have become an important part of her musical language.

Fowler moved to London in 1969 and taught for several years at Wykeham Secondary School. Her first big success came in 1970 when one of the works she had written while in Utrecht, *Hours of the Day* (1968) for four sopranos, two oboes and two clarinets, won a prize from the Akademie der Kunste in Berlin. The following year she was a joint winner of a Radcliffe award for her string quintet *Ravelation* (1970–71). Other works written in 1971 include the humorous piece *Chimes, Fractured* for double woodwind, organ, bagpipes and percussion which had been inspired by hearing the organ and bells playing in Liverpool Cathedral while a traditional Scottish wedding was taking place outside, and *Veni Sancte Spiritus – Veni Creator*, a choral work for 12 solo singers based on plainsong.

In 1971 Fowler married British computer designer Bruce Patterson, a keen amateur musician whom she had met through singing in a choir. She had two sons, born in 1973 and 1976, and although she found that working from home while bringing up small children placed restrictions on her composition, she produced several important works during the 1970s. The complex orchestral work *Chant with Garlands* (1974) uses elements from the Aboriginal musical culture of Australia such as regular pulsating figures that are reminiscent of the sound of the didgeridoo as well as passages evoking Aboriginal chanting. In *Voice of the*

Shades (1976–7) for soprano, oboe or clarinet and violin, Fowler's text uses 'made-up' words created by the same strict procedures as those by which the musical pitches were chosen. The result is a lyrical, almost hypnotic work.

Fowler has always been concerned to find a musical path somewhere between extreme complexity and extreme simplicity that would enable her to express her own sense of excitement at the creation of music. During the 1980s she moved away from writing music where a complex texture was of prime importance. Several of her works continued to use elements of Aboriginal music such as *When David Heard* (1982) for choir and piano, based on Aboriginal chanting, and *We Call to You, Brother* (1988) for flute, cor anglais, cello, percussion and two trombones in which one of the trombonists doubles on the didgeridoo and the percussion used includes traditional clap sticks.

Several works are concerned with exploring the possibilities within a single line of music. *Line Spun with Stars* (1982) for flute or violin, cello and piano creates beautiful melodic lines interspersed with 'star patterns' or note clusters. Fowler uses a similar technique in the atmospheric *Threaded Stars* (1983) for solo harp. *Blow Flute: Answer Echoes in Antique Lands Dying* (1983) for flute explores the challenges of working with straightforward pitch and rhythmic material and builds a wonderfully contemplative fluid line. Fowler often revises or reworks her pieces. *Echoes from an Antique Land*, which grew out of *Blow Flute*, exists in three different versions for different instrumental ensembles.

In some of her works with text, Fowler is concerned to express women's experiences. Her setting of the Magnificat, *Tell Out my Soul* for soprano, cello and piano, was written in 1980 and revised in 1984. Fowler sees the text of the Magnificat as an expression of a particularly feminine kind of joy. The expression of woman's experience is more explicit in her BBC commission of 1989, *And Ever Shall Be* for mezzo-soprano, oboe, clarinet, trombone, string trio and percussion, which sets four traditional songs dealing with various significant moments in a woman's life.

Erika Fox
b. 1936

Erika Fox's earliest musical experience was of the ecstatic devotional music of the Hassidim. An only child, she grew up in an intensely religious Jewish community. Her grandfather was a rabbi and the house in which she lived acted as a synagogue. Born in Vienna, Fox had come to England as a refugee at the age of three. She first started making up pieces of music when she came across a piano in the house in Leeds to which she was evacuated with her mother during the Blitz.

When she was about nine years old, Fox began having piano lessons with Milicent Silver and later won a piano scholarship to the Royal College of Music where she took composition as a second subject. In 1961, as was expected of a woman from her background, Fox married and devoted herself to bringing up her two children and running a household. During the late 1960s her desire to develop a career and to compose increased. She started taking composition lessons from Jeremy Dale Roberts whose

influence and support were extremely important. She also attended summer schools at Dartington and took a few lessons from Harrison Birtwistle.

Inspired and encouraged by these teachers and by the example of her close friend, the New Zealand composer Gillian Whitehead, Fox began to write her first mature works, such as *Eight Songs from Cavafy* (1968) for mezzo-soprano, flute, oboe, bassoon, violin and piano and *In Memoriam Martin Luther King* (1969) for cello and oboe. Although her first fully developed works were not written until she was in her mid-30s, Fox has produced a wide range of music from opera and music theatre through large-scale pieces for big ensembles to smaller chamber works. She is particularly inspired in her work by literature and painting, especially the works of an artist such as Francis Bacon whom she feels expresses strong emotions through a detached and distanced technique.

Fox's music is strikingly individual, and rather than being developmental in the Western Germanic tradition, is often built on the basis of repetition, echoing the repetitive phrases within the narrow range of notes of the Hassidic music she grew up with as a child. A strong sense of structure is central to Fox's complex works, which often involve very detailed pre-compositional planning. In several pieces, such as *To Veronica* (1976) for piano, she uses the letters from relevant words to produce the pitches and rows that she will use in a work.

Fox has always been particularly drawn to music theatre. Many of her instrumental pieces contain theatrical elements in that she asks players to move or speak during the performance. An early example is found in *Lamentations for Four* (1973) for two cellos and percussion, in which the two percussionists move between different positions on the stage. One of Fox's most important early works is the as-yet-unperformed chamber opera *The Slaughterer* (1975), based on a story by Isaac Bashevis Singer and drawing on childhood memories of her horror of chickens being killed by the ritual slaughterer who visited her grandfather's house. Fox compiled her own libretto, finding the peace and quiet to work on this and other compositions in a garden shed.

East European and Jewish traditions are very important in Fox's work. She is drawn to a wide range of music, including the exciting rhythms and rough, immediate vocal style of flamenco as well as the music of Russia and Eastern Europe, from Hungarian gypsy music to the work of composers such as Béla Bartók, Dmitri Shostakovich, György Kurtág and Igor Stravinsky. Fox's tributes to Stravinsky include *In Memoriam Igor Stravinsky* (1971) for wind quintet, piano and percussion and *On Visiting Stravinsky's Grave at San Michele* (1988) for piano.

From the late 1970s onwards Fox's music was increasingly being commissioned by a variety of performers and ensembles, including Lontano, for whom she wrote *Paths where the Mourners Tread* (1980) for ensemble, and the Yehudi Menuhin School, for whom she wrote *Litany for Strings* (1981). Fox has held various teaching posts, including running a composition workshop in the junior department of the Guildhall School of Music and Drama.

Melody is very important to Fox and some of her main sources of melodic inspiration are Jewish liturgical chant and Hassidic folk music. In 1983 she visited Jerusalem and that year produced three major works, *Quasi una Cadenza* for horn, clarinet and piano, *Kaleidoscope* for flute, cello, harp and vibraphone (which won a Finzi award that year) and the intensely powerful *Shir* for wind quintet, trumpet, trombone, string

Erika Fox

quartet, double bass, percussion and piano. 'Shir' means song in Hebrew, and this work includes part of the Song of Songs, spoken by the instrumentalists.

Fox's interweaving of Jewish elements with the language of Western serial music can be clearly heard in a work such as *Osen Shomaat* (1985), a title which translates as 'the hearing ear', a phrase taken from the Bible. This piece for small orchestra was written for a wedding and introduces an unmistakable Hassidic-like melody which

contrasts strongly with the more complex serial textures.

In 1990 Fox's music theatre work *The Bet* was performed all over England. This piece for narrator, puppets, flute, piano, double bass, percussion and voices has a text by Elaine Feinstein and was choreographed for the puppets by John Roberts. The following year Fox's opera *The Dancer Hotoke*, commissioned by The Garden Venture at The Royal Opera House, was performed at the Riverside Studios in London. With a libretto by poet Ruth Fainlight based on a Japanese Noh play, *The Dancer Hotoke* tells the story of how the warlord Kiyomori becomes infatuated with Hotoke after she has danced for him and casts aside his previous favourite Gio. Gio goes into the wilderness to become a Buddhist nun and is joined by Hotoke who feels too much remorse to take Gio's place. Fox uses an instrumental ensemble of oboe, three brass, piano and percussion. With a typical distancing gesture, she has the central dance of this story performed by a puppet, accompanied by percussion alone.

The work of Ruth Fainlight has a particular resonance for Fox. Before working on *The Dancer Hotoke* she had set Fainlight's poetry in *Letters and Notes* (1990) for soprano, viola, cello and clarinet, and the two women are working together on a number of ongoing opera projects. Immediately after finishing *Hotoke*, Fox set parts of Fainlight's series of 27 Sibyl poems as *Meditation on Sibyls* (1991) for mezzo-soprano, violin, viola, cello, horn, trumpet and trombone. *Meditation on Sibyls* can be seen as an exploration of artistic creativity, presenting two differing states and kinds of music, one contemplative and inward-looking, the other wild and ecstatic.

Eleanor Everest Freer
1864–1942

Eleanor Everest Freer came from a family of musicians. Her father Cornelius Everest was a church organist and theory teacher while her mother Amelia was a singer. Freer was born in Philadelphia, Pennsylvania in 1864 and was given her first music lessons by her parents. She played the piano, sang and composed from an early age. Later, she was encouraged to study singing by the singer Christine Nilsson and financially supported by George Childs.

In 1883, at the age of 19, Freer went to Paris to study with the singer and teacher Matilde Marchesi, whose other pupils at that time included Nellie Melba and Emma Calvé. During her three years abroad, she also took some composition lessons from Benjamin Godard. Freer became the first pupil to be allowed to teach Marchesi's distinctive teaching method. On her return to the United States in 1886 she taught the piano and singing in Philadelphia, and between 1889 and 1891 travelled to New York twice a week to teach at the National Conservatory of Music.

In 1891 she married medical student Archibald Freer and the couple spent the first eight years of their married life in Leipzig where Freer continued to study music and had a daughter, while her husband studied medicine. In 1899 the Freers returned to the United States and settled in Chicago. For five years from 1902 to 1907, Freer took composition and theory lessons from Bernard Ziehn and began to concentrate on composition. She became very active in the musical life of the city and started to publish her songs and piano pieces, such as the *Lyric Studies for Piano* (1904), op. 3.

Freer was to produce over 150 songs in a colourful but firmly tonal idiom to a wide variety of English texts, including some verses by her husband but concentrating on better-known British poets such as William Shakespeare, John Donne, Robert Herrick, John Milton, Percy Bysshe Shelley, Alfred

Tennyson, Robert Browning and others. One of her most impressive achievements in the field of song was a cycle setting 44 of Elizabeth Barrett Browning's *Sonnets from the Portuguese*, which was published in Chicago in 1939.

It is for her work with opera that Freer is best known, including the composition of her own 11 operas, most of which achieved performances. She was always concerned to make opera as accessible as possible and in 1921 established the Opera in Our Language Foundation in Chicago. Three years later, this became the American Opera Society of Chicago with Freer as its first president. She wrote her first opera in 1921 at the age of 57. It is a simple, tuneful retelling of the Pied Piper story, *Legend of the Piper*, op. 28, to a libretto by J.P. Peabody. First performed in 1924 in Indiana, it was published and given another performance in Chicago the following year. This work was followed by *Massimiliano, the Court Jester, or The Love of a Caliban*, op. 30, which was performed in Nebraska, together with *Legend of the Piper*, in 1926.

Her next opera *The Chilkoot Maiden*, op. 32, was written in 1926 to a libretto by J.J. Underwood based on an Alaskan legend and premiered in Alaska in 1927. Most of her operas are based on European stories or subjects. For some, such as *Joan of Arc* (1929), op. 38, Freer wrote her own libretto. One of her operas with an American subject was *Scenes from Little Women* (1934), op. 42, a two-act work based on the novel by Louisa M. Alcott. *The Brownings go to Italy* (1936), op. 43, with a libretto by G.A Hawkins-Ambler after Robert and Elizabeth Barrett Browning was Freer's last opera.

Freer played an important part in various music clubs in Chicago and was also a patron of the Women's Symphony Orchestra of Chicago. This orchestra, which had been founded in 1925, gave several performances of Freer's orchestral music including her *Four Modern Dances* in 1931 and her *Spanish Ballet Fantasy*, taken from her opera *A Legend of Spain*, performed to an audience of 20,000 in the summer of 1935. Freer died in 1942 at the age of 78.

Virginia Gabriel
1825–1877

Virginia Gabriel was born in Surrey into an Irish military family in 1825. She had an extensive musical education, taking piano lessons from Johann Peter Pixis, Theodor Dohler and the great virtuoso Sigismond Thalberg, as well as studying composition with violinist and composer Bernhard Molique. She may also have had some composition lessons with the Italian opera composer Saverio Mercadante.

One of Gabriel's earliest surviving works appears to be the song 'The blind boy' to words by Colley Cibber, which was published by Jullien and Co. around 1836 when she was about 11. In the early 1850s, when she was in her 20s, Gabriel started publishing many of her piano pieces and songs to Italian and French texts. These early vocal works, such as the romanza 'Isacco' or the recitative and aria 'Ciel, che veggio!' are complex, operatic pieces with elaborate harmonies, fluid melodies and written-out flourishes. She was also setting English texts, publishing ballads such as the

impetuous 'Weep not for me', sung by Charlotte Dolby (later to become Sainton-Dolby). Gabriel's early piano works are showy, difficult pieces such as L'Espieglerie which she describes as a 'caprice en forme de valse', the nocturne La Previdenza or the 'romance sans parole', La Reine des Aulnes.

Gabriel's first commercial success was the ballad 'The Skipper and his Boy' to words by Hamilton Aidé, written for and sung by Dolby. By 1865, it was in its third edition. Throughout the 1860s and 70s Gabriel produced a steady stream of songs and ballads in a style that was often simpler than that of her early works but which still incorporated an Italianate technique in its rich harmonies and expressive vocal lines. These works proved to be extremely popular and Gabriel soon became one of the best-selling composers of the day. 'When Sparrows Build', a dramatically impassioned work to words by Jean Ingelow, first published in the 1860s, had reached a 30th edition by the end of the decade and was arranged as a 'Reverie' for piano in 1878. In 1880, after Gabriel's death, the publishers Metzler sold the copyright on her song 'Ruby', to words by J.J. Lonsdale, for £418 10s and the copyright on 'When Sparrows Build' fetched £390.

Gabriel capitalized on her success by reworking some of her earlier songs for the amateur ballad market, replacing the Italian texts with English ones. In 1865 she produced the popular 'Nightfall at Sea', with words by Arthur Matthison, from her 'Ave Maria' of 1857. An English version of 'Ciel, che veggio!', 'On the Threshold', was published in 1870.

In the mid–1860s Gabriel began writing music for the theatre. *Widows Bewitched*, to a libretto by Hamilton Aidé, was first performed at the Royal Gallery of Illustration in Regent Street in August 1865 and later ran for several weeks, performed by the Bijou Operetta Company, at St George's Hall in 1867. As might be expected, the overture and songs of this work show Gabriel making use of her more elaborate, operatic style. Her later operettas are often simpler. *The Lion's Mouth*, a burlesque opera with a libretto by Alfred Thompson, was performed at Lady Collier's house in Eaton Place in May 1867, and the

operetta *A Rainy Day* with a libretto by a Miss H. Smith was given an amateur performance at the Gallery of Music in May 1868.

Gabriel also continued to produce vocal music and a few piano pieces. Her ballads were still extremely popular and financially successful, but in 1870 Gabriel had to pay for the publication of her cantata *Dream-Land, or Light through Darkness* herself, although it was performed that year at Covent Garden. Gabriel sent another of her cantatas, *Evangeline*, with a text based on Henry Wadsworth Longfellow's poem, to William Sterndale Bennett asking for help in getting it performed. In 1873 it was played in Brighton and at Covent Garden. Another cantata, *Graziella*, does not appear to have survived.

Several of Gabriel's later operettas had libretti by George March whom she married in 1874, a few months before her 50th birthday. *Who's the Heir* and *Lost and Found* were performed at the Royal Gallery of Illustration in 1869 and 1870, with *Lost and Found* also performed at the Royal Alexandra Theatre in Liverpool later that year. Their operetta *The Shepherd of Cournailles* was given a performance in Liverpool two years after Gabriel's sudden death in August 1877 at the age of 52, after a carriage accident.

Miriam Gideon
b. 1906

Miriam Gideon is best known for her lyrical and dramatic vocal chamber works with their imaginative use of texts from various cultures in many different languages. She was born into a German-Jewish family in Colorado where her father Abram Gideon taught philosophy and modern languages at the State Teachers' College. Her mother Henrietta Shoninger had been a schoolteacher before her marriage.

The family moved several times while Gideon was a child. In 1915, when she was nine, they moved to Chicago, and it was here that she had her first piano lessons from a cousin. The following year the family moved to New York and Gideon took piano lessons from Hans Barth at the Yonkers Conservatory of Music. In order to further her musical studies, Gideon went to live with her uncle in 1921, at the age of 14. Henry Gideon was the music director of Temple Israel, a large reform synagogue in Boston. Gideon played the organ at the Temple, continued her piano lessons, studied at Boston Girls'

High School and then at the College of Liberal Arts, Boston University, where she majored in French. After graduating from Boston in 1926 at the age of 19, Gideon returned to New York and started to compose, taking courses in music at New York University with various teachers, including Marion Bauer.

Her earliest surviving songs, mostly settings of German and French poets such as Pierre Louys and Heinrich Heine, date from 1929. From 1931 for three years she studied composition with Lazare Saminsky, Russian composer and music director of the Temple Emanu-El. During this time she had her first public performance, of *Dances for Two Pianos*, at a League of Composers concert. On Saminsky's suggestion she then studied for eight years with Roger Sessions who was a considerable influence on her own music. Her early songs, such as her settings of Joseph Eichendorff's 'Lockung' (1937) or James Joyce's 'She Weeps Over Rahoon' (1939) demonstrate an exquisite lyricism within an essentially conservative and tonal idiom.

Gideon went to live and study in Europe in 1939, but had to return when war broke out later the same year. In 1941 Gideon wrote the first work that she was not later to withdraw, the one-movement *Lyric Piece* for strings. This was first performed in April 1944 by the London Symphony Orchestra, and broadcast in the United States in a version for string quartet as part of the American Music Festival the following year.

During the early 1940s Gideon taught music in private schools in New York as well as studying at Columbia University for an MA in musicology from 1942 to 1946. For 10 years from 1944 she taught harmony, composition and music history at Brooklyn College. Here she met the English professor Frederic Ewen whom she married in 1949. She has also taught at the City University of New York, the Cantors' Institute at the Jewish Theological Seminary and the Manhattan School of Music.

In March 1945 Gideon's *The Hound of Heaven,* a setting of part of a long poem by 19th-century Catholic poet Francis Thompson for baritone, oboe and string trio, was first performed at the Temple Emanu-El. A commission from Saminsky for the centenary cele-brations of the synagogue, the work

was repeated by the International Society for Contemporary Music the following year. In this work Gideon's individual musical style, which changed little over the next 50 years, is already clearly apparent. She has described it as 'freely atonal', using chromaticism and dissonance without serial techniques. Other early works included a String Quartet that was performed at Yaddo Festival in September 1946 and *How Goodly are thy Tents,* a setting of psalm 84 for women's voices with organ or piano, written in 1947.

In the early 1950s Gideon wrote several works for orchestra, both with and without voices: *Sonnets from Shakespeare* (1950) for voice, trumpet and string orchestra; the concentrated *Symphonia Brevis* (1953) for orchestra; and a setting of the Hebrew prayer *Adon Olam* (1954) for soloists, chorus and chamber orchestra, first performed at Temple Chizuk Amuno in Baltimore.

In 1957 Gideon wrote her first work in which she used poetry both in its original language and in translation. *Mixco,* for voice and piano, is an atmospheric setting of a poem by Guatemalan poet Miguel Angel Asturias, with each verse heard first in Gideon's own English translation and then in the Spanish original, with different musical treatment for the two different languages. Gideon was to use this technique again in several other works including *The Condemned*

Playground (1963) and *Songs of Youth and Madness* (1977), a setting of four poems by Friederich Hölderlin with their English translations by Michael Hamburger, for voice and orchestra. *The Condemned Playground* is an elaborate setting of three poems for soprano, tenor, flute, bassoon and string quartet. The first poem, 'Pyrrha', is heard in the Latin original by Horace and in John Milton's English translation; 'Hiroshima', an English poem by Gary Spokes, is also heard in a Japanese translation by Satoka Akiya; and the final poem, 'The Litanies of Satan', uses Charles Baudelaire's French original and the English translation by Edna St Vincent Millay. Once again, Gideon used contrasting musical styles for original and translation, pointing to different ways of understanding or illuminating the same text. *The Condemned Playground* is one of her few works to specify whether the voice should be male or female, rather than simply medium or high.

Gideon received a Doctorate of Sacred Music in Composition from the Jewish Theological Seminary in 1970, and the following year became the first woman to be commissioned to compose a Jewish service. Her *Sacred Service* for cantor, soloists, chorus, flute, oboe, trumpet, bassoon, viola, cello and organ was first performed by the Temple in Cleveland, Ohio. In 1974 another service, *Shirat Miriam*

L'shabbat for cantor, chorus and organ, was commissioned and performed by the Park Avenue Synagogue in New York. In both works Gideon used elements of traditional Jewish musical material together with her own personal voice. Jewish materials had occasionally been heard in other works, as in her use of cantillation or traditional chanting motives in *Three Biblical Masks* (1958) for organ, later revised for violin and piano, and based on the characters in the Purim story.

In 1975 Gideon became the second woman composer to be elected to the American Academy and Institute of Arts and Letters. She continued to draw on a wide range of texts for her vocal compositions including ancient Greek poetry in *Voices from Elysium* (1979) for high voice and instruments; German poetry from the 13th to the 20th century in *The Resounding Lyre* (1979, a reworking of *Spiritual Madrigals* of 1965) for high voice and instruments; American poetry from the 17th to the 20th century in *Spirit above the Dust* (1981) for voice and instruments; and Hebrew texts for *Woman of Valor* (1982) for high voice and piano. She also continued to write works without voices, although such music often refers to a text of some kind. Her Piano Sonata (1977) uses melodic fragments from songs by Hugo Wolf and Robert Schumann and the titles of its three movements were given headings taken from a Swinburne play.

During the later 1980s and into the 1990s, Gideon has composed a series of inventive vocal works including *Creature to Creature* (1985), a setting of poems from Nancy Cardozo's whimsical bestiary *Creature to Creature: An Animalculary,* for high voice, flute and harp. *Steeds of Darkness* (1986) for voice, flute, oboe, cello, percussion and piano, setting an Italian poem by Felix Pick together with its English 're-creation' by Eugene Mahon, is a powerful and intense work confronting the sorrow and inevitability of death.

Ruth Gipps
b. 1921

Ruth Gipps' output includes an impressive list of orchestral, vocal and chamber music, at the centre of which stand her five symphonies. Gipps is part of a generation of British composers, including men such as George Lloyd, Robert Simpson and Adrian Cruft, whose resolutely tonal symphonic works, building on the musical tradition of composers such as Arthur Bliss and William Walton, have been largely ignored by the musical establishment.

Her parents, Bryan Gipps and Swiss pianist Hélène Johner, met at the Frankfurt Conservatoire in Germany. Their daughter was born in Bexhill-on-Sea in East Sussex and had piano lessons with her mother from a very early age. An extremely precocious child, she made her public debut at the Grotian Hall in London at the age of four and performed one of her early piano pieces at a public concert in Brighton in 1929 at the age of eight. Two years later Gipps performed the first movement of a Haydn piano concerto with the Hastings Municipal Orchestra and continued to perform throughout her teenage years.

In 1937, at 16, Gipps entered the Royal College of Music where she took up the oboe, studied the piano with various teachers and composition with R.O. Morris, Gordon Jacob and Ralph Vaughan Williams. Many of her works were performed at the College, including *Knight in Armour* (1940), op. 8, a symphonic poem inspired by Rembrandt's painting 'Young Warrior'. Gipps won several prizes as a student, including Cobbett prizes for her string quartet *Sabrina* (1940), op. 13, first performed by the Society of Women Musicians in 1946, and her piano quartet *Brocade* (1941), op. 17.

While studying at the College, Gipps also passed the exams for the B.Mus. from Durham University, writing a Quintet for oboe, clarinet and string trio, op. 16, as part of her final exams. This was premiered at the Wigmore Hall in July 1941, her first adult work to be given a public performance. One of the musicians for this performance was the clarinettist Robert Baker whom Gipps had first met three years previously and whom she married in 1942, while he was on leave from the RAF. Later that year her Oboe Concerto, op. 20, was performed by her college friend Marion Brough with the Modern Symphony Orchestra; and at the last night of the Proms, Henry Wood conducted her symphonic poem *Knight in Armour*.

Gipps continued to study, taking piano lessons from Tobias Matthay and oboe lessons from Leon Goossens, and to perform as a pianist and oboist. She also continued to compose, writing her Symphony no. 1 in F minor, op. 22, in 1942. Her symphonic poem of the following year, *Death on a Pale Horse*, op. 25, was given its premiere by the City of Birmingham Orchestra conducted by George Weldon. A few months later, Gipps took the post of second oboist with the CBO and moved to Birmingham. Weldon was very supportive of her work as a composer and the CBO gave several performances of her music, including the premiere of her Symphony no. 1 in 1945, an occasion when Gipps played cor anglais in the orchestra for her own work and was then the soloist in a performance of Alexander Glazunov's Piano Concerto no. 1.

Gipps' son Lance was born in 1947, and the following year she became the second woman to receive a doctorate in composition from Durham University. Her examination work was the inventive choral work *The Cat*, op. 32, for contralto, baritone, double chorus and orchestra, setting various texts about cats. Many of Gipps' works were written for family and friends. An early Clarinet Concerto (1940), op. 9, and a *Rhapsody* for clarinet and string quartet (1942), op. 23, were composed for Baker. A Violin Concerto, op. 24, was written for her violinist brother Bryan Gipps in 1943 and a Piano Concerto, op. 34, for her mother in 1948.

Gipps worked in a variety of musical jobs while she was living in Birmingham. Weldon taught her to conduct and made her chorus 'master' of the City of Birmingham Choir, but refused to believe that a woman should conduct public concerts. She also earned money by performing as a concert pianist, writing programme notes, giving lecture-recitals and composing incidental music for BBC Midland. Other compositions from this time included the short piece *Cringlemire Garden* (1952), op. 39, for string orchestra, and a setting of Christina Rossetti's *Goblin Market* (1953), op. 40, for two soprano soloists, three-part female choir and strings or piano.

In 1954 Gipps returned to London. By this time, at the age of 33, she was having problems with her right hand which she had injured when she was a child, and decided to concentrate on building a career as a conductor rather than as a pianist. She began working as a guest conductor with various orchestras but still came across great resistance to the idea of a woman conductor, especially when applying for any permanent conducting posts.

In 1955 she founded the One Rehearsal Orchestra, or as it was later known, the London Repertoire Orchestra. This was an orchestra that gave students and amateurs the opportunity to read through and learn repertoire, by rehearsing two different programmes a week as well as giving concerts of more thoroughly rehearsed works. A few years later, in 1961, Gipps also founded the Chanticleer Orchestra, a professional orchestra that gave many opportunities to young British soloists as well as making a point of performing music by living British composers such as William Alwyn, Arthur Bliss and Malcolm Arnold. Arnold wrote his *Variations on a Theme of Ruth Gipps*, first performed in 1978, especially for the orchestra, using a theme from Gipps' *Coronation Procession* (1953), op. 41. By forming her own orchestras, Gipps was able to build a conducting career and to sidestep the persistent neglect of her own music by the BBC and the rest of the musical establishment.

Both orchestras gave premieres of her large-scale works, which were often then performed by other orchestras. Gipps conducted the Chanticleer Orchestra in the first performance of her Concerto for violin, viola and orchestra (1957), op. 49, and the London Repertoire Orchestra in the first performances of her Symphony no. 3 (1965), op. 57, Horn Concerto (1968), op. 58, Symphony no. 4 (1972), op. 61, and Symphony no. 5 (1982), op. 64. The Fifth Symphony, which was dedicated to William Walton, is, like so much of Gipps' music, a rich and dramatic work with fluent melodies and exciting climaxes. The last movement is a Missa Brevis for orchestra with instrumental themes whose rhythmic patterns set phrases from the liturgy of the mass.

As well as conducting and composing, Gipps has taught at a number of institutions including Trinity College of Music, the Royal College of Music and Kingston Polytechnic. In 1967 she was chair of the Composer's Guild of Great Britain and played an important part in establishing the British Music Information Centre which opened that year. In 1981 she was awarded the MBE for services to music. After her retirement from the London Repertoire Orchestra in 1986, Gipps took various posts conducting choral societies and choirs in Sussex (where she has lived since 1982) and playing the organ in local churches. Her later music focuses in particular on wind instruments with works such as the *Sinfonietta* (1989), op. 73, for 10 wind and tam tam written for the Rondel Ensemble, *A Wealden Suite* (1991), op. 74, for four different clarinets, *Cool Running Water* (1991), op. 77, for bass flute and piano and *Pan and Apollo* (1992), op. 78, for two oboes, cor anglais and harp.

Dorothy Gow
1893–1982

The youngest of six children from a Scottish family, Dorothy Gow, who never married, was born, lived and died in London. Despite the support and encouragement of many well-known musicians and composers, she was plagued by acute shyness and a lack of confidence in her own abilities as a composer. She continued to write her tightly constructed and intensely lyrical music throughout her life although she would only work when she was sure that no-one could overhear her. Attending performances of her compositions put her through agonies.

One of her earliest works to survive, a piece for flute and piano, is dated 1919. Although The Music Society was performing her work as early as 1922, Gow did not start studying at the Royal College of Music until 1924 when she was 31 years old. Her composition tutors were R.O. Morris and Ralph Vaughan Williams, who remained an enthusiastic supporter of Gow's music throughout his life. Gow was a student at the College for 10 years and made important friendships there with Grace Williams, Elizabeth Maconchy and particularly with Elisabeth Lutyens. Amongst Gow's sketches is a game of musical consequences played by herself, Williams and Vaughan Williams. Some of her sketches also show her experimenting with serial techniques. Towards the end of her time at the College, Gow won several composition prizes including the Signor Foli scholarship in 1931 and the Octavia Travelling Scholarship, which took her to Vienna to study with Egon Wellesz in 1932.

Four of Gow's early works were performed at the important Macnaghten–Lemare concerts. The earliest of these was a *Fantasy String Quartet*, written sometime in the 1920s and performed in 1932. Opening with a ferocious 'con fuoco' theme in the second violin, this is a robust work with moments of quieter lyricism. Reviewers of these early concerts often found Gow's work frighteningly intellectual, yet gave grudging praise. At a Macnaghten–Lemare concert given in December 1934, two works by Gow were heard – her Second String Quartet, described in the programme as 'a string quartet in one movement', and *Three Songs for Tenor and String Quartet*. A review in *The Evening News* described '... moods, tensions and intentions, half revealed and half bleakly veiled ...', while the *Daily Telegraph* felt that her music 'shows a close acquaintance with the most up-to-date harmonic idioms ... she has ideas and does not despise emotion'.

Alan Rawsthorne had earlier written to Anne Macnaghten that 'the Gow songs were beautiful ... They seem entirely free from that woolliness which characterises most English modern music'. The texts Gow set in the *Three Songs* are 'Hey Nonny No', 'Tristia' and 'I mun be married on Sunday'. She gives no authors but 'Hey Nonny No' is an anonymous 17th-century lyric and 'I mun be married' is by the 16th-century writer Nicholas Udall. These first and last movements are energetically rhythmic while the central slow movement, 'Tristia', is beautifully sustained and very dissonant. Gow's music had several other performances during the 1930s. Her *Prelude and Fugue* (1930–31) for orchestra, played at a Macnaghten–Lemare concert in 1934, was later broadcast by the BBC, and her Oboe Quintet (1936) was performed at the London Contemporary Music Centre.

Her best-known work is the short, intense *String Quartet in One Movement*, completed in 1947 and published, at the prompting of Vaughan Williams, by Oxford University Press in 1957. He wrote to her, 'I am so glad the quartet is out at last, and I hope a lot of people will play it, and you will now get over your fearful diffidence, and will write a LOT MORE MUSIC.' It was first performed by the Aeolian String Quartet at a London Contemporary Music Centre concert in 1950, played by the Macnaghten Quartet and the Allegri Quartet several times in the 1950s and broadcast by the BBC in 1958. Malcolm Williamson felt this work was 'supremely satisfying music written in a pure, unique, distinctive style'. Sometime in the 1960s Gow herself wrote about the piece in a typically self-deprecating way: '... when it was first played it was considered by many to be harsh and intellectual, but now in these days of indeterminate music, I fear it would be considered mushy and very sentimental!'.

During the 1950s several of Gow's other works were played at various concerts in London, including *Two Pieces* (1954) for oboe and *Theme and Variations* (1955) for violin. She was extremely self-critical and destroyed much of her music, especially after she suffered a stroke in 1978. Her latest work to survive, *Piece for Violin and Horn,* was broadcast by the BBC in 1972. Shortly afterwards, Elisabeth

Lutyens wrote to her: 'I've always thought you potentially almost the best composer I've met, if ill health had not dogged you ... But it was a struggle in those far off days if one had an unconventional ear, wasn't it?'

Jane Guest
*c.*1765–after 1824

Jane Mary Guest was born in Bath where her father worked as a tailor. Unusually for a child who was not from a family of musicians, she started appearing in public as a pianist as early as four or five. She studied with the well-known singer and teacher Venanzio Rauzzini as well as with Johann Christian Bach. In 1780 the novelist Fanny Burney visited her in Bath and heard her play.

Guest seems to have made her London debut as a pianist at the end of the 1770s, and some time soon afterwards moved to the capital where she became well known as a virtuoso performer, praised in the press and by the music historian Charles Burney in his *A General History of Music* (1789). In 1783 she performed at the Hanover Square Grand Concert series (possibly playing her own piano concertos) and also that year published her op. 1, a set of piano sonatas with accompaniment for flute or violin. The sonatas were dedicated to Queen Charlotte and subscribed to by many of the most prominent musicians of the time, including Burney, Rauzzini, William Shields and Dr Hayes, the professor of music at Oxford, as well as members of the aristocracy. In the 1783–4 season Guest ran her own series of five subscription concerts at the Tottenham Street Rooms, and the following year played a piano concerto in Bristol.

In 1789 Guest married Abram Miles and may at this point in her career have moved back to Bath where she taught and performed in the 1790s, playing her own piano concertos in concerts directed by her old teacher Rauzzini. She continued to publish music under her married name and in 1806 was appointed music instructor to Princess Charlotte, the daughter of the Prince of Wales. She also taught music to Princess Augusta of Salms.

Guest published a variety of music, including accompanied sonatas, other works for the piano and many songs, duets and glees for several voices. Some of her vocal music became very popular. Her ebullient ballad 'The Bonnie Wee Wife' to words by Robert Burns was sung by a variety of well-known singers at oratorio concerts and music festivals. It was printed in many editions, including one issued as late as 1874.

As well as the early sonatas mentioned above, Guest's works for piano include another, more complex sonata with an optional violin accompaniment. This work has three movements: *allegro con spirito*, an *adagio* based on a theme by Purcell and a final waltz. Guest's other piano works, such as *La Jeanette, La Georgiana* or *La Jolie Julienne,* are also fairly difficult pieces. They often take the form of a slow introduction ending with a cadenza followed by a faster dance movement such as a waltz or a polacca. Guest's piano concertos have not survived and were probably never published. The date of her death is unknown, although she was still alive in 1824.

Faustina Hasse Hodges
(1822–1895)

Faustina Hasse Hodges' father was the British composer and organist Edward Hodges. He had four children (the youngest named John Sebastian Bach Hodges!), all of whom worked as organists. Faustina Hodges was born in Malmesbury in 1822. Her father emigrated to New York in 1838 and she joined him there in 1841 at the age of 19. She worked as an organist in Brooklyn during the 1850s and also taught organ, piano and voice at the Troy Female Seminary run by Emma Willard. She began publishing her music in the 1850s and continued to write and publish until her death. In the late 1870s she was working as the organist for two churches in Philadelphia.

Hodges' father returned to England in 1863 after the death of his wife and died there four years later. Hodges ensured that his life and works were remembered, publishing one of his cathedral services in 1874. Several years later, in 1891, she published an edition of his works, *The Kyries,*

Chants and Tunes Composed by Edward Hodges with a list of Dr. Hodges' Works (Musical and Literary) and an Illustrative Comment in which she also included sacred vocal music by herself, two of her brothers and her nephew. She also wrote his biography, published a year after her death.

Hodges produced a variety of keyboard and vocal music. Two secular sentimental songs from 1859, 'Dreams' and 'The Rose Bush', were especially popular and she also wrote comic works such as the song 'The Indignant Spinster' from the 1860s. Two late songs, both setting words by William Henry Gardner, 'Yearnings' and 'Remember Me', were published two years before her death. Her keyboard works include transcriptions of songs and nocturnes as well as piano pieces such as the simple *Rêverie de Soir*, subtitled 'Rimembranza'.

Several sacred vocal works have survived, including her setting of the 'Te Deum' and a vocal trio 'The Holy

Dead'. Her hymn tune 'Cleveland' was written for the Bishop of Western New York, Rev. Arthur Cleveland Coxe, when he preached at Westminster Abbey. It is included in her edition of her father's works along with two of her settings of the Kyrie and several hymns, some of which are for children to use at home.

Imogen Holst
1907–1984

Imogen Holst's father was Gustav Holst, one of the leading British composers of the early 20th century. She herself is usually remembered for her work on her father and his music, her work with English folk music and with Benjamin Britten and the festivals at Aldeburgh. But she was also a composer, and although other musical work seems to have taken priority she has left a small but fascinating body of music that was written throughout her life.

Holst's first music lessons, as well as a love of early English music and of folk song, came from her father. She began to compose as a child, and from 1921 to 1925 attended St Paul's Girls School, where her father was director of music, taking piano lessons from Adine O'Neill. Holst also loved ballet and dance and at 16 joined the English Folk Dance Society. In 1926 she entered the Royal College of Music where she took conducting and ballet classes as well as studying the piano with Kathleen Long and composition with George

Dyson and later, Gordon Jacob. She was very successful at the College, winning a composition scholarship during her first year. Several of her chamber works were performed at informal student concerts, and in 1928 she won the Cobbett composition prize for her *Phantasy String Quartet*. The following year she won an Arthur Sullivan prize for composition and had her overture *Persephone* conducted by Malcolm Sargent at the Patron's Fund Concerts.

Holst was a member of the Society of Women Musicians who put on a performance of her prize-winning string quartet in the summer of 1930. This was also the year in which she won an Octavia scholarship of £100. She spent the award travelling and studying in Austria, Germany, Holland and Hungary as well as investigating stone circles in Sweden and Greek temples in Sicily. In Vienna she met up with Grace Williams, who was also on an Octavia scholarship. Back in London in 1931, two of her works, a

Quintet for oboe and strings and a Suite for viola, were performed at early Macnaghten–Lemare concerts.

During the 1930s Holst worked as a freelance musician and teacher and joined the staff of the English Folk Dance and Song Society. In 1933 she conducted a brass band in a perform-ance of her suite *The Unfortunate Traveller* at a concert in Carlisle Cathedral. She became increasingly involved in arranging folk music with works such as *A Book of Tunes for the Pipes* (1932) or her arrangements of *Four Somerset Folk-Songs* (1934) collected by Cecil Sharp. She also published a wide variety of teaching pieces for choirs, string players and pianists. Two of her part-songs for women's voices, published by Cramer, were performed at one of the 25th anniversary concerts of the Society of Women Musicians in 1936.

Holst's father had died in 1934, and a few years later she wrote the first of her many books about him, *Gustav Holst: A Biography* (1938). During the early years of the war she worked for CEMA (Council for the Encouragement of Music and the Arts, the forerunner of the Arts Council of Great Britain), travelling throughout the Southwest of England encouraging music in rural communities. Then from 1942 until 1951 Holst lived and worked in the lively, exciting artistic community at Dartington in Devon which she had first visited in 1938. Here she estab-

lished a thriving music department, initially aiming to train teachers for the Rural Music Schools, as well as organizing musical activities for those who lived on the estate. Learning from the work with amateurs that her father had started at Morley College in London, Holst stressed the importance of music-making, including composi-tion, for everyone, regardless of experience or ability.

During her years at Dartington, she wrote her second book about her father, *The Music of Gustav Holst* (1951), and went to India for two months, where she studied and taught at Rabindranath Tagore's Santiniketan University in West Bengal. She also continued to make arrangements, especially for women's voices, and to compose. In 1943 a concert of her music was given at the Wigmore Hall in London as a present to her 'from three hundred of the friends who have made music with her during the last few years'. The works played included first performances of her Suite for string orchestra, *Serenade* for flute, viola and bassoon and *Three Psalms* for chorus and string orchestra. In 1946 Holst wrote a String Quartet which does not appear to have been performed until after her death. This is a complex and dissonant work consist-ing of a set of variations followed by a scampering scherzo in an irregular but rhythmic metre. Later music from the 1940s included the part-song for women's voices, *In Heaven it is always*

Imogen Holst conducting the
Snape Maltings Training Orchestra, 1977

Autumn (1947) to a text from a sermon by John Donne.

Holst had first met Benjamin Britten and Peter Pears at Dartington. After leaving and taking on freelance work, one of her jobs was to orchestrate Britten's *Rejoice in the Lamb* for the 1952 Aldeburgh Festival. For the next 12 years she worked primarily as Britten's devoted music assistant at Aldeburgh. During this time she wrote several books about music including *The Story of Music* (1958), written in collaboration with Britten, *Henry Purcell* (1961), *Tune* (1962) and *An ABC of Music* (1963). Holst also continued to write her own music. The 1950s saw some of her best-known arrangements, including the collection of songs *Singing for Pleasure*, published in collaboration with the National Federation of Women's Institutes in 1957. She also became known for her vital and energetic conducting, especially with the Purcell Singers, a professional group which she directed from 1953 to 1967.

From 1964, Holst concentrated on writing about, editing and promoting the work of her father, although she continued to be involved in a wide range of other music activities. Her publications included guides to J.S. Bach (1965), Britten (1966), William Byrd (1972) as well as Gustav Holst (1974) in the Faber and Faber 'Great Composers' series and *A Thematic Catalogue of Gustav Holst's Music* (1974). She was an active artistic director of the Aldeburgh Festival from 1956 to 1977, and in 1975 she was awarded a CBE.

Holst still managed to find time to compose. From the 1960s onwards she was frequently asked to write music for a variety of amateur groups. She also composed substantial works for professionals, producing music in her more individual style. Such works include the brief String Trio of 1962 and the solo cello piece, *The Fall of the Leaf* of 1964, written for cellist and composer Pamela Hind O'Malley. This beautifully judged work consists of

three studies on a mournful theme from a 16th-century keyboard piece in the Fitzwilliam Virginal Book. In 1965 Holst wrote a cantata *The Sun's Journey* to words by John Ford and Thomas Dekker for the national music festival of the National Union of Townswomen's Guilds.

Her later works included the intense, three-movement String Quintet (1982) and her last completed piece, *Homage to William Morris* (1984) for double bass and bass voice. Her String Quintet was commissioned for the Cricklade Festival, and Holst described this work as a depiction of the Thames whose source is near Cricklade. The first movement, Prelude, represents the mysterious birth of the river. By the next movement, a fast-moving, muted Scherzo, it has become a stream reflecting the glitter of sunlight and splashes of rain. The last movement, Variations, uses a theme from her father's final notebook and depicts the London Thames by which he lived and worked, one last tribute to the man whose music and ideals were so important to her own work.

Helen Hopekirk
1856–1945

Helen Hopekirk was born in Edinburgh in 1856. Her earliest musical studies were with Professor G. Lichtenstein and the Scottish composer Alexander Mackenzie. In 1876, when she was 20, she went to Leipzig where she studied at the Conservatory for two years, making her debut as a pianist with the prestigious Leipzig Gewandhaus Orchestra in November 1878. Her first British appearance was at the Crystal Palace concerts the following year, and she quickly established a career as a pianist, performing throughout Europe and Britain. By this time she was already composing, although she does not appear to have had any formal composition training. Her earliest surviving work is a song, 'Sigh my lute', setting words by Lewis Novra, which was published in London in about 1880.

In 1882 Hopekirk married the Scottish painter and music critic William Wilson who became her concert manager. In December of the following year she embarked on a four-year tour of the United States, which started with a New York recital and an appearance with the Boston Symphony Orchestra. In 1887 she went to Vienna where she spent two years continuing her piano studies with the Polish pianist Theodor Leschetizky. Hopekirk embarked on her second American tour in 1890, playing her own Sonata in E minor for violin and piano at a concert in Boston in March 1891. From this time on, composition played an increasingly important part in her professional life. She spent two years, from 1892 to 1894, in Paris taking composition lessons, and at the end of this time composed a *Concertstück* for piano and orchestra. The first performance of this work was given in Edinburgh in 1894 by the Scottish Orchestra conducted by Georg Henschel. In the same year Augner published her *Five Songs* to words by Robert Burns and Heinrich Heine.

Sometime in the late 1890s Hopekirk's husband was injured in an accident and became unable to work, a situation that may have influenced her decision to take up the offer of a post teaching the piano at the New England Conservatory in Boston. She and her husband settled in Boston in 1897 and eventually became American citizens. That year Oliver Ditson published six of her songs, mostly settings of Burns, and a *Melody in G* for violin and piano. Hopekirk soon became involved in the musical life of Boston, and made important friendships with other women composers such as Margaret Ruthven Lang and Mabel Daniels, as well as taking part in the fight for women's suffrage. She gave regular recitals which often included her own works. In 1900 the Boston Symphony Orchestra performed her Piano Concerto in D major, doubtless with Hopekirk herself playing the solo part. The following year she resigned from her job at the Conservatory and concentrated on private teaching, establishing a work pattern whereby she practised the piano and composed in the morning and gave piano lessons in the afternoons.

Hopekirk was very proud of her Celtic heritage. She frequently returned to Scotland and had always been particularly interested in setting the works of Scottish poets such as Robert Burns. In 1904 she published *Five Songs* to words by Fiona Macleod (the pseudonym of William Sharp), followed by more settings of the same poet, *Six Songs* (1907). She also developed an interest in the Scottish folk music that

she had heard as a child and in later visits to the Scottish Highlands. During a visit to the Western Isles in 1903 she was fascinated by the music sung at a traditional funeral. She spent time investigating old collections of folk song in the Advocates' Library in Edinburgh and found a clear distinction between the pastoral lowland songs and the truly Celtic music of the Highlands which she found of much more interest, pointing to its essential sadness and 'weird quality'. In 1905 she edited and arranged a collection of *Seventy Scottish Songs*, which became very popular. Her use of traditional Scottish rhythmic and harmonic material in her own music can be clearly heard in a work such as *Iona Memories*, four pieces for piano published by Schirmer in 1909. The use of modal melodies and the dotted rhythm of the Scotch snap can also be seen in her works with less obviously Scottish titles. She continued to make arrangements of Scottish folk music for several years, with works such as the piano transcriptions of *Five Scottish Folk-Songs* which were published in 1919.

Hopekirk returned to Scotland once more in 1919 when she and her husband spent a year in Edinburgh. In February 1920 she gave a concert in Glasgow where she played her Piano Concerto in D major and selections from a more recent work, *Serenata*, a classical suite of simple pieces for piano, dedicated to Arthur Foote and published that year by the Boston Music Company. In 1926 Wilson died but Hopekirk continued to perform and compose. She gave a farewell concert of her own works in April 1939 at the age of 82, six years before her death in 1945.

Mary Howe
1882–1964

Mary Howe came from a prominent and wealthy Washington family. Although she was born at her maternal grandparents' house in Richmond, Virginia in 1882, she grew up in Washington and lived there all her life, playing an important part in the musical life of the city. Her father, Calderon Carlisle, was a lawyer with both Scottish and Spanish ancestors. Like many girls of her class, Howe was taught privately and her education included piano lessons. As a teenager she frequently performed at private concerts and parties. In 1900, when she was 18, she started taking piano lessons at the Peabody Conservatory in Baltimore.

Howe spent much time travelling abroad, especially after her father died in 1901. On one of these trips in 1904 she spent four months in Dresden taking piano lessons from Richard Burmeister. In 1912 Howe married lawyer Walter Howe and had her first child. This was also the year in which she started performing in a piano duo with Anne Hull. During the next few years Howe had two more children, performed with Hull at private concerts and music clubs and started to compose. In about 1920, when Howe was in her late 30s, the duo started performing with professional symphony orchestras. At this time composition became increasingly important to Howe. She took lessons from Gustav Strube at the Peabody Conservatory and later studied with Nadia Boulanger during a year spent in France in 1933.

Much of Howe's early work consists of piano pieces, several of which were performed at Peabody. She also made many arrangements, especially of works by J. S. Bach, for her two-piano duo. In 1923 Howe appeared as pianist in a performance of her *Andante and Scherzo* for piano quintet, and the following year Howe and Hull included their own transcriptions in their New York debut concert. At about this time Howe got to know Amy Beach. She became one of the first members of the

Society of American Women Composers of which Beach was the president, and in 1925, with Hull, gave the first performance of Beach's Suite for two pianos.

1925 also saw the first public performance of a large-scale work by Howe. This was *Chain Gang Song* for chorus and orchestra, given a public rehearsal by the New York Symphony Orchestra at the Worcester Music Festival. Howe had originally written the work for a choral group she conducted in Washington and then revised it for male-voice chorus and orchestra. Inspired by her memories of an African–American convict chain gang laying dynamite in North Carolina and singing as they hit the drill into the stone with iron hammers, the work is based on chain-gang tunes collected by J.M. Carlisle and Kathleen Doyle. It was a success, described by Marion Bauer's sister Emilie Bauer in *The Musical Leader* as 'a powerful piece of writing with no trace of femininity and astonishing skill in the handling of her resources'.

The following year Howe was asked by conductor Georges Barrère, who was to become an enthusiastic performer of her music, to orchestrate three of her works. The most successful of these was her revision of a piano piece, *Stars*. This short work gradually builds to an expansive climax, then dies away to end with a shimmering harp glissando. It was frequently performed

with *Sand,* another short orchestral work. Written in 1930, *Sand* makes extensive use of staccato triplet figures, representing the gritty quality of sand. Howe was to write over 20 orchestral works as well as a variety of chamber, vocal and piano music. Much of it was written at the MacDowell Colony where she spent most of her summers after her first visit in 1926.

Howe was involved in many aspects of music in Washington. In 1925 she had helped Carl Engel organize the first of the Coolidge Chamber Festivals, having been to the Berkshire Festivals organized by Coolidge in Pittsburgh, Massachusetts. In 1930 she raised the money needed to found the Washington-based National Symphony Orchestra, and remained closely involved with the orchestra, which gave several performances of her music, for many years. Two works performed by the NSO were *Castellana* (1935) for two pianos and orchestra and *Spring Pastoral* (1937). Both, like many of Howe's works, had originally been written for smaller forces and were then orchestrated. *Castellana*, based on four Spanish folk songs that she remembered being sung by cousins of her father, became one of her most popular works.

In April 1939 a recital of Howe's songs was given in Washington. Howe herself had also started singing, having formed a madrigal group, 'The Four Howes', with her three children.

They sang a variety of madrigals, catches and glees to raise money for the various projects in which Howe was involved. In the early 1940s Howe wrote several works for string quartet, including *Three Pieces after Emily Dickinson* and two orchestral works, the richly colourful *Paen* and the orchestral suite *Potomac*. During the war she threw herself into volunteer war work but still found time to compose, producing works such as *Prophecy 1792* (1943) for chorus and piano to words by William Blake and *To the Unknown Soldier* (1944) for tenor and piano or orchestra to a poem by Nicholas Levy.

Howe continued to compose into her 70s. In 1952 the National Symphony Orchestra gave a concert consisting entirely of her works. In 1955, the year after her husband died, Howe went to Vienna where the Vienna Symphony Orchestra played *Stars* and *Sand* and gave the first performance of her majestic orchestral work *Rock* which explores the different qualities of rock, from impregnable and lonely to magnificent and undeniable. In 1959 her autobiography, *Jottings*, was privately printed, and Galaxy published a seven-volume edition of her songs. Howe died five years later, at the age of 82.

Dorothy Howell
1898–1982

Dorothy Howell caused a sensation in the British musical world when her symphonic poem *Lamia* was performed at the Proms in 1919 when she was only 21. She was born in Birmingham, and as a child received a convent education in Birmingham, Belgium and London. Her first pieces were published in 1911 while she was still at school although her father, himself an amateur organist and choirmaster, discouraged any publicity. She entered the Royal Academy of Music in 1913 at the age of 15 where she studied composition with John McEwen, piano with Percy Waller and later Tobias Matthay and violin with Gladys Chester. In 1914 Howell won the Hine prize for composition of an English ballad. But most of her earliest compositions were for the piano, many of which were published by the Anglo-French Music company including *Pieces for Bairns* (1917), *Toccata* (1918), *Five Studies* (1919) and the intricately rhythmic *Humoresque* (1919). In March 1919 Howell made her debut as a pianist in a recital at the Aeolian Hall at which she played the *Five Studies* and *Humoresque*.

1919 was also the year of *Lamia*. Howell had started work on the piece, based on the poem by John Keats, two years previously. When she had finished the score McEwen advised her to show it to Henry Wood who immediately accepted it for the Proms and gave the first performance on September 10. The work was such a success that it was played five times that season and was soon being heard all over England. In 1921 the score was published by Novello. It is a powerful work that makes much use of the whole-tone scale and what were seen at the time as 'modern harmonic idioms'.

During the next few years a remarkable number of Howell's works were performed at important London concerts. In February 1920 her *Two Dances* for orchestra were heard at the Queen's Hall. Two other orchestral works were given first performances at the Proms: music from her ballet *Koong Shee* in 1921 and her Piano Concerto in D minor in 1923 with Howell herself as soloist. Her spirited *Phantasy* for violin and piano, which had won a Cobbett prize in 1921 was first performed at the Wigmore Hall in 1924 and published by Augener the following year. *The Rock*, an orchestral overture written after a visit to Gibraltar, was performed at the Proms in 1928, and several works were commissioned and performed by the pioneering Bournemouth Symphony Orchestra.

In 1924 Howell was appointed professor of harmony and composition at the Royal Academy, a post she held, together with other teaching jobs in Oxford, Cheltenham, Malvern, London and Birmingham, for the next 46 years until she retired in 1970 at the age of 72. She continued to compose and to perform although she never achieved the fame and position in English musical life that had been predicted for her in the 1920s. Even by 1928 Ethel Smyth was complaining that there was no entry for Howell in the new edition of *Grove's Dictionary*. Performances of her music became much less frequent and she found it increasingly hard to get her works published. In 1929 Oxford University Press published her *Three Preludes* for piano and Hawkes &

Son published her part-song for unaccompanied women's voices, *If you will come to Corté*, to words by Rose Fyleman, whose poetry Howell had set several times before.

In the 1930s Howell wrote many vocal teaching pieces as well as editing *Fifty Songs for Schools* (1933) with Henry Richards. Her *Three Divertissements* for orchestra were commissioned for the 1940 Proms but the performance was cancelled when the Queen's Hall was bombed two days before. The work was not heard for another 10 years. Howell herself worked in the Women's Land Army during the war. Her published work from the 1950s includes a Sonata for violin and piano, broadcast from BBC Birmingham in 1953 and published in 1954, and *Two Pieces* for violin and piano, published in 1956. Much of Howell's later music was liturgical, including several works written for the nuns of Stanbrook Abbey. She made several Mass settings including *Missa Simplex* (1960), *A Simple Mass for the People* (1965), *An English Mass for Ampleforth* (1967) and *A Short English Mass for Congregation* (1967). Other sacred works included the motet *Coeli enarrant gloriam Dei* (1961) and *Four Anthems of Our Lady* (1966). Howell died in 1982, shortly before her 84th birthday.

Jean Eichelberger Ivey
b. 1923

Jean Eichelberger Ivey was born in Washington, DC in 1923. As a child she played the piano and the organ as well as starting to compose. She studied music at Trinity College, graduating in 1944, and then went to the Peabody Conservatory in Baltimore to study for a master's degree in the piano, graduating in 1946. She also received a master's degree in composition from the Eastman School of Music in 1956, studying during the summers.

While studying, Ivey taught the piano, organ and theory at various colleges and worked as an organist and a pianist, touring in the United States, Latin America and Europe in the late 1950s. She included in her recitals her own piano works, such as *Theme and Variations* (1952) and *Pianoforte Sonata* (1957). Other early works, all in a basically tonal language, included *Little Symphony* (1948), *Scherzo* (1953) for wind septet and *Festive Symphony* (1955). In 1958 she married Frederick Maurice Ivey.

In the early 1960s Ivey became interested in electronic music, intrigued by the variety of sounds, textures and colours that can be instantly created by working in a studio. Her first work for tape was *Pinball* (1965), a collage of clicks, rattles, bells and other sounds from a pinball machine, which she made at Brandeis University Electronic Studio. This piece was later used in the film 'Montage V: How to play Pinball' by Wayne Sourbeer. In 1967 she wrote *Continuous Form* which was used in the short breaks between television programmes in combination with visual images put together by Sourbeer. In the same year Ivey set up one of the first electronic music workshops for schoolteachers, and in 1969, when she took a job at the Peabody Conservatory, founded the Electronic Music Studio there. The first work to be made at the Studio was her *Cortege – for Charles Kent* (1969), a lament for one of the past directors of Peabody, created entirely from electronically produced sounds.

Ivey continued to write music for acoustic instruments with works such as *Tribute: Martin Luther King* (1969) for baritone and orchestra, and also began increasingly to write for various combinations of acoustic instruments or voice together with electronic tape. In 1972 she received a doctorate in music from the University of Toronto, specializing in electronic music. From the 1970s Ivey worked increasingly with voice, setting a wide range of texts. *Hera, Hung from the Sky* (1973) for mezzo-soprano, wind, percussion, piano and tape, uses a powerful poem by Caroline Kizer about the goddess who was punished for daring to think herself equal with Zeus by being turned into a constellation of stars. Ivey was attracted by Kizer's reinterpretation of the myth from a woman's point of view, and created a vivid, exciting work with an intensely dramatic vocal line.

Another of her works to reinterpret a familiar myth was *Testament of Eve* (1974) for mezzo-soprano, orchestra and tape, first performed by the Baltimore Symphony Orchestra in 1976. For this virtuoso work Ivey set her own text, which she had written nearly 10 years previously. Lucifer, sung by a taped voice, debates with Eve, sung by the live mezzo-soprano, who chooses knowledge and growth rather than simple pleasure. *Solstice* (1977) for soprano, flute, percussion and piano is another work for which Ivey wrote her own text, describing the

winter solstice when the sun appears to stand still, and evoking the memory of ancient solstice festivals from different cultures. She asks the performers to play with a 'sense of awe and mystery' and uses expressive flute and vocal lines coloured with piano and percussion to create an absorbing and dream-like piece.

Ivey's later works from the 1970s set William Shakespeare, in *Prospero* (1978) for bass-baritone, horn, percussion and tape, and Walt Whitman, in *Crossing Brooklyn Ferry* (1979) for baritone and piano. Between 1980 and 1982 Ivey worked on her first opera, *The Birthmark,* to her own libretto after Nathaniel Hawthorne, telling the story of a scientist who wants to remove his wife's birthmark, but as he succeeds and the birthmark fades, she dies. In the 1980s Ivey wrote several orchestral works, including *Sea-change* (1982) for orchestra and tape, first performed by the Baltimore Symphony Orchestra and a Cello Concerto (1983–5), as well as instrumental and vocal chamber music such as *Ariel in Flight* (1983) for violin and tape and *Notes toward Time* (1984), three songs for mezzo-soprano, flute and harp to poems by Josephine Jacobsen. Ivey celebrated 1994, her 70th-birthday year, with premieres of her three-movement orchestral work *Forms in Motion*, originally written over 20 years earlier in 1972, and *My Heart is Like a Singing Bird*, a new work for a chorus of women's voices and flute choir to a text by Christina Rossetti.

Carrie Jacobs-Bond
1861–1946

Born in Janesville, Wisconsin in 1861, Carrie Jacobs-Bond was playing the piano by ear at the age of four. She had piano lessons from local teachers and was inspired by hearing a concert given by the virtuoso American pianist Julia Rivé-King. But she gave up all study when she made her first marriage to Mr E.J. Smith at the age of 18. This was not a happy marriage. Jacobs-Bond had a son in 1881 but the couple eventually separated and divorced.

In 1886, when she was 25, Jacobs-Bond married Dr Frank Bond and moved with her son Frederick to Iron River in Northern Michigan. Bond encouraged her to continue with her music and to write down the songs that she was composing, as long as this remained a private hobby. When the family was thrown into financial difficulties during the Panic of 1893, Jacobs-Bond, in spite of her husband's disapproval, managed to get two of her songs published in an attempt to add to the family income.

Two years later, Bond died suddenly when he fell and hit his head after being pushed over by a little girl. Completely devastated and left with almost no money, Jacobs-Bond had to find a way to support herself and her son. They moved to Chicago where she tried many ways of earning a living, including taking in lodgers and selling hand-painted china as well as attempting to get her songs published and promoting them by singing at parties and after-dinner concerts for a fee of $10. Her memoirs detail how painful such public exposure was to a woman of her class and expectations.

After spending several years dealing with dishonest publishers and having her songs rejected by Tin Pan Alley publishers who found them too classical, Jacobs-Bond decided in 1901 to form her own publishing company, Carrie Jacobs-Bond and Son of Chicago. With the financial help of singer Jessie Bartlett Davis, she issued her first collection which was modestly titled *Seven Songs as Unpretentious as the Wild Rose* and included the sentimental 'I love you truly', which became one of her best-known works. Gradually learning the world of the music business, Jacobs-Bond realized that she needed well-known singers to promote her music. In 1901 the Quaker singer David Bispham gave a concert in Chicago consisting entirely of her songs. Other singers who performed her work included Ernestine Schumann-Heink.

Jacobs-Bond also continued to promote her music herself, travelling to New York and Washington and to England. In London she sang at a party where Enrico Caruso was also performing and was appalled at the indignity of being served refreshments in a separate room from the guests. She also sang at a concert in the White House for the Roosevelts. Jacobs-Bond's tuneful and undemanding songs, mostly to her own melancholy words, soon became extremely popular. Her biggest success came in 1910 when she first published the song, 'A Perfect Day', inspired by a sunset in California. During the first world war Jacobs-Bond had endless letters from soldiers who had kept up their morale by singing it, and it was sung by thousands on the streets of New York on Armistice Day. This simple song, which has been published in over 60 versions and is still sung today, sold over eight million sheet-music copies.

These incredible sales ensured the success of Jacobs-Bond's music business which by this time included a retail outlet, the Bond Shop.

Continually suffering from bad health, Jacobs-Bond began to spend the winters in Southern California, giving recitals for employees of the Santa Fe Railroad in order to earn the money for the journey. She eventually settled in California, moving her business to Hollywood in 1920. She also started writing articles for newspapers, was one of the founders of the California Federation of Music Clubs and became friends with a number of movie stars including Gracie Fields. In 1927 she published her memoirs, *The Roads of Melody*. Although she was shattered by the suicide of her son, she continued to compose songs.

In October 1934 Jacobs-Bond was a guest of honour, with Amy Beach, at a concert given by the Women's Symphony Orchestra of Chicago at the Century of Progress Exhibition in Chicago. In 1940 she published a collection of poems, *The End of the Road*. Her last songs, such as 'My Mother's Voice' (1942), 'There's some-body waiting for me' (1942) and 'Because of the Light' (1944) were published when she was in her 80s. She died in 1946 at the age of 85.

Minna Keal
b. 1909

When Minna Keal was 80 her first orchestral work, a symphony, was performed at the 1989 Proms by the BBC Symphony Orchestra conducted by Oliver Knussen. Keal had completed the work four years previously and it was only the third work she had completed after taking up composition again after a gap of over 45 years. She was born Mina Nerenstein in the East End of London in 1909. Her parents were Russian-Jewish immigrants who had arrived in London from Byelorussia a few years previously and ran a Hebrew publishing and book-selling business in Petticoat Lane. As a child, Keal listened to her mother singing Hebrew folk songs and her Uncle Leibel playing the violin by ear. She also had piano lessons and listened to endless records of violin and operatic virtuosi.

Keal's father died in 1926 when she was 16. Two years later she entered the Royal Academy of Music where she studied the piano and took composition lessons with William Alwyn, winning a bursary for composition in her second year. Several of her chamber works were performed at the Academy and at concerts in Whitechapel Gallery and at the People's Palace including a *Fantasie* in C minor for violin and piano, a *Ballade* in F minor for viola and piano and *Three Summer Sketches* for piano. This early music is deeply passionate with vibrant melodies and rich harmonies.

In 1929, at the age of 20, Keal left the Academy under pressure from friends and relatives, and gave up her musical studies in order to help her mother with the family business. She married in the early 1930s and had a son. Although she had stopped composing, she continued to play the piano and her early works were occasionally heard. In 1933 her *Fantaisie* and *Ballade* were played at a concert at the Jewish Institute.

Keal led an eventful life. During the 1930s she set up a local committee to help Jewish children escaping from

Minna Keal

Nazi Germany and became very involved in left-wing politics at the time of the Spanish Civil War. When her marriage broke up during the second world war she moved to Slough and worked in an aircraft factory. It was here that she met her future second husband, engineering fitter Bill Keal, although they were not to be married until 1959. Keal continued to be active in politics. She had joined the British Communist Party in 1939, organized a Communist Party branch at the aircraft factory, worked on the *Daily Worker* and was involved with the Workers' Music Association, including singing in the WMA Choir. In 1942 her *Fantasy Sonata* for viola and piano was played at a concert given by the Anglo-Soviet Friendship Committee. In 1963 the Keals moved to Chesham and Keal took a job in the fur trade as well as taking piano lessons at the Guildhall School of Music. When she retired in 1969 at the age of 60, she began taking a few pupils, having qualified as a piano teacher.

Keal first met composer Justin Connolly in the early 1970s when he was examining one of her piano pupils for the Associated Board examinations. After he saw some of Keal's early compositions, Connolly encouraged her to start writing again. In 1974 her son gave her some composition lessons with Connolly as a Christmas present. Apart from some piano pieces, the first work Keal wrote was a String Quartet, op. 1, which she completed in 1978 and was first performed in public in 1989. This work is immediately in an entirely different musical language to that of her early works – dissonant and atonal although still as intense and heartfelt. Keal's next composition was a Wind Quintet, op. 2, which she completed in 1980. Connolly then encouraged her to write an orchestral piece and she started work on her Symphony.

In 1982 Keal started taking lessons with Oliver Knussen. The Symphony, written in a specially built extension to her home in Buckinghamshire, took five years to complete. Originally planned as an orchestral suite in five movements based on poems written by her husband, Keal turned the work into a four-movement symphony expressing what she described as 'the turmoil of human existence and the spiritual search for serenity and permanence'. The first three movements of the work were played at St John's, Smith Square in London in 1984, and the whole work was first heard as a BBC broadcast in 1988. Surprising audiences with its grit and power, it is a passionate work based on an eight-note chord and a theme using all 12 notes of the scale.

Since the success of her Symphony, Keal has continued to compose, treating her state pension as the equivalent of a student grant! Her next work was *Cantillation* for orchestra with a prominent solo violin part, completed in 1988 and first performed by the European Women's Orchestra, conducted by Odaline de la Martinez in 1991. Taking its title from the style of chanting in Jewish synagogues, *Cantillation* is a powerfully expressive work with the violin taking on the role of a fierce, lamenting voice. Her Cello Concerto, a large work which she started writing in the late 1980s and felt might take her the rest of her life, was scheduled for performance at the 1994 Snape Proms. At the time of her Proms debut in 1989, Keal explained what her return to composition meant to her: 'I felt I was coming to the end of my life, but now I feel as if I'm just beginning. I feel as if I'm living my life in reverse.'

Barbara Kolb
b. 1939

Rich sounds and vivid instrumental colours and textures are central to the music of Barbara Kolb, who uses a variety of often complex techniques to create her own highly individual and enticing musical language. Kolb was born in Hartford, Connecticut where her father, Harold Kolb – jazz pianist, composer and conductor of popular music – was the director of music for the WITC radio station. As a young girl Kolb frequently sang on one of his radio programmes and started playing the E♭ clarinet when she was 11.

After leaving school in 1957, Kolb went to the Hartt School of Music at the University of Hartford where she studied the clarinet and began to compose, graduating in 1961. For the next four years Kolb taught clarinet and theory at Hartt while studying for a master's degree in composition with Arnold Franchetti. In 1964 she first went to study at Tanglewood, taking composition lessons from Gunther Schuller and Lukas Foss. During the early 1960s she was also earning a living by playing the E♭ clarinet in the Hartford Symphony Orchestra and Hartford Summer Band, a job which she hated, finding it entirely lacking in any opportunity for self-expression.

In 1965 Kolb moved to New York where she worked as a music copyist for four years, supplementing this income with various grants and awards for her music. Her first published work, *Rebuttal* for two clarinets, dates from the same year. In 1966 she was awarded a Fulbright scholarship to study in Vienna but, finding the musical life and teaching there conservative and dull, she returned the award and came back to the United States. During these years she often worked at the MacDowell Colony, and spent the summer of 1968 at Tanglewood taking further lessons from Schuller.

In 1969, Kolb became the first American woman to receive the Prix de Rome, and spent the next two years living and working in Rome. This period saw a succession of works, often for unusual combinations of instruments, in which she began to develop her highly distinctive voice. *Trobar Clos* (1970) for chamber ensemble, commissioned by the Fromm Foundation for performance at Tanglewood and based on a medieval poetic form using patterns of repetition, was followed by *Solitaire* (1971) for piano and tape using pre-recorded vibraphone. The music, which allows the performer a certain degree of choice, is built up with repeated fragments of melodies, including a quotation from Chopin's Prelude in A♭ Major, which combine to create a spellbinding and richly sonorous pattern of sound. *Soundings* (1971–2), for chamber ensemble and tape, was commissioned by the Koussevitsky Foundation. The title refers to the technique of measuring the depth of water by establishing the echo time of signals bounced off the bottom of the sea. With harmonies based on a row built from the whole-tone scale, Kolb's music conjures up vivid impressions of the depths of the sea.

With her reputation as a composer growing rapidly, Kolb received several short-term appointments on her return to the United States. In the summer of 1973 she was composer-in-residence at the Marlboro Music Festival, Vermont, and in the same year was appointed assistant professor of music theory at Brooklyn College, New York for two years. In 1974 and 1975 she was composer-in-residence at the American Academy in Rome. Kolb continued to write chamber music that incorporated the use of taped sound with works such as *Spring River Flowers Moon Night* (1974–5) for two pianos and pre-recorded tape. This fundamentally still and contemplative piece was inspired by a poem by the eighth-century Chinese poet Chang Jo-Hsu. In *Looking for Claudio* (1975) for guitar and tape, the tape uses the pre-recorded sounds of a mandolin, six guitars, vibraphone, chimes and three humming voices which weave with the guitar to produce a web of mysterious and enthralling music. In 1975 Kolb revised *Soundings* for orchestra and two conductors, and the new version was premiered by the New York Philharmonic conducted by Pierre Boulez and David Gilbert. In this version the work toured Japan under Seiji Ozawa and the Boston Symphony Orchestra, and Kolb revised it again in 1978.

From 1976 to 1977 Kolb lived and worked in Paris on a Guggenheim Fellowship. During this time she worked on two very different works. *Appello* (1976) for piano takes its title from the Italian word meaning 'call'. It is in four movements, with each based on a different tone row taken from Pierre Boulez's *Structures 1a* and exploring a different kind of call. In *Homage to Keith Jarrett and Gary Burton* (1976) for flute and vibraphone, Kolb explores her love of jazz and escapes from some of the discipline of the techniques she had been using in a work like *Appello*. *Homage* is based around a short improvisation on an early Jarrett piece, 'Grow your own'.

In 1978 Kolb was a visiting professor at Temple University, Philadelphia and started work on her orchestral piece *Grisaille* (1978–9). The title refers to a Renaissance technique of painting using tones and shades of grey, and the work was inspired by the iridescent graphite pictures of Hans Schiebold and the textures of music by Claude Debussy and Pierre Boulez. Kolb based the whole work around a single chord and builds to a dramatic climax. In *Chromatic Fantasy* (1979) for narrator, amplified alto flute, oboe, soprano saxophone, trumpet, amplified electric guitar and vibraphone, Kolb uses a prose poem by Howard Stern. Each of the work's three sections presents a different version of the poem, at first a shortened version, followed by the complete text and ending with random words and phrases. The complex, chromatic music supports the discursive text.

Kolb has been involved in a variety of different musical projects. For three years from 1979 she was Artistic Director of Contemporary Music at the Third Street Music School Settlement where she organized the concert series 'Music New to New York'. In 1981 she spent several months in Italy working with film-maker James Herbert on a

tape collage for his film *Cantico* about the life of St Francis. The following year she embarked on the development of a music-theory instruction course for blind and otherwise disabled people, sponsored by the Library of Congress and completed in 1986.

Between 1983 and 1984 Kolb spent nine months on a residency at IRCAM (Insitute de Recherche et de Co-ordination Acoustique/Musique) in Paris. This experience of working with computer-generated music led to the composition of *Millefoglie* (1984–5) for flute, oboe, clarinet, bass clarinet, trombone, percussion, amplified harp, cello and computer-generated tape and ensemble, commissioned by IRCAM and first performed in Paris. As the name suggests, the music is built out of many different layers of harmony and rhythm, combining fragmented gestures with more lyrical passages. From 1984 to 1985 Kolb was visiting professor of composition at the Eastman School of Music in Rochester, New York but since then has lived off her work as a composer. Her chamber music from this time includes *Umbrian Colours* (1986) for violin and guitar and *Extremes* (1989) for flute and cello.

Since the mid–1980s Kolb has received an increasing number of commissions for large-scale works. *The Enchanted Loom* (1988–9) for orchestra is a dramatically expressive work which was commissioned by the Atlanta

Symphony Orchestra and first performed in Georgia in 1990. In *Voyants* (1991) for piano and chamber orchestra, commissioned by Radio France, Kolb uses the piano as a voyant or seer predicting disastrous future events which are finally realized by the orchestra in a huge and terrifying climax. The short orchestral piece *All in Good Time* (1993) was commissioned by the New York Philharmonic Orchestra for their 150th anniversary. In this work, Kolb explores different aspects of time. The floating middle section, centring around a dream-like passage for soprano saxophone, is framed by two outer sections of intense and exciting rhythmic vitality.

Margaret Ruthven Lang
1867–1972

Margaret Ruthven Lang's father, Benjamin Johnson Lang, was an important figure in Boston's musical life at the end of the 19th century. He had studied in Europe and worked as organist and conductor with many of Boston's important musical institutions such as the Handel and Haydn Society, the Apollo Club and the Cecilia Society. He wrote music himself but apparently never felt it was good enough to be published. Lang's mother was an amateur singer and Lang's first musical experiences doubtless came through her parents. Benjamin Lang obviously took his daughter's musical ambitions seriously and provided her with support and encouragement as well as a good musical education. She studied the piano with her father and took violin lessons with Louis Schmidt.

Lang started writing music at an early age, producing a movement of a piano quintet when she was 12, and in 1886, at the age of 19, went to Munich where she studied the violin and took lessons in counterpoint and fugue with Victor Gluth. She returned to Boston the following year and continued her composition studies with leading New England composers George Chadwick and Edward MacDowell.

Lang's early songs to German and English texts began to be performed in Boston soon after her return from Germany. At a recital in December 1887, Myron Whitney gave the first public performance of her songs. The next month, at the first meeting of the Boston 'Manuscript Club', five of Lang's songs were sung, including 'Ghosts', which was published the following year. She was greatly helped in these early performances by her father. Groups with which he was involved, such as the Cecilia Society and the Apollo Club, gave many of the early performances of her work. One of the most auspicious of these was the 1890 performance at the Apollo Club of *The Jumblies*, op. 5, witty settings of poetry by Edward Lear for baritone solo, men's chorus and two pianos. These musical pastiches were published by Schmidt, who was to publish much of her chamber and vocal music. Lang followed up their success with two later Lear collections, *Nonsense Rhymes and Pictures* (1905), op. 42, and *More Nonsense Rhymes and Pictures* (1907), op. 43.

In the early 1890s Lang's songs began to be heard outside Boston. In 1889 'Ojalà', a setting of words by George Eliot, had been performed at the Paris Exposition in a concert of American music. This song was performed again in 1890 at the inauguration of the Lincoln Concert Hall in Washington, DC, and in 1892 a recital consisting entirely of works by Lang was given in New York. Her songs were popular both with the general public and with singers such as Ernestine Schumann-Heink, Alma Gluck and John MacCormack. She adapted her music to the texts she was setting, with inventive touches such as the opening vocal melisma in 'Oriental Serenade' from *Three Songs of the East* (1892), op. 8, or the bare unison passage in 'The Sky-Ship' to words by Frank Sherman from *Four Songs* (1892), op. 9. Some of her songs, such as the well-known 'An Irish Love Song' (1895), op. 22, and 'An Irish Mother's Lullaby' (1900), op. 34, display an interest in working with folk material.

Benjamin Lang obviously tried to promote his daughter's work wherever possible. In 1892 he wrote to the conductor Theodore Thomas to suggest that he programme Lang's setting of Walter Scott's *The Wild Huntsman* for solo voices, chorus and orchestra. Her father's position in Boston musical society obviously gave Lang unprecedented access to opportunities denied to most women of her generation. Towards the end of her life she remembered as a young woman getting Arthur Nikisch and the Boston Symphony Orchestra to play through some Grieg for her so that she could listen to the orchestration! In 1893 her *Dramatic Overture*, op. 12, became the first work by a woman to be played by the Boston Symphony Orchestra in its 12-year history. Later in the same year her overture *Witchis*, op. 10, was performed several times at the World's Columbian Exposition in Chicago, having been selected along with two other works from 21 entries and one of only three other works by women to be played outside the Women's Building. Other performances of large scale works followed. In 1895 *Sappho's Prayer to Aphrodite* for contralto and orchestra was performed in New York, and the following year *Armida*, op. 24, for soprano and orchestra was performed by the Boston Symphony Orchestra. In 1901 Lang's *Ballade* in D minor, op. 36, for orchestra was played at a Women in Music Grand Concert given by the Baltimore Symphony Orchestra.

Unfortunately most of Lang's orchestral works were not published and have not survived. It seems that

Lang herself may have destroyed them. She continued to compose after her father's death in 1909 although while he was alive she had depended on his approval of a piece before offering it for publication. Her later works include *Wind* (1913), op. 53, an impressionistic setting of a text by John Galsworthy for double chorus of women's voices which was commissioned by the St Cecilia Chorus of New York; *The Heavenly Noel* (1916), op. 57, a setting of words by Richard Lawson Gales for mezzo-soprano, women's chorus, organ, piano, harp and string quartet, performed by the Choral Music Society of Boston in 1917; and *Elegy* (1917), op. 58, for piano. For no apparent reason, Lang appears to have stopped writing music at this time although she was to live for another 55 years, dying in 1972 at the age of 104.

Libby Larsen
b. 1950

Libby Larsen's exuberantly tuneful and excitingly rhythmic music draws on very American roots in jazz and popular song as well as owing something to the pioneer spirit of the early American settlers. She is a highly successful and practical composer who makes her living from commissions without a full-time academic post, although she has been a visiting professor and lecturer at several institutions. Her work makes contemporary classical music relevant to generations that have grown up with rock music, television and video.

Born in Wilmington, Delaware, Larsen grew up in the midwest, near the lakes of Minnesota, in a house full of the sounds of the Broadway musicals and stride boogie piano recordings her mother loved. Larsen sang and played the piano from an early age as well as being fascinated with dance and ballet. At school she sang in choirs and began to compose songs and choral pieces. She studied music at the University of Minnesota, graduating with a degree in

music theory in 1971, although at one time she had considered training to be a professional singer.

After graduation, Larsen worked as a secretary at an insurance company, spending her coffee breaks writing chamber operas such as the 'quasi-ragtime' *Psyche and the Pskyscraper* for coloratura soprano, tenor, baritone and chamber ensemble, based on a story by O. Henry, and *Lovers*, based on a story by Liam O'Flaherty, for tenor and mezzo-soprano, oboe and harpsichord, with male and female dancers to represent the lovers in their youth.

After six months Larsen returned to the University of Minnesota to study with Dominick Argento, Eric Stokes and Paul Fetler for further degrees in composition, receiving her master's degree in 1975, the year in which she also married James Reece, and her doctorate in 1978. In 1973, together with composer Stephen Paulus, she founded the Minnesota Composers

Forum, an organization set up to provide composers with practical help in business matters such as applying for fellowships and negotiating contracts as well as to organize concerts and recordings of local composers' works.

Vocal music has always been very important in Larsen's output and her early works for voice demonstrate her accomplished word setting, using a wide range of texts, from Rainer Maria Rilke in *Three Rilke Songs* (1977) for soprano, harp, flute and guitar to H.D. in *Eurydice* (1978) for soprano and string quartet, and Belle Star (Jesse James' lover) in *Three Cowboy Songs* (1978) for soprano and piano. Larsen's early instrumental works include her celebration of speed and boogie woogie, *Four on the Floor* (1977) for violin, cello, bass and piano, and the more sedate *Aubade* (1982) for flute, a work echoing jazz improvisation.

In 1983 Larsen was appointed one of the Minnesota Orchestra's two composers-in-residence, a position she held for the next four years, during which time her daughter was born. The opportunities for composing that the residence was to give her proved extremely useful for her development as an orchestral composer. Earlier orchestral works had included *Three Cartoons* (1980), *Pinions* (1981) for violin and chamber orchestra and *Deep Summer Music* (1982) which had been premiered by the Minnesota Orchestra.

Overture – Parachute Dancing (1984) was commissioned by the American Composers Orchestra and was inspired by a Renaissance court dance in which the dancers danced along walls holding silk umbrellas and then jumped off using the umbrellas as parachutes. Since her childhood, Larsen has been fascinated by 'everything having to do with wind, sky and water' and built the piece around the sense of danger, motion and colour in the dance, using brass and percussion in particular to create a sense of excitement. The work ends with a loud climax followed by falling string glissandi as the dancers float overhead and then land with a gentle thud. Larsen's first work as composer-in-residence for the Minnesota Orchestra, *Symphony: Water Music* (1984), was inspired by 'the motions and rhythms of nature' and in particular by the lakes of Minnesota.

Larsen has been particularly drawn to the history of the American pioneers. *The Settling Years* (1987) for chorus, woodwind quintet and piano sets three pioneer texts. The boisterous first movement, 'Comin' to Town', opens with an ear-piercing round-up whistle and uses whoops and whistles throughout to punctuate the lively choral writing. The second movement 'Beneath These Alien Stars' uses lush, slow-moving harmonies and is followed by a rousing finale, 'A Hoopla', complete with foot stamping. In *Songs from Letters* (1989) Larsen

Libby Larsen

sets part of a diary kept by Calamity Jane in the form of letters to her daughter Janey. Another work using pioneer texts is *Ghosts of an Old Ceremony* (1991), a music-theatre piece for orchestra and dancers written in collaboration with choreographer Brenda Way, which includes the narration of extracts from the journals of pioneer women.

Larsen has often used texts by women that are particularly expressive of women's experiences. At the suggestion of the singer Arleen Auger, she used six of Elizabeth Barrett Browning's *Sonnets from the Portuguese* in her 1988 song cycle of the same name. Both Larsen and Auger felt that the poems explored issues still relevant to women today as well as providing a heartfelt expression of mature love. Setting the poems for soprano and chamber ensemble, Larsen created a powerfully moving work with rich harmonies and soaringly lyrical vocal lines. Another important work using a text by a woman is Larsen's music drama piece *Mrs Dalloway* (1993) with a libretto by Bonnie Grice based on Virginia Woolf's novel. In *Mary Cassatt* for soprano, trombones, orchestra and art slides, first performed by the Grand Rapids (Michigan) Symphony Orchestra in 1994, Larsen celebrates female creativity in the visual arts.

A wide variety of popular music has continued to provide an importance source of inspiration for many of Larsen's works, from the energetic orchestral piece *Collage: Boogie* (1988) to her two concertos of 1992: *Marimba Concerto: After Hampton* and *Piano Concerto: Since Armstrong*. The influence of certain aspects of rock music and rock concerts is particularly apparent in what has probably been Larsen's most successful work, her seventh opera, *Frankenstein, the Modern Prometheus* (1990). This is a compelling multi-media work that raises fascinating questions about the uses and abuses of technology. Larsen studied the construction of screen-plays and television commercials before writing her tight, sparse libretto, based on the novel by Mary Shelley. *Frankenstein* makes use of an earlier orchestral piece, *What the Monster Saw* (1987), and the monster's viewpoint is central to the work, presented to the audience on large video screens. Larsen scored the work for an amplified chamber ensemble with three different keyboards, and developed a set consisting of ropes and ladders that extend out over the audience, drawing them into a closer, almost cinematic experience of this enthralling work.

Nicola LeFanu
b. 1947

As a child Nicola LeFanu was fascinated by drama and the theatre. The daughter of composer Elizabeth Maconchy and William LeFanu, she was taught to read music by her mother at a young age but did not show any interest in learning to play the piano until she was about 10. Her first attempts at making up music were the tunes she invented for songs in the many plays that she wrote and performed with friends throughout her childhood. As a teenager she began to be more involved in music and started to compose for instruments. She took up the cello in her last years at school in Wiltshire and had composition lessons with Jeremy Dale Roberts, writing music that was already distinctly her own.

Determined to keep her composing separate from academic work, LeFanu chose to study music at St Hilda's College, Oxford, where there was no element of composition in the course. She studied with Alexander Goehr in the university vacations and wrote music for college friends to perform. In 1965, during her first term at Oxford, she wrote *Soliloquy* for oboe, a work that was almost immediately taken up professionally, broadcast and published by Novello. After graduating from Oxford in 1968, LeFanu attended a summer school in Siena with Goffredo Petrassi before spending a year at the Royal College of Music studying with Humphrey Searle and taking private lessons with Thea Musgrave. During her time at the College her *Variations* for oboe quartet, commissioned after the success of *Soliloquy*, won a Cobbett prize.

After leaving the College in 1969, LeFanu taught music at Francis Holland School in London for three years. She also took classes in conducting and music theatre at Morley College and then became the tutor for the music-theatre class which worked on her first theatrical piece, *Anti World* (1972). This work for dancer, soprano, baritone, alto flute and percussion, first performed at the Cockpit Theatre, set Soviet samizdat texts by Natalia Gorbanevskaya and Andrei Vosnesensky and explored issues of control and freedom, concentrating on the relationship between the dancer and the musicians.

In 1973 LeFanu's first orchestral work *The Hidden Landscape* was commissioned by the BBC and performed at the Proms. That year LeFanu was awarded a Harkness Fellowship to study in the United States with Earl Kim and Seymour Shifrin, providing her with an important opportunity to widen her experience of contemporary music and further develop her own serially based language. During her time in the States she wrote a cycle of 15 songs, *The Same Day Dawns* (1974) for soprano, flute, clarinet, violin, cello and percussion, and conducted its first performance in Boston. *The Same Day Dawns* sets translations of Tamil, Chinese and Japanese poems that LeFanu has described as '... words of unendurable love and longing, of loneliness, distance and death...', and for which she created a very intimate sound-world in which the voice and instruments often move in a single line of music.

In 1975, after her return to Britain, her orchestral work *Columbia Falls* was premiered in Birmingham by the City of Birmingham Symphony Orchestra and repeated the next day at the Royal Festival Hall in London. Various

different landscapes are often a starting point for LeFanu's music. *Columbia Falls* was inspired by the hills and moors of Maine and also by the countryside of the north of England and the music of Australian composer David Lumsdaine. It presents a continuous arch with the strings, brass and wind finally coming together at a dramatic climax.

From 1975 to 1977 LeFanu was Head of Music at St Paul's Girls School in London. She took six months leave in 1976 which she spent in Australia writing her chamber opera *Dawnpath* for baritone, soprano, male dancer and five instrumentalists. This work grew out of her experience of the Australian wilderness but also from her travels in the southwestern states during her 18-month stay in the United States. LeFanu constructed her own text out of two Native-American creation myths in which the first man sings the rest of the world into being and the first woman then chooses mortality and a life in the light over immortality and darkness.

From 1977 to 1994 LeFanu taught composition at King's College, London University, a job she shared from 1981 with David Lumsdaine, whom she had married in 1979. In 1994 she became the Professor of Music and head of the music department at York University. Sharing the post at King's College gave LeFanu more time to compose, and since the late 1970s she has produced a series of powerfully expressive works that communicate a wide range of emotions and ideas, often exploring the issues that she finds important in the world today.

In 1981 LeFanu wrote one of her most successful and inventive works, which combines exploration of human emotions with a vivid evocation of place. *The Old Woman of Beare*, for soprano and 13 instruments, is a dramatic and moving work for which LeFanu adapted a 9th-century monologue in which an ageing Irish courtesan reflects on her life and death. The singer speaks much of the text, singing the rest with a virtuosic intensity supported by the varied and exciting textures of the instrumentalists. The work produces a remarkable musical expression of a woman's passionate memories combined with the wildness of the coast of southwest Ireland.

LeFanu used early Irish poems again, together with Japanese and English poetry, in *A Penny for a Song* (1981) for soprano and piano. In 1982 LeFanu's son Peter was born. From the autumn of 1984 LeFanu spent a year in Australia. During this time she wrote the saxophone quartet *Moon over Western Ridge, Mootwingee* (1985) which was inspired by the extraordinary space of the Australian outback and uses quarter tones to create an equally extraordinary sound-world. LeFanu has since written a Saxophone

Concerto (1989) and *Ervallagh* (1993) for alto saxophone and piano.

While in Australia she also started work on *Mary O'Neill,* a radio opera for voices commissioned by the BBC and first broadcast in 1989. *Mary O'Neill*, with a libretto by Sally McInerney based on an initial story by LeFanu herself, explores issues of dispossession and empire through the story of an Irish woman who emigrates to Argentina. She marries an Argentinian and the opera follows the fate of her two mixed-race sons and their descendants to the present day. LeFanu uses the 17 unaccompanied voices to create a rich range of music from lyrical solos to evocations of the forest.

In the later 1980s LeFanu wrote several important chamber works such as *Invisible Places* (1986) for clarinet and string quartet, a piece inspired by Italo Calvino's *Invisible Cities*. Her String Quartet (1988) makes use of quarter-tones, as does *Lament 1988* for oboe doubling cor anglais, clarinet doubling bass clarinet, viola and cello. A dark, angry work, *Lament 1988* marked two anniversaries, the 70th birthday of Nelson Mandela and the 200th anniversary of the invasion of Australia by white settlers.

In 1987 LeFanu was one of the founding members of the organization Women in Music, set up to encourage and celebrate women's contributions to all kinds of music. Her article 'Master Musician: An Impregnable Taboo?' attracted considerable media attention with its statistics documenting the music establishment's neglect of work by women composers. In the early 1990s LeFanu had three full-length opera commissions. The move to writing opera was one that LeFanu had long prepared for, with works such as *Dawnpath* and *The Old Woman of Beare,* and one which drew her early love of theatre and working with other people together with her ability to create finely judged, eloquent music.

The first of these operas was *The Green Children,* a children's opera written for the King's Lynn Festival in Norfolk. LeFanu worked closely with librettist Kevin Crossley-Holland, the Baylis Programme at English National Opera, the ensemble Gemini and the 200 local children who were involved in composing parts of the work as well as performing it. She conducted the first performance at the festival in the summer of 1990. *The Green Children*, set in the 12th century, is based on a local story in which villagers discover two green children who have come from another world in which everything is green and explores society's fear of those who are different. LeFanu initially found using her own complex language in a way that could be performed by children and amateurs to be a challenge but one that eventually enriched her music.

Blood Wedding (1991–2), with a libretto by Deborah Levy based on the play by Federico Lorca, was commissioned by The Women's Playhouse Trust for a production that was directed, designed, written, composed and conducted entirely by women. *Blood Wedding* is the story of love destroyed by the pressures and conventions of a strict society, of a woman who is in love with a man, Leonardo, whose family are feuding with the family of the man she is about to marry. The lovers run away on her wedding day with tragic results. LeFanu translated the violent passion of Lorca's play into dramatically expressive music with two big love duets and a central role for the groom's mother, a repressed but powerful woman who is also Death in the second act. LeFanu uses a broad musical language ranging from simple moments using almost modal harmonies to the strange microtones of the forest scene, with fragments of popular songs for the wedding festivities.

LeFanu's third opera is *The Wildman* (1994–5), written for performance at the Aldeburgh Festival in the summer of 1995. With a libretto by Kevin Crossley-Holland based on the legend of the Orford Merman, it explores, like many of LeFanu's works, issues of tolerance and the place of the stranger in the community.

Liza Lehmann
1862–1918

Liza Lehmann came from a family of musical women. Her grandmother was well known in Edinburgh as an amateur singer and harpist whose daughter, Lehmann's extremely self-critical mother Amelia, wrote a great deal of vocal music but destroyed most of it, publishing a few songs under the pseudonym 'A.L.'. Lehmann's sister Alma, who married Charles Goetz, also wrote and published music. Their father was the German painter, Rudolph Lehmann, who had settled in Britain.

Lehmann was born in London but spent the first five years of her life in Italy, and Italian was her first language. The family then returned to London but continued to spend every winter on the continent, in France, Italy or Germany. Lehmann's first musical memories were of the soirées her parents held in their house. She had her first singing lessons from her mother and studied the piano with Alma Haas. She continued her vocal studies with Alberto Randegger and attended classes taught by Jenny Lind. While the family were abroad she also had some composition lessons from Raunkilde in Rome and Wilhelm Freudenberg in Wiesbaden.

From an early age, Lehmann wanted to write music but felt that women were not usually taken seriously as composers. Coming from a family of artists and musicians there were no objections to her taking up a musical career and she was encouraged by her mother to become a professional singer. Her father apparently wanted her to develop her artistic talents and become a painter.

Lehmann had sung in public since the age of 17 but made her professional debut at a Monday Popular Concert in 1885 at the age of 23. For the next nine years she made a successful career as a singer appearing at concerts, private parties and festivals all over Britain. One of the features of her recitals was her performance of old English music by composers such as Henry Purcell,

Thomas Arne and James Hook. She spent many hours in the British Museum copying out this unknown repertoire and published several arrangements of such music which was well suited to her small soprano voice. Lehmann also included her own songs in her concerts and published several of them, including an *Album of Twelve German Songs* (1889). Three years later Chappell published two instrumental works, a *Romance* for piano and a *Romance* for violin and piano. Lehmann took further composition lessons from Hamish MacCunn but always felt that she did not have the time she wanted to devote to composition.

In 1894, at the age of 32, Lehmann decided to marry and give up her singing career. Her future husband was Herbert Bedford who had been a successful student at the Guildhall School of Music but had then became a partner in a City firm although he continued to compose. In July 1894 Lehmann gave a farewell concert which included a few of her songs and two piano pieces, *Abdallad* and *Valse de Sentiment*. Also on the programme was Bedford's *Ave Maria* for contralto, chorus, cello, piano, harp and organ. Lehmann always claimed that she gave up her career as a singer without the slightest regret and her retirement gave her the time she had always longed for to concentrate on composing. After their marriage the Bedfords lived in Pinner with

Lehmann's friend Maude Valérie White as a neighbour. The two women often met to play each other their work.

Lehmann's greatest success as a composer came in 1896 with her song cycle *In a Persian Garden*, a setting for four voices and piano of Edward Fitzgerald's extremely popular translation of the *Rubáiyát* of Omar Khayyám. The work was initially refused by various publishers for having so many singers and being too difficult for the profitable amateur market. Lehmann's friend, the society host Mrs Edward Goetz who wrote music herself, finally persuaded Metzler to publish it and gave the first performance at a concert in her house. This concert was reviewed enthusiastically by Hermann Klein in *The Sunday Times*. Public performances soon followed and the work became extraordinarily popular, especially in the United States.

The song cycle with four voices and piano was not a form that was often used at this time and it was one that Lehmann was to do a great deal to popularize. The various solos, duets and quartets of *In a Persian Garden* are held together by the recurrence of several themes. Lehmann's vocal writing moves between a dramatic, declamatory recitative and a more lyrical style, as in the exquisite tenor solo 'Ah, Moon of my Delight'. The piano accompaniment uses rich harmonies that some contemporary critics found startlingly modern. Lehmann followed this work with a cycle setting 12 sections of Alfred Tennyson's *In Memoriam* for solo voice and piano. This never achieved the popularity of *In a Persian Garden* although Lehmann considered it one of the best of all her works. It was first sung by Robert Kennerley Rumford and taken to the United States by David Bispham.

Bedford's business was affected by the Boer War, and the family, which by now included two sons, moved to Wimbledon. Lehmann continued to write, producing two large works for voice and orchestra – *Endymion*, a setting of Henry Wadsworth Longfellow for soprano and orchestra, and *Young Lochinvar*, a setting of Walter Scott for baritone, chorus and orchestra which was premiered at the Kendal Festival in 1899 in a performance conducted by the festival organizer Mary Wakefield. Later that month it was performed at the Crystal Palace. In 1900 Lehmann wrote the first of her many lighter works. *The Daisy-chain* was a song cycle for four voices and piano setting children's poetry by Robert Louis Stevenson, Alma Tadema and others. This became nearly as popular as *In a Persian Garden*, and Lehmann followed it in 1902 with another cycle *More Daisies*. In the same year she wrote the incidental music for a production by Henry Irving of Ludwig Fulda's play *The Twin Sister* which ran for two months at the Duke of York's Theatre.

In 1904 Lehmann became the first woman to be commissioned to write a musical comedy when she was asked to compose the music for *Sergeant Brue*, a farce by Owen Hall. Asked to ensure that the music was not as complex and modern as *In a Persian Garden*, Lehmann later felt that she had probably made it 'even more commonplace than it need have been'. It was a big success, running in London for nine months as well as touring the provinces. Two years later, in 1906, Lehmann wrote her light opera *The Vicar of Wakefield* with a libretto by Laurence Housman after Oliver Goldsmith. Apart from problems with a furious Housman after his script had been cut and altered, the work was well received and played for 37 performances at the Prince of Wales Theatre. W.S. Gilbert came to the first night and was so impressed that he suggested to Lehmann that they work together, an offer she turned down.

Lehmann was a prolific composer. The sales of her music may have played an important part in the family finances. She clearly divided her compositions into the ambitious or serious work and the lighter, more popular pieces , becoming increasingly frustrated by the success of, and demand from her publishers for, what she regarded as lightweight music. Her 'serious' works included *The Golden Threshold, an Indian Song-garland* (1906), settings

Liza Lehmann

of lyrics by the Indian poet and suffragette Sarojini Naidu and the cantata *Leaves from Ossian* (1909), to words by Norman McCann which was published by Chappell but never performed in London. At one provincial performance, Bedford had to 'play' a missing bassoon part on a brown paper tube!

Four Shakespearean Part-Songs, published by Novello in 1911, were well received by the critics, but to Lehmann's intense disappointment her opera *Everyman*, 'written with love, conviction and sincerity' and staged by the Beecham Opera Company at the Shaftesbury Theatre for a couple of performances in December 1915, was a failure, perhaps because the audience was not expecting such a solemn work. Other 'serious' works include her songs 'Magdalen at Michael's Gate' (Henry Kingsley, 1913) and 'When I am dead my dearest' (Christina Rossetti, 1918).

The lighter music that sold so well included the marvellously witty *Nonsense Songs* (1908), settings of lyrics by Lewis Carroll from *Alice in Wonderland,* and the Belloc settings *Four Cautionary Tales and a Moral* as well as sentimental songs such as 'There are Fairies at the Bottom of the

Garden' (Rose Fyleman) or 'Daddy's Sweetheart' (Curtis Hardin-Burnley). In 1909 Lehmann made the first of two tours of the United States, where she was received enthusiastically. Her travels inspired the song cycle *Prairie Pictures* (1911) and *Cowboy Ballads* (1912) with words taken from John Lomax's *Cowboy Songs and other Frontier Ballads*.

A form Lehmann tried to promote without lasting success was the recitation with piano accompaniment. Her cycle *In Memoriam* had ended with a section for spoken voice over the piano and she later wrote accompaniments for Oscar Wilde's *The Happy Prince* (1908), Jean Ingelow's *The High Tide – On the Coast of Lincolnshire 1571* (1912) and Nancy Price's *Behind the Nightlight* (1913).

By the time she was in her 50s, Lehmann had become an important role model for other women as well as a successful and popular composer. She was the first president of the Society of Women Musicians when it was formed in 1911, and a few years later accepted a professorship at the Guildhall. She published several teaching works such as *Practical Hints for Students of Singing* (1913), *Useful Teaching Songs* (1914) and *Studies in Recitative* (1915).

After the war broke out in 1914, Lehmann's son Rudolph joined the army, only to die of pneumonia while he was in training. Lehmann was devastated by his death and became ill herself, dying shortly after completing her memoirs *The Life Of Liza Lehmann* in 1918 at the age of 56.

Tania León
b. 1943

Tania León was born in Havana, Cuba where her grandmother encouraged her early interest in music. As a child she had piano lessons at the Carlos Alfredo Peyrellade Conservatory and gave her first public performance at five. In the early 1960s she graduated from the Conservatory with a degree in music education, having also studied as an accountant. León then worked in television in Havana for a short while before moving to New York in 1967, where she has lived ever since, and continuing to study music, taking up the trombone and the bassoon while making a living as an accountant.

In 1968 León met choreographer Arthur Mitchell who was forming the Dance Theatre of Harlem. She became the company's musical director and worked with it for 11 years, from 1969 to 1980, founding its music department, music school and orchestra. At Mitchell's request she soon started writing music for the company, producing her ballet *Tones* in 1970. León's other ballets written for the Dance

Theatre of Harlem in the 1970s included *The Beloved* (1972), *Dougla* (1974), written in collaboration with Geoffrey Holder, and *Spiritual Suite* (1976) with Marian Anderson as narrator.

It was also through the Dance Theatre of Harlem that León first started to conduct when, with no previous experience, she was asked to conduct at the Spoleto Festival in Italy while the company was on its first European tour in 1971. She later studied conducting with Laszlo Halasz and at the Juilliard with Vincent LaSilva as well as taking conducting classes at New York University and at Tanglewood. León has become a highly respected and sought-after conductor, working with orchestras throughout Europe and South Africa as well as the United States.

In the 1970s León studied composition at New York University with Ursula Mamlok. She was also involved with various musical projects including founding (with Julius Eastman and Talib Rasul Hakim) and directing the Brooklyn Philharmonic's Community Concerts Series in 1977. The following year she worked as conductor and musical director for the Broadway musical *The Wiz* and went on to work as composer, conductor and musical director for several other shows.

León went back to Cuba for a visit in 1979, and returned to the United States determined to acknowledge her rich heritage (African, Chinese, Cuban, French and Spanish) in her works and to incorporate some of the varied sounds and rhythms of her country's music into her own highly personal musical language. She began writing works in a wide variety of genres including *Concerto Criolio* (1980) for piano and orchestra, *De-Orishas* (1982) to various texts, including a Yoruban poem, for unaccompanied voices, and *Ascend* (1983), a fanfare for brass and percussion commissioned by Queen's Symphony Orchestra. In 1985 León wrote *Batá*, an orchestral piece dedicated to her father and first performed by the Bay Area Women's Philharmonic. Batá are the religious drums used for Afro-Cuban rituals and festivals. Leon's work uses lyrical orchestral fragments with interjections from the percussion building to an intense rhythmic climax. A solo piccolo, a memory of her father's whistling, ends the piece with an echo of the opening. Also in 1985, León began teaching at Brooklyn

Tania León

College where she was made Music Director of the resident orchestra in 1991 and Professor of Music three years later, in 1994.

León has described *A La Par* (1986) for percussion and piano as her first work to explore the dichotomy between Cuban folk-music traditions and the classical European tradition in which she had been trained at the Conservatory in Havana. In the first movement León creates a world of insistent rhythmic patterns and complex harmonies, followed by the hazy dream of the central slow movement with its memory of a distant rumba. The third movement builds an elaborate and percussive dance. León's other chamber works from the late 1980s include the powerful *Rituál* (1987) for piano; *Pueblo Mulato* (1987), settings of poems by Nicolas Guillen for soprano, oboe, guitar, double bass, percussion and piano; the brief *Parajota Delaté* ('for J from T', 1988) for flute, violin, clarinet, cello and piano, written for León's friend Joan Tower; and the compelling *Batéy* (1989) for six singers and six percussionists, composed in collaboration with the Dominican-born pianist and composer Michel Camilo.

In 1988 the American Composers Orchestra commissioned León's *Kabiosile* for orchestra and solo piano. León has described this short work as 'a salute to my ancestors', and it celebrates the African god Chango. Using lively rhythms and jazzy harmonies, it creates a frenzied dance alternating with slower, more meditative moments. Another work with a prominent part for a soloist is *Indígena* (1991) for chamber orchestra

and trumpet, commissioned by the Solisti Chamber Orchestra of New York. This evokes the world of the Caribbean carnival and in particular the virtuoso trumpeter who dominates the *comparsa*, a group of revellers.

Important commissions have continued into the 1990s. In 1992 the Cincinnati Symphony Orchestra commissioned and premiered *Carabalí* for orchestra. The title refers to the people of Zaire who fought against the slave traders, a people whom León has described as 'a symbol of a spirit that cannot be broken'. In the same year the City University of New York Brass Ensemble commissioned and premiered *Crossings* for the inauguration of President Clinton. In 1993 León started a two year residency as 'Revson Composer' with the New York Philharmonic Orchestra. Premieres of León's works in 1994 included her first chamber opera, based on Wole Soyinka's play *A Scourge of Hyacinths* for the Fourth Munich Biennale, *Para Viola y Orquesta* for viola and orchestra and a work for jazz percussionist Max Roach and the Uptown String Quartet.

Mary Linwood
1755/6–1845

Mary Linwood was a remarkable woman. As well as writing a variety of music, publishing four volumes of *Leicestershire Tales* (1808) and running an establishment for young ladies in Leicester, she was famous in the later 18th century for her needlework copies of famous paintings. Linwood articulated her concerns about the position of women in the society of her day. In a letter of 1809 one of her relatives reports her hope 'that the soul may be considered in Woman, as in Man, altho' some *ignorant* or *illiberal* authors contend they have not any!'.

Linwood was born in Birmingham in 1755 or 1756 and went to school there. She later moved to Leicester where she was to spend most of her life. The first examples of her embroidered pictures, mostly copies of works by British painters such as Thomas Gainsborough and Joshua Reynolds, were shown at exhibitions of the Society of Artists in 1776 and 1778. In April 1787 she was introduced to Queen Charlotte. Others who admired her work included Catherine II, Empress of Russia, and Napoleon, who presented her with the Freedom of Paris. The Royal Academy refused to show her pictures, but the undaunted Linwood organized her own exhibition at the Pantheon on Oxford Street in May 1787. As well as being shown at the Hanover Square Rooms and various venues outside London, her work (somewhere between 60 and 100 pictures) was mounted as a permanent exhibition in Leicester Square and was regarded as one of the sights of London until Linwood's death in 1845.

Nothing is known about Linwood's musical education although both she and her sister Ann, who also wrote music, must have received the lessons in singing and piano playing that were part of every genteel young lady's education. Only a few works by Linwood have survived although she doubtless wrote many more. In 1828 two canzonets, 'Let us hence!' and 'Pretty Fairy' appeared in *The Harmonicon* followed by 'a dialogue', 'The Sabbath Bridal', in 1832. On

May 4, 1840, when she was in her 80s, Linwood's oratorio, *David's First Victory*, was performed at the Queen's Concert Rooms at Hanover Square conducted by Sir George Smart. The work, dedicated to Queen Adelaide, was published soon afterwards with the following assured preface:

> On announcing the fact that the Words, the Composition and the Instrumentation of this Oratorio are all the production of the same hand, the Author is actuated (as she trusts) by a natural wish to claim for herself whatever it may contain that is worthy of commendation. Being however not more emulous of praise than desirous of sound criticism, she publishes the work in the full confidence of obtaining a just award from a liberal and discriminating public.

Telling the biblical story of David and Goliath, *David's First Victory* is an impressive, if rather old-fashioned work with rousing choruses and moments of high drama. It was not Linwood's only large-scale work; she also wrote the score and libretti for two operas. Although there are no records of performances for either work, two ballads, 'I ponder on those happy hours' from *The Kellerin* and 'Leave me to sorrow awhile' from *The White Wreath*, were published and sung by the two acclaimed singers Charlotte Dolby (later Sainton-Dolby) and John Sims Reeves. Both ballads show an appealing tunefulness with some rather unexpected vocal leaps and harmonic twists.

Kate Loder
1825–1904

Unfortunately, little of Kate Loder's music appears to have survived although she is known to have written an opera, *L'Elisir d'Amore*, orchestral music, a variety of chamber music, piano and organ pieces, songs and teaching works. Loder came from a highly successful family of composers and musicians. Her father, George Loder, was a flautist; her mother, Fanny Philpot, was the leading piano teacher in Bath; and her aunt, Lucy Anderson, was the first woman pianist to play at a concert of the Philharmonic Society, piano teacher to Queen Victoria and a professor of the piano at the Royal Academy of Music. Loder's brother, George Loder, was a conductor and composer who spent much of his life in the United States and Australia.

Kate Loder is said to have demonstrated perfect pitch at the age of three. At this time her health was thought to be too delicate for her to have piano lessons but she played the piano by ear. From the age of six she had lessons from one of her mother's teaching assistants and later studied for a year with Henry Field. In 1838, aged 13, Loder came to London as a student at the Royal Academy of Music where she studied the piano with her aunt, Lucy Anderson, and harmony and composition with Charles Lucas. She won the King's Scholarship in 1839 and again in 1840, the year in which she made her performing debut in Bath and London.

Loder left the Academy in 1844 and began to make a successful career as a pianist. In that year she played Felix Mendelssohn's Piano Concerto in G minor in the composer's presence at one of Lucy Anderson's concerts at His Majesty's Theatre. Loder was apparently invited to study with Mendelssohn in Germany but he died before she could take up the offer. In 1847 she made her debut at the important Philharmonic Society concerts, playing a piano concerto by Carl Maria von Weber. Building on her success as a performer, Loder became well known as a teacher. Many of her compositions were studies and teaching pieces for the piano. In 1844 she became a prof-essor of harmony at the Royal Academy, a very unusual appointment for a woman. Amongst her pupils was composer Landon Ronald who claimed that '... her influence on my early musical days was deeply marked'.

One of the earliest performances of Loder's music appears to have been that of an overture played at a Royal Academy concert in 1844. Two years later, in 1846, the Society of British Musicians gave the first performance of her four-movement String Quartet in G minor which was received with great applause. The Society of British Musicians also performed her Sonata for violin and piano in 1847. Other chamber works included a String Quartet in E minor and a Piano Trio which was performed by the Musical Artists Society in 1886.

Loder published several works for the piano in the 1850s. Some were teaching pieces, such as the *Twelve Studies for the Pianoforte*, dedicated to Lucy Anderson. Others were more elaborate works such as her *Three Romances, Grand Valse Brillante* or *Pensée Fugitive*. Her two Piano Sonatas do not seem to have been published and are lost, but her surviving piano pieces show a clear sense of structure and pianistic feeling.

In 1850 Loder met Henry Thompson whom she married in December 1851. She gave her last public performance in 1854 at a Philharmonic Society concert. In the early days of the Thompsons' married life, Loder's income from performing and teaching was the main support of the household while her husband was setting himself up as a doctor in Wimpole Street. He was later to become an eminent surgeon, knighted in 1867 and made a baronet in 1899.

Loder had her first child in 1856 and two more in 1859 and 1860. Although her public career as a pianist was over, she remained an important figure in British musical life. She continued to teach and to compose, writing vocal and organ music as well as piano and chamber works. For those that were published after her husband's knight-hood, Loder appeared on the title page as Lady Thompson. She was a friend to many eminent musicians including Joseph Joachim and Clara Schumann. In 1871 the first British performance of Johannes Brahms' *Deutsches Requiem* took place at Loder's house in Wimpole Street with herself and Cipriani Potter playing the accompaniment on the piano. From the early 1870s onwards Loder became gradually paralysed from an unspecified illness although she continued to compose and outlived her husband, dying in August 1904.

Elisabeth Lutyens
1906–1983

Elisabeth Lutyens was a composer of often demandingly radical yet always intensely expressive works whose musical language was constantly changing and developing throughout her life. A composer of 12-tone music at a time when it was not accepted or understood in Britain, she fought hard for her works to be heard. Often struggling with alcoholism, depression and the pressures of being financially responsible for her family, her pride in her professionalism and her music remained central and essential to her life.

Lutyens came from a distinguished upper-class family. Her father was the architect Sir Edwin Lutyens. Her mother, Lady Emily Lytton, became an ardent follower of theosophy, a belief system strongly influenced by Hinduism and whose followers aimed to achieve self-perfection through reincarnation. Lutyens started to learn the violin when she was about seven years old. She later took up the piano, began to write her own music and became determined to be a composer. She was encouraged by her aunt, Constance Lytton, a militant suffragette who had studied the piano in her youth.

Lutyens was sent to boarding school in Kent and finishing school in London before being allowed to study music in Paris for a few months in 1923. She attended classes in harmony and counterpoint at the Ecole Normale, lived with composer Marcelle de Manziarly and became excited over the music of Claude Debussy. For the next three years Lutyens became involved in theosophy, travelling with her mother and sister to study with theosophists in Europe, India and Australia. She did manage to arrange a few composition lessons at times, including a period in London when she studied with theosophist composer John Foulds.

In 1926 Lutyens returned to England and enrolled at the Royal College of Music where she studied composition, with the viola as second subject. Her composition teacher Harold Darke arranged for several of her works to be played while she was at the College. Lutyens got to know the other women composers studying at the College at this time and became particularly close to Dorothy Gow. She also spent much of her time at a cottage she had built in Suffolk and played the organ at a local church, exploring pre-Baroque music.

In 1931, after she had left the College, Lutyens spent some time in Paris studying counterpoint with Georges Caussade. On her return to England, anxious to obtain professional performances of her music, Lutyens suggested to violinist Anne Macnaghten and conductor Iris Lemare that they organize a series of concerts featuring music by unknown British composers. Macnaghten and Lemare ended up doing most of the actual organizing and the Macnaghten–Lemare concerts, as they were known, became an extremely important forum for new British music during the 1930s. Many of Lutyens' early works, including several song settings, were performed at the concerts although they were all later withdrawn. Another early work was her ballet *Birthday of the Infanta*, performed by the Carmargo Society in 1932 in a production designed by Rex Whistler and directed by Constant Lambert.

Lutyens married singer Ian Glennie in 1933. She had her first child in 1934 and twins two years later in 1936, continuing all the time to compose. In 1938 she first met Edward Clark, one of the leading figures in contemporary music circles of the time. Nearly 20 years older than Lutyens, Clark had studied music with Arnold Schoenberg and, until his resignation in 1936, had been responsible for introducing much new European music to Britain through his post as a programmer for the BBC. Lutyens travelled with Clark to Poland in 1939 to hear her second string quartet played at the International Society for Contemporary Music Festival there, and on her return to England left Glennie to move in with him.

The late 1930s and early 1940s were exciting but difficult years for Lutyens. She started to use serial techniques in her music, and always claimed that she had developed her 12-tone language from listening to the independent part-writing of Henry Purcell's *Fantasias* and in almost total ignorance of the work of Schoenberg and the second Viennese school. Her first work using this technique, and one of the first that she later acknowledged, was the *Chamber Concerto no. 1* (1939–40) for nine instruments, the first in a set of six chamber concertos composed during the 1940s. Other works of the time were less revolutionary, such as the *Three Pieces for Orchestra*, written in 1939 and performed at the

Proms in 1940.

During the early years of the war Lutyens and Clark lived near Newcastle. In 1941 Lutyens had another child and married Clark the following year after Glennie finally agreed to a divorce. At this time Clark had no regular employment and although various members of her family gave her financial help, Lutyens was essentially the main breadwinner for herself, her husband and four children. In 1943 she returned to London where she earned money copying music, and gradually moved into writing music for radio and films. Her first film score was for the documentary *Jungle Mariners* made by the Crown Film Unit in 1944. Writing film music was to be a vital source of income for most of her life. Unlike many other composers of the time, Lutyens regarded providing music for films simply as a way to make money and composed music in a completely different, far more accessible style than that of her concert scores.

During this time Lutyens began frequenting the pubs of Fitzrovia, making friendships with writers and musicians such as Dylan Thomas, Stevie Smith, Louis MacNeice and Alan Rawsthorne. Her 'serious' music of this time included the haunting cantata for soprano and strings (including a solo violin, mandolin, guitar and harp), *O saisons, O chateaux!* of 1946. The text is from

Arthur Rimbaud's *Les illuminations* and the lamenting invocation of the soprano is accompanied by richly individual string writing.

In the early 1950s Lutyens suffered a bad nervous breakdown after which she gave up drinking. Her family and Ian Glennie helped her look after the children and she spent a few years living apart from Clark, able to concentrate exclusively on her work. This was the period when she felt she had finally found her own individual musical language and produced some of her most striking works. Unfortunately her music was regarded as too advanced for the musical establishment of the time and she had many fierce battles, especially with the BBC, trying to get her works performed. Her new-found maturity can be heard in her String Quartet no. 6 (1952) which she wrote in a single sitting, or the extraordinary unaccompanied vocal work of the same year, *Motet – Excerpta tractatus-logico philosophici*, a tightly organized setting of text by the philosopher Ludwig Wittgenstein. However astringent Lutyens' writing may have seemed, it always remained deeply lyrical, as in the first of her *Music for Orchestra* series (1953–5) or her expressive cantata for soloists, chorus and orchestra, setting words by Chaucer, *De Amore* (1957).

A change in the reception of her music began with the successful first performance in 1962 of the powerful

Quincunx (1959–60) for baritone, wordless soprano and orchestra. This work is structured throughout on the idea of the quincunx pattern of five points in the corners and middle of a square or rectangle. The central slow movement, dominated by the strange, floating beauty of the wordless soprano, is introduced by the unaccompanied baritone singing lines from Thomas Browne's *The Garden of Cyrus*. The outer movements highlight the different sections of the large orchestra in turn. Clark, who loved the work, died a few months before its first performance.

During the 1960s Lutyens became an important figure in British musical life. A changing musical climate led to a readiness to accept more adventurous music and her works began to be heard far more frequently. Lutyens had been teaching since the 1950s and her pupils included composers such as Alison Bauld, Richard Rodney Bennett, Brian Elias, Robert Saxton and Malcolm Williamson. She also developed friendships with the new generation of radical composers such as Harrison Birtwhistle and Alexander Goehr.

Lutyens' own language continued to develop during the 1960s, moving away from the austerity of her early works to a simpler, more immediately expressive idiom. Much of her music of this time was vocal, including *And Suddenly It's Evening* (1966), a setting of four poems by Salvatore Quasimodo

for tenor and ensemble, and *Essence of our Happiness* (1968) for tenor, chorus and orchestra, a setting of three mystical texts by ninth-century writer Abu Yasid, John Donne and Rimbaud. Lutyens also wrote three operas in the 1960s including *The Numbered* (1965–7) for solo singers, three actors, chorus and an orchestra using mandolins and electric guitars with a libretto based on Elias Canetti's *Die Befristeten*. It has yet to be performed.

Lutyens was never happy in her relationships with her various publishers and when in 1969 she won an award from the City of London, she used the money to form her own publishing company, Olivan Press. In the same year she was awarded the CBE. In 1972 her autobiography *A Goldfish Bowl* was published. This is a fascinating if somewhat unreliable account of her life and career which also focuses on the neglected achievements of Edward Clark.

Throughout the 1970s and into the 1980s, Lutyens continued to compose prolifically and to become more and more outspoken in her views on music and the establishment. Some of her best-known music was written at this time, including the moving *Requiescat* (in memoriam Igor Stravinsky, 1971) for soprano and string trio, the series of four different *Plenum* works and the dramatic oboe quartet *Driving Out the Death*. Written in 1971, this is a highly expressive work based on ancient rituals of the changing seasons representing life and death. Lutyens herself died in 1983 at the age of 76. One of the ways in which she described her life was apparently: 'Innumerable compositions, two husbands, three lovers, four children, one abortion and *nobody* knew.'

Elizabeth Maconchy
b. 1907

Regarded in the early 1930s as one of the most individual and striking composers of her generation, Elizabeth Maconchy fulfilled her early promise with the creation of a lifetime of powerful and deeply lyrical music. She once said: 'I compose because I have to, from that there is no escape.'

Born in Hertfordshire in 1907 to Irish parents, Maconchy started writing her own piano pieces from an early age. After the end of the first world war, the family moved back to Ireland. They lived near Dublin and Maconchy had lessons in harmony and counterpoint as well as continuing to have piano lessons. But she had little opportunity to hear any music other than that she created for herself. The only orchestral music she heard while living in Ireland was a performance of Beethoven's Seventh Symphony given by the Hallé Orchestra in 1922 when she was 15.

That same year her father died, and in 1923 her mother brought the family to London where Maconchy entered the Royal College of Music. She studied the piano with Arthur Alexander but gradually began to concentrate on composition, studying initially with Charles Wood and then with Ralph Vaughan Williams. Vaughan Williams, who believed in allowing his pupils to develop their own personal voices, was an extremely supportive teacher. Maconchy later described learning from him as 'like turning on a light'.

Maconchy was soon regarded as one of the most brilliant College students. She won several prizes and had works played at College concerts and at the Patron's Fund concerts, where student works were given professional performances. She also made important friendships with the other College composers including Dorothy Gow and in particular Grace Williams, with whom she started exploring the works of modern composers such as Béla Bartók.

In 1929 Maconchy won an Octavia Travelling Scholarship and went to

Vienna, Paris and Prague where she studied for two months with Karel Jirák. In 1930 she won a Cobbett prize for her Fantasy String Quintet and returned to Prague to hear Jirák conduct the first public performance of her Piano Concerto. The same year saw Maconchy's first big success in Britain. She had sent a score of her orchestral suite *The Land*, written in 1929, to conductor Henry Wood who gave the work its first performance at the Proms in August 1930 to enthusiastic reviews. *The Land* is based on the poem of the same name by Vita Sackville-West. The four sections of the piece follow the four seasons, starting with the bleak dissonance of winter. The stirrings of spring provoke dances from the strings and woodwind while summer opens with a languid flute theme over a repeated, rocking accompaniment. Autumn ends the piece in a blaze of brass. Just a week before this premiere Maconchy had married Irish scholar William LeFanu.

Maconchy was closely involved with the early Macnaghten–Lemare concerts. Her prize-winning string quintet was played at one of the first concerts in 1931, having been previously performed at a concert given by the Society of Women Musicians. In 1932, the year that her Piano Concerto was broadcast by the BBC, Maconchy developed tuberculosis, the disease that had killed her father. She left London for Kent and cured herself by living in a hut at the bottom of the garden. In spite of this isolation, her music continued to be performed and broadcast throughout the 1930s. She had 11 performances at the Macnaghten–Lemare concerts and in 1933 won a Daily Telegraph Prize for her Oboe Quintet. Her Piano Concerto was played by Harriet Cohen at the Proms in 1936, and two works for her favourite instrument, the viola – a concerto and a sonata – were given premieres in London in 1938. Her music was also played abroad at concerts in Poland, Belgium and Hungary and at the International Society for Contemporary Music Festivals in Prague and Paris in 1935 and 1937.

Some British critics thought that Maconchy's work was too modern and intellectual, qualities they found especially disturbing in music written by a woman, while others immediately recognized its originality and strength. Maconchy has described her music as 'an impassioned argument', something apparent nowhere so much as in her series of 14 works for string quartets, written throughout her life and central to her musical output. Her first quartet with its biting, syncopated rhythms was premiered at a Macnaghten–Lemare concert in 1933 and her intense second quartet, written in 1936, was first performed the following year at the International Society for Contemporary Music Festival in Paris. Her third quartet, first performed at a BBC contemporary music concert in London in 1938, is in one continuous,

*Elizabeth Maconchy and Nicola LeFanu
at an SPNM concert, Spitalfields 1993*

cyclic movement. Maconchy's string quartets clearly show her fascination with a counterpoint of melodic lines and rhythm as well as her technique of building a work from one initial fragment or phrase.

Maconchy's first daughter, Anna, was born in 1939 and her second, composer Nicola LeFanu, in 1947. She has said that she had to learn to compose between feeds. As well as making bread and clothes for the family, growing vegetables and keeping hens, she continued to write powerful music in a wide range of genres throughout the 1940s and 1950s. Although her works were heard less frequently than in the 1930s, they were still being broadcast and performed all over Europe. Maconchy's fourth string quartet was written in 1942 and 1943, during the war. It is a dark, uneasy work in four movements, all growing out of the opening pizzicato cello motif. Her fifth quartet, written in Ireland in 1948, opens with a slow introduction to the richly contrapuntal first movement. This is followed by an energetic *scherzo*, an expressively mournful slow movement and the vigorous dancing of the final allegro. Maconchy's orchestral works from this period included a dramatic Concertino for clarinet and string orchestra (1945), a Bassoon Concerto (1952) and the overture *Proud Thames* (1952) which won a London County Council competition for a coronation overture and was premiered by the BBC Symphony Orchestra conducted by Malcolm Sargent.

In the later 1950s, following a creative block after her seventh string quartet (1956), Maconchy turned to opera for the first time. Over the next few years, she produced a series of three one-act operas: *The Sofa* (1956–7) with a libretto by Ursula Vaughan Williams, *The Departure* (1960–61) with a libretto by Anne Ridler and *The Three Strangers* (1958–67) with a libretto she wrote herself based on a short story by Thomas Hardy. These works were followed by several operatic works for children and amateurs including *The Birds* (1967–8) and *The Jesse Tree* (1969–70). During the 1960s Maconchy continued to write orchestral, vocal and chamber works including her

ninth string quartet (1968), the slow movement of which is a heartfelt lament written during the Soviet occupation of Prague.

The 1970s and 80s were a period of great productivity for Maconchy and a time when she was receiving a large number of commissions from many different performers, institutions and festivals. Although continuing to write music of all genres, she turned increasingly to vocal music. *Ariadne* (1970), a dramatic monologue setting words by Cecil Day Lewis for soprano and orchestra, was first performed in Norfolk in 1971. *The Leaden Echo and the Golden Echo* (1978) for chorus, alto flute, viola and harp sets Gerard Manley Hopkins, whose poetry had a particular appeal for Maconchy. Her large choral piece *Héloïse and Abelard*, based on the story of the two 12th-century lovers in Abelard's *Historia Calamitatum*, was commissioned by Croydon Philharmonic Society in 1979. Another vocal work, for solo soprano and six instruments, was the hauntingly beautiful *My Dark Heart* (1981), a setting of three of Irish writer J.M. Synge's prose translations of Petrach's Sonnets. Orchestral music from this period includes *Epyllion* (1975) for cello and strings and *Music for Strings*, first performed at the Proms in 1983. Maconchy also continued to write much chamber music, adding several important works to her series of string quartets.

Michael Tippett remembered visiting Maconchy in her hut in Kent during the 1930s to find her agonizing over what she felt was a decision between 'social and political work' and her work as a composer. She ended up by combining the two in her continuous support for new music, serving as chair of the Composers' Guild of Great Britain and president of the Society for the Promotion of New Music as well as being involved in the Workers' Music Association and being endlessly supportive of individual composers. This work, as well as Maconchy's enormous contribution to the music of the 20th century, was recognized when she was made a CBE in 1977 and a DBE in 1987.

Adela Maddison
1866–1929

Adela Maddison was born in 1866 into an Irish family. Her father, Louis Symonds Tindal, was a vice-admiral. Nothing is known about Maddison's early musical education but she was doubtless given the piano lessons deemed appropriate for a girl of her class. Two of her early works, *Brer Rabbit*, a polka for piano and the simple, tuneful song 'Will You Forget?' to words by G. Bendall, were published by Metzler in 1882. The following year, at the age of 16, she married Frederick Brunning Maddison, a lawyer who acted as one of the directors of Metzler. The firm continued to publish Maddison's music throughout the 1880s and 90s.

Maddison had two children, a daughter, Diana, born in 1886 and a son, Noel, born a few years later. The family lived at Hyde Park Corner and Maddison seems to have led a glamorous life, frequently visiting Paris, Bayreuth and St Moritz as well as Ascot and Buckingham Palace. She continued to write music, and in 1895

published a collection of *Twelve Songs*, her op. 9 and op. 10 combined, setting the work of various poets including Algernon Swinburne, Dante Gabriel Rossetti, Alfred Tennyson and Heinrich Heine. The music is sometimes predictable but more often uses rich and unexpected harmonies, always with fluent vocal lines.

The Maddisons moved in musical circles and at some time in the mid–1890s got to know Gabriel Fauré, whose music they were to promote enthusiastically and who appears to have given Maddison composition lessons. Fauré thought very highly of Maddison and her music and was probably behind the publication of her *Six French Songs* by the French firm Choudens in 1896. In the same year two of her songs, 'Ob ich dich liebe' and 'Im Traum', were performed by David Bispham in a concert at St James's Hall. The concert also included Fauré's Piano Quartet, op. 15.

Fauré was by now a family friend,

staying at the Maddison villa in Brittany that autumn. He dedicated his seventh piano prelude to Maddison and several of Fauré's songs were published by Metzler with her English translations. She also provided the English text for a performance of his *La Naissance de Venus* when it was performed at the Leeds Festival in 1898. That year one of Maddison's Rossetti settings from her op. 9 was published in a French translation in *Le Figaro* where she was described as a 'remarkable' pupil of Fauré.

Fauré's biographers seem certain that the relationship between Maddison and Fauré became a sexual one, or at least that she left her husband in order to be with him. She certainly seems to have settled in Paris towards the end of the decade, but in such a cosmopolitan age this may have been nothing more than a desire to move in French musical circles. The only suggestion that she had abandoned her family to become Fauré's lover is found in the diary of Madame de Saint-Marceaux.

Music certainly remained central to Maddison's life. In 1899, *Koanga*, an opera by Frederick Delius, was played at her Paris house in the presence of Fauré and the Princesse de Polignac, one of the most influential music patrons of the day and a close friend and supporter of Fauré. Maddison continued to write music herself. In 1900 Fauré wrote to the poet Albert Samain to ask his permission for

Maddison to publish her settings of two of his poems, 'Silence' and 'Hiver', describing the latter as a little masterpiece.

In 1904 a concert of Maddison's music was given in Paris. At this time her relationship with Fauré seems to have become more remote. Sometime soon afterwards she moved to Berlin where she organized concerts of French music and started to compose on a larger scale. She also appears to have been reunited and to have lived with her husband before his death sometime before 1910. The music she was writing included an *Irische Ballade* for orchestra, a copy of which Ethel Smyth offered to take to Delius to see if he could get it performed by Thomas Beecham and the Musical League. No performance appears to have taken place and the *Ballade* has not survived.

The work which Maddison spent several years composing and which produced her greatest triumph was the four-act opera *Der Talisman* which was given eight performances in Leipzig in November 1910. The libretto was based on the play by Ludwig Fulda which tells the story of the conceited King who walks naked through the town, believing that the non-existent cloak he is wearing is magic and visible only to those who are neither wicked nor foolish. A critic in *The Times* described the work as the first 'real success' of a British opera in Germany and the music as 'melodious and interesting'. Unfortunately it has not survived.

While she was in Berlin, Maddison developed a very close friendship with a German woman, Martha Mundt. Whether or not this was a sexual relationship is again unknown. The couple lived together and moved in some of the best-known lesbian circles of the time. The Princesse de Polignac was renowned for her affairs with women and one of Maddison's oldest friends was Mabel Batten, a singer and dedicatee of many of her songs as well as the first lover of the writer Radclyffe Hall. Before the first world war, Maddison and Mundt were living in France where Mundt worked as a secretary for the Princesse de Polignac. Whenever Mundt and Maddison were in England they visited Batten and Hall. During the war, Maddison and Mundt had to escape from France where Mundt, as a German citizen, was regarded as an undesirable, even, to Maddison's disgust, by her employer the Princesse de Polignac. They arrived in London with very little money and nowhere to live and seem to have depended on help from friends such as Batten and another amateur society singer, Elsie Swinton.

In 1915 Augener published several of Maddison's songs. These songs appear to be the first of her music written after she left London in the 1890s to have survived. In the early years of the century she complained that people described her music as 'Wagner, Debussy and Fauré served in a gravy of my own'. The Augener songs are in a far more impressionistic style than the early songs, especially the beautiful *Trois Melodies*, settings of Edmond Harancourt. The other songs include settings of German poetry (also given in English translation) as well as a long and dramatic setting of part of a Henry Wadsworth Longfellow poem, 'Sail On, O Ship of State' which was dedicated, with permission, to the King.

Some time during the war Maddison became involved with Rutland Boughton's Glastonbury Festival and moved to live at Tor Down in Glastonbury. She provided the incidental music for Miles Malleson's play *Paddly Pools* which was performed at Glastonbury in 1917 and again in 1918. One of Maddison's songs from 1918 was 'National Hymn for India' to words by K.N. Das Gupta, who had produced a play at Glastonbury in 1917 and was organizer of the Union of the East and the West, to whom the song is dedicated. In 1920 a selection of Glastonbury works produced at the Old Vic in London included Maddison's ballet *The Children of Lir*. None of the Glastonbury music appears to have been published or to have survived.

By the 1920s Maddison and Mundt appeared to be dividing their time between Geneva and England, where Maddison organized several concerts. An evening of her music at the

Wigmore Hall in 1920 included her Piano Quintet as well as a selection of songs. In 1924 she put on a concert at the Hyde Park Hotel which included a performance of Arnold Bax's Oboe Quintet. Her Piano Quintet was published in 1925 by Curwen who had issued a group of four songs the previous year. These songs see Maddison's music becoming more condensed and experimental. They include the hauntingly atmospheric 'The Heart of the Wood', setting an anonymous Irish poem in a translation by Lady Gregory, and the brief and intense setting of 'Tears' from Cranmer Byng's translations of Chinese poetry in the *Lute of Jade* for which Maddison used a dissonant harmony built on fourths. Maddison became ill during the last years of her life and died in an Ealing nursing home in 1929 at the age of 62.

Ursula Mamlok
b. 1928

Born in Berlin, Ursula Mamlok's earliest musical memories are of her uncle playing popular songs on the piano. She started copying the music that he was playing and making up her own pieces. At the age of nine she began studying the piano and music theory with the composer and musicologist Gustav Ernst. When the Nazis came to power, Mamlok's family realized that they would have to leave Germany. Ernst went to Holland and offered to take Mamlok with him but she stayed with her family. In 1939, when Mamlok was 11, they managed to escape to Guayaquil in Ecuador. Ernst was killed by the Nazis and Mamlok's grandparents died in Auschwitz.

In Ecuador there was little opportunity for Mamlok to continue her music studies so she and her mother tried to arrange for her to study in the United States. Mannes College of Music in New York offered her a scholarship on the basis of the compositions she had sent them, and at the age of 13 she travelled alone to New York. The rest of her family were unable to get permission to join her until sometime later and Mamlok survived on her own, living off an anonymous grant in a basement in the Bronx. She studied composition with George Szell who proved to be a disappointingly conservative teacher. In 1944 Mamlok had her first experience of more avant-garde music when she attended a summer institute at Black Mountain College in North Carolina, organized to celebrate Arnold Schoenberg's 70th birthday. She arranged to take lessons with Roger Sessions who had been at the institute and worked with him for a year.

Mamlok spent many years continuing to study, defining her music language and finding the system that she felt she needed in order to compose. She had lessons from various composers including Stefan Wolpe and Ralph Shapey. During this time she wrote and published several piano works for children. In 1955, at the age of 27, she won a scholarship to study at the

Manhattan School of Music where she found that her teachers disliked her dissonant idiom built on a serial system using flexible rhythms and simple structures. Nevertheless, she obtained both her bachelor's and master's degrees.

In the 1960s, Mamlok's music began to receive performances and critical attention. Her *Variations for solo flute* (1961), which explores different ways of working with a tone row, remains one of her most frequently performed works. Her intense and demanding String Quartet (1962) demonstrates her use of repetition as a clear structural device. *Concert Piece for Four* (1964), written for flute, oboe, viola and percussion, shows the playful, light-hearted side of Mamlok's work. Although she is probably best known for her chamber music, Mamlok has also written a number of vocal works such as her delicate settings of Rabindranath Tagore, *Stray Birds* (1963) for soprano, flute and cello and dedicated to John F. Kennedy, or the descriptive *Haiku Settings* (1967) for soprano and flute.

In 1967 Mamlok took her first teaching post at New York University where she taught until 1976 when she joined the faculty of the Manhattan School of Music. She continued to concentrate on writing chamber music with works such as the intricate *Sextet* (1977) for flute, clarinet, bass clarinet, violin, double bass and piano and *When*

Summer Sang (1980) for flute, clarinet, violin, cello and piano, a tranquil piece full of the calls and chattering of birds that was written in the country while she was recovering from a serious illness. *Panta Rhei* ('Time in Flux', 1981), for violin, cello and piano, is a short complex work in three sections which explores a variety of sounds, textures and moods.

In the early 1980s Mamlok wrote a series of three serene works entitled *From My Garden* in which the performers also play crotales (small metal cymbals). *From My Garden* no. 1 is for violin; no. 2 is for oboe, French horn and piano; and no. 3 is for viola. Another garden piece is Mamlok's song cycle *Der Andreas Garten* (1986) which sets nine poems by her husband Dwight Mamlok, another German refugee whom she had married in 1949 and who took up writing (under the name of Gerard Mamlok) after his retirement. The poems are about the garden of the Mamloks' summer home in San Mateo, California. The strain of living in earthquake territory over the San Andreas Fault is brought out through the underlying tensions in the music.

Although Mamlok had written a few orchestral works in the 1950s, her first orchestral commission, for which she wrote an Oboe Concerto, came in 1976 from the City University of New York. Nearly 20 years later she received her next orchestral commission when the

San Francisco Symphony Orchestra asked for a work at the suggestion of their composer-in-residence George Perle. *Constellations*, a short, four-movement work, was first performed in February 1994. Like much of Mamlok's music it is constructed out of various transformations of the opening material, moving from a dramatic brass fanfare through an angular scherzo and a more lyrical slow movement to the joyful dance of the finale.

Meredith Monk
b. 1942

Meredith Monk is one of the world's most popular and critically acclaimed performance artists. She works with music and movement to create extra-ordinarily vivid theatre pieces in which voices dance and bodies sing, pieces that seem to communicate timeless feelings and experiences. Central to all her work is her use of her own voice. Over the years she has developed an incredible range of sounds using many different techniques to produce sighs, moans, sobs, wails, calls, overtones and beautiful patterns and webs of sound. She rarely uses words yet her vocal music can express a wide range of emotions and ideas. She has written of her belief that 'the voice is a language: a world of continuing discoveries'. Sometimes her music is for voice or voices alone and sometimes it is accompanied by a piano or an organ or other instruments playing repetitive accompanying figures.

Monk comes from a long line of Jewish musicians. Her great-grandfather was the cantor of a synagogue in Moscow and her grandparents founded the Zellman Conservatory of Music in New York. She was born in Lima, Peru while her mother, popular singer Audrey Marsh, was on tour, and grew up in New York and Connecticut. Monk sang before she talked and had voice and piano lessons from an early age. She also studied movement in the form of Dalcroze eurhythmics. After leaving her Quaker boarding school in Pennsylvania she went to Sarah Lawrence College in Bronxville, New York. There she studied various aspects of performing arts and graduated in 1964.

That year Monk moved to New York City where she soon became part of the 'downtown' avant-garde, and worked with the Judson Dance Theatre, producing performance pieces such as *Cartoon* (1964) and *Duet for Cat's Scream and Locomotive* (1966). In 1967 two of her pieces, including *Dying Swan with Sunglasses* for solo voice and echoplex, were performed at Expo

67 in Montreal, Canada. In 1968 Monk formed her interdisciplinary performance group, The House, based in her New York loft. This has now become The House Foundation for the Arts.

In 1969 Monk managed to obtain the Guggenheim Museum in New York as the performance space for her 'theatre cantata' *Juice*, a work for two violins and 85 performers who sang and also played jew's-harps. In the early 1970s Monk did some teaching at various colleges while arranging performances of her works, often in her own New York loft. In 1971 she first performed *Vessel: An Opera Epic*. This work, which she has described as a 'performance tapestry', is very loosely based on the life of Joan of Arc. It used 150 performers and took place at three different sites with the audience taken in buses from Monk's loft to the Performing Garage and then to a parking lot. Most of the music in the original performance was for solo voice and organ which Monk sang and played herself although there was also some ensemble vocal music. Monk later rearranged some of the music for vocal trio. In comparison to later works, the music uses fairly simple vocal techniques, creating repetitive patterns over rich harmonies from the organ.

Many of Monk's works centre around the experience of women. *Education of the Girlchild* (1972–3), is an extra-ordinarily static theatre piece for six solo voices, electric organ and piano which won first prize at the Venice Biennale in 1975 and has been described as 'a biography of womankind'. In an extended solo at the end of the piece, Monk follows the span of a woman's life from old age and death back to the earliest years of life through a remarkable range of vocal sounds moving to inarticulate sobs over slowly repeated piano chords.

Monk made her first film, *16 millimeter earrings*, in 1966, and film has continued to play an important part in her work. The opera *Quarry* (1976) for 38 voices, two pump organs, two soprano recorders and tape is a work that explores images of the Holocaust and includes the projection of a black-and-white film made by Monk in which a bleak quarry is gradually peopled.

In 1978 Monk founded the Meredith Monk Vocal Ensemble, a tightly knit group of performers who come, like her, from mixed performance back-grounds and with whom she works very closely on her pieces. She has described singing with other people as like 'touching souls'. One of the first works performed by the group was *Dolmen Music* (1979) for six solo voices, cello and percussion which grew out of Monk's fascination with the standing stones that she had seen while on tour in Brittany. In this piece she recreates an ancient culture, centring on the way on which its people communicated. Using the six individual voices of the group, Monk produced a richly resonant work that seems at the same time to be both very old and very new.

Much of Monk's work in the early 1980s dealt with the realities of life in the United States. Her film *Ellis Island* (1981–2) looked at the experience of immigrants (including her own family) at the turn of the century while *The Games* (1983), created in partnership with her long-term collaborator Ping Chong, looked at the possibilities of a future after nuclear war. In *Turtle Dreams* (1983), a theatre piece for four solo voices and two electric organs, Monk explored life in a contemporary urban environment like New York City.

In 1984 Monk wrote a vocal concerto *Book of Days* for five voices, chorus and electric organ. She later reworked this music for her film of the same name which uses 10 voices and a variety of instruments

Meredith Monk

such as hurdy-gurdy, dulcimer, bagpipe, synthesizer, cello and shawm. This work centres round a young Jewish girl from the 14th century who has visionary dreams of the 20th century and draws explicit parallels between medieval and modern times, both apocalyptic ages of violent conflict and fear of plague. It is a powerful piece, creating, as Monk puts it, 'a sense of displacement that encourages the viewer to see and hear our own world in a fresh way'. In 1990 Monk recorded a purely musical version of the work. Her contract with the German record label ECM has led to recordings of much of her music being available in versions reworked to suit the very different medium of the CD and the home listener.

Recognition by the classical-music establishment came with a commission from Houston Grand Opera. *Atlas*, an opera in three parts, was first performed in Houston in 1991 to an enthusiastic critical response. It is loosely based on the life and writings of the American explorer Alexandra Daniels and the central female character is sung by three different performers, including Monk, as she moves through the different experiences and explorations of her life. Together with her chosen companions she travels to different places in the world, facing ghosts, demons and hardships, in what becomes a physical and a spiritual quest. The opera uses 18 vocalists and an instrumentation, on which Monk worked with the musical director Wayne Hankin, of two keyboards, clarinet, bass clarinet, horn, sheng, shawm, two violins, viola, two cellos and percussion. There are moments when the performers use actual speech but most of the work is conveyed through wordless vocal music.

While Monk was working on *Atlas* at an artists' retreat in the Canadian Rocky Mountains, her surroundings prompted her to start work on *Facing North* (1990–91) which became a collaboration with Robert Een, one of the members of the Meredith Monk Vocal Ensemble. Originally a concert work, Een and Monk developed it into a theatre piece which explores the survival of two figures in the snowy wilderness of the north and creates beautiful vocal images of a bleak, still world and the people who survive there.

Mary Carr Moore
1873–1957

Mary Carr Moore was born in Memphis, Tennessee but her family moved frequently, settling in Napa Valley, California in 1881. By this time Moore was eight years old and had already started having music lessons. She attended various schools during the 1880s and continued to take singing and piano lessons as well as studying theory with her great-uncle John Pratt who had studied music in Leipzig. Moore's parents had wanted to send her to Europe to finish her musical training but Moore damaged her voice at a week-long revival meeting and her father lost most of his money so she stayed in the United States.

In 1889 Moore moved with her family to San Francisco and stayed there after her parents moved to Lemoore, a town several hundred miles away. She continued her musical studies, rebuilding her voice and studying composition with Pratt. A few of the songs and piano pieces that she wrote at this time have survived. In 1890 she began teaching music and took a job singing at the First Baptist Church. In 1894 her operetta *The Oracle,* for which she wrote the text and the music as well as singing the leading role, was given two performances by a local social club. Moore was featured in all the local newspapers and later clearly remembered the shame and disgrace that she felt at this public exposure.

Moore had always been sickly and, having been ordered by her doctor to rest, she moved to Lemoore to live with her parents in 1895. She took up teaching again but composed little during this period, although in 1896 she wrote six songs, duets and part-songs for the suffrage campaign. In 1898 she married a doctor, John Claude Moore, and had her first child in September. Moore continued to teach after her marriage and by the time they moved to Seattle in 1901, was earning more money than her husband.

She stopped teaching shortly before the birth of her second child in April

1904, but was very active in women's music clubs in the city. She also continued to compose. Most of her works were songs and choral pieces written for churches or the clubs and many were published. She was keen to promote American music, and in 1909 became the first president of the Seattle chapter of the American Music Society. Moore's marriage was never very happy and in 1905, after a miscarriage, she attempted to kill herself. After a reconciliation her third child was born in 1907.

In 1908 Moore's mother Sarah Carr, who was a writer and journalist, started work on an opera libretto telling the story of the 1847 killing of two missionaries, Marcus and Narcissa Whitman, near Walla Walla. Moore began work on the music in late 1909 and finished the full score of the four-act opera *Narcissa* in the summer of 1911. Both Moore and her mother were committed to telling this story from a woman's point of view and felt it was important to present a sympathetic portrayal of Native Americans, redressing the 'growing shame' of their treatment by white settlers. After unsuccessful attempts to interest various producers in the work, a performance financed by Moore's husband and conducted by Moore herself was given in Seattle in 1912. The critics were complimentary, finding the work original and pleasingly American. Encouraged by the success of this opera, Moore went

to New York in 1913 in order to promote her music but returned to Seattle after six months having achieved very little. Her marriage started to disintegrate again and she finally divorced her husband in 1914.

Moore moved back to San Francisco in 1915. In need of money since she was now self-supporting, she started teaching again as well as continuing to compose and publish and involve herself in the life of the music clubs. In 1917 she married pianist Arthur De Celles *dit* Duclos and opened the Mary Carr Moore School of music in their home. This venture only lasted a year before Moore became ill and gave up teaching although she continued to compose.

In the early 1920s Moore began to experiment with impressionistic textures and harmonies that were regarded as more modern. Her works from this time include another opera to a libretto by her mother, *The Flaming Arrow* (1920), later revised and retitled *The Shaft of Ku'pish-ta-ya,* which was given several successful performances, and a song-cycle *Beyond These Hills* (1923–4) for four soloists and piano on poems by Gilbert Moyle.

In 1925 Moore conducted a revival of *Narcissa*. The following year, having left her second husband, she moved to Los Angeles where she taught composition privately and at the Olga Streeb Piano School and the California

Christian College. She continued to work with local music clubs and societies as well as to compose. Her compositions from the later 1920s and the 1930s included two String Quartets and a Trio, a symphonic poem *Ka-mi-a-kin* and a Piano Concerto, all in classical Germanic style, as well as four operas. The first of these was the Italianate *David Rizzio* with a libretto by Emanuel Browne, completed in 1928 and first performed in 1932. *Legende Provencale* (1929–38), based on a play by Eleanore Flaig, took Moore nearly 10 years to write and was never produced during her lifetime although it is considered to be one of her finest works. *Los Rubios* (1931) was written for the celebrations for the 150th anniversary of Los Angeles, and *Flutes of Jade Happiness* (1932–4) was an operetta for amateurs.

Always a staunch supporter of American music, Moore became involved with the Federal Music Project and had several large-scale works performed by the Federal Music Project Symphony Orchestra of Los Angeles. In 1930 she formed the Society for the Advancement of American Music and was later involved with the Californian Society of Composers. She found the new music of the ultra-modern movement literally hard to stomach, apparently leaving performances in order to throw up! In 1945, at the age of 72, Moore conducted two performances of *Narcissa* at the Philharmonic Auditorium. Two years later she retired from the California Christian College (renamed Chapman), although she continued to teach privately, and died 10 years later at the age of 84.

Thea Musgrave
b. 1928

Thea Musgrave was born near Edinburgh in Scotland. Music played an important part in her life as a child, but when she entered Edinburgh University in 1947 at 19 it was to study medicine with a view to becoming a doctor. She soon changed to studying music, taking composition with the Austrian composer Hans Gál. After graduating in 1950, Musgrave went to Paris where she studied with Nadia Boulanger, both at the Conservatoire and privately, until 1954, winning the Lili Boulanger Memorial Prize in 1952.

Musgrave's early works were written in an accessible, tonal language and soon attracted attention, especially in Scotland. Her first commission, for which she wrote *A Suite O'Bairnsangs* for voice and piano, came in 1953 from the Scottish Festival at Braemar. The same year she wrote *A Tale for Thieves*, a one-act ballet based on Chaucer's *The Pardoner's Tale*, for her old school Moreton Hall in Shropshire. Her first big success was a work commissioned by BBC Scotland, the dramatic *Cantata*

for a Summer's Day (1954) for narrator, chorus and chamber ensemble with a text by Alexander Hume and Maurice Lindsay.

In 1955, shortly after her return from Paris, Musgrave moved to London. Here she worked as the coach and accompanist for the Saltire Singers who commissioned and performed several of her works, as well as teaching for Morley College and London University's Extra-Mural Department. She was increasingly exposed to the music of a variety of contemporary composers such as Charles Ives, Milton Babbitt and members of the second Viennese school, both at the Dartington summer schools run by William Glock and the summer course at Tanglewood in the United States. This led to a gradual change in her musical language which became much more chromatic, expressive and abstract, as can be heard in the angular vocal writing of *Five Love Songs* (1955) or the String Quartet (1958). By the end of the 1950s

Musgrave was using 12-tone rows to construct her music in works such as *Triptych* (1959) for tenor and orchestra which was premiered at the Proms in 1960.

In the mid-1960s Musgrave worked on an uncommissioned three-act opera, *The Decision*. The libretto by Maurice Lindsay was about a 19th-century Scots miner, who was trapped for 23 days in an Ayrshire coalpit, and his lover, the pit-foreman's wife, who dies after giving birth to their child. The opera was completed in 1965 and first performed by the New Opera Company at Sadler's Wells in 1967.

Working on writing music for dramatic situations and characters led to another change in Musgrave's music. Over the next few years she developed an instrumental style that she described as 'dramatic-abstract' in which the instruments work out dramatic situations and confrontations. The individuality of instruments and instrumental groups was further emphasized by Musgrave's use of 'asynchronous music', where the instruments retain a certain freedom within a system of cueing.

Her characterization of instruments can be heard in a work such as Chamber Concerto no. 2 'In Homage to Charles Ives' (1966) in which the viola player insistently turns the motifs of the work into popular tunes such as 'Swanee River' and 'All things bright

and beautiful'. In Chamber Concerto no. 3 (1966) and Concerto for Orchestra (1967), players stand to play solo passages or cadenzas. This theatrical idea is taken further in the Clarinet Concerto (1968) in which the clarinettist struggles with the conductor for control of the orchestra and moves around the concert platform to play with the various concertante groups. In *Night Music* (1969) for chamber orchestra, the two horns move from their seats to opposite sides of the orchestra for a fiercely confrontational passage.

Musgrave also explored the relationship between the solo instrument in a concerto and the players of the same instrument in the orchestra. In her Horn Concerto (1971) the orchestral horns, who move to play from different positions, appear to interrupt and mock the soloist, while in the Viola Concerto (1973) the soloist seems to instruct the orchestral violas who sit at the front of the orchestra in the position usually occupied by the first violins. Musgrave herself conducted the premieres of these two works and has become increasingly known as a conductor of her own music.

The Viola Concerto was written for viola player Peter Mark whom Musgrave had met in 1970 while she was a visiting professor at the University of California at Santa Barbara for three months. They married in 1971 and settled in the

United States the following year. Another work written for Mark was *From One to Another* (1970) for viola and tape. The tape, which used processed viola sounds, was made in collaboration with composer Daphne Oram, as was the tape which had been used in Musgrave's ballet *Beauty and the Beast* (1968–9). Musgrave combined this use of electronic music and the dramatic techniques developed in her instrumental music in *The Voice of Ariadne* (1972–3), a vivid chamber opera. The libretto, by Amalia Elguera, was based on a short story by Henry James about a man who becomes obsessed by the statue in his garden. The unearthly voice of the statue is written for the electronic tape.

In 1973 Musgrave made a series of eight programmes about electronic music for the BBC, aiming to make this relatively new medium more accessible to the general listener. This was also the year of her richly complex choral work *Rorate Coeli* for five soloists and chorus which sets two poems about the Nativity and the Resurrection by the 16th-century Scots poet William Dunbar. The following year Musgrave received both a Koussevitsky Award and a Guggenheim Fellowship, recognition of the esteem in which her work was held in the United States.

From the mid-1970s Musgrave concentrated on writing opera. *Mary Queen of Scots* (1975–7) uses her own libretto based on a play by Amalia Elguera about the years that Mary spent in Scotland, her relationships with men and questions of power. First performed in Edinburgh, the opera incorporates 16th-century dances and is more tonal than much of Musgrave's earlier work. In 1975 Mark was appointed director of the Virginia Opera Association in Norfolk, Virginia which has since given several performances of Musgrave's operas including the premieres of *A Christmas Carol* (1978–9), based on the novel by Charles Dickens, and *Harriet, the Woman Called Moses* (1985), based on the life of Harriet Tubman, an escaped 19th-century slave who returned to Maryland to help others escape along the Underground Railroad. Tubman's inspirational story had attracted Musgrave as a representation of 'every woman who dared to defy injustice and tyranny'. Just as she had used tradi-tional British carols in *A Christmas Carol,* Musgrave used spirituals and African–American folk music in *Harriet.*

Musgrave's opera *Simón Bolívar,* written for performance by Virginia Opera in 1995, tells another story of a national hero, the man who liberated Venezuela, Columbia, Ecuador, Peru and Bolivia from the Spanish in the early 19th century, and makes use of traditional Spanish and Latin-American music. Her other dramatic works include the radio opera *An Occurrence at Owl Creek Bridge* (1981) and *Echoes Through Time* (1988) for singers, dancers, speaker and instrumental ensemble. Musgrave has also continued to write inventive instrumental and vocal chamber music and orchestral works. *Rainbow* (1990), a celebratory work for orchestra including synthesizer, was commissioned for the opening of Glasgow's new concert hall. Her Wind Quintet (1992) uses some of her earlier 'asynchronous' techniques and Musgrave has described it as 'a kind of mini-drama without plot'. *Wild winter*, a set of moving lamentations for voices and viols using texts about war in English, French, Italian, Spanish, German and Russian, was commissioned for the 1993 Lichfield Festival. Three works were premiered at the 1994 Cheltenham Festival: the bass clarinet concerto *Autumn Sonata*; the choral work *On the Underground Set no. 1* and *Journey through a Japanese Landscape* for marimba and wind orchestra (with piano, harp and percussion), inspired by Japanese haiku.

Caroline Norton
1808–1877

Although Caroline Norton is far better known as a writer and campaigner for legal reform than as a composer, she published many songs with her own words and music. Several of these became extremely popular and were an important source of income for her at a time when she was forced to be financially self-reliant.

Norton was a granddaughter of singer Elizabeth Linley and playwright Richard Brinsley Sheridan. Her father, Tom Sheridan, died in 1816 when Norton was eight years old. She and her six brothers and sisters were brought up by their mother, novelist Caroline Henrietta Callander, at Hampton Court where they were given a home by Frederick, Duke of York. Norton began writing stories and poems as well as composing songs at an early age. She was the only daughter of the family to be sent away to school, possibly an attempt to instil a sense of discipline into a rather unruly child.

In 1827, at the age of 19, Norton made

her disastrous marriage to barrister and MP George Norton. She published her first collection of poems, *The Sorrows of Rosalie, a Tale, with other Poems*, anonymously in 1829. It was a success, reaching a fourth edition within a year. The Nortons were not well off and Norton used the proceeds of the book to buy herself a pianola and to help with the expenses of her first child who was born in July of that year. In 1830 she published her second collection of poems, *The Undying One and other Poems,* which contained many of the lyrics of her songs.

During the early 1830s Norton edited and contributed to several magazines and started publishing her songs as well as having two more sons and continuing to write and publish her poetry. She became well known as a writer, beauty and wit in London literary society, and was much in demand for her after-dinner performances of her own and other people's songs in her deep contralto voice. But her relationship with her violently abusive husband continued to deteriorate. In 1836 it finally broke down completely, and after a notorious trial involving Lord Melbourne, Norton discovered that as a woman separated from her husband she had no legal right to keep her children. Her three sons consequently remained with their father who would not let her see them. Norton refused to give in to this treatment and embarked on a campaign to change the law. She published pamphlets on the subject and used her society connections to get a bill introduced in Parliament. In 1839 the Infant Custody Act was finally passed which, in certain circum-stances, allowed a mother access to her children.

Norton refused to accept money from her husband and supported herself through her writing and composition, although as a married woman she was unable to own property. George Norton even tried to claim her earnings for himself. Enraged by such injustice, Norton campaigned for the Matrimonial Causes (Divorce) Act of 1857. Her separation from her husband, determination to live on her own and involvement in legal campaigns and court cases caused scandal and great damage to her repu-tation in an age when society women were supposed to keep firmly out of the public eye. George Norton died in 1875, and four months before her own death in 1877 Norton married her old friend, Sir William Stirling-Maxwell.

Some of Norton's earliest songs were published in collaboration with her older sister Helen (1807–67). Two collections were issued in the early 1830s: *A Set of Ten Songs and Two Duets, the words and music by two sisters* and *A Set of Twelve Songs ... by Mrs Price Blackwood and the Hon*[ble]. *Mrs Norton*. Helen, who had married Price Blackwood (later to become Baron Dufferin) in 1825 at the age of 18, went on to write several more songs, for many of which she wrote her own words, although she often remained anonymous in her published works.

Norton did not care about public exposure and published a variety of vocal music or, as she put it, 'melodies and songs for young girls and women to sing in happier homes than mine'. She issued a third collection of songs, *A Set of Seven Songs and a Duet by the Hon*[ble]. *Mrs Norton*, writing the words of all the songs but the music for only three of them, the rest being supplied by a Miss A. Cowell. A typical ballad by Norton from the 1830s is 'The Fairy Bells', a mournful piece with tinkling piano figures to illustrate the bells of the title. The first song in the volume *Songs of Affection*, a later collection from the early 1850s, was set to music by Augusta (or Mrs Henry) Ames although all the rest of the music is by Norton. Like most of Norton's work, these songs have simple, tuneful vocal lines although the piano parts can be quite elaborate. *Songs of Affection* is a gloomy collection full of laments for lost love, with the exception of *Juanita,* a song that was Norton's best-known and best-selling composition. Apparently written one evening in 1851 for one of her children to sing to a guitar, it was issued in many different arrangements, including a piano version by Brinley Richards which was being reprinted as late as 1913. The music for *Juanita* has a decidedly Spanish feel with an imitation of guitar strumming in the piano part and Mediterranean-style ornaments in the voice. Another successful song in the same vein was 'Maraquita: A Portuguese Love Song'. Another popular volume from the early 1850s was *Sabbath Lays*, a collection of songs for which Norton set a selection of her religious poetry.

Jane O'Leary
b. 1946

Although Jane O'Leary was born, grew up and studied in the United States, something of the wild, open spaciousness of the west coast of Ireland, where she has lived since 1972, has found its way into her music. She was born in Hartford, Connecticut to an artist mother and an architect father. Intrigued by her older sister's piano lessons, she first made her teach her how to play a piece and then begged her parents to let her have piano lessons herself. O'Leary studied music at Vassar College for four years, majoring in performance. While at Vassar, she took up the harpsichord and began to compose in her final year.

After graduation, O'Leary went to Princeton graduate school to major in music theory but changed to composition after a year. She spent four years at Princeton studying with Milton Babbitt and others while hearing many performances of her music. She met her Irish husband there and moved with him to Galway on the west coast of Ireland in 1972. It was here that she

finished her doctoral thesis. O'Leary continued to compose while teaching piano and theory, and had various works performed at occasions such as the Dublin Festival. An important turning point in her career as a composer came in 1976 when she founded the chamber group Concorde, which has become of central importance for the performance of contemporary music in Ireland and has provided a vital forum for O'Leary's own music. Soon after this she had her first child.

O'Leary has put an immense amount of energy into many different music projects in Ireland, from founding 'Music for Galway' to serving as chair of the Contemporary Music Centre and on the board of the National Concert Hall. In 1981 she was elected to Aosdána, an academy of artists set up by the Irish government to honour writers, visual artists, film-makers and composers. Apart from the important recognition and encouragement that this provided at a crucial point in her career, it also allowed her to apply for a grant that she has received every year since 1983. This grant gave her the time to concentrate on composition and enabled her to work as a full-time composer.

Also in 1983, O'Leary's second child was born, and her music, starting with the lyrical String Quartet she wrote that year, broke away from the serial technique on which she had been heavily dependent to a freer, more melodic style. Several of O'Leary's works are inspired by places and nature: *from the flatirons* (1984–5) for chamber orchestra of flute, oboe, clarinet and strings was written while she was visiting Boulder in Colorado, home of the mountain range the Flatirons. Other chamber or string-orchestra works include *the petals fall* (1986–7) and *sky of revelation* (1988–9), both premiered by the Dublin Irish Chamber Orchestra.

Most of O'Leary's works are for small groups or solo instruments. She has written several pieces for her own instrument, the piano, such as *Reflections: A Set of Five Images for Solo Piano* (1985–6), and *When the Bells have Stopped Ringing* (1989) which explores the bell-like resonance of a grand piano. Other chamber works include *A Silver Thread* (1988) for violin and percussion. This piece was choreographed by Ian Montague who then worked with O'Leary on *A Woman's Beauty* (1991), a setting of

W.B. Yeats for speaker, flute, percussion and dancer. O'Leary enjoys putting poetry together with music and often incorporates readings into concerts given by Concorde. The poetry of Brendan Kennelly has a particular resonance for her, often inspiring the titles of her music. She has also set several of his poems in her vocal works such as the unaccompanied choral piece *Filled Wine Cup* (1982).

O'Leary's first full-scale orchestral commission came from the Irish broadcasting company RTE. *Islands of Discovery* (1991) was first performed in 1992 by the National Symphony Orchestra. Determinedly not a symphony, *Islands of Discovery* is a descriptive work in five movements and was inspired by the image of Christopher Columbus setting off on his journey into the unknown in 1492. The movements explore various ideas connected with the voyage, such as exploration, contemplation, anxiety and discovery as an opening up of new questions. The central movement grew from Columbus's remark that, although his body might walk elsewhere, his heart was always in his native city of Genoa, using the textural contrast between a solo violin and the full orchestra.

The one-movement Piano Trio (1992) also explores different textures, especially the contrast between long, sustained notes and more percussive, staccato writing. O'Leary herself has suggested that the piece represents the visual image of 'a grassy meadow randomly dotted with the bright colours of wildflowers'. Poetic images are often an important starting point for O'Leary. *Silenzio della Terra* (1993), a duet for flute and percussion, is based on an early poem by Mario Luzi. The work opens with rhythmic fragments from the lowest register of the flute accompanied by tom-toms but is essentially contemplative, making much use of silence.

Pauline Oliveros
b. 1932

As a child, Pauline Oliveros used to tune the radio to the hiss, whistles and static between stations. This fascination with listening intently to any and all sounds has remained central to her work in music. Oliveros was born in Houston, Texas. Both her mother and grandmother were piano teachers and she had her first piano lessons from her mother. At 13, Oliveros took up the accordion, and although she later taught herself the tuba and studied the French horn, the accordion has always remained the instrument through which she expresses herself.

While still at school, Oliveros knew that she wanted to be a composer, and in 1949 went to the University of Houston to study music. She majored in the accordion and also took composition lessons that she found conservative and dull. Her first work, *Ode to a Morbid Marble* (1951) for piano, dates from this time. In 1952 she moved to San Francisco where she worked for a while as an accordion player and music teacher before enrolling at San Francisco State College in 1954, also taking private composition lessons with Robert Erickson. She graduated in 1957 and continued to work as a freelance musician.

Oliveros soon became interested in improvisation, forming an improvising group with Terry Riley and Loren Rush in 1957. Her music became more experimental. *Variations for Sextet* (1959–60) for flute, clarinet, trumpet, horn and cello is in a complex, freely atonal style until the cello plays a single long note for 20 seconds after which the other players take up similar drone-like notes. In the extremely difficult work *Trio for Flute, Piano and Page-Turner* (1961), which was the last piece in which Oliveros used traditional notation, the page-turner silently presses down notes on the piano so that they will resonate without actually sounding.

In 1961, Oliveros formed another improvisation group, called Sonics,

Pauline Oliveros

with Morton Subotnick and Roman Sender. They also established the electronic music studio at San Francisco Conservatory, which later became the San Francisco Tape Center. Oliveros had been interested in electronics ever since her mother had given her a tape recorder in the early 1950s, and she had found that working with tape was one way of reproducing some of the unusual sounds that she was hearing. Her first electronic composition, *Time Perspectives*, was made in 1961, using environmental sounds recorded on a home tape recorder. In the same year she wrote *Sound Patterns,* a textless work for unaccompanied choir which imitates some of the sounds of electronic noise such as percussive envelopes, ring modulation and white noise.

In the early 1960s Oliveros started to introduce a visual element into her work, creating theatre pieces such as *Duo for Accordion and Bandoneon with Possible Mynah Bird Obbligato* (1964) and *Pieces of Eight* (1965) in which imagery from Robert Louis Stevenson's *Treasure Island* combines with alarm clocks and a bust of Beethoven with flashing red eyes. Works that were commissioned by individual players also became theatre pieces built round the character of the player such as *Theater Piece for Trombone Player* (1966) created for Stuart Dempster in which he plays hosepipes over a tape of his own trombone playing.

The San Francisco Tape Center relocated to Mills College in the mid–1960s, and Oliveros became its director. Her electronic work from this period included *Bye Bye Butterfly* (1965) which combined white noise with a recording of part of Puccini's *Madame Butterfly*, and *I of IV* (1966), a purely electronic studio piece. In 1967, Oliveros joined the music faculty at the University of California at San Diego where she taught a variety of music and became director of the Center for Music Experiment. She continued to work with electronic music until the end of the decade. One of her most widely performed pieces was *In Memoriam Nicola Tesla, Cosmic Engineer* (1968/9) which was commissioned by the Merce Cunningham Dance Company.

By the early 1970s Oliveros was becoming increasingly interested in various aspects of Asian culture, such as t'ai chi, Tibetan Buddhism, meditation, karate and the symbolism of mandalas. A sense of ritual and ceremony became central to her work as did a growing feminist awareness. In 1970 she wrote an article published in the *New York Times* entitled 'And Don't Call Them Lady Composers'. The same year she wrote *To Valerie Solanas and Marilyn Monroe in Recognition of their Desperation*, a work for any group of players which involves each performer choosing five pitches to use to produce a 'calm and meditative' piece.

At this time Oliveros was working with a group of ten women, called the ♀ Ensemble, on some of her best-known works, the 24 *Sonic Meditations*. These are a series of prose directions to be performed by everyone present, with no-one acting as an audience. They involve the participants in intense listening to sound and sometimes in remembering or imagining sound. The first meditation, 'Teach yourself to fly' (1971), was dedicated to Amelia Earhart, and instructs the participants to focus on their own deep, concentrated breathing and then slowly allow their vocal cords to vibrate.

Meditation plays a central part in Oliveros's extraordinary ceremonial theatre works of the mid–1970s such as *Crow Two* (1975), commissioned by the State University of New York at Buffalo, which uses a series of meditations. *Rose Moon* (1977), commissioned by the Wesleyan Singers, lasts for two hours and uses an elaborate mandala form. The players form a series of circles. On the outer ring runners wearing bells take turns in running round the circumference of the performing space. In the next circle, percussion players hit their instruments as they feel the runners pass behind them and also chant names for the moon and of people they want to remember. The next two circles consist of a procession of seven people with a moon rattle and twelve performers who meditate, sing and move with large cloths. At the centre of the mandala stand a naked man and a naked woman.

Oliveros also created works that she performed herself, such as *The Pathways of the Grandmother* (1976) for accordion and voice, a memorial to her grandmother who had died in 1973, or *Horse Sings from Cloud* (1977) for accordion, built on a series of ascending chords. The audience is often involved in the performance of a piece. *Exchanges* (1979) grows out of the performers and audience making sounds, listening and imitating the sounds that they are hearing. In *MMM, a Lullaby for Daisy Pauline* (1980) the audience make humming sounds using the consonant 'm' with various different vowels.

In 1981, Oliveros moved to Mount Tiemper in New York State and the same year set up the Oliveros Foundation, a non-profit-making arts organization that she uses as a platform for her musical projects. Since the 1980s she has released several important recordings that have taken her work to a wider audience. *The Wanderer* (1984) included the title work performed by Oliveros and the Springfield Accordion Orchestra as well as an ensemble version of *Horse Sings from Cloud*. *The Well and the Gentle* (1985) included music recorded in a drained reservoir in Germany as well as two parts, 'The Well' and 'The Gentle', from her piece *The Well*. This work is for any group of players who are provided with two scales, a rhythmic pattern and the five words: listen, match, merge, support and soar.

To describe her work, Oliveros has developed the term 'Deep Listening', which she has defined as 'listening in every possible way to everything possible to hear no matter what you are doing'. In 1988, together with composer Paniotis and trombonist Stuart Dempster, she formed The Deep Listening Band to make *Deep Listening*. This recording was made in the Fort Worden Cistern, an abandoned water tank in Port Townsend, Washington. The tank, which once held two million gallons of water, is 14 feet deep, 186 feet in diameter and has a 45-second reverberation. The performers used a didgeridoo, conch shells and pieces of metal as well as accordion, trombone and voice to create a timeless web of sound that draws the listener into its own magical world. A second recording, *The Ready Made Boomerang*, was recorded in the cistern in 1990 when Oliveros, Paniotis and Dempster were joined by singer and performance artist Thomasa Eckert and clarinettist William O. Smith. In the same year the Deep Listening Band made

Trogolodyte's Delight, recorded in the Tarpaper Cave in Rosendale, New York.

Another aspect of Oliveros' Deep Listening work is the Deep Listening Chorus which is open to anyone. The participants meet once a month to 'lie on the floor and make sounds' and have given performances of Oliveros' meditation pieces. In 1993, Oliveros was involved in more conventional work when she collaborated with her friend, the playwright Ione, on *Nzinga: The Queen King*, performed as part of the Next Wave Festival of the Brooklyn Academy of Music. This theatre work is based on the life of the mighty 17th-century queen who, dressed in man's clothes, ruled Ndongo for 40 years, successfully keeping the Portuguese out of the country. Oliveros worked on the music and the sound design for *Nzinga*, using an ensemble of African musicians on stage who play traditional music and improvise on Oliveros' own music which provides commentary and support for the action of the play. In her work on this project Oliveros was able to concentrate on the creation of music that expresses a sense of community, something that has always been of central importance in her remarkable and powerful work.

Daphne Oram
b. 1925

Daphne Oram was born on the last day of 1925 in Devizes, near the Salisbury Plain. She has always been fascinated by sound and exploring different ways of producing it. As a child she had piano lessons and was intrigued by the reverberations produced when she sang into a grand piano as well as by the different noises made by sticking objects under the strings, creating an early version of a prepared piano. With her brother she built a basic trans- mitter as well as endlessly playing with transformers and valves. Oram continued to study the piano when she went to Sherborne School for Girls and also played the organ in Sherborne Abbey where she was excited by the possibility of building up massive resonant chords.

In 1943, at the age of 17, Oram took a job at the BBC, turning down a place at the Royal College of Music. At the BBC, she was trained in aspects of studio engineering, such as the use of micro- phones and how to control the output of a musical performance, so that she could work as a music balancer, a job that required technical engineering knowledge as well as a musical training. With many men absent because of the war, several women were being trained in these technical areas at this time. During her years at the BBC Oram worked with many of the most famous performers of the time including Myra Hess, Kathleen Ferrier, Alfred Cortot and Solomon. She also worked on broadcasts from the Proms and the Glyndebourne opera season.

From 1944, Oram also began her experiments in converting graphic information into sound. These were prompted by an incident on her BBC engineering training course. The students were given a demonstration of an oscilloscope which showed wave pattern forms when musical sounds were fed into it. Oram wanted to know if a system that worked the other way round was possible, whether musical sound could be produced from graphical wave patterns. Her question was dismissed but this only fuelled

Oram's determination to produce such a system, something that was to become her life's work. She began building pieces of equipment, such as a tape head, out of old radio components and other bits and pieces. By the late 1940s she had access to an early tape recorder and was fascinated by the possibilities for manipulating sound that it offered. When Oram tried to persuade the BBC to investigate the potential that magnetic tape and electronically produced music could offer she met with considerable resistance, at one time being told that the BBC had an orchestra to make every sound it needed. As early as 1950 she submitted a work to the BBC for 'orchestra, five microphones and manipulated recordings'.

When tape recorders first arrived at the BBC, Oram started working at night, moving all the tape recorders together to set herself up a studio. Finally, in 1957, she was allowed to set up what became known as the radiophonic unit. Meanwhile a committee was being established to look into setting up a radiophonic workshop. The impetus behind this move came from the drama, rather than the music, department. One of the earliest broadcasts of a radiophonic work was made in October 1957 when Frederick Bradnum's *Private Dreams and Public Nightmares*, subtitled 'A Radiophonic Poem', was heard on the third programme. For this work Bradnum had specified sounds such as 'a

comet-like shriek' or 'a developed sound like a cry'. These sounds were produced by Oram, together with Desmond Briscoe and others from the BBC's drama department.

Early in 1958 Oram produced the first electronic soundtrack for a television play, *Amphitryon 38*. Later that year the BBC Radiophonic Workshop was officially opened, with Oram as one of the directors. But she was already disillusioned with the direction in which the workshop was heading, to the production of sound effects for drama rather than towards musical experimentation. In October of that year she was sent to the 'Journées Internationales de Musique Experimentale' in Brussels. This conference, attended by other experimental composers such as Roberto Gerhard, Humphrey Searle and Karlheinz Stockhausen, confirmed her belief that there were exciting possibilities in the development of electronic music, and when she returned to England she resigned from the BBC in order to set up her own studio at her home in a converted oast house in Kent.

Working in her own studio enabled Oram to continue her experiments in converting graphic information into sound. Having cashed in her BBC pension in order to buy basic studio equipment, in 1962 she was given a Gulbenkian grant to start work on designing and building what was to become her Oramics system. Oram describes this system as a 'photo-electric digital/analogue compositional machine'. Oramics allows the composer to manipulate many different parameters of sound. Components of sound (such as pitch, envelope, rhythm, dynamics, vibrato, reverberation, timbre and so on) are drawn onto 10 parallel tracks of 35-millimetre film. These are then transported through the photoelectric sound-generating system by a motor.

In the early 1960s Oram started a highly successful series of concert lectures, at venues such as the Mermaid Theatre in London and at the Edinburgh Festival, where she explained electronic music to fascinated audiences, playing music by composers such as Karlheinz Stockhausen, Bulent Arel, Luigi Nono and Luciano Berio as well as works of her own such as *Four Aspects* (1959) which had been written in order to demonstrate the possibilities of electronic composition. In 1965 she received another Gulbenkian grant towards her work.

Oram also made a living by producing electronic music for theatre, ballet, exhibitions, radio, television, commercials and feature and documentary films. In 1961 she wrote the music for the film *The Innocents*, based on Henry James' *The Turn of the Screw*, although the music is often credited to Georges Auric who in fact

only provided the music for the opening credits. Oram's music for the theatre included her work for Fred Hoyle's science-fiction play *Rockets in Ursa Major* (1962). Her *Episode Metallic* (1965) was written to be played with *Nucleus*, a sculpture by Andrew Bobrowski on permanent exhibition at the Mullards Electronics Centre. In the same year *Pulse Persephone* was commissioned for the 'Treasures of the Commonwealth Exhibition' at the Royal Academy of Arts. Each room of the exhibition housed exhibits from a different part of the Commonwealth and had corresponding music from the appropriate country. Oram's tape was for the British room and she built it up using single sounds from each part of the Commonwealth such as a note from a steel pan and another from an African drum. She also used a note of Oramics and a note of an electric guitar (as a tongue-in-cheek reference to the popular music of the time). Underpinning the rest of the tape is an extremely low, shifting pulse which could be felt through the floor at the original exhibition. *Pulse Persephone* creates exciting, primeval sounds and was later used for a ballet, *Alpha Omega*, choreographed by Seraphina Lansdowne.

Oram has also often worked in collaboration with other composers. The tapes for three of Thea Musgrave's works, the ballet *Beauty and the Beast* (1968–9), *Soliloquy* (1969) for guitar and tape and *From One to Another*

(1970) for viola and tape were all made in collaboration with Oram and in her studio. Oram also worked with her BBC colleague, Ivor Walsworth, on two works for piano and tape (using Oramics), *Contrasts Essconic* (1969) and *Sardonica* (1972). Both works were premiered by Walsworth's wife, pianist Joan Davies. In 1972 the New London Ballet gave the first performances of *Xallaraparallax,* a ballet choreographed by Seraphina Lansdowne to music commissioned from Oram. It was performed at the Brighton Festival and then toured throughout the world, including Europe, Hong Kong and South America. In the same year, Oram's book *An Individual Note of Music, Sound and Electronics* was published, a fascinating discussion of the basics of electronic sound, including a lucid explanation of her own work on Oramics.

Oram has continued to write music for a variety of uses. Teaching and explaining the opportunities and possibilities of electronic sounds and music has also remained important. From 1982 to 1989 she taught at Christ Church College, Canterbury. In the late 1980s she worked on a project called 'Out and Round About with Music' (O.R.A.M), which aimed to take older people out to hear music. But central to her work is the development of Oramics, a research project that it is still in progress. With grants in the mid–1980s from the Ralph Vaughan Williams Trust and the Arts Council, Oram is transferring the system to Risc computer technology. She sees her work continuing for many years to come, comparing the growth of Oramics (and indeed of electronic music in general) to the growth of instruments such as the piano which took a very long time to realize their full potential.

Morfydd Owen
1891–1918

Morfydd Owen died while still in her 20s, yet she had already written a substantial body of work, much of which is still performed, especially in her native Wales. She was born in 1891 in Trefforest near Cardiff in South Wales where her parents ran a drapery business. Owen started writing hymn tunes at a young age and as a child was given piano lessons. When she was 16 she started having private lessons in both composition and piano from composer David Evans, and while she was still at school her hymn tune 'Morfydd' was published.

In 1909, at the age of 18, Owen went to study music at University College in Cardiff where many of her compositions were performed at student concerts, including a *Romance* for violin and piano, the part-song *My Luve's Like a Red, Red Rose* and many songs. She graduated in the summer of 1912, writing an *Ave Maria* for mezzo-soprano, chorus and orchestra for her final examinations and in September moved to London to

continue her studies at the Royal Academy of Music. Her composition teacher at the Academy was Frederick Corder, and she also started to study singing. Owen was very successful at the Academy, winning the Charles Lucas medal for composition and the Oliveria Prescott prize for general excellence in her first year as well as being awarded the Goring Thomas scholarship which she held for four years.

In March 1913, Owen made her first appearance in London at a student concert in the Bechstein Hall, singing four of her own songs, including the Welsh lullaby 'Suo Gan'. The orchestral *Nocturne* in D♭ that had won her the Lucas medal was played at an Academy concert later that year. Many other works were heard at the Academy during her years as a student, including the baritone solo 'England, give ear!' from her cantata *Pro Patria* for soprano, baritone, chorus and orchestra, performed at an Academy concert in December 1915.

In London, Owen developed two separate circles of friends. One of these revolved around the Welsh Presbyterian Charing Cross chapel, a focal centre for many Welsh people in London. She particularly valued her friendship with Herbert and Ruth Lewis and their daughter Kitty who organized private concerts in their house at which Owen and her friends performed. During 1916, Owen lived with them for a while. Before moving in, she reassured them that she never practised the piano, just played through her compositions and practised singing for 15 minutes four times a day.

Through Ruth Lewis, who was a leading member of the Welsh Folk-Song Society, Owen became involved in transcribing and writing accompaniments for collections of Welsh folk songs. They collaborated on a volume of *Folk-Songs Collected in Flintshire and the Vale of Clwyd* (1914), and many years after Owen's death, Ruth Lewis used more of her work in her *Second Collection of Welsh Folk-Songs* (1934). Owen herself often gave lectures and talks on Welsh folk music.

Her other circle of friends, which was not one approved of by the Welsh chapel-goers, included the poets D.H. Lawrence and Ezra Pound and several Russian émigrés. Shy but extremely attractive, Owen was rumoured to have had 15 proposals of marriage before she was 21. Her Russian friendships led to a fascination with Russian folk song, and in 1915 she applied for a fellowship from the University of Wales to study the folk music of Russia, Norway and Finland, proposing to travel to Petrograd to collect material. The University gave her a £100 grant but the war made such travel impossible and Owen stayed on at the Academy instead.

Owen's career as a singer continued to grow throughout 1916. She often sang at concerts given for the troops, and made her professional debut at the Aeolian Hall in London in January 1917 at a concert given by the London Trio where she sang some of her own compositions. The next month, to the dismay of the Lewises and her parents, she married the psychoanalyst Ernest Jones who was twelve years her senior. Jones was seen as part of her 'Bohemian' circle of friends and Ruth Lewis refused even to meet him. He appears to have attempted to dissuade Owen from her strongly held religious beliefs and possibly from her musical career. Owen remained at the Academy until the summer of 1917, and she continued to compose and perform after her marriage, although a letter from Jones to Sigmund Freud claimed that the Aeolian Hall concert was to be her last public appearance.

In 1917, Chapell published Owen's setting of words by Ethel Newman, 'For Jeannie's Sake'. Her *Two*

Madonna Songs were heard on 19 April at Isodore de Lara's 'All British Concert' at the Steinway Hall and were published that month, although they had been written several years previously. They are very different from the much more conventional 'For Jeannie's Sake', which has an obvious popular appeal. Both are very intense songs and Owen herself is said to have often been overcome with emotion while singing them. 'To our Lady of Sorrows' sets a poem by Wilfred Hinton and is a dramatic, impassioned song, with a chilling piano opening. 'Slumber Song to the Madonna', a setting of words by Alfred Noyes, has a pulsating piano accompaniment and strange, unexpected harmonies.

In July 1917, Owen gave the first performance of Harry Farjeon's song cycle *A Lute of Jade* and in September sang at the Birkenhead National Eisteddfod. In 1918, several of her more popular songs were published by Boosey, including more settings of Ethel Newman. In the summer of 1918, while on a visit to Jones's father in Wales, Owen suddenly developed acute appendicitis, and in spite of an emergency operation she died on 7 September, apparently from delayed chloroform poisoning, shortly before her 27th birthday.

Owen's orchestral music included a tone poem *Morfa Rhuddlan* and a suite *Death Music: The Passing of Branwen*. She also wrote several works for voice and orchestra, including *Sea Drift*, *Cycle of Four Sea Songs*, *My Sorrow* and *Toward the Unknown Region*. Much of Owen's vocal and piano music was published in a memorial edition (1923–4), edited by Jones and Corder , a collection which shows the distinctive quality of so much of her writing, especially in the imaginative and heart-felt songs.

Priti Paintal
b. 1960

Priti Paintal, who was born in New Delhi, grew up surrounded by a wide variety of music. Her maternal grandfather had been brought up in a German Missionary School in the Himalayas and subsequently ensured that all his children and their children grew up with a love of Western classical music. Paintal's interest in classical Indian music was encouraged by her uncle, a singer who taught in the music department at Delhi University. As a teenager she also used to listen to the music of fusion artists such as Chick Corea and Keith Jarrett as well as the more straightforward rock of groups like the Rolling Stones.

Paintal played the piano from an early age and later took up the sitar and the tabla, although she was more interested in learning about the structure of Indian music than in becoming a performer. After a while she started to write down the music she was improvising at the piano, and later had some orchestration lessons from the conductor of the Delhi Symphony Orchestra. From 1977, Paintal studied anthropology at Delhi University. After graduating with a bachelor's degree in 1980, she spent two years working for a master's degree in ethnomusicology, conducting field work into tribal and folk music in villages in the Himalayas. By this time she knew that she wanted to concentrate on composition and had several important performances of her early works. In 1981 her orchestral piece *Anubhav* was played by the Delhi Symphony Orchestra and *Abyas Kriti* for piano was broadcast on All India Radio.

In 1982 Paintal was awarded a British Council Scholarship to study composition at York University. She stayed at York for a year and then moved to the Royal Northern College of Music where she spent two years studying composition with Anthony Gilbert, graduating with a master's degree in composition in 1985. She has described her reaction to studying recent Western classical music as one of 'bewilderment which over the years has matured into

Priti Paintal

indifference'. During this time her own music moved from an early lyrical style to the more complex, post-serialist idiom of works such as *Ayodhya* (1986) for flute, clarinet, cello and two percussion, commissioned by Yorkshire Arts and played at the Huddersfield Festival. Paintal's vocal works of this period were more lyrical. These included *A Sanskrit Love Poem* (1986) for mezzo-soprano and clarinet and *Gandharva Music* (1987) for mezzo-soprano, piano and percussion.

Using a rhythmic and repetitive Sanskrit mantra as its text, this work provided a clear indication of the modal harmonies and emphasis on rhythm that was becoming central to Paintal's music.

Paintal soon developed her own individual voice which drew on the melodies, harmonies and rhythms of both classical and folk music from India and the rhythmic patterns of African music and of Western composers such as Igor Stravinsky. This voice is clearly present in her powerfully poignant chamber opera *Survival Song* (1988), with a libretto by Richard Fawkes set in South Africa, which was commissioned and performed by the Garden Venture of the Royal Opera House. In the same year Paintal founded Shiva Nova, a group of musicians from Asian and Western traditions playing sitar, tabla, flute, cello and keyboards. This combination of musicians who work with notated music and musicians trained in improvisation aims 'to unite soundworlds not cultures'. Works written by other composers for Shiva Nova include Eleanor Alberga's *The Edge* (1991) and Nicola LeFanu's *Sundari and the Secret Message* (1993) which also uses a storyteller.

In Paintal's early music for the group, only the sitar and tabla players improvised. This music included works such as *Evening Rhythms* (1988), for Shiva Nova with mezzosoprano, and *For Us* (1988), for Shiva Nova with tape. The frequently performed *Euroasian Quintet* (1989) for the group explores rhythmic improvisation with the sitar and tabla picking up and expanding on the vivacious notated rhythms of the flute, cello and keyboards. The fast rhythmic sections of the piece surround a lyrical slow passage for flute, cello and sitar. In her dynamic settings of South African poetry, *Black and White Songs* (1991), Paintal adds two vocalists to the instrumental line-up of Shiva Nova.

From the early 1990s, Paintal's works include several written for ensembles other than Shiva Nova. *Scarlet Mountain Dances: Music for Guilty Lovers* (1990) was commissioned by the East of England Orchestra. The instrumentation for this work includes three improvising Asian instruments. Written in the Himalayas, it is in five movements which depict stages in the story of the 'eternal love triangle', from the initial meeting through a courtship dance, betrayal and confrontation to a final resolution. Paintal's string quartet *Bound by strings of rhythm* (1992) has been performed by both the Bingham and Balanescu string quartets. This is an exciting work with vital driving rhythms alternating with slower, more meditative music dominated by the cello. *How long is a piece of string?*, a chamber-orchestra piece for the Bournemouth Sinfonietta, was premiered at the 1994 Chard Festival of Women in Music in Somerset.

In 1992 Paintal's full-length opera *Biko*, commissioned by the Royal Opera House, was premiered at the Birmingham Rep and repeated at the London International Opera Festival. To a libretto by Richard Fawkes, this opera tells the story of the South African hero, Steve Biko. Much of the text is spoken, and Paintal's vocal writing and word-setting remain direct and clear throughout the work, with the singers instructed to sing in a straightforward rather than an elaborately operatic style. The music is simple and appealing, based around two main themes representing freedom and love.

In the early 1990s Paintal began incorporating more improvisation into her work with Shiva Nova and inviting musicians from other improvising cultures to play with the group. These musicians included the kora player Tunde Jegede and jazz marimba player Orphy Robinson. Paintal's *Polygamy* (1993) for Robinson and Shiva Nova is an inventive work based around a central theme, in which the marimba, sitar and tabla play entirely improvised music, the flute and piano parts are notated and the cello improvises as well as playing notated music, all coming together to create an intense and dazzling sound-world.

Maria Parke
1775–1822

Maria Parke's father and uncle were both prominent London oboists. She was the eldest of John and Hannah Parke's 10 children and first appeared in public at the age of nine, singing at the Handel Memorial Concert of 1784. She made her debut as a pianist a year later, playing a concerto after the first part of Handel's oratorio *Samson*. Parke appeared as singer and pianist at most of the important concert series and venues of the 1780s and 90s, including the Professional Concerts, the concerts given by the Academy of Ancient Music, and at Ranelagh Gardens. She also performed outside London, singing in Gloucester Cathedral and the Oxford Music Room.

In April 1794, Parke stood in for the famous singer Gertrude Mara at Salomon's Haydn concerts. Something of her character can be seen in a review of her performance: 'Miss Parke improves rapidly, and if her efforts continue, she will become an honour to the divine art she professes; especially as she evidently studies passion, and prefers it to that tinsel, mechanical execution, which repetition soon renders disgusting.' Haydn was obviously taken with the 19-year-old singer. He sent her one of his piano sonatas and played the pianoforte at her benefit concert at the Hanover Square Rooms in May that year, an occasion described as 'the most brilliant assemblage of female fashion any public rooms have displayed through the season...'. Parke herself sang and played one of her own piano sonatas.

Parke continued to perform into the 19th century. At the age of 40, in 1815, she married John Beardmore of Mayfair and retired. She gave birth to a son but died in 1822 at the age of 47. It is important not to confuse Parke's published work with that of Maria Hester Reynolds (later Mrs Park). Most of Parke's music was composed in the early years of the 19th century. She wrote two sets of conventional sonatas – *Three Grand Sonatas* for the pianoforte, op. 1, and *Two Grand*

Sonatas for pianoforte with an optional violin accompaniment, op. 2. Her other surviving piano work, *A Divertimento and Military Rondo*, takes the form of a sonata with an *allegro* first movement followed by an slow *andante grazioso* and ending with the 'Rondo à la Militaire'.

Parke's vocal music includes what appears to be her earliest published work, the song 'I have often been told and began to believe' to words by Rev. Newman which was sung at the Vauxhall Gardens and issued in about 1787 with an accompaniment for horns, violins, bassoons and pianoforte. Her other surviving vocal works are two duets, 'What is Beauty' and the stately 'God of Slaughter quit the Field'.

Susan Parkhurst
1836–1918

Almost nothing is known about Susan Parkhurst's early life. She was born Susan McFarland in Leicester, Massachusetts, and her first recorded appearance was as a soloist and accompanist at a Methodist concert in New York in 1860 at the age of 24. She married and had a daughter but her husband died in action in 1864.

Mrs E.A. Parkhurst, as she was known professionally, was most active, as both performer and composer, in the 1860s, presumably earning a living for herself and her daughter Effie. But she did not have to remain self-supporting for long, marrying John Duer in 1868. Parkhurst produced songs in a wide variety of styles: comic songs, sacred and gospel tunes, political and patriotic songs. Many of these songs became extremely popular, along with those of her friend Stephen Foster whom she had met through their mutual publisher Horace Waters.

Parkhurst's most famous song was the temperance ballad 'Father's A Drunkard and Mother is Dead', a pathetic tale told through the eyes of a child. Another temperance ballad was 'I'll Marry No Man if he Drinks'. Parkhurst also wrote piano music, including sets of variations on 'Yankee Doodle' and 'Blue Bells of Scotland' and a *Funeral March to the Memory of Abraham Lincoln*. She died in New York in 1918.

Julia Perry
1924–1979

Julia Perry was born in Kentucky but the family soon moved to Akron, Ohio where she grew up in a house full of music. Her father, a doctor, played the piano, and both her older sisters played the violin. Perry wanted to be a composer from an early age. After graduating from Akron High School, she studied piano, violin, voice, conducting and composition at Westminster Choir College in Princeton, New Jersey.

While she was at college, Perry published her first work, *Carillon Heigh-Ho*, and spent the summer of 1946 in Birmingham, Alabama training a choir to sing one of her compositions. In 1948, at the age of 24, she graduated from Westminster with a master's degree. Her examination work was the cantata *Chicago* for baritone, narrator, chorus and orchestra to a text by Carl Sandburg. That same year she moved to New York where she continued her composition studies at the Juilliard School of Music, worked as an opera coach for the Columbia Opera

Workshop and started seeing her music published and performed. In 1950 her sacred cantata *Ruth* for chorus and organ was first performed in New York.

Perry spent much of the 1950s in Europe. After taking composition lessons from Italian avant-garde composer Luigi Dallapiccola at Tanglewood in 1951, she won two Guggenheim Fellowships in 1952 and 1955 to study with him in Italy. While she was in Europe on her first fellowship she also took the opportunity of taking composition lessons from Nadia Boulanger in Paris and won a Boulanger Grand Prix for her Viola Sonata. She also spent several summers studying conducting at the Accademia Chigiana in Siena, and in 1957 conducted a successful concert tour in Europe funded by the US Information Agency.

Perry's early works were largely vocal. Her first piece to attract attention was the *Stabat Mater* (1951) for contralto and string orchestra, dedicated to her mother. Like much of Perry's music, it is in a basically tonal language that makes extensive use of expressive dissonances with dramatic yet always lyrical vocal writing. It was followed by two vocal pieces for which Perry used her own texts, the anthem *Ye Who Seek the Truth* (1952) for tenor, chorus and organ, and *Song of our Saviour* (1953) for unaccompanied chorus, a work which clearly shows Perry's delicate blending of African–American music idioms such as spiritual-like melodies or call-and-response structures with the 20th-century Western techniques she was learning from Dallapiccola and Boulanger. At this time Perry was also publishing several arrangements of spirituals such as 'Free at Last' (1951) and 'I'm a Poor Li'l Orphan in this Worl'' (1952).

In 1954 the Columbia Opera Workshop performed Perry's one-act opera *The Cask of Amontillado* with a libretto after Edgar Allen Poe. She was to write several other stage works including a three-act opera-ballet *The Selfish Giant* (1964) with a libretto after the play by Oscar Wilde and another three-act opera *The Symplegades* about the 17th-century Salem witch trials.

By 1959 Perry was back in the United States and began to concentrate on writing instrumental and orchestral music. Over the next 12 years she wrote 12 very different symphonies including Symphony no. 1 for violas and string basses and her 11th symphony, *Soul Symphony* (1972), which makes extensive use of African–American folk idioms. She also wrote other orchestral pieces such as *Requiem for Orchestra* (1959) based on themes by Antonio Vivaldi, *Pastoral* (1959) for flute and strings and her 1962 revision of an earlier work, *A Short Piece for Orchestra*. This was performed in 1965 by the New York Philharmonic Orchestra, the first time they had played a piece by a woman since the late 1940s.

Perry also wrote more experimental works such as *Homunculus C.F.* for harp, piano and 10 percussion players, composed during the summer of 1960. The 'homunculus' of the title refers to the 'little man' created by Faust's assistant; 'C.F.' stands for the central chord of the 15th (made up of two major sevenths) round which the work is based. In the first three sections of the piece Perry explores in turn three of the basic elements of music: rhythm, melody and harmony. The fourth section combines the three elements, building to a dramatic climax at which the full chord of the 15th is heard.

During the 1960s Perry lectured and taught at various colleges and institutions, such as the Florida A & M University in Tallahassee and the Atlanta University Centre, as well as continuing to compose. She won several important prizes, such as an

American Academy and National Institute of Arts and Letters award in 1964. She had several severe strokes in 1973 which left her right side paralysed and led to long periods in hospital. Perry eventually began composing again, although none of her later works such as *Five Quixotic Songs* (1976) for bass-baritone and instruments or *Bicentennial Reflections* (1977) for tenor and instruments were published. She moved back to Akron where she died in April 1979 at the age of 55.

Poldowski
(Irene Wieniawska)
1879–1932

Poldowski was the pseudonym chosen by the youngest daughter of the famous Polish violinist Henri Wieniawski and his Irish wife Isobel Hampton. She was born in Brussels in 1879, the year before her father died 'penniless' in Moscow. As a child, she studied music with a Miss Ellis and then, from the age of 12, at the Brussels Conservatory. The famous tenor Gervase Elwes heard her play some of her own compositions when she was 14, describing them as 'very remarkable, showing great originality, and, for her age, great finish …'.

In her late teens Poldowski came to London where she continued to study, taking piano lessons with Michael Hambourg and composition lessons with Percy Pitt. In 1900 she published two songs under her own name, settings of Alfred Tennyson, 'O Let the Solid Ground' and W.B. Yeats, 'Down by the Sally Gardens'. A year later, at the age of 22, she married Sir Aubrey Dean Paul, an amateur baritone who sometimes sang in public under the

name of Edward Ramsey. After the birth of her son Aubrey in 1902, Poldowski went to Paris for further musical study with André Gédalge.

In 1904 Aubrey died and, pregnant with her second child, Poldowski returned to London. Sometime after the birth of Brian and before the birth of her daughter Brenda in 1907, Poldowski returned to Paris and took lessons from Vincent d'Indy at the Schola Cantorum. In 1908 seven of Poldowski's songs were performed at Bechstein Hall by Gervase Elwes, accompanied by the composer on the piano. From this time on her songs, mostly to French texts, were often heard at concerts in London, sung by singers such as Elwes and Maggie Teyte. Several were published in Paris, later to be issued in London by her principal publisher, Chester. These early songs show the clear influence of her time in France, with harmonies and textures reminiscent of Claude Debussy, but are also distinctly individual. Poldowski was particularly drawn to the poet Paul Verlaine, setting at least 18 of his lyrics throughout her life. Her early Verlaine settings include the dream-like 'Brume', the joyous 'Mandoline' with its strumming piano accompaniment and the beautifully simple 'L'Heure exquise'.

In January 1912, Henry Wood performed Poldowski's *Suite Miniature de Chansons à Danser* for eight woodwind instruments at Queen's Hall. He felt she had 'exceptional talent' and encouraged her to write an orchestral work for him. Later that year her *Nocturne* for orchestra with an amazing array of 21 woodwind instruments (including hecklephone and corno di bassetto) was premiered at the Proms. In July of the same year Poldowski gave a concert of her works, including a Violin Sonata in D minor, at the Aeolian Hall. The reviewer from *The Times* recognized the impressionistic quality of her work: '...grass may be green and cornfields golden, and mountains blue, and they are in her picture; but what she painted it for, and what she would wish it to be judged by, is the effect upon them of light and atmosphere'.

During the war Poldowski appears to have been working on an opera to a libretto by Maurice Maeterlinck but this work does not seem to have been finished or, if it was, to have survived. In the 1919 Prom season, Wood conducted the first London performance of Poldowski's *Pat Malone's Wake* for

piano and orchestra, with the composer as soloist. She continued to write and publish songs such as her two Albert Samain settings: the complex and chromatic 'Pannyre aux talons d'or' (1919) with no key signature and the exquisite 'Soir' (1920) with an accompaniment for piano and oboe d'amore.

During the early 1920s Poldowski's works were heard frequently in London and Paris and she organized several concerts of her music in London and New York. Her musical language did not go down well with the more conservative music critics. In 1923 she published two pieces for violin and piano, *Berceuse de l'Enfant mourant* and *Tango*, which a reviewer for *The Musical Times* described as 'exceedingly and unnecessarily difficult', going on to add that 'the Berceuse has all the air of having been written to provide a swift, if not a sweet, ending for the sufferings of the "enfant"...'.

Caledonian Market, a collection of eight short piano pieces, was published in the same year. These are highly inventive and often very tongue-in-cheek pieces in a dissonant style, occasionally reminiscent of Erik Satie. Each piece is highly descriptive, from the tinkling of the mechanical 'Musical Box' to the miaows of 'Child Talking to the Cat'. The third piece, 'Bloomsbury Waltz', paints a gently mocking picture of British refinement. The music is slow, quiet and stilted with directions to the pianist such as 'mincingly', 'wooden' and 'genteel'. Leigh Henry reviewed *Caledonian Market* in *The Chesterian* after Poldowski played it at a Music Society Concert in 1923, saying 'Irony glints throughout ... but there is also a sensitively tender humanity ...'.

The more progressive journals such as *The Chesterian* or *The Sackbut* usually gave Poldowski's music excellent reviews. *The Chesterian* was published by Poldowski's own publishers and she herself contributed several interesting articles on music. These included 'Man and Modernism' (1923), a fascinating discussion of what Poldowski saw as man's debilitatingly intellectual and theoretical attitude to music, even to the modern music of the day in which he is simply 'evolving yet another theory out of the material which was essentially Eve's'. Several writers in the 1920s saw Poldowski's music as embodying a new and distinctly female voice. In 1924 Yvonne Pert described her as 'the most spontaneously feminine composer up to the present' and her music as 'instinct with the feminine quality of moods, the feminine reaction to images and atmospheres, the feminine impulses expressed in new varieties of rhythm and harmonic colour ...'.

In 1924 Poldowski published two songs to poetry by William Blake – 'Song' and 'Reeds of Innocence'. A reviewer from *The Musical Times* felt that the latter had 'happy touches ... as well as some harshnesses that seem quite inappropriate'. Poldowski also continued to set French texts, with songs such as 'A Clymène' (1927) to a poem by Paul Verlaine and 'Narcisse' (1927) possibly to her own text and with an accompaniment for muted string quartet. Her late instrumental works included a *Pastorale* (1927) for clarinet in C and piano, *The Hall of Machinery – Wembley* (1928) for piano and a *Sonatine for Pianoforte* (1928).

Despite the early support of Henry Wood and some enthusiastic reviews, most of Poldowski's large-scale work remained unpublished, including the Violin Sonata, *Tenements* for orchestra, the symphonic drama *Silence* and a light opera *Laughter*. Some of these works were never performed. In a letter of 1924 to Chester she pointedly remarked, 'I have not had the luck to either produce my bigger works or get them published'. Towards the end of her life Poldowski may have been living apart from her husband and seems to have found herself in financial difficulties as the royalties from her music were assigned to her creditors while she was still alive. She died of bronchitis in January 1932, just a few days before a concert of her music had been due to take place at the Dorchester Hotel.

Oliveria Prescott
1842–1919

Born in London in 1842, Oliveria Prescott started studying composition with George Macfarren at the Royal Academy of Music in the early 1870s when she was already in her 30s. Her earliest surviving works date from her early student days. A song 'There is for every day a bliss', sub-titled 'a thought from St Basil' with words by J.W.H., was published in 1873. Two more works were published the following year: the four-part 'Song of Waterspirits' to words by E. Evans and 'Ask me no more', a song setting words from Alfred Tennyson's *Princess* with an interesting obbligato cello part. These were followed by two four-part anthems with organ accompaniment, 'Our conversation is in heaven' and 'The righteous live for evermore', found to be 'highly creditable' by *The Musical Times* in 1878.

Prescott remained at the Academy for seven years. In both 1876 and 1877 she was highly commended for the Academy's Charles Lucas medal for composition, and several of her early works, such as a Symphony and *Magnificat* for solo voices, chorus, orchestra and organ were heard at student concerts in St James's Hall. In April 1879 her *Concert Finale* for orchestra was played at a concert organized by the French pianist Jenny Viard-Louis. Unlike most of Prescott's other large-scale music, this work was published, although only in an arrangement for piano duet.

From the early 1880s Prescott was involved with the Musical Artists Society and served on the council for a time. The society gave many performances of her chamber music including 'a sacred work' (probably the *Magnificat*) in 1880, her Piano Quartet in G major in 1888, her String Quartet in C minor in 1892 and her String Quartet in G major, subtitled 'Be Happy', in 1894. *The Musical Times* found her C-minor quartet to be 'remarkable for vigour and terseness ... the whole work abounds in clever and effective passages'.

Prescott, who never married, also worked as a journalist and a lecturer. She gave various talks and lectures to schools and associations in London, including the Music School in Baker Street run by composer Clara Macirone, the Church of England High School and the Musical Association who heard a paper on 'Musical Design, a help to Poetic Intention' on 10 May 1892. A series of articles she had written for *The Musical World* were published as *Form or Design in Music* in 1880, with a revised edition issued in 1894. In this work Prescott identified three main elements of form: the balance of different keys, the recurrence of ideas and the observation of rhythm. She also made an interesting distinction between form as it is heard and form as it is seen written down, as well as, unusually for the time, describing form in music as a progressive and fluid concept. In 1904 she published *About Music, And What It Is Made Of*, a book which included the contribution of women to musical life, from Tudor virginal and lute players to the composers who were her contemporaries:

In a book written by a woman we may not omit the part which women have of late played in the orchestra of our musical world. Abroad, Mdlle Holmès, Mdlle Chaminade and others, and in England Virginia Gabriel, Alice Mary Smith, Maude Valérie White, Rosalind Ellicott, E.M. Smyth – and, may we add, the present writer? – have, among others, done work which has its share of influence in the making of what is now the modern musical style.

Prescott's membership of the Incorporated Society of Musicians, which included her works at a meeting in June 1911, and the Society of British Composers shows how important she felt her contribution to musical life to be. Yet very little of her music other than part-songs was ever published. Lists of her works, most of which have not survived, show that she composed several orchestral works including two symphonies, three overtures and a Piano Concerto in A major, subtitled 'Joy'. Only one of her six vocal works with orchestra, *Lord Ullin's Daughter*, was published, although with the orchestral accompaniment arranged for piano. This is a dramatic choral ballad telling the story of eloping lovers who are drowned in a storm at sea. One of her two children's operettas, *Carrigraphuga (The Castle of Fairies)*, a musical comedy in three acts written for the Guild of the Holy Child at St Etheldreda's, Fulham, was published in 1914 by Weekes & Co. Prescott died five years later, shortly after her 77th birthday.

Florence Price
1888–1953

Florence Price was born into an African–American middle-class family in Little Rock, Arkansas. Her father, James Smith, was a dentist who also wrote a novel and painted in his spare time. Her mother, Florence, had been a schoolteacher before her marriage and gave Price her first piano lessons. Price first performed the piano in public at the age of four and later took up the organ and the violin. She also began composing at an early age and had a piece of music published by the time she was 11.

After leaving school at the age of 14, Price became one of the very few African–American students at the New England Conservatory of Music in Boston where her principal studies were in piano and organ. During her student years she apparently wrote a symphony which was performed in Boston but which has not survived. In 1906, aged 19, Price graduated from the Conservatory and moved back to the South. For the next few years she taught music at the Arkadelphia

Academy in Cotton Plant and Shorter College in North Little Rock. In 1910 she moved to Atlanta, Georgia where she was head of the music department at Clark University.

Two years later, in 1912, Price returned to Little Rock, married lawyer Thomas J. Price and stopped teaching in public institutions. She had two daughters, born in 1917 and 1921, as well as a son who died in infancy. After her marriage, Price gave private violin, piano and organ lessons, although as an African–American she was refused admission to the Arkansas Music Teachers' Association. She also continued to compose, winning prizes for her music in magazine competitions.

In 1927 the Prices moved to Chicago, a decision doubtless made in part to escape the racial violence of the South. Throughout the early years of the 20th century many African–Americans from the impoverished, prejudiced South moved to Northern cities such as

Chicago, Washington and New York. These were the years of the 'Harlem Renaissance', the flowering of African–American art, literature and music that spread far beyond New York City. In Chicago, Price started to study composition, taking a variety of courses with different teachers, including Carl Busch, Leo Sowerby and Wesley LaViolette, at institutions such as the Chicago Musical College and the American Conservatory of Music. She continued to give private music lessons and wrote teaching pieces for the piano and music for radio commercials.

In 1928 four of Price's piano pieces were published but her first big success came in 1932 when she won first prizes in the Wanamaker Competition for her Symphony in E minor and her Piano Sonata in E minor, as well as receiving honourable mentions for her orchestral piece *Ethiopia's Shadow in America* and her *Piano Fantasie no. 4*. The following year Frederick Stock and the Chicago Symphony Orchestra gave the first performance of the Symphony at the Auditorium Theatre and repeated it later in the year for the Chicago World's Fair. Like most of Price's music, the Symphony is in an expressive, late-romantic idiom.

Price rarely quoted African–American folk music directly in her works but often used aspects of its rhythms or melodies. The third movement of the Symphony, for instance, is called 'Juba' and uses the rhythmic patterns of this old dance which involved syncopated clapping and thigh-slapping. Price's next large-scale work, the *Concerto in One Movement* in D minor for piano and orchestra, also used juba rhythms as well as opening with a typically spiritual-like melody. Price herself was the soloist in the first performance of this work in June 1934 at Orchestra Hall as part of the Commencement Exercises of Chicago Music College where she was taking composition courses. The concerto was played again in the autumn of that year by the Women's Symphony Orchestra of Chicago conducted by Ebba Sundstrom at the Century of Progress Exhibition in Chicago with Price's pupil, composer and pianist Margaret Bonds as soloist. The following year a highly successful gala concert of Price's music was organized in her home town, Little Rock.

Price continued to write a succession of orchestral works, including concertos, symphonies, overtures and a suite for orchestra. None of these works was published and they survive only in manuscript, although they were performed at concerts in the United States and in Europe. John Barbirolli commissioned Price to write a suite for strings based on spirituals, possibly the *Chicago Suite*, which he performed in Manchester. In November 1940, Price's Symphony no. 3 in C minor was premiered in Detroit.

She also continued to write piano pieces and vocal music. In 1941, her *Songs to the Dark Virgin*, settings of poetry by Langston Hughes, were published. They were sung by Marian Anderson and proved immediately successful. Price was always best known for her songs and spiritual arrangements. Her 1936 arrangement of 'My Soul's Been Anchored in the Lord', was recorded by Anderson and Leontyne Price among others. In 1942 Price's husband died. She continued to teach and to compose, writing her Second Violin Concerto the year before her death in 1953 at the age of 65.

Priaulx Rainier
1903–1986

Priaulx Rainier started composing comparatively late in her life and, almost entirely self-taught, developed a highly personal, complex and uncompromising musical language. She worked slowly and often in isolation, producing about 30 chamber, vocal and orchestral works. Rainier was born in Natal, South Africa close to the border with Kwazulu in 1903. Although she always denied using explicit references to African music, many critics have seen links with the place of her birth in the all-important rhythmic patterns and use of space in her music.

Early musical experiences came from the Western classical music played by her two older sisters, one of whom, Nella, was to give Rainier her first piano lessons. Rainier had violin lessons from the age of seven, and when the family moved to Cape Town in 1913, when she was 10, she became a violin student at the recently established College of Music. In 1920, at the age of 17, she won a University of South Africa Overseas Scholarship to study the violin at the Royal Academy of Music in London where she was to be based for the rest of her life. She studied with Hans Wessely and then with Rowsby Woolf and made a first attempt at composition, producing a string quartet movement in 5/8 time which ended on a discord. In 1925, after leaving the Academy, Rainier took up a teaching post at Badminton School and also worked as a violinist. One of the ways in which she made a living was by playing in cinemas.

In the mid-1930s Rainier had a serious car accident in which she damaged her shoulder. While recuperating, she started writing a duo for violin and piano which was later played by her violinist friend Orrea Pernel at a Wigmore Hall concert with pianist Harriet Cohen. Impressed by the music she produced, some friends clubbed together anonymously to give her a small sum of money so that she could concentrate on composing. In 1937 she went to Paris to study for 10 weeks

Priaulx Rainier

with Nadia Boulanger, the only composition teaching she ever received. That year she wrote the *Three Greek Epigrams* to words from Anyte of Tegea, followed in 1939 by her String Quartet. This was her first successful work, originally performed at the National Gallery Concerts in 1940 and then at the Wigmore Hall in 1944. It opens with a dark, intense *Allegro molto serioso* movement, followed by a short scherzo with driving rhythms. The slow movement builds a mournful lyricism out of motifs from the first movement, and the work ends with the biting, rhythmic dance of the finale.

In 1943 Rainier became a professor of composition at the Royal Academy of Music. She quickly gained a reputation as an excellent teacher but the job left her with little time for composition. In the following years there were few performances of her music. During the war, as well as working as an air-raid warden and on the land in Hertfordshire, Rainier developed some important friendships. One of these was with William Glock, who was working as a journalist and had reviewed her String Quartet for *The Observer*. He was later to become BBC controller of music.

Another friendship was with Michael Tippett and through him with Benjamin Britten and his lover, singer Peter Pears, who was to commission several works from Rainier. At this time Tippett was working for Morley College in London and asked Rainier to write a piece for the college orchestra. Rainier produced the powerfully rhythmic *Sinfonia da Camera* for string orchestra. William Walton was heard to say at the first performance given at the Central Hall in Westminster in 1947 that Rainier must wear barbed-wire underwear! In the late 1940s Rainier met Igor Stravinsky whose works were extremely important to her and whose love of dynamic rhythms so closely matched her own.

Most of Rainier's close friendships were not with other composers but with artists in different mediums. Always enthralled by movement and dance she lived for a while with dancer Pola Nirenska and her husband Jan. Another close friend was the writer Elizabeth Sprigge. The two women lived in separate flats in the same house in London and frequently travelled abroad together. But perhaps her most important friendships were with visual artists such as Henry Moore and Lucien Freud and especially with Barabara Hepworth and Ben Nicholson. The ideas of these two artists about the relationship between space and form and the movement of lines were to have important parallels in Rainier's music and in particular in her telling use of silence. Hepworth and Nicholson worked in St Ives in Cornwall and Rainier began to divide her time between St Ives and London, finding that she could find the concentration she needed to compose in the studios she rented in St Ives. In 1953, Rainier and Hepworth, with the help of Michael Tippett, organized an Arts Festival in St Ives.

Rainier's music from the 1940s included two songs for voice and guitar, *Dance of the Rain* and *Ubunzima*, written in 1947 but not heard until the 1970s, as well as the popular *Barbaric Dance Suite* for piano of 1948. In 1952 the Worshipful Company of Musicians awarded her the Collard Fellowship of £300 a year for three years. Over 30 years later she became the first woman to be elected to the livery of the Company. The fellowship enabled her to give up some of her teaching and spend more time on composition. In 1953 her *Cycle for Declamation*, a passionate setting of John Donne's *Devotions* for unaccompanied voice, commissioned by Peter Pears, was first performed. In 1956 he also sang in the first performance of her deeply moving *Requiem* for solo tenor and unaccompanied chorus at the Victoria and Albert Museum with the Purcell Singers conducted by Imogen Holst. The words for *Requiem* had been written for Rainier by David Gascoyne 16 years before.

In the early 1960s Rainier had a severe

accident which led to her retirement from her job at the Royal Academy of Music. This gave her even more time to compose. Elisabeth Lutyens was instrumental in getting her a Civil List pension in the mid-1960s which must have eased any financial worries. This gesture led to a long-lasting correspondence between the two composers. Rainier's letters show a sense of resignation at the lack of recognition for her music at the same time as a determination to continue producing it. She was particularly impressed by Lutyens' persistent battles for her own music.

The early 1960s were a time when Rainier's language changed, becoming more chromatic and fragmented. It was also a time when she began to receive more commissions, both from the BBC and from a variety of performers who admired her music. Yet performances of her music, especially any second performances after a premiere, were still infrequent and the critics were often antagonistic towards what were often mediocre performances of her admittedly difficult music. One of the first works in which Rainier's change of language was noticed was her first BBC commission, *Quanta* (1962) for oboe quartet. This striking work is a musical expression of the quantum theory in physics, of energy existing apart from matter, heard as clusters of notes which fragment without seeming to move anywhere. A string of BBC commissions and performances followed, including a Cello Concerto for Jacqueline du Pré that was premiered at the Proms in 1964 and a BBC Invitation Concert of her works in 1967 which included first performances of the String Trio (1966) and the Suite for Cello (1963–5). In the same year Rainier's orchestral suite *Aequora lunae*, dedicated to Barbara Hepworth and commissioned by the BBC, was premiered at the Cheltenham Festival.

Commissions continued in the 1970s. Peter Pears asked for another work, to be first performed at the Aldeburgh Festival in 1971. This was *The Bee Oracles* for tenor, flute, oboe, violin, cello and harpsichord, a setting of Edith Sitwell's poem 'The Bee-Keeper' based on an old Indian text. There were also two more performances of Rainier works at the Proms. The first, in 1973, was the premiere of *Ploërmel*, a dramatic and colourful work for wind and percussion inspired by the sound of bells and the play of light in the town of the same name that Rainier had visited while travelling in France. Her publishers, Schott, refused to publish the work, to Rainier's disappointment. The second Proms performance, in 1978, was of her violin concerto *Due Canti e Finale*, commissioned by Yehudi Menuhin and first heard at the Edinburgh Festival the year before.

Rainier continued to compose into the 1980s. Her last works included *Grand*

Duo (1980–82) for cello and piano, a work that has received many performances, and *Wildlife*, subtitled 'Celebration' (1984), for violin and orchestra, written for the 25th anniversary of the Jersey Wildlife Trust and first performed by Yehudi Menuhin and the Jersey Youth Orchestra in 1984. Two years previously Rainier had been awarded an honorary doctorate from the University of South Africa, having given a lecture tour in her native country a few years before. She died while on holiday in France in the autumn of 1986, working on settings of Rainer Maria Rilke's *Sonnets*.

Shulamit Ran
b. 1949

Shulamit Ran's German father and Russian mother emigrated to Israel in the early 1930s and their daughter was born in Tel Aviv. As a child, Ran believed that the music she could hear when she read poetry was a part of the poetry itself. She discovered the piano when she was about eight years old and started having lessons. Her piano teacher wrote down some of the songs Ran had been making up and sent them to the Israeli Broadcasting System. Ran was extremely excited by hearing her music on the radio and determined to continue being a composer. She studied both piano and composition with various teachers at the Tel Aviv Academy of Music and privately, making her debut as a pianist at the age of 12.

In 1962, when she was 14, Ran came to the United States with her parents when she won a piano scholarship to study at the Mannes College of Music in New York. She also continued to compose, taking composition lessons at Mannes with Norman Dello Joio. In 1963 she played her *Capriccio for Piano and Orchestra*, a work she describes as 'Gershwinesque', with the New York Philharmonic conducted by Leonard Bernstein in a performance broadcast on national television as part of the 'Young People's Concerts' series. In 1967 Ran graduated from Mannes, and in the same year premiered her *Symphonic Poem for Piano and Orchestra* with the Kol Israel Radio Orchestra conducted by Gary Bertini.

Over the next six years Ran performed throughout the United States as well as in Europe and Israel. In 1971 she played her brilliantly virtuosic *Concert Piece for Piano and Orchestra*, written the previous year, with the Israel Philharmonic Orchestra conducted by Zubin Mehta. She also wrote music for other instruments, including *O The Chimneys* (1969), an intense setting of five poems by Nelly Sachs about the Holocaust, for mezzo-soprano, flute, clarinet, cello, piano, percussion and tape. It was hearing a recording of this work that prompted Ralph Shapey to offer Ran a post in the music faculty at the University of Chicago in 1973. She accepted, gave up performing and moved to Chicago.

For over 10 years, with access to performances by the University of Chicago's Contemporary Chamber Players, Ran concentrated on writing chamber music, further developing her freely atonal and deeply expressive musical language. She took composition lessons from Shapey and spent a sabbatical year from 1977 to 1978 composing on a Guggenheim Fellowship. Her chamber music from the 1970s includes *Ensembles for 17* (1975), a setting of the final speech from William Shakespeare's *Othello* for soprano and 16 instruments, and *Double Vision* (1976) for woodwind quintet, brass quintet and piano. *Hyperbolae* (1976) for piano explores the extravagant connotations of its title with dramatic music that grows from the basic material of the opening bars. *Apprehensions* (1979), a setting of a poem by Sylvia Plath for voice, clarinet and piano, opens with a wordless lament from the singer. The feeling of lamentation continues throughout the work, with a powerfully moving vocal line using the full range of the voice with wide leaps, speech, sprechgesang, whispers, lyrical melismas and dramatic declamation. In this piece Ran felt she had found a 'new freedom of expression'. Several of her works from the early

1980s were for stringed instruments, including *Excursions* (1980) for violin, cello and piano, String Quartet no. 1 (1984) and *Fantasy Variations* (1984) for solo cello.

In 1986 Ran, who had previously been married to conductor and composer Cliff Colnot, married surgeon Dr Avraham Lofton with whom she has had two children. In the same year the American Composers Orchestra commissioned and premiered *Concerto for Orchestra*, Ran's first large-scale orchestral piece since her early works for piano and orchestra. In this four-movement work she explored the idea of each instrument or group of instruments acting and reacting as characters in a drama.

She was a visiting professor at Princeton University in 1987, and also underwent an operation to remove a tumour from the base of her skull. In the same year she followed her *Concerto da Camera I* (1985) for woodwind quintet with *Concerto da Camera II* for clarinet, piano and string quartet, a richly detailed and often impassioned work. Another important chamber-music piece, the String Quartet no. 2, subtitled 'Vistas' (1989), was written for the Taneyev String Quartet of Leningrad.

From 1989 to 1990 Ran took a year's sabbatical from her teaching post to write her three-movement Symphony, commissioned by the Philadelphia

Orchestra. In 1991 this work won a Pulitzer Prize in music. The year previously Ran had become composer-in-residence for the Chicago Symphony Orchestra. As well as providing opportunities for writing orchestral works, the post also put her in charge of the orchestra's contemporary music and educational programming. Feeling passionately that contemporary classical music has little opportunity for being heard, Ran has put a great deal of energy into successfully bringing new music to a wider audience, both through Chicago Symphony Orchestra concerts and her work with the radio station WFMT. Her concert series at Chicago's Orchestra Hall, 'Oh Them Rats Is Mean In My Kitchen', explored the links between classical and more popular music culture.

Although Ran was becoming increasingly involved in composing orchestral music, excited by the challenges and possibilities it offers, she also continued to write chamber music with works such as *Mirage* (1990) for flute, clarinet, violin, cello and piano which explores some of the sounds and rhythms of Middle Eastern music and *Inscriptions* (1991) for violin. In 1991 WFMT commissioned *Chicago Skyline* for brass and percussion which was first performed by the Chicago Symphony Orchestra conducted by Pierre Boulez. Ran's first large-scale work for the Chicago Symphony Orchestra was *Legends* (1992–3), a two-movement composition for an orchestra with a huge percussion section. Ran chose the title to communicate some of the aspects of storytelling that she felt were present in the piece, such as timelessness, heroism and mystery. It was first performed by the Chicago Symphony Orchestra, conducted by Daniel Barenboim in October 1993 to enthusiastic reviews. Ran has described composing as 'like going on an unknown voyage ... you never know where the piece will leave you'.

Caroline Reinagle
1818–1892

Caroline Reinagle was the daughter of actor and writer Mary Ann Orger, a popular performer on the London stage who was herself the daughter of a theatre musician. She briefly gave up performing when she married a Quaker from High Wycombe, but by the time her daughter was born she was appearing regularly at Drury Lane.

Nothing appears to be known about Reinagle's musical education but she established a career as a pianist from an early age as well as composing music. In May 1843 she was the soloist in a performance of her own Piano Concerto. For the next few years, while Reinagle was still in her 20s, her chamber works were regularly heard in London, especially at concerts given by the Society of British Musicians. In 1844 her Piano Trio was given its first performance, and in the same year the Society of British Musicians played her Piano Quartet no. 1. Three years later the Society also gave a performance of her Piano Quartet no. 2 in E♭ major. Her other chamber works of the 1840s

included a Sonata for cello and piano in G major but none of these works was published and they do not appear to have survived in manuscript. Only one work written before her marriage in 1846 has survived, a *Tarantella* for piano, published under her maiden name by Cocks & Co. as her op. 4. This is a fast, lively piece which builds to a dramatic climax.

Some sources give Reinagle's husband as an Arthur Reinagle but it seems most likely that she married the organist, teacher and composer Alexander Reinagle, who lived and worked in Oxford. After her marriage Reinagle worked as a piano teacher and continued to compose, publishing her songs and works for piano, including many teaching pieces. She may well have continued to write chamber music, but none has survived. One of her most substantial works is the Piano Sonata in A major, op. 6, published sometime after her marriage but before 1850 and dedicated to W.F. Donkin, a professor of astronomy at Oxford. This is a difficult, well-structured work in four movements that opens with a long *allegro moderato*, followed by a spirited *scherzo* and a tuneful *andante*, ending with an intricate *allegro cappriccioso*.

In 1862 *The Musical Times* serialized Reinagle's long article 'A Few Words on Pianoforte Playing' which gives instruction in aspects of technique such as correct accents, fingering and ornamentation. It is obviously aimed at a female reader, giving instructions on spreading chords for those with moderately sized hands, and in the final paragraphs referring to the

pianist as 'she'. Most of Reinagle's surviving songs date from the 1860s and include several settings of Adelaide Procter and Robert Browning. Her vocal writing is always fluent with complex piano accompaniment. In 1877 Reinagle's husband died in Kidlington, outside Oxford. She continued to compose, publishing in about 1880 *Two Songs* setting 'Come not when I am dead' by Alfred Tennyson and 'When I am dead, my dearest' by Christina Rossetti. These are dedicated to her cousins, Mr and Mrs Lazenby who lived at Tiverton, the town in which Reinagle died in 1892 at the age of 73.

Maria Hester Reynolds

(Maria Hester Park)

dates unknown – active from 1792

The works of Maria Hester Reynolds (who later married and became Maria Hester Park) are often mistakenly credited to Maria Parke, who was better known as a performer but appears to have written much less music. Reynolds was also a singer and pianist as well as a composer. Little can be traced about her life although she was one of the most prolific of 18th-century women composers. She first appears in Oxford where she seems to have been the harpsichord player for the permanent orchestra at the Music Room from 1772 to 1779. She also sang at the concerts held in this important music venue. The earliest surviving Oxford Music Room programme lists her singing a song by Sacchini in November 1773. In February 1779 she held a benefit concert at the Music Room.

Reynolds' earliest published works are her op. 1 sonatas of 1785 (dedicated to the Countess of Uxbridge) for harpsichord or pianoforte. By the time her op. 2 set of three keyboard sonatas was published in about 1790 she was living in London, at 121 Pall Mall. Her op. 3 set of six three- and four-part glees (including 'the Dirge in Cymbeline') was published after her marriage. From this point on, her name appears as Maria Hester Park with a few instances of M.H. Park, maybe an early attempt to disguise her gender.

Reynolds published at least 13 sets of work with opus numbers as well as other works that were not credited with numbers. Not all of these have survived, but those that have show her working in a variety of genres and styles. As well as the set of glees (her only surviving vocal music) and many sonatas for piano or harpsichord (often with violin accompaniment), Reynolds published divertimenti and duets for harp and piano, smaller pieces such as a waltz and a divertimento for the piano as well as a Piano Concerto (usually attributed to Maria Parke).

Although many of Reynolds' works, such as the opp. 1 and 2 keyboard sonatas, are simple pieces and obviously aimed at the genteel amateur market, other works are more complex and virtuosic, such as the second of the op. 4 keyboard sonatas or the Piano Concerto. These were probably works that Reynolds performed herself at concerts. The second sonata of the op. 13 set, although designated as a sonata 'for the Piano Forte, with an accompaniment for a Violin', has in fact a fully independent violin part. The Piano Concerto, op. 6, is a three-movement work with a lively first movement in sonata form, a lyrical slow movement and a vivacious final rondo.

Marga Richter
b. 1926

Marga Richter sees her work as a way of sharing her experience of the world and her feelings of mystery, beauty, joy, pain and loneliness. She has said, 'Music is the way I speak to the silence of the universe.' Her parents first met when her father heard her mother, soprano Inez Chandler, singing in Germany during the first world war. Their daughter was born near Madison, Wisconsin, in 1926, just before the family moved to Minnesota. Richter had piano lessons from the age of three and began composing at 12. At 14 she accompanied her mother in a public performance of one of her works.

In 1943, when Richter was 17, the family moved to New York so that she could study at the Juilliard School of Music. After initially majoring in piano she changed to composition when her piano teacher, Rosalyn Tureck, left the Juilliard. Richter's early music made extensive use of dissonance and all 12 notes of the octave. While she was still a student, several of her works, includ-ing a Sonata for clarinet and piano (1948) and the song cycle for voice and piano *Transmutation* (1949), were performed at a Composer's Forum concert in New York.

Richter graduated from the Juilliard with a master's degree in 1951 and two years later married academic Alan Skelly. She had two children, in 1956 and 1958, and until the early 1970s her family took priority over her composition. Nevertheless, several of the inventive and individual works that she wrote during these years became very well known.

In the later 1950s MGM took the unusual step of issuing a series of her works on record including her Concerto for piano and violas, cellos and basses (1957), *Lament* (1956) for string orchestra, *Aria and Toccata* (1957) for viola and string orchestra, *Transmutation* and *Two Chinese Songs* (1953) for voice and piano as well as a Piano Sonata (1954) that they had commissioned. MGM also issued two records of Richter performing music for children by herself and other composers. *Lament* for string orchestra is one of Richter's best-known pieces, an intense, grief-laden work dedicated to her mother who died of cancer on the day that Richter finished the score. The music, built on a single theme, gradually grows through a series of repetitions to a deeply felt climax and then slowly dies away.

Some of the first works Richter had written after her graduation had been for dance. In 1964 Harkness Ballet commissioned a work from her and she produced *Abyss*, an expansion and orchestration of her *Aria and Toccata*. This work was performed by many different ballet companies and played as a concert piece. A second ballet, *Bird of Yearning* (1967–8), was also commissioned by Harkness.

In 1968 Richter saw a painting by Georgia O'Keefe, *Sky Above Cloud II*, in a magazine and was immediately inspired to start writing a piece of music. She worked on the piano concerto *Landscapes of the Mind I* for the next six years. It is a work that seeks to convey spaciousness and serenity contrasted with turbulence and a feeling of isolation. The orchestra includes an amplified tamboura and the second section of the work is based around the classical Indian raga *marva*. When the work was first performed in 1976 it was an immediate success. In 1971, while she was writing *Landscapes of the Mind I*, Daniel Heifetz had asked her for a violin and piano piece. Richter wrote *Landscapes of the Mind II* for him and in 1978 wrote *Landscapes of the Mind III* for piano, violin and cello.

During the 1970s Richter relaunched her career. She started teaching at Nassau Community College and taking private piano pupils as well as performing her own piano works. In 1972 she was one of the founders of the Long Island Composers' Alliance, and three years later was involved in founding the League of Women Composers.

Many of Richter's works are inspired by places and the feelings that they evoke in her. *Blackberry Vines and Winter Fruit* (1976) for orchestra grew out of the winter landscape of Vermont where she spends part of the year. It opens with a desolate three-note rising and falling motif that is heard throughout the work. The bleak landscape is soon filled with fragments of orchestral colour and the music moves to a threatening climax after which it dies away. *Sonara* (1981) for two clarinets and piano was written after she had visited Arizona for the first time and uses the hollow tones of the clarinets to express the beautiful loneliness of the desert. *Out of Shadows and Solitude* (1985) for orchestra was inspired by a documentary on the Andes and the condor, while *Qhanri* (1988), subtitled 'Tibetan Variations', for cello and piano was written after Richter had been travelling in Tibet and uses a Tibetan chant that she heard there.

Richter's music creates a world which is often very beautiful and at the same time almost unbearably poignant, as in *Seacliff Variations* (1984) for violin, viola, cello and piano which presents a variety of moods in its intense exploration of a simple theme. Another moving work is *Into My Heart* (1990), settings of seven poems by various authors for chorus, oboe, violin, brass sextet, timpani and percussion which is dedicated to the memory of Richter's husband who had died in 1988. On a lighter note is the short orchestral piece, *Quantum Quirks of a Quick Quaint Quark* (1991), a work inspired by the image of 'boundless good-humoured energy' and later transcribed for organ and for piano.

Richter often makes use of borrowed material that she then radically changes. *Düsseldorf Concerto* (1981–2) for flute, viola, harp, percussion and strings, commissioned by Düsseldorf New Music Ensemble and first performed in Salzburg, uses material from Robert Schumann, Johannes Brahms, Ludwig van Beethoven, Sofia Gubaidulina and the hymn tune 'Open my eyes that I may see'. The prologue from Claudio Monteverdi's *Orfeo* is used as the theme of *... beside the still waters* (1992), subtitled 'variations and interludes' for piano, violin, cello and orchestra. The interludes of this work grew out of improvisation around J.S. Bach's C major Prelude. Much of the music is permeated with early Baroque textures which grow into dramatic and occasionally chilling outbursts. Towards the end of the work the piano plays the Bach prelude accompanied by a hauntingly dissonant melody from the violin and cello. This is followed by long cadenzas from each solo instrument before the orchestra remembers the *Orfeo* material and the work ends.

Helen Roe
b. 1955

Helen Roe was born in Bournemouth in 1955. Her father was a parish priest (later to become Bishop of Ely), and one of Roe's earliest musical experiences was singing in the church choir. She had piano and violin lessons and started to write music at an early age, producing an Oboe Concerto in D major when she was about nine. The family moved to Abingdon in Oxfordshire in the early 1960s, and Roe had harmony and counterpoint lessons from local composer Bryan Kelly. When she was in her early teens the family moved to Durham where Roe continued to write music for her school friends to play. After leaving school in 1973 she studied composition with composer David Lumsdaine for a year and finally began to find ways to structure her musical ideas.

In 1974 Roe went to study music at Jesus College, Oxford while continuing to study with Lumsdaine in the vacations. She later had lessons from other composers, including Nicola LeFanu and Peter Wiegold. Her piano piece *Ash Wednesday*, written as an exercise for Lumsdaine, was broadcast as part of the BBC Young Composers' Forum in 1976. Roe has described the work as a 'meditation' on T.S. Eliot's poem which she also used to generate some of the structures and harmony of the music.

Her next work to be heard on the radio was the intense *Die Blaue Blume*, written in 1975, first performed the following year in Oxford and broadcast in 1977. For high soprano with oboe, clarinet, viola, cello and percussion, *Die Blaue Blume* uses four poems from Johann Wolfgang Goethe's play *Wilhelm Meister*, with the pensive 'Kennst du das Land' as the central text of the piece. In the first of the work's three cycles, verses from all four poems are used. In the second cycle, 'Kennst du das Land' begins to be heard as the central song, interrupted by fragments of the other poems. In the third cycle 'Kennst du das Land' is heard on its own. The final text that Roe has created in this way focuses on a feeling of not belonging and a yearning for something other. Once again the pitches and harmonies of this work, which is dominated by a passionate vocal line, are generated by patterns thrown up from the text.

Roe graduated from Jesus College in 1978. The same year saw the first performance of *Close by the place where ...*, a piece for flute, clarinet, viola and cello which worked elements of a Bach prelude into the tone row used to generate the harmonic material. In 1978 Roe also married Nigel Timms who had been a student of Lumsdaine's at Durham University. For two years after her marriage she concentrated on composing, while working part-time in a bar. Her major work from this period was her String Quartet (1980), commissioned by the Radcliffe Trust, which works a transformation of the opening material through a series of refrains. Roe then embarked on a year of teacher-training. During this time she and Timms organized a composers' co-operative called Soundpool for which she wrote several works, including one for solo violin, *Notes towards a definition* (1981), which later became a test piece for the Carl Flesch International Violin Competition.

Roe's three sons were born between 1981 and 1985, a period when she was writing shorter works such as *Verbum supernum prodiens/Conditor alme siderum* (1983) for flute and guitar and *Five Edington Melodies* for solo oboe or clarinet. Most of Roe's works since the mid-1980s have used text in a variety of different ways and she has developed increasingly complex methods of exploring these texts and using them to build her musical structures. She wrote her own words for *And the angel departed from her* (1986) for mezzo-soprano, flute, horn, marimba and string trio. Roe suggests that the work be performed with the singer looking into a mirror with her back to the audience. *And the angel* creates a powerfully rapt vision of the Virgin Mary at Advent, a woman waiting for the birth of her child. Once again the text influences the harmony of the work which is based on several plainsong advent hymns, including the antiphon *Alma Redemptoris mater.*

In the 1988 piano piece *My mind's white truth,* Roe explored the phonemic shape of the phrase 'my mind's white truth' from one of John Donne's *Divine Poems* and used the resulting pattern of degrees of resonance to generate the shape of the work. The shape of each of the four movements follows the shape of each word. This interest in using phonemic patterns was continued in her two e.e. cummings settings, *this is the garden* (1987) for tenor, flute, clarinet and string quartet and *joyful your complete fearless and pure love* (1988) for tenor, clarinet and hand drums.

During the 1990s Roe has focused her

work on opera and music theatre. She met writer Russell Hoban at a meeting of the English National Opera's Contemporary Opera Studio in 1989 and the two then collaborated on the 'entertainment' *Some Episodes in the History of Miranda and Caliban* (1990) for two singers, narrator, ensemble and tape. Roe felt that Hoban's densely allusive libretto needed very straight-forward music so that the text could be clearly heard and understood. She produced a mixture of different kinds of text setting (spoken word; rhythmically notated speech; a recitative-type approach and lyrical song or duet) and, in terms of her own complex, post-serial idiom, radically simple yet very effective music. This simplification of her musical language can also be seen in the music-theatre piece *Two Queens of the Ile of Britain* (1991) for two sopranos who also play the harpsichord and bells and for which Roe created her own text from

the writings of Mary Queen of Scots and Elizabeth I.

In 1992 Roe was awarded the Gemini Fellowship for composers from the Worshipful Company of Musicians, a two-year grant to enable her to write her long-planned opera based on Hans Christian Andersen's *The Little Mermaid* and Henrik Ibsen's *The Lady from the Sea*. These are both works that Roe sees as being 'concerned with a conflict in a woman between the life she's born to and expected to live and something from outside that she yearns towards ...'. While working on this project she also completed a chamber-music piece *Divide Light if you dare* (1992) for clarinet, piano and string quartet and worked with a group of composers, poets and an installation artist on *Song Cycle*, a collaborative music-theatre work for the Women's Playhouse Trust.

Clara Kathleen Rogers
1844–1931

Clara Kathleen Rogers was born in Cheltenham in 1844. Her earliest music lessons came from her mother, the daughter of the cellist Robert Lindley, and her father John Barnett, a singing teacher and composer of many operas and songs. In 1857 her mother took Rogers and her older sister and brother, Rosamond Liszt (named after her godfather) and Domenico (named after Dragonetti), to Leipzig to study at the Conservatoire. At 12, Rogers was the youngest student the Conservatoire had ever accepted. She studied the piano and singing as well as taking Hans Richter's class in harmony and counterpoint. In 1858 the young Arthur Sullivan came to study at the Conservatoire and soon became close to the whole family, including Rogers' cousin John Barnett who was also studying there.

At 14, Rogers wrote a string quartet, primarily to impress Sullivan who then arranged for it to be played. It seems to be this performance that prompted the authorities to arrange for composition classes at the Conservatoire to be made available for women. Rogers graduated in 1860 and decided to concentrate on singing as a career. She took further lessons in Berlin and Milan before making her debut in Turin under the name Clara Doria. Rogers spent several years working as an opera singer in Italy before reluctantly returning to England. Here she maintained that her father ruined her chances of an operatic career by writing an angry letter to the influential impresario who was going to promote her about his advertising techniques. After this she had to concentrate on singing in oratorio and at concerts.

In 1872 Rogers went to the United States on tour with the Parepa-Rosa Opera Company, making her American debut singing in Michael Balfe's *The Bohemian Girl* in New York. The next year she settled in the United States, first in New York and then in Boston, where she performed and taught singing. In 1875 she embarked on an eight-month tour with the violinist Camilla Urso which took them all over the United States and Canada. Three years later she married the lawyer Henry Munroe Rogers. After her marriage Rogers retired from performing in public but continued to teach, although even this level of professional musical activity went against the advice of most of her friends. She felt that it was impossible for her to abandon her career completely and luckily her husband agreed with her. She became involved in several local music clubs and founded a Bach Club in 1883. She also gave weekly musicales at her house which were frequented by Boston musicians and composers such as Edward MacDowell, George Chadwick, Benjamin Lang and Arthur Foote.

Rogers had continued to compose, and after giving successful performances of her songs at various clubs, she offered some of them to Arthur Schmidt for publication. Her first set of *Six Songs* was published in 1882 and was described in the *Musical Herald* as 'one of the most poetic and genuinely beautiful that we have seen for a long time'. From that moment on she put all the energy that she had previously used in performing into her composition. Most of her works were songs and she always regretted that she had not been given the training to compose orchestral music. She wrote several piano pieces, including a *Scherzo* (1883), op. 15, and a

Romanza (1895), op. 31.

Her chamber music included a Cello Sonata and a *Sonata Dramatice* in D minor, op. 25, for violin and piano that was played in 1888 at the first meeting of the Manuscript Club. This club aimed to give performances of works by little-known composers and included in the same programme some early songs by Margaret Ruthven Lang. Rogers' violin sonata lives up to its title, opening with a robust, forthright theme which dominates the first movement. The slow second movement has some beautiful, lyrical writing for the violin with a delicate piano accompaniment and is followed by an ardent *allegro giocoso* with some wonderfully operatic moments.

In 1893 several of Rogers' songs were performed at the Woman's Musical Congress held during the World's Columbian Exposition in Chicago, including 'Out of my own Great Woe', a deeply felt setting of a poem by Heinrich Heine in a translation by Elizabeth Barrett Browning and 'Ah, Love but a Day' to words by Robert Browning, whose work had a special appeal for Rogers. She wrote two song cycles, op. 27 (1893) and op. 32 (1900), and several solo songs using his poetry.

Teaching was very important to Rogers and she had firm ideas about how singing should be taught, writing her first book on the subject,

The Philosophy of Singing, in the early 1890s. This was followed by *My Voice and I* (1899), a psychological study of singing, and *Clearcut Speech in Song* (1927). She also wrote two volumes of autobiography, *Memories of a Musical Career* (1919) and *The Story of Two Lives* (1932). In 1902 Rogers accepted Chadwick's offer of a post as a professor of singing at the New England Conservatory which she interrupted in 1903 with a journey round the world with her husband. They visited Japan, China, Hong Kong, India and Egypt before returning home through Greece and Italy. The music that Rogers heard on her travels does not seemed to have impressed her. In her account *Journal-Letters from the Orient* (1934) she described a performance of Indian music that she heard in Delhi, finding it 'not pretty' and having 'all sorts of disturbing flourishes'.

Rogers was also unimpressed by the ultra-modern music of the 1920s which she found monotonous. Her own music, much of which remained in manuscript, always retained the harmonies and structures of the romantic music of her youth. She appears to have stopped composing some time before she died in 1931 at the age of 87.

Charlotte Sainton-Dolby
1821–1885

Charlotte Sainton-Dolby was probably the best-known contralto of her day, acclaimed throughout England and Europe for her singing of ballads and oratorio. She was born Charlotte Dolby in London in 1821 into a middle-class 'trading' family and sent to school at Mrs Sulch's establishment where she received her first piano lessons. She later took private piano lessons and started to train her voice. When her father died and the family were left with little money, it was decided that Sainton-Dolby should train for a musical career. She entered the Royal Academy of Music in 1832 at the age of 11 and studied there for over five years, being elected a King's Scholar in 1837.

In 1840 Sainton-Dolby was one of the founder members of the Royal Society of Female Musicians. She started appearing in public in the early 1840s, singing her first solo at a Philharmonic Society concert in 1842. She appeared at a wide variety of London concerts, including Ann Mounsey Batholomew's series of Classical Concerts at Crosby Hall in the mid-1840s. In 1847 Felix Mendelssohn arranged for her to appear at the distinguished Gewandhaus Concerts in Leipzig. He also wrote several works for her, including the contralto part in his oratorio *Elijah*.

Music by Sainton-Dolby appeared in print as early as the 1850s. Her earliest published song was 'Lady, I think of thee', issued in 1856. She also published her own arrangements of the songs in her repertoire such as 'Charlie yet' (1853), a 'jacobite melody ... newly arranged by C.H. Dolby', or an even earlier edition of 'Bonnie Dundee', ' ... as sung by Miss Dolby ... by whom the symphonies & accompaniments are arranged'.

In 1860 Sainton-Dolby married the French violinist Prosper Sainton who had settled in England in 1845. The couple had one son, Charles. Sainton-Dolby continued to perform, hyphenating her new married name to her own. She became particularly associated with the songs and ballads of Claribel as well as singing the work of many other composers. In 1870, at the age of 49, she left the public stage to concentrate on teaching and composing. In 1872 she founded her famous Vocal Academy and published a *Tutor for English Singers*. The Vocal Academy gave regular London concerts which often included Sainton-Dolby's own works. Most of these are simple songs and ballads that became very popular, especially her many settings of lyrics by ballad writer F.E. Weatherly such as 'When we are old and grey' and 'The White Cockade'.

Sainton-Dolby also wrote four cantatas. The most popular was the earliest, *The Legend of Dorothea*, first performed in June 1876 at St James's Hall and published in 1876 with individual numbers also printed separately, including a 'Triumphal March' arranged for piano and piano duet. This is a large-scale work for five soloists and chorus, telling the story of the early Christian martyr Dorothea and the non-believer Theophilus. It was followed by *The Story of the Faithful Soul* to words by Adelaide Procter, a simpler work on a smaller scale which was given its premiere at a concert given by pupils from her Vocal Academy at the Steinway Hall in June 1879 and published in 1880. A third cantata *Thalassa, the Sea Maiden* was never published.

Charlotte Sainton-Dolby

Sainton-Dolby's final cantata, *Florimel* for female voices to a text by J.A. Blaikie, was published posthumously by Novello. The work, dedicated to Alexander Mackenzie, with a virtuoso part for the heroine, tells the story of a princess who sets up an 'order of shepherdesses' who have no communication with men on the outside world. It was first performed at Sainton-Dolby's memorial concert on 24 April 1885 at Prince's Hall.

Daria Semegen
b. 1946

Daria Semegen was born in West Germany to Ukranian parents and came to the United States as a refugee at the age of four. She started studying the piano at six. Fascinated by being able to write down the sounds of music, she soon started composing piano pieces. Her various piano teachers taught her theory and she continued to compose. A string quartet she had written was performed while she was still at school.

Semegen studied at the Eastman School of Music for four years, graduating in 1968. She made her first experiments with tape at this time, creating a piece called *Six Plus* with fellow student Bob Ludwig. This used a tape collage of a chamber ensemble work together with a live performance of that same piece. Most of her student works were acoustic and written in a complex serialist idiom. They included pieces such as *Suite for Flute and Violin* (1965), the William Blake setting *Silent, Silent Night* (1965) for tenor and piano, and *Study for 16 Strings* (1968).

After graduating from Eastman, Semegen won a Fulbright scholarship and spent a year in Poland studying with Witold Lutoslawski and exploring electronic music at the Warsaw Conservatory and the Polish Radio Station. In 1969 she wrote *Poème Premier: Dans la Nuit*, a setting of a text by Henri Michaux for baritone and orchestra, given a first performance six years later in 1975. On her return to the United States that year she went to Yale University to study for a master's degree with Bulent Arel, a composer with whom she was to work for many years. A piece from this period, *Jeux de Quatres* (1970), a 'game' for clarinet, trombone, piano and cello in five short movements, shows Semegen experimenting with aleatoric devices and developing her own system of notation. She has compared working with aleatoric music to creating a three-dimensional mobile.

In 1971, after receiving her master's degree from Yale, Semegen was awarded a postgraduate scholarship to study at the Columbia-Princeton Electronic Music Center. She worked at the Center for five years, studying with Vladimir Ussachevsky and doing some teaching herself. She also worked as a sound engineer for the Boulton Collection of World Music and on preparing material for recordings. In 1971 she collaborated with Arel on an electronic film score, *Out of Into*, and the following year completed her first significant work for two-channel tape, *Electronic Composition No. 1*. This work was built around two contrasting kinds of sound: long, sustained sounds and short, fast sounds.

Semegen continued to write acoustic works. Her *Music for Violin Solo* (1973) was played at the 1978 International Society for Contemporary Music World Music Days in Finland and published by Columbia University Press in 1981. She was later to follow this work with a series of acoustic pieces with similar titles: *Music for Clarinet Solo* (1980), *Music for Cello Solo* (1981), *Music for Contrabass Solo* (1981) and *Music for Violin and Piano* (1988) which was the first McKim commission from the Library of Congress to be given to a woman.

It is for electronic music, however, that Semegen is best known. Like Jean Eichelberger Ivey, she has compared working alone with electronic music in a studio to working as a painter or sculptor who creates her work without relying on others to realize her

conception. Semegen herself has produced paintings that have been exhibited at the Eastman Gallery. In 1974 she joined the music faculty at the State University of New York at Stony Brook where she helped to design and run the Electronic Music Studios with Bulent Arel as director. Her first works created at Stony Brook, although they had been started at the Columbia-Princeton Center, were the experimental *Spectra Studies* (1974–6).

In 1977 she worked with choreographer Mimi Garrard on *Arc: Music for Dancers*, creating the music after Garrard had worked out the choreography and the complicated lighting arrangements which were computer-generated and had to be synchronized exactly with the music. She worked with Garrard again on *Epicycles* (1982), a piece for three female dancers. In 1979 Semegen followed *Electronic Composition No. 1* with *Electronic Composition No. 2: Spectra*. Once again the piece explores two contrasting sounds, a sustained drone or pedal point and a group of differing and detached sounds, but this time using more complex and sophisticated equipment to create the sounds.

In 1980 Semegen became co-director of the Stony Brook Studios, and was made director in 1989. She has continued to explore new ways of creating sounds and music with works such as *Rhapsody* (1990) for the Yamaha MIDI piano and *Arabesque* (1992) for two-channel tape, created using analogue and digital equipment as well as traditional tape splicing. *Arabesque* was commissioned as a tribute to Bulent Arel and was first performed at a League of Composers/International Society for Contemporary Music concert.

Alice Mary Smith
(Mrs Meadows White)
1839–1884

The daughter of an upper-class family, Alice Mary Smith studied music privately with William Sterndale Bennett and George Macfarren and started publishing her songs in the late 1850s. These early songs included 'Sing on sweet thrush' to words by Robert Burns and 'Weep no more!' to words by the early 17th-century playwright John Fletcher. Both were described as 'canzonets', probably to distinguish them from simpler and less prestigious 'ballads'. Another early work published at about this time was *Vale of Tempe*, a difficult and atmospheric rondo for piano.

In 1861, at the age of 21, Smith had a Piano Quartet in B♭ major performed at a play-through of new works by the Musical Society of London. This organization had been formed in 1858 by a group of professional and amateur musicians as a body that would promote concerts, provide less formal opportunities for playing through new compositions and give lectures on music. The Musical Society performed Smith's String Quartet in D major in November 1862, a Symphony in C minor the following year and an *Introduction and Allegro* for piano and orchestra in 1865. Her overtures *Endymion* and *Lalla Rookh* were given play-throughs in 1864 and 1865. Other early works by Smith were heard at concerts given by the New Philharmonic Society. These included a Piano Quartet in D (1864), and another String Quartet.

In 1867 Smith married Frederick Meadows White, a QC with a keen interest in music who acted as honorary counsel to the Royal Society of Musicians. After her marriage she continued to publish her music as Alice Mary Smith, adding her married name in brackets afterwards. The same year Smith was elected a Female Professional Associate of the prestigious Philharmonic Society. Two years later she published an *Impromptu* for piano and a *Melody and Scherzo* for cello and piano. Smith also continued to write and publish her songs, duets and part-songs. Some of these became very popular, in particular the wistful duet 'Maying' to words by Charles Kingsley which was first published in about 1870 and still being reprinted as late as 1944.

In the 1870s Smith's music, always well-structured with elegantly expressive melodies, began to be heard further afield. She revised *Endymion* for performance at the Crystal Palace in 1871, and the following year her Clarinet Concerto was played at the Norwich Festival. The New Philharmonic Society continued to programme her works. The overture to *The Masque of Pandora*, first heard at a New Philharmonic Society concert in July 1878, was also heard at the Crystal Palace Saturday Concerts and at the Liverpool Philharmonic Society. The overture *Jason, or the Argonauts and Sirens* was first performed at a New Philharmonic Society concert in June 1879 and was heard again at a Crystal Palace Saturday Concert in May 1881. Such numerous performances of large-scale works at prominent venues were unusual, especially for a woman composer.

Smith's achievements in the 1870s and 80s generated an intense debate about the position of women as composers and whether it was possible for a woman to become a 'great composer'. Stephen Stratton's ground-breaking paper given to the Royal Musical Association in May 1883 on 'Woman in

Relation to Musical Art' referred to press comments about some of Smith's works including the charge that one of her cantatas was 'simply a striking reproduction of masculine art' and that another 'proves that talent is of neither sex'. In the discussion following the paper Frederick Meadows White was asked to comment and he reassured the audience that ' ... there is nothing inconsistent with the little eminence my wife has attained in music with the good management of domestic affairs'.

In the 1880s Smith concentrated on writing large-scale vocal works with orchestra, perhaps because such music could be easily performed by the many choral societies throughout the country. Her first such work, *Rudesheim or Gisela* for soloists or chorus with small orchestra, had been given its first performance at the Fitzwilliam Musical Society in Cambridge in 1865. Over 10 years later came her second and best-known cantata. This was the dramatic *Ode to the North-East Wind*, a setting of Charles Kingsley's poem for chorus and orchestra, first heard with piano accompaniment at a Musical Society concert in 1878 and then performed in full by the Hackney Choral Association in November 1880.

In 1882 Smith's cantata *Ode to the Passions* for soloists, chorus and orchestra to words by the 18th-century poet William Collins was premiered at the Three Choirs Festival in Hereford. A reviewer found that the first London performance of this work at St James's Hall on April 30 1883 'revealed new beauties, both in the vocal and orchestral details – an unfailing proof of careful and earnest workmanship which merits record'. It is an elaborate work full of sharply contrasting music to portray the various passions.

Smith's last two completed cantatas were both further settings of Kingsley. *Song of the Little Baltung* for men's voices and orchestra was first performed by the Lombard Amateur Musical Association in 1883 and *The Red King* was first heard at a Musical Society concert in 1885 just before Smith's early death in December of that year at the age of 45. Another cantata, *The Valley of Remorse,* to a text by a Miss Bevington, was left unfinished.

Ode to the North-East Wind, Ode to the Passions, Song of the Little Baltung and *The Red King* were all published by Novello and continued to be performed by choral societies throughout England well into the 20th century. Apart from a few smaller instrumental pieces and the choral works mentioned, none of Smith's chamber or orchestral music, including a Second Symphony in G major which was never performed, was published. Luckily, however, many of her manuscripts have recently been rediscovered.

Julia Smith
1911–1989

Although Julia Smith lived and worked in New York for most of her life, she was born in Denton, Texas and her music often uses folk idioms from the music of both the Native Americans and the white settlers in that part of the United States. Smith was a prolific composer who wrote many orchestral works and six operas as well as chamber and vocal music. She was given her first piano lessons by her mother, who had studied voice and piano at college.

Smith studied for her first degree at North Texas State College, where she composed the college 'alma mater' song, and graduated in 1930 at the age of 19. She then moved to New York where she embarked on further musical study at the Juilliard School of Music, taking piano lessons with Carl Friedberg who encouraged her to compose and about whom she later wrote a book. Smith also took courses at New York University towards a master's degree which she was awarded in 1933. That same year she was given a composition fellowship at the Juilliard to study with Rubin Goldmark, who was initially reluctant to accept her as a pupil, claiming that all his other women students had eventually given up their careers to look after their families.

Smith first met the pioneering conductor Frederique Petrides in a conducting class at New York University and the two women soon became close friends. In 1933 Smith became the pianist of Petrides' newly formed all-woman orchestra, the Orchestrette Classique. The Orchestrette gave several premieres of Smith's early works such as the *Little Suite Based on American Folk Tunes*, first performed in the Aeolian Hall in New York in February 1936; *Episodic Suite*, first performed in 1937; and *Hellenic Suite*, a work based on Greek folk materials, dedicated to Petrides and first performed in 1941.

In the mid-1930s, while still studying at the Juilliard, Smith undertook a variety of part-time jobs as teacher and arranger. In 1938 she married engineer Oscar Vielehr who proved to be a supportive husband, even copying orchestral parts for her at times. In February 1939 Smith had her first big success when her opera *Cynthia Parker* was premiered at the North Texas State College in a performance partly sponsored by the Juilliard. She had begun work on the opera in 1934, against the advice of Goldmark. To a libretto by Jan Isbel Fortune set in Texas, it tells the story of a white girl brought up by Comanches. In her setting, Smith incorporated Native American themes into a traditionally European operatic style.

Later in 1939 the Juilliard Orchestra gave the first performance of Smith's Piano Concerto, a three-movement work using folk and jazz idioms. In the same year she graduated from the Juilliard. As well as continuing to compose and perform, Smith took up a number of teaching positions over the next few years, working at the Juilliard (1940–42) and the New Britain (Connecticut) State Teachers' College (1944–6) as well as founding a music-education department at Hartt College in Connecticut (1941–6).

During this time she wrote several chamber works and the short orchestral piece *Liza Jane*, as one of 20 composers commissioned by CBS to write a work based on an American folk tune. She also continued to write opera. *The*

Stranger of Manzano to a libretto by John William Rogers, completed in 1943, was premiered in Dallas in 1946, and her children's opera *The Gooseherd and the Goblin* to a libretto by Josephine Royle, commissioned by Hartt College, was first performed in 1947. In the same year she started studying for a doctorate at New York University, working on composition with Marion Bauer and writing a thesis on the music of Aaron Copland which was eventually published in 1955.

Smith's *Folkways Symphony* was first performed in January 1949. The four movements of this work have the titles 'Day's a-breakin'', 'Night Herding Song', 'Cowboy's Waltz' and 'Stomping Leather', and it makes extensive use of Western-American hoedown and fiddle tunes. In the following years Smith wrote two more operas: *Cockcrow* (1953) to a libretto by Constance D'Arcy Mackay, and *The Shepherdess and the Chimney Sweep* (1963), also to a libretto by Mackay after a story by Hans Christian Andersen. *Our Heritage*, a patriotic large-scale choral orchestral work to a text by Arthur Sampley, was commissioned by the Texas Boys choir and first performed in 1957. Smith's continuing use of infectious, dance-like rhythms can be heard in one of her most successful chamber works, the String Quartet of 1964.

Always a strong supporter of other women composers, in the late 1960s

Smith organized a chamber-music concert of works by five women composers from all over the United States which was widely reported in the media. She was then asked by the National Federation of Music Clubs to compile a *Directory of American Women Composers*, published in 1970. She was chair of the Federation's Decade of Women and in 1971 she successfully lobbied the National Endowment for the Arts to start giving large-scale grants to women composers. Smith herself continued to compose into her 60s and 70s. Her later works included her sixth opera *Daisy* (1973), telling the story of Juliette Gordon Low, the founder of the Girl Scouts in the United States, and her song-cycle *Prairie Kaleidoscope* (1982), settings of O.M. Ratcliffe for soprano and string quartet. Smith died in New York in 1989.

Ethel Smyth
1858–1944

Ethel Smyth was a woman of immense and sometimes overwhelming vitality, which found its way into everything she did, from playing tennis and golf, bicycling and mountaineering to supporting women's campaigns for the vote and their right to play in orchestras. She made no secret of the importance of her relationships with women, and her many friends and lovers played central roles in her tempestuous life. Above all, she poured endless passion and energy into her music and her continuous battles to ensure that it was heard.

Smyth was born into an upper-class family in Sidcup, just outside London, in 1858. In 1867 her father, a general in the army, moved the family to Frimley, near Aldershot in Surrey. One of Smyth's governesses had studied music at the Conservatory in Leipzig. Entranced by her playing of Beethoven, Smyth decided, at the age of 12, that she too would one day go to Leipzig and study music. But she had to face the opposition of her father who refused even to consider the idea of one of his daughters studying for a profession in the musical world.

In the mid-1870s Smyth had some harmony lessons from Alexander Ewing, an officer in the army service corps, which were stopped abruptly when her father discovered what he thought to be a compromising letter from Ewing to his daughter. Showing characteristically headstrong determination, Smyth decided to make her family's life so miserable that they would have to let her go to Leipzig. She refused to sing and play the piano after dinner, attend church or go riding, an activity which she adored. Eventually her father relented and in the summer of 1877, at the age of 19, Smyth left for Germany.

Smyth found the teaching at the Leipzig Conservatory disappointing, and only studied there for a year. Instead she took private lessons from Heinrich von Herzogenberg whose talented wife Lisl was one of the first of the women with whom Smyth was to fall passionately in love. Through the Herzogenbergs, Smyth became part of a musical circle that included Clara Schumann and Johannes Brahms, who nicknamed her 'the Oboe'.

Smyth's music began to be heard in Leipzig. Some of her earliest works were two collections of songs to German texts, later published by Peters as her opp. 3 and 4. She also wrote several piano works including three sonatas and *Variations on an Original Theme (of an Exceedingly Dismal Nature)*. Her String Quintet, with its vigorous driving rhythms and poignant slow movement, was performed at the Leipzig Gewandhaus in 1883 and published as her op. 1 by Peters the following year. At this time Smyth became caught up in a complicated relationship with Lisl von Herzogenberg's brother-in-law Harry Brewster, an Anglo-American writer and philosopher. Although they did not at this point become lovers, their feelings for each other caused an unbreachable rift between Smyth and the Herzogenbergs. Smyth was devastated at the loss of Lisl, but consoled herself with other friendships and Marco, first of the many dogs who were her perpetual companions.

During the late 1880s Smyth concentrated on writing chamber music. In 1887 her dramatic Sonata in A minor for violin and piano, op. 7, was performed by Adolph Brodsky and

Fanny Davies at the Leipzig Gewandhaus and published by J. Reiter Biedermann. The critics were not universally impressed. One of them found the work to be 'deficient in the feminine charm that might have been expected of a woman composer'. Meanwhile Smyth was being encouraged to study orchestration and write orchestral music by Pyotr Tchaikovsky.

By 1890 Smyth had settled back in England, and in the spring of that year August Manns conducted her four-movement orchestral work *Serenade in D* at the Crystal Palace, followed in October by her *Overture to Shakespeare's Antony and Cleopatra*. Early in 1890 Smyth had started work on her Mass in D, inspired by the devout Catholicism of her friend Pauline Trevelyan. In the autumn of 1891, Smyth played the work to Queen Victoria. Smyth's own performances of her music, playing the piano and singing as many parts as she could, were always commanding and exhilarating occasions.

After pressure from Smyth's well-connected friends, such as Lady Mary Ponsonby, one of the Queen's maids of honour, and the Empress Eugénie, widow of Napoleon III, Joseph Barnby and the Royal Choral Society finally performed the Mass at the Royal Albert Hall in January 1893. The audience and most of the critics were impressed and one of Smyth's sisters' hunting friends called it 'slashing stuff'. From the sombre opening of the Kyrie through to the ebullient joy of the final Gloria, it is a compelling and heartfelt work. The Empress Eugénie, always a devoted supporter of Smyth and her music, paid for it to be published.

Smyth had always wanted to write opera, and in 1892 had begun work on *Fantasio*, a two-act comic opera to a German libretto, based on a play by Alfred de Musset. She wrote the libretto herself in collaboration with Harry Brewster, with whom she had started corresponding after he came to the performance of her *Serenade* in 1890. He later became her only male lover but she always refused to marry him. 'No marriage, no ties, I must be free,' she once wrote to a friend.

Smyth finished the score of *Fantasio* in 1894 and embarked on a long struggle to get it performed. Knowing that new opera stood a far greater chance of being produced on the continent than in England, she concentrated on getting the work staged in Germany. It was eventually produced at Weimar in 1898 and published the following year. By this time Smyth was at work on her second opera, the one-act music-drama *Der Wald*, working again with Brewster on the libretto. This work, described by Brewster as 'a short and tragic story of passion', was first produced in Berlin in April 1902 and then performed at Covent Garden in July of the same year, an occasion that

Smyth described as 'the only really blazing triumph I have ever had'.

Brewster also wrote the libretto, originally in French, for Smyth's next and greatest opera, *The Wreckers*, based on a legend that Smyth had heard on a walking holiday in Cornwall in the 1880s. In a late 18th-century Cornish fishing community the villagers lure ships onto the dangerous rocks of the coast so that their cargo can be looted. Two lovers, Mark and Thirza, who is the wife of the village headman, defy their community and light a warning beacon. But they are caught by the villagers and sentenced to die in a cave that will gradually fill with the incoming tide.

Smyth worked on the music for *The Wreckers* between 1902 and 1904, and at one point wrote to a friend, 'I feel awfully full of power – deadly sure of what I am doing.' This is a remarkable work, full of evocations of the sea and of what Smyth called 'the desperate rugged coast'. Her vocal writing is intense and demanding, especially in the long, impassioned love duet for Thirza and Mark in the second act. *The Wreckers* was first performed in a savagely cut production in Leipzig in 1906. *The Times* nevertheless described it as 'one of the very few modern operas which must count among the great things in art'. In spite of all Smyth's efforts it was not given a complete performance in Britain for another three years.

Ethel Smyth in 1916

Smyth described her music for *The Wreckers* as in her 'latest manner' and 'absolutely out of the German wood'. In the early years of the century, her works were beginning to show much more of a French influence, with lighter textures and impressionistic harmonies. At this time she was frequently in Paris, attracted by her adoration for the influential and openly lesbian music patron, the Princesse de Polignac whom she first met in 1903 and who often included Smyth's works in performances at her famous salon. Some of the most striking examples of Smyth's new musical style were her four sensuous songs of 1907, settings of French texts for mezzo-soprano or baritone accompanied by flute, harp, string trio and percussion. They were admired by Claude Debussy when he heard them at a private party in London.

In 1908 Brewster died from cancer of the liver. Smyth spent some time in Venice with her sister and then returned to England to campaign for an English production of *The Wreckers*. She finally achieved this in June 1909 with a production funded by the American millionaire Mary Dodge and conducted by Thomas Beecham at His Majesty's Theatre. Dodge also gave Smyth the money to build her house, Coign, near Woking. In 1910 Smyth was awarded a honorary doctorate from Durham University and wrote two works for chorus and orchestra, the ebullient *Hey Nonny No!* to an anonymous 16th-century text, and a setting of Christina Rossetti's *Sleepless Dreams*.

Also in 1910, Smyth first met Emmeline Pankhurst and, falling in love with her, offered to devote the next two years to the militant suffragette cause. One of her first contributions was to write the rousing chorus, 'The March of the Women'. With a text by Cecily Hamilton, this anthem was sung at all the suffragettes' massed processions and marches. Smyth also used it as the final movement of *Songs of Sunrise*, a collection of three pieces for unaccompanied chorus. This work was first performed at a grand concert of Smyth's music given at the Queen's Hall in April 1911 by the Crystal Palace Choir and the London Symphony Orchestra, conducted by Smyth herself when Beecham failed to appear.

In 1912 two movements of an uncompleted string quartet that Smyth had written 10 years previously were played at the first public concert of the Society of Women Musicians. She decided to finish the work by adding two more movements, producing her only instrumental chamber work since the works of the 1880s. Her involvement with the campaign for the vote continued and in March 1912, during a mass suffragette demonstration, she threw a stone through the window of the Colonial Secretary's house, was duly arrested and spent three weeks in Holloway Prison.

During the next few months Smyth cut down on her involvement in the suffragette campaign. In June 1913 her atmospheric settings of poems by Arthur Symonds, *Three Moods of the Sea*, for mezzo-soprano or baritone and orchestra, were premiered at the Queen's Hall. Towards the end of that year Smyth went to Egypt for several months to write one of her most overtly feminist works, the lively comic opera, *The Boatswain's Mate*, to her own libretto based on a short story by W.W. Jacobs. The central character of the opera is Mrs Waters, the strong-willed landlady of the Beehive who successfully outwits her bumbling suitor as he stages a robbery of her house so that he can then save her. Smyth pointedly incorporated 'The March of the Women' into the overture. She managed to get both *The Wreckers* and *The Boatswain's Mate* scheduled for performance in Germany during 1915 but both productions were cancelled due to the outbreak of war. *The Boatswain's Mate* was finally premiered at the Shaftesbury Theatre in London in January 1916.

Smyth had begun to hear ringing and booming in her ears as early as 1913, and by the end of the war knew that she was slowly losing her hearing. She still continued to compose although she also turned to writing her extra-ordinary stream of memoirs and essays, starting with two volumes of autobiography, *Impressions that Remained*, published in 1919. Her next

opera was the neo-classic 'dance-dream' *Fête Galante* (1921–2), with a libretto by Edward Shanks based on a story by her friend Maurice Baring. It was first performed in Birmingham in June 1923 with a London performance a few days later. This was followed by the less successful comic opera *Entente Cordiale* (1923–4) to her own libretto, given a first public perfor-mance in Bristol in 1926.

The 1920s saw increasing recognition for Smyth. She was made a DBE in 1922, and many of her works were revived, including several perfor-mances of *The Boatswain's Mate* by Lilian Baylis at the Old Vic and the first performance since 1893 of the Mass in D. Her inventive Double Concerto for violin and horn (1926) was premiered in 1927 by Jelly d'Aranyi and Aubrey Brain with the Queen's Hall Orchestra conducted by Henry Wood, another staunch supporter of Smyth's music who performed many of her works at the Proms. *The Prison* (1929–30), her last large-scale work, was a setting for soprano and bass soloists, chorus and orchestra of her own adaptation of one of Brewster's philosophical works. First performed in Edinburgh in 1931, conducted by Smyth herself, it was repeated the same year in London.

During the 1930s Smyth developed an intense friendship with Virginia Woolf and published more memoirs and other writings. Her music continued to be heard in concerts and broadcast on the

BBC. In 1940 she published her fourth volume of autobiography, *What Happened Next*, and then started another, to be called *A Fresh Start*. She died before it was finished, in May 1844 at the age of 86.

Bruno Walter, writing in *The Times* in 1912, described Smyth as 'a composer of quite special significance' while believing that recognition for her work would 'only come gradually and in the teeth of opposition'. Although by the end of her long life Smyth was regarded as little more than a typical English eccentric who wrote amusing memoirs, she herself never stopped believing that future generations would give her powerful and exciting music the hearing that it deserves.

Emma Steiner
1852–1929

Frustratingly little is known about the remarkable life of Emma Steiner. She is thought to have been born in Baltimore, Maryland in 1852. Her father, Frederick B. Steiner, was a colonel, and Steiner doubtless had the usual piano lessons given to girls of her class. She started writing music at an early age, producing a piano duet at nine and part of a grand opera *Animaida* at 11. Her song 'I envy the Rose', written when she was 12, was later sung in the United States and Europe.

Although Steiner's family disproved of a musical career for a woman of her background, she moved to Chicago and started working as assistant musical director for Edward E. Rice in the Rice and Collier 'Iolanthe' Company. She went on to conduct for various other light-opera companies. In 1889 her own operetta *Fleurette* was produced in San Francisco and two years later performed in New York to good reviews. Steiner wrote six more operas, including *Day Dreams* (based on the same story as Pyotr Tchaikovsky's

Sleeping Beauty), *Brigands*, *The 'Burra Pundit'* and *The Man from Paris*, as well as musical dramas and ballets. She also wrote songs and piano pieces, some of which were published.

Steiner continued to get increasingly important conducting engagements, giving performances of light and grand opera as well as instrumental works. In December 1894 she conducted the Anton Seidl Orchestra in New York in a concert of her own works, and three years later arranged a series of concerts in which she conducted members of the New York Metropolitan Orchestra. In 1902 she worked for a season as music director for Heinrich Conried, who apparently wanted to appoint her as conductor at the Metropolitan Opera House but did not dare. Soon after this Steiner became seriously ill and was ordered to rest. She decided instead to go prospecting in the tin mines 100 miles northwest of Nome, Alaska and then spent the next ten years mining and travelling in Alaska.

On her return to New York Steiner took up her musical career again. In 1914 her *Gavotte Menzeli* for piano and orchestra was published as her op. 400. In 1921 she gave a concert of her own works that she called 'Harmony and Dischord' at the New York Museum of Natural History, including songs, opera extracts and instrumental music. Four years later, in 1925, a Golden Jubilee Concert in her honour was given at the Metropolitan Opera House. Several of her works were played including extracts from her operas and an orchestral work *The Flag – Forever May It Wave*. The proceeds from this concert went towards her latest project, a Home for Aged and Infirm Musicians that she was establishing at Bay Shore, Long Island with her friend Margaret Macdonald, who had been the librettist for one of her operas. The venture was not a success and financial worries may have precipitated her death in February 1929.

Elizabeth Stirling
1819–1895

Elizabeth Stirling was born in Greenwich, London, in 1819. She studied the piano and the organ as a girl, and in 1837, at the age of 18, gave an organ recital at St Katherine's Church, Regent's Park which was reviewed in *The Musical World*:

> This young lady ... was the unceasing object of general astonishment, and performed for nearly three hours in continuation the most difficult pedal fugues and preludes of Bach, with a degree of precision and mastery, which may almost be said to be unrivalled. We hope to see justice done to Miss Stirling. The prejudice against lady organists cannot remain, with such an example opposed to it.

At 20, Stirling became the organist of All Saints' Church in Poplar, a post she retained for nearly 19 years. She studied harmony privately with James Hamilton, author of several books on the theory of music, and with George Macfarren. Her first work to appear in print seems to have been the simple, strophic song 'It was the early winter' to anonymous words which were probably her own. This was published in 1851 when Stirling was in her early 30s. Over the next few years she became well known for her part-songs, many of which were published in *The Musical Times*. One of her most successful works was the part-song *All among the Barley* to words by 'A.T.' which was published in the *Novello Part-Song Book* series and *The Musical Times* as well as in Stirling's own collection *Nine Choral Songs* (1858).

In 1856 Stirling submitted a setting of Psalm 130 for five-part chorus and orchestra for the music degree at Oxford University. The work was passed by the examiners but, as a woman, Stirling could not be awarded the degree and her work was not performed. It was not for another 65 years, in 1921, that women were able to receive music degrees from Oxford University.

Stirling continued to compose, writing a great deal of music for the organ. These were works she would have used in her job as church organist, and many of them would have remained in manuscript. Her published organ works include *Six Pedal Fugues ... and eight other movements* (1857), a collection she dedicated to George Macfarren. Five of the pedal fugues are based on English psalm tunes, including a chorale by Thomas Tallis. Stirling's fugal writing is complex and academic with difficult pedal parts and is deliberately old-fashioned, almost in the style of J.S. Bach whose music she continued to perform throughout her career.

In 1858 Stirling left All Saints' when she was offered the post of organist at St Andrew's Church in Undershaft. She stayed at St Andrew's for the next 22 years. In 1863, when she was 44, Stirling married Frederick A. Bridge, and in the same year published the song 'England's Prayer for the Prince and Princess of Wales' to his words. She continued to perform in public after her marriage, giving a concert at which she played the piano in London in 1866. She also continued to compose, writing songs, part-songs and organ works as well as publishing many arrangements of Bach, Handel and Mozart for the organ. Stirling died in 1895 at the age of 76.

Louise Talma
b. 1906

Louise Talma's parents were both American musicians. She was born in France where her opera-singer mother, Alma Cecile Garrigue, was working in 1906. Talma's father, pianist Frederick Talma, died when she was very young, and her mother gave up her singing career and turned to teaching in order to be able to devote herself to bringing up her daughter. Music was important throughout Talma's childhood, and she was given her first piano lesson as a fifth-birthday present.

In 1914, when she was seven, Talma and her mother returned to the United States and settled in New York. At the age of nine she embarked on writing an opera to Victor Hugo's *Notre Dame de Paris*. Although she had developed a keen interest in chemistry and was considering studying the subject at college, Talma chose to study to be a musician when her mother became ill, a career in which she knew she could make a living. She initially wanted to become a pianist, and after graduating from high school in 1922, at the age of 15, went to the Institute of Musical Art where she studied for the next eight years.

In 1926, Talma first attended the summer school held at the American School at Fontainebleau in France, and was to return every summer for the next 13 years. For the first two years she studied the piano with Isidore Philipp but from 1928 started taking composition lessons from Nadia Boulanger. It was Boulanger who convinced Talma that she had the ability and talent to become a composer and who was probably one of the most important influences in her development as a composer, in particular by introducing her to the works of Igor Stravinsky whose neoclassic style was reflected in Talma's early music. Talma herself was later to be the first American to teach at the Fontainebleau school. In the late 1920s Talma received her first commissions when she was asked to write two choral works by Gerald Reynolds, director of the Women's University Glee Club.

In the early 1930s, her mother's illness grew worse. Talma had to concentrate on looking after her and earning enough money to support them both. She had been teaching at the Manhattan School of Music from 1926 to 1928. In 1928 she began to teach at Hunter College, City University of New York where she was to stay for over 50 years, becoming a full professor in 1952. She herself studied at night school to get her qualifications, a bachelor's degree in music from New York University (1931) and a master's degree from Columbia University (1933). Talma composed little during these years.

In 1943 her mother died. Talma spent the summer at the MacDowell Colony and started composing again. That summer she wrote her Piano Sonata no. 1, first performed at a League of Composers concert by Talma herself, and the first song of her *Terre de France* cycle. She was to spend many summers working at the MacDowell colony which was vitally important not only in giving her the space and peace in which to write music but also in introducing her to other artists such as the 'Boston composers', including Lukas Foss and Irving Fine, who were writing in a similarly neoclassic style. At a concert during that first MacDowell summer, Foss, who was to become a close friend, joined Talma in a performance of her light-hearted piano duet *Four-Handed Fun* (1939).

Talma had her first big success in 1945 when her orchestral *Toccata*, written the year before, was performed by the Baltimore Symphony Orchestra. This is a brilliant, strongly rhythmic work which won a Juilliard publication award. Many of Talma's early works from the 1940s and early 50s are vocal, such as *Terre de France* (1943–5), a song-cycle for soprano and piano to texts by Charles Pierre Peguy, Du Ballay, Pierre de Ronsard and Charles d'Orléans; her oratorio *The Divine Flame* (1945–8), setting words from the Bible for mezzo-soprano, baritone, chorus and orchestra; and many settings of poems by Gerard Manley Hopkins, including *The Leaden Echo and the Golden Echo* (1950–1) for soprano, double chorus and piano. She also wrote works for her own instrument, the piano, including the jazzy *Alleluia in Form of Toccata* (1945) for piano. In 1946 and again in 1947 Talma won coveted Guggenheim Fellowships.

In the early 1950s Talma began using serial techniques in her music, although she constructed her rows so that her music remained based in tonality and retained the lyricism and clarity of her earlier style. The first work in which she used 12-tone rows was *Six Etudes* (1954) for piano. Each etude has a different row and is based round a specific piano technique, such as playing pianissimo (very quietly) or frequently crossing the hands. Another early serial work is her String Quartet (1954).

At the MacDowell Colony in the summer of 1955, Talma completed *La Corona*, her intense setting of seven sacred sonnets by John Donne for unaccompanied chorus. This work was not given a first performance until 1964. Another piece completed in 1955 was Talma's Piano Sonata no. 2, a difficult four-movement work, combining tonal and serial techniques, which she had started writing in 1944 and then taken up again in the early 1950s. Talma dedicated this work, together with *Three Bagatelles* (1955) for piano, to the writer Thornton Wilder whom she met at the MacDowell Colony. Wilder was very impressed by Talma's music and asked her to write an opera with him. Talma eventually agreed and Wilder supplied a libretto based on his play *Life in the Sun*. Talma spent nearly five years on the work, *The Alcestiad,* including 10 months in Rome on a Senior Fulbright Research grant, and finished it in 1958. It was first performed in Frankfurt am Main in March 1962 by the Frankfurt Opera Company with the libretto translated into German, where it received a 20-minute ovation. Other works from the early 1960s included a Violin Sonata (1962) and *Dialogues* (1964) for piano and orchestra.

Talma had converted to Catholicism in 1935 during her mother's illness, possibly influenced by Boulanger. Religious and sacred texts were always important to her although she wrote little music for liturgical use in the church. In 1959 she was commissioned by the Koussevitsky Music Foundation to write a chamber work and composed *All the Days of My Life,* a cantata for tenor, clarinet, cello, piano and percussion to words from the Bible, which was completed in 1965. Vocal or choral works with secular texts from this time included her setting of various words of John F. Kennedy, *A Time to Remember* (1966–7) for three choirs and chamber orchestra, and one of her best-known works *The Tolling Bell* (1967–9) for baritone and orchestra. This work, which Talma described as 'in the nature of an elegy to the fallen', uses text from Christopher Marlowe's *Doctor Faustus* and a John Donne sonnet as well as lines from Hamlet's famous soliloquy, taking the fundamental interval of the fifth as the equivalent of the words 'to be'. In the 1960s Talma wrote two text books, *Harmony for the College Student* (1966) and *Functional Harmony* (with J. Harrison and R. Levin, 1970).

Talma continued to write music in all genres throughout the 1970s and 1980s. She became increasingly recognized as one of America's leading composers, and won several prestigious awards; in 1974 she became the first woman composer to be elected to the National Institute of Arts and Letters. Her later vocal works include a divertimento for three voices and chamber ensemble *Have You Heard? Do You Know?* written over six years (1974–80) to her own text about a young couple, Fred and Della, their neighbour Mildred and their dreams of escape from the strain of modern life; a setting of Wallace Stevens' *Thirteen Ways of Looking at a Blackbird* (1979) for voice, treble instrument (flute, oboe or violin) and piano; and a rare liturgical work, *Mass for the Sundays of the Year* (1984).

Her later instrumental works include two works given first performances by Joan Towers' Da Capo Chamber Players: *Lament* (1980) for cello and piano, based on a Bedouin melody that Talma had heard in Jordan; and the four-movement piece *The Ambient Air* (1980–3) for flute, violin, cello and

piano which opens with the song of a nightingale transcribed for the flute. An earlier piece that also used bird song was *Summer Sounds* (1973) for clarinet and string quartet. Talma also continued to write piano and orchestral music with works such as *Kaleidoscopic Variations* (1984) for piano and *Full Circle* (1985) for orchestra with a prominent piano part. *Full Circle*, a concentrated work which moves between passages of calm, almost mournful lyricism and lively, driving rhythms, was first performed by The Prism Orchestra conducted by Robert Black a few days before Talma's 80th birthday in 1986.

Hilary Tann
b. 1947

Although Hilary Tann has lived and worked in the United States since 1972, the mountains, mists and landscape of her native Wales have retained their importance as the inspiration for much of her music. Tann was born in the Rhondda Valley and wrote her first piece of music, a waltz she called 'The Wye Valley', when she was about six years old. She studied music at the University of Wales at Cardiff from 1965 to 1968 and then went to Southampton University to do graduate research into the music of Roberto Gerhard.

In 1972, Tann went to Princeton University as a visiting fellow and stayed on there to study composition. From 1973 to 1977 she held a Princeton University Fellowship and worked as a teaching assistant. She then taught for three years at Bard College in Annandale, New York before joining the staff at Union College in Schenectady, New York where, from 1992 to 1995, she was chair of the Department of Performing Arts. In

1981 she received her doctorate from Princeton. Tann sees herself as an economic migrant, finding that she can earn a living from academic teaching in the States and use the long summer vacation to concentrate on composition.

Tann's early works include *Templum* (1975–6) for computer-synthesized tape and *As Ferns* (1979) for string orchestra without basses. In the 1980s much of her music was written for one or two performers, short pieces creating their own vividly atmospheric sound-worlds. *Duo* (1981) for oboe and viola is a meditative piece in which the two instruments weave slowly around each other. *A Sad Pavan Forbidding Mourning* (1982) for guitar grows out of quotations from 'A Sad Pavan for These Distracted Tymes' by the 17th-century composer Thomas Tomkins. In *Doppelganger* (1984) the piano creates a glistening web of sound broken by still chordal passages. *Windhover* (1985), for either flute or soprano saxophone, grew from the vision of a bird of prey, combining slow hovering with the swooping excitement of flight.

A larger chamber work, *Winter Sun, Summer Rain* (1986) for flute, clarinet, viola, cello and celeste was commissioned by the Welsh Arts Council and first performed at the Vale of Glamorgan Festival. This entrancing piece contrasts two images, the snow-covered landscapes and blurred forms of North America and the bright, shimmering reflection of the sun, coming out from the clouds after rain, in the raindrops hanging on plants and trees in a Welsh summer.

In 1989 Tann was commissioned by the local Schenectady Symphony Orchestra to write an orchestral work. She originally intended to write a piece celebrating freedom but as she was working on the piece heard news of the Tiananmen Square massacre in China. *The Open Field*, subtitled 'In memoriam Tiananmen Square, June 1989', is a tightly constructed, 10-minute work which opens with dramatic brass fanfares over threatening timpani rolls. It moves through mournful lyricism from the strings, mingling with fragments of Ludwig van Beethoven's 'Ode to Joy', and ends with the return of triumphant yet disturbing flourishes from the brass.

Tann was first attracted to the music and culture of Japan through hearing the vertical bamboo shakuhachi flute and through the image of the 13th-century mendicant monks who walked the length and breadth of Japan looking for the single sound that would enlighten the world. One of her earliest works to use the shakuhachi, *Llef* (1988) for shakuhachi and cello, is also a very Welsh work. Llef means 'cry from the heart' in Welsh, and Tann has written that the piece 'recalls the rain-swept stone walls of the Welsh country side'. In 1989 Tann co-edited a symposium of articles on Japanese music in the journal *Perspectives of New Music*, and in 1990 she wrote another work for shakuhachi, *Mei Shin*, which can also be played on bass clarinet.

In the autumn of 1990 Tann went to Kansai University of Foreign Studies, near Kyoto in Japan, where she studied the shakuhachi and Noh performance traditions. During her time in Japan she wrote *Of Erthe and Air* for flute, clarinet and frame drums which takes its title from a poem by the 14th-century poet John Trevisa. The two wind instruments alternate between passages of busy forward-moving music and moments of calmer stillness, accompanied all the time by an insistent variety of sounds from the drums.

The 1990s have brought Tann a series of important commissions from both Britain and the United States. The short fanfare overture *Through the Echoing Timber* (1991) was commissioned by the Pro Musica orchestra of Columbia, Indiana, and the Glens Falls

Symphony Orchestra commissioned a work to commemorate the 100th anniversary of the Adirondack Park, a large semi-wilderness area in New York State. Tann conducted the first performance of *Adirondack Light* in October 1992. It is a work for narrator and chamber orchestra and uses the poem 'A Lesson from the Hudson River School: Glens Fall, NY 1848' by Jordan Smith which is about a Boston man's journey into the Adirondacks. Tann found many parallels between the Adirondacks and South Wales and incorporated Adirondack folk songs, originally from Ireland and Wales, into her music which also reflects images of light and water.

In 1994 Tann was composer-in-residence at the Presteigne Festival at which several of her works were played, including the premieres of *Water's Edge* (1994), transcribed for string orchestra from the original piano duet, and *The Cresset Stone*

(1993) for violin. A cresset stone was a hollowed stone used in medieval times as an oil light. In her piece, Tann used part of a medieval Gregorian chant to create a work described as 'a meditation on stone and light'. As Tann is a long-standing member of the International League of Women Composers and editor of the *ILWC Journal* from 1982 to 1988, it was fitting that she should be commissioned to write the opening overture, played by the European Women's Orchestra, of the 1994 Cardiff Festival which celebrated the music of women composers. The title of Tann's work, *With the heather and small birds* (1994), is taken from the end of 'Nant y Mynydd' ('The Mountain Stream') by the Victorian Welsh poet, John Ceiriog Hughes, a poem reflecting on his exile from Wales and which echoes Tann's own feelings: '. . . my heart is in the mountain, with the heather and small birds'.

Phyllis Tate
1911–1987

Phyllis Tate was born in Gerrards Cross, just outside London, in 1911. At 10 she was expelled from school for singing a bawdy music-hall song that she had been taught by her architect father at an end-of-term concert. She had no further formal schooling but among other projects, such as producing a paper called 'Catland News', taught herself to play the ukulele. Inspired by the jazz craze of the 1920s, she started writing foxtrots and blues, and joined a concert party that gave concerts for charity. At one of these performances she was noticed by composer Harry Farjeon who offered to give her music lessons.

In 1928, at the age of 17, she entered the Royal Academy of Music where she studied composition with Farjeon as well as taking lessons in conducting, timpani and piano. As a music student, she became, in her own words, 'frightfully arty', wearing sandals and a large black hat. Several of her works were performed at the Academy, including an operetta *The Policeman's Serenade*

and a Symphony, which, with chacteristic modesty, she later described as 'ghastly'. On leaving the Academy in 1932, she found supporters of her music in Norman Peterkin and Hubert Foss of Oxford University Press who helped to arrange concerts of her works. Some of her early music was also heard at the Macnaghten–Lemare concerts in the mid–1930s, including her first published work, 'Cradle Song' (William Blake) for tenor and piano. Her Cello Concerto was performed by the Bournemouth Symphony Orchestra in 1934, and on hearing Tate play through this work, Ethel Smyth remarked, 'At last I have heard a *real* woman composer!'.

In the 1930s Tate was also writing and arranging commercial light music under pseudonyms such as Max Morelle. In 1935 she married music publisher and clarinettist Alan Frank, and her first child was born in 1940. Although she was told that being a mother would mean the end of her composition, Tate actually found that 'oddly enough my output appeared to increase'. She later destroyed most of her pre-war music. The first work she was prepared to acknowledge was her brilliantly virtuosic Concerto for alto saxophone and strings, written as a BBC commission in 1944. This was followed by the two works that brought her to public attention, an inventive four-movement Sonata for clarinet and cello that was performed at the London Contemporary Music centre in 1947, and the sombre *Nocturne for Four Voices*, a setting of a poem by Sidney Keyes for four soloists with string quartet, double bass, celesta and bass clarinet written in 1945 and broadcast in 1947. Both works showed her life-long interest in unusual textures and instrumental combinations.

Phyllis Tate

Tate finished her String Quartet in F major just before the birth of her second child in 1952 and after several years of illness. It is a powerful work with a sorrowful slow movement and an intense introduction to the vigorously playful finale. Words were always of great importance to Tate in firing her imagination, and from the 1950s onwards she turned increasingly to vocal and choral music. *The Lady of Shalott* (1956) sets the poem by Alfred Tennyson for tenor, viola, two pianos and a vast array of percussion. Opening with an insistently ominous piano accompaniment, the work always keeps up the suspense of the story. Sir Launcelot is represented by a military side drum and the piano builds to a dramatic climax as the Lady of Shalott finally looks out of her window. It is only after the curse has come upon her that the viola enters, with mournful falling glissandi.

The text for *A Secular Requiem* (1967) is the strange poem 'The Phoenix and the Turtle' attributed to William Shakespeare. Tate reworked an earlier setting for tenor and ensemble to produce this dramatic work for chorus, organ and orchestra. A typically atmospheric work is the ghostly *Apparitions* (1968) for tenor, harmonica, string quartet and piano. Tate delighted in writing music for the stage. In 1960 her opera *The Lodger*, written in 1958, was performed at the Royal Academy of Music. This was a musical thriller with a libretto by David Franklin based on a Jack-the-Ripper novel by Marie Adelaide Belloc-Lowndes. Tate also wrote a television opera, *Dark Pilgrimage* (1963), to another libretto by David Franklin, a setting of John Gay's *The What D'ye Call It* and several stage works for children. One of Tate's ambitions, unfortunately never realized, was to write a musical on the eventful life of Isabella Beeton, making songs from the recipes in her book *Mrs Beeton's Household Management*.

Tate was always very critical of her own work and destroyed a great deal of it. She had no interest in writing large-scale orchestral music but continued to compose a wide range of chamber works, increasingly searching for greater economy or, as she put it, using few notes but the right ones. Her *Variegations* (1970) for viola is a richly inventive work, exploring a variety of moods, sounds and textures. Other late instrumental works included *Explorations around a Troubadour Song* (1973) for piano, *The Rainbow and the Cuckoo* (1974) for oboe and string trio, *Sonatina Pastorale* (1974) for harmonica and harpsichord and *Prelude – Aria – Interlude – Finale* (1981) for clarinet and piano.

From the mid–1950s Tate lived in Hampstead, North London, and became involved with local music clubs and choral societies as well professional bodies such as the Composers' Guild of Great Britain and the Performing Right Society. Several of her later choral works were written for organizations with which she was associated, such as *St Martha and the Dragon* (1977), to a poem by Charles Causley for narrator, soprano, tenor, chorus, children's chorus and chamber orchestra, written for the Barnet and District Choral Society of which she was the president.

Tate strongly believed that music should be accessible, that it should entertain and give pleasure. She died in

1987 at the age of 76. Composing had always remained extremely important to her, and some years before her death she claimed that ' ... writing music can be *Hell*; torture in extreme; but there's one thing even worse; and that is *not* writing it'.

Joan Tower
b. 1938

Joan Tower was born in New Rochelle, New York, but grew up in South America. Her father was a mining engineer and the family moved frequently, living in Bolivia, Peru and Chile. In spite of this travelling childhood, Tower always managed to find piano lessons wherever her family was living. She returned to the United States as a teenager in 1955 and three years later went to Bennington College, Vermont, to study music. At Bennington, Tower started writing music and hearing it played, although the main focus of her musical activity was as a pianist.

Tower graduated in 1961 and went to Columbia University, where she studied for a master's degree in theory and history of music. Much later, in 1978, she received a doctorate in composition from Columbia. Tower had many different composition teachers during her years of study, including Otto Luening, Ralph Shapey and Darius Milhaud. Her early works, dating from the 1960s, such as

Percussion Quartet (1963) or *Movements for Flute and Piano* (1968) are complex and angular, using elaborate serial techniques.

Like so many performers who are also composers, Tower discovered that one of the best ways to combine making a living with making opportunities for her music to be heard was to form her own ensemble. In 1969 she founded the Da Capo Chamber Players, a group consisting of flute, clarinet, violin, cello and piano that specializes in playing contemporary music and commissioning new works. The Da Capo Players have been extremely successful, winning a prestigious Naumburg award in 1973.

Tower's early music for the Da Capo Players, such as *Prelude for Five Players* (1970) or the virtuosic *Hexachords* (1972) for flute, continued to be written in a strictly organized serial language. During the early 1970s, however, her music gradually became less austere and she slowly moved away from using serial techniques. This change can be heard in the difference between the two movements of *Breakfast Rhythms I and II* (1974–5) for solo clarinet and five instruments. A gap of a year separated their composition. Whereas the first movement uses serial techniques to create a jagged sound-world, the second uses pentatonic and whole-tone scales and is far more lyrical and impressionistic.

Tower's chamber works from the late 1970s and early 1980s are often inspired by particular images. She wrote a series of three pieces in memory of her father which each explore the properties of a different mineral or precious stone. *Platinum Spirals* (1976) for violin grew from the flexibility and malleability of this metal. *Black Topaz* (1976) for piano and six instruments reflects the ability of topaz to 'transform into different hues' while *Red Garnet Waltz* (1977) for piano captures the shiny, hard-edged quality of the stone. One of Tower's best-known chamber pieces is the shimmering *Petroushkates* (1980) for flute, clarinet, violin, cello and piano which builds on material from Stravinsky's ballet *Petrushka* and the image of the gliding grace of an ice skater. Another work drawing on grace and speed is the virtuosic *Wings* (1981) for clarinet, inspired by the soaring and diving of a falcon.

In 1979 Tower had arranged her

chamber piece *Amazon* (1976) for orchestra but her first full-scale orchestral work, *Sequoia*, was written in 1981 as a commission from the American Composers Orchestra. *Sequoia* was inspired by the grandeur of the Californian sequoia, a huge tree with tiny leaves. Working with this image, Tower explores the ideas of balance and contrast in a vigorous work that was immediately successful and has since been frequently performed. Since the success of *Sequoia,* Tower has concentrated on writing orchestral music, although she has never stopped writing chamber music, with works such as *Noon Dance* (1982) for flute, clarinet, violin, cello, piano and percussion, *Fantasy... Harbor Lights* (1983) for clarinet and piano, and String Quartet (1994).

In 1984 Tower stopped performing with the Da Capo Players in order to concentrate on composition, although she continued to teach at Bard College in Annandale, New York where she has worked since 1972. From 1985 to 1988 she was composer-in-residence for the St Louis Symphony Orchestra. Her first work for the orchestra was *Silver Ladders* (1986). Like the earlier 'mineral' works, *Silver Ladders* reflects some of the properties of the metal, perhaps in particular the contrast between silver as heavy and solid and silver as something delicate and intricate. The other central image of this dynamic work is found in the persistent upward ladder-like movement of the orchestra. Instantly popular, it won an international Grawemeyer Award and has been performed all over the world.

That year Tower also wrote the first in her series *Fanfare for the Uncommon Woman*. The first fanfare, for brass and percussion, was a tribute to Aaron Copland (composer of *Fanfare for the Common Man*) and 'to adventurous women who take risks'. The second, written in 1989 and also for brass and percussion, was dedicated to the general manager of the St Louis Symphony Orchestra, Joan Briccetti. The third fanfare, written in 1991 for double brass quintet, was followed by the orchestral *For the Uncommon Woman* (1992) while *Fanfare for the Uncommon Woman (No. 5)* (1993) was written for trumpet quartet. These frequently performed works are good examples of Tower's energetic use of exciting rhythmic patterns. The driving rhythmic impulse of Tower's music makes it ideal for dance. Her ballet score *Stepping Stones* was choreographed by Kathryn Posin for Milwaukee Ballet who gave the first performance in April 1993.

Tower's concern for writing music that works for its performers, doubtless born from her many years as a pianist, can be seen in her series of concertos, from *Music for Cello and Orchestra* (1984) through the virtuosic concertos for piano (1985), clarinet (1988) and flute (1989) to the colourful Concerto for Violin (1992). A rather different work is *Island Prelude* (1989) for oboe and string orchestra, also arranged for oboe and string or wind quintet. This is an essentially lyrical, slow-moving piece with rich harmonies from the accompanying instruments. Recalling her South-American childhood, Tower drew on an image of a brightly coloured bird gliding and swooping over a lush tropical island. Tower's biggest orchestral work, the dramatic *Concerto for Orchestra* (1991), was first performed by the St Louis Symphony Orchestra, one of three commissioning orchestras. The music gradually builds from a threatening opening to a series of powerful climaxes interspersed with quieter moments of stillness for small groups of instruments.

Julia Usher
b. 1945

Born in Oxford in 1945, Julia Usher spent her earliest years in the United States where her parents moved immediately after the second world war. She had piano lessons from the age of five and took up the flute at her South London secondary school when the family returned permanently to Britain in 1959 when she was 14. Usher began composing in her last years at school, writing music for the annual Shakespeare production and experimenting with the unusual harmonies that have always been a part of her musical language. She went on to study music at Newnham College, Cambridge, where she had composition lessons in her final year with Richard Orton. She was very involved in the musical life of Cambridge and heard several of her works performed by friends.

After being refused a job with the BBC, Usher decided to take up teaching and improve the situation of contemporary music in schools. She took her Postgraduate Certificate of Education at York University where her attitude to music was transformed by exposure to jazz and improvisation. During her teaching practice in Hull she met her future husband, fellow teacher Rodney Usher. After they married, Usher taught for a while in Hull before the birth of her first son. Although she continued to write, winning a competition for a flute piece before the birth of her second son, it was not until she won a prize for her clarinet quintet *Encounter* in 1974 that she began to take herself seriously as a composer. That year the family moved to London and Usher took a few composition lessons with composer Robert Sherlaw Johnson. While composing, Usher continued to work in education, initially in teacher training and then teaching for three years in a school for children with disabilities.

Having grown up with a deep love of literature instilled by her mother, Usher writes most of her own texts, and much of her music is inspired by strong visual or verbal images. This can be clearly seen in a work such as *Ordnance Survey* (1979), subtitled 'Seven Pieces mapped for tenor, flute, clarinet, viola, cello'. This complex, contrapuntal piece grew from the visual idea of maps and their relationship to the landscape. Each short movement with its graphic musical images explores a different aspect of the landscape. *A Chess Piece* (1980) for three clarinets and soprano sets three of her own poems about choice and freedom and musically represents an actual chess game whose moves are marked in the score.

In 1980 Usher and composer Enid Luff set up Primavera, a music publishing company for their own works which operates from Usher's home in South London. Usher trained as a music therapist in 1985, and has since worked in the music-therapy department of Queen Mary's Hospital in Carshalton. Her work in music therapy brought about a change in her attitude towards the harmonic foundations of music. A departure from her usual contrapuntal, linear style can be seen in her choral work *A Grain of Sand in Lambeth* (1987). This work was commissioned by the Blake Society of St James's Church, Piccadilly in London and is a setting of visionary texts by William Blake for choir, brass, flute, oboe, piano, string quartet and four metal sound sculptures made by artist Derek Shiel. A powerful medita-

tion on ideas of time, space and the relationship of the individual to the rest of the world, *A Grain of Sand* moves from passages of chilling ferocity, such as the clanging of Shiel's sculptures representing Los' anvils and furnaces in the sixth movement, 'Bowlahoola', to moments of calm, still beauty such as the seventh movement, 'A memorable fancy'.

Given Usher's preoccupation with visual and verbal imagery, it was perhaps inevitable that she should move into the world of music theatre. From 1988 to 1990 she worked on *The Orford Merman*, a retelling of a 12th-century Suffolk legend in which the merman, who does not speak and is feared and reviled by the local inhabitants when he is brought to shore, is played by a dancer and represented musically by a French horn. Exploring the themes of language and communication, Usher used speech rather than song for the five other roles which are played by an actor. In 1993, Usher's music-theatre piece *Hope's Perpetual Breath* for tenor, dancer, flute, clarinet, cello, harp and percussion, based on texts by Chinese writer Lu Hsun, was first performed by InterArtes, the cross-cultural combined-arts group formed by composer Ho Wai-On. *Hope's Perpetual Breath* centres around regret at the passing of youth but ends with a powerful image of hope.

Nancy Van de Vate
b. 1930

Nancy Van de Vate is a prolific composer with an intense love of travel and of the music that she has found on her journeys from Hawaii to Indonesia and Eastern Europe. She is best known for her large orchestral works which use a variety of sounds from huge tone clusters to expressive, lyrical melodies. She was born Nancy Hayes in Plainfield, New Jersey, and played the euphonium in high school and with the New Jersey All-State Band as well as studying the piano. She made her professional debut as a pianist at the age of 15, and a year later was studying the piano in New York. In 1948 she spent a year at the Eastman School of Music as a piano major before transferring to Wellesley College in Massachusetts, graduating in 1951 with a major in theory.

She married Dwight Van de Vate in 1952, and continued to study the piano. After she moved with her husband and baby to Mississippi in 1955 she began to study composition at the University of Mississippi, receiving her master's degree in 1958. Vate chose to concentrate on composition rather than performance because she felt it was a career that she could work at from home while bringing up her three children. She also gave private piano lessons and worked for a short while as an instructor in music at the University.

In 1958 Vate's sombre but moving *Adagio* for orchestra, written the previous year as part of a projected three-movement work, was performed in Alabama, the first professional performance of one of her works. Another orchestral work, the tuneful *Variations for chamber orchestra* (1958) was first heard in 1960. In 1963 the family moved to Florida. Vate continued to teach the piano and took further composition lessons as well as teaching at Memphis State University and the University of Tennessee. She also became involved in the Southeastern Composers League, and in 1966 her Sonata for viola and piano (1964) was performed at a concert organized by the League.

Vate received a DMA in composition from Florida State University in 1968. For her doctoral dissertation she wrote a Piano Concerto, the last large-scale orchestral work she was to write for over 10 years. Moving with her family to Tennessee in the same year, Vate played viola in the Knoxville Symphony Orchestra and taught at Knoxville College. Her works from this period include the 12-tone *Six Etudes for Solo Viola* (1969), String Quartet no. 1 (1969), *Four Sombre Songs* (1970), settings of Georg Trakl, Edgar Allan Poe, William Blake and Paul Verlaine for mezzo-soprano and piano which she orchestrated in 1992, and *An American Essay* (1971), settings from Walt Whitman's *Leaves of Grass* for chorus.

During 1972 Vate discovered the music of Edgar Varèse and also studied electronic music for the first time. This exposure to different ways of thinking about sound and texture in music proved to be of vital importance for her own works. The change in her music can be heard in works such as *Three Sound Pieces for Brass and Percussion* (1973) or *Suite for Solo Violin* (1975). During this time Vate began to campaign for recognition for women composers, writing an article 'Every Good Boy (Composer) Does Fine' for *Symphony News* and in 1975 founding the League of Women Composers. The same year she moved to Hawaii where

she taught at the University of Hawaii and various other colleges and worked as a music critic for the *Hawaii Observer*. It was in Hawaii that she first heard and grew to love the music of Asia.

Vate's own music written during her years in Hawaii uses a variety of sounds and techniques. *Concertpiece for cello and orchestra* (1976) is an expressive, almost romantic work which makes much use of percussion. Six of the *Nine Preludes for Piano* written between 1974 and 1978 use serial techniques while *Letter to a Friend's Loneliness* (1976), a setting of two poems by John Unterecker for soprano and string quartet, is for the most part freely atonal. *Music for Viola, Percussion and Piano* (1976) introduces, amongst lyrical tunes and jaunty rhythms, the tone clusters that were to become so important a part of Vate's writing in the 1980s. One of the last works Vate wrote in Hawaii was *Dark Nebulae* (1981) for orchestra, which brought together many of her experiments over the previous decade to create a powerful work of dense orchestral sounds with lyrical individual lines from solo instruments.

Having divorced her first husband in 1976, Vate married Clyde Smith three years later, and from 1982 to 1985 they lived in Indonesia and travelled widely. The influence of gamelan music can be heard in the pentatonic harmonies and insistent rhythms of a work such as *Gema Jawa* (1984) for string orchestra. Clear echoes of the music of Asia can also be heard in *Pura Besakih* (1987), an orchestral work of calm serenity with an underlying edge of threatening disaster, inspired by a Balinese Hindu temple built on an active volcano. Vate's orchestral work *Journeys* (1981–4) was written in Indonesia, the United States and Eastern Europe and uses vivid tone colours drawn together by a central four-note motif.

In 1985 Vate settled in Vienna and has developed strong links with musicians in the Czech Republic, Slovakia and Poland where her music is very popular and frequently performed. She has continued to develop the massive orchestral language of *Dark Nebulae* and *Journeys,* producing a series of intensely expressive orchestral works. *Distant Worlds* (1985) and Violin Concerto no. 1 (1985–6) are two very different orchestral works using solo violin. *Distant Worlds* is highly dissonant with extensive use of percussion whereas the violin concerto is an almost traditional work.

Chernobyl (1987), for orchestra with electronics, was written after the nuclear disaster in the Soviet Union and builds slowly to an almost unbearable climax of noise followed by a more tonal final section built around a descending 'weeping motif'. Another work inspired by a specific event is *Katyn* (1989) for orchestra and chorus,

commemorating the Katyn Forest massacre of over 4,000 Poles by the Soviet troops. Vate uses Gregorian chant, a motet by Josquin des Pres and a Polish folk song, together with her characteristic orchestral clusters, to create a moving memorial. Her *Krakow Concerto* (1988) for orchestra with a virtuoso percussion ensemble who play alone in the second and fourth of the five movements, opens with a solo trumpet playing the melody that is heard hourly from St Mary's Church in Krakow.

Vate and her husband founded the record company Vienna Modern Masters in 1990. As well as seeking out little-known works by a wide variety of composers from all over the world, the company has issued most of Vate's significant works, from the *Adagio* of 1957 through the chamber works of the 1970s to her most recent orchestral pieces. Obtaining live performances of contemporary orchestral music is notoriously difficult, and by setting up the company Vate has ensured that her music reaches a wide public.

In the 1990s Vate has written a viola concerto and a second violin concerto, and has turned increasingly to vocal music with works such as *How Fares the Night?* for violin, women's chorus and orchestra. She has also worked on two operas, *The Shadow of the Glen*, after the play by J.M. Synge and an anti-war opera, *All Quiet on the Western Front*.

Errollyn Wallen
b. 1958

Although she showed little interest in popular music until her mid-20s, Errollyn Wallen has become one of the most versatile composers of her generation, working with many different kinds of music, from opera and string quartets to jazz-influenced popular songs, to all of which she brings her own individual voice.

Born in Belize, Wallen moved to London with her family when she was two. As a child she was preoccupied with ballet although she also wrote poetry and took piano lessons, having been taught to read music by a cousin. Her interest in playing the piano and writing music grew while she was at boarding school in Sussex. After running away from school at 17, she continued to study music by correspondence course as well as winning a national poetry competition judged by one of her favourite poets, Philip Larkin.

Wallen then spent some time in New York taking courses at the Dance Theatre of Harlem before returning to England to study music at Goldsmith's College, London University. After graduating, Wallen continued her studies at King's College with Nicola LeFanu. She left King's with a master's degree in composition in 1983 and joined Pulse, an alternative cabaret band with an emphasis on systems music that performed on the comedy circuit. Although primarily a performer with the group, Wallen wrote several songs to perform with them.

After leaving Pulse in 1985, Wallen worked as a freelance keyboard player before meeting Steve Parr in 1986. Together they set up Wallen Parr, a recording studio and music-production company in North London. Wallen started writing music for corporate videos, film and television, as well as moving back into the world of classical concert music with works such as her Second String Quartet (1988). In this four-movement work Wallen moves through a variety of moods from gently rocking, dance-like rhythmic patterns to the exquisite, almost mournful, lyricism that is an essential part of her musical language.

In 1987 she joined Graeme Fitkin's group Nanquidno (four players on two pianos) for which she wrote works such as *The Girl in My Alphabet* (1990), which she describes as a deconstruction of a jazz standard. Wallen was composer-in-residence for the Newcastle Electric Music 3 Festival in 1988, for which she wrote *Take* for tape, soprano and piano. She also continued to write music in a more popular style and in 1989 put together *Cities of the Red Night*, an album of her imaginative, quirky songs. Writing and performing her songs remains an important part of Wallen's musical career. She sings them in a tightly knit trio of bass, drums and piano, which she plays herself, often joined by her brother, jazz trumpeter Byron Wallen.

In 1989 Wallen received her first commission, from the ensemble Gemini, for which she wrote a tribute to Philip Larkin. *It all depends on you* sets four of his poems for soprano, tape and two players on clarinets and saxophone. Framed with long, pulsating notes, the work moves through different moods, throwing out snatches of the jazz that Larkin loved and capturing moments of quiet lyricism. In 1990 Wallen composed one of her most popular works, *In Our Lifetime* for baritone and tape. Written

to celebrate the life of Marcus Garvey and the imminent release of Nelson Mandela, Wallen wrote her own text incorporating the words, and at one point the music, of the African National Congress anthem, *Nkosi Sikel i'Afrika*. The work uses multi-track recording of singer Mike Henry's voice to create a richly layered and deeply moving lament. First performed a week before Mandela was released, *In Our Lifetime* had an immediate impact and was choreographed in 1993 by Christopher Bruce for the London Contemporary Dance Company.

Always preferring to work with musicians who have strong classical backgrounds and yet have also worked with more popular kinds of music, Wallen formed a loosely based group called Ensemble X to perform her works. Their first concert at London's South Bank Centre in 1990 was received enthusiastically by the critics. Wallen's works performed by the group include *Jelly Dub Mix* (1990) for string quartet, saxophone and tape; *Having Gathered his Cohorts* (1991), a setting of three of her own poems for baritone and two clarinets, written 'in anger and despair' during the Gulf War; and *I Hate Waiting* (1991), also to her own text, for clarinet/voice, clarinet/sax/bass clarinet, piano/voice, acoustic/electric bass, trumpet, percussion, tape and live electronics, which brings together popular and more classical elements as well as improvisation.

Errollyn Wallen

Not all Wallen's works are written for Ensemble X. The beautiful lament *Dark Heart* (1991), a setting of a poem by the medieval poet Christine de Pizan for soprano and piano, was written for singer Nicola Walker-Smith. In 1993 Wallen's first opera, *Four Figures with Harlequin* to her own libretto, was premiered by The Garden Venture of the Royal Opera House. The work uses both spoken and sung text, telling of 'a journey into the subconscious where a lost boy searches to be born' and uses an actor who does not sing, an actor who does sing, a soprano, a jazz singer and a boy singer, all accompanied by a six-piece ensemble and tape. In the same year Wallen worked on *1 2 3 4*, electronic music for Union Dance Company's piece *Driving Force*.

Important commissions continued into 1994 with *Are you worried about the rising costs of funerals? – Five Simple Songs* for soprano and string quartet for Birmingham Contemporary Music Group; *No Chicken in the West End* for percussion group Ensemble Bash; and *Song Cycle* for the Women's Playhouse Trust, produced in collaboration with other composers, poets and an installation artist. In April 1994 Wallen's first orchestral work, Concerto for Percussion and Orchestra, commissioned by the BBC, was premiered as part of their Young Musician of the Year competition. Written for a vast array of percussion, this work opens with arresting single drumbeats that develop into a rhythmically complex solo for drums in which the orchestra gradually joins. Drums dominate the first movement with a central jazz-like passage for vibraphone accompanied by rich string harmonies. The slow movement centres on the marimba, creating intense, dream-like music and the concerto ends with an effusive finale of elaborate, syncopated rhythms and a carnival atmosphere.

Elinor Remick Warren
1900–1991

Elinor Remick Warren spent most of her life living and working in Los Angeles on the west coast of the United States, away from what is usually regarded as the musical mainstream of the east coast. Her music is unashamedly traditional, in the forms and style of late 19th-century romanticism. She is perhaps best known for her vocal, choral and orchestral works.

Born in Los Angeles in 1900, Warren was the only child of parents who were keen amateur musicians. Her mother Maude had studied the piano with a pupil of Franz Liszt, and her father, businessman James Warren, had at one time hoped to be a professional singer. Warren herself had piano lessons from the age of five and began writing music while she was at Westlake School for Girls. At 15 she started having composition lessons, and three years later Schirmer published her first work 'A Song of June'. After graduating from high school Warren spent a year at home studying the piano and composition and then a year at Mills College in Oakland, California.

In the early 1920s Warren went to New York for four years where she continued to study and to work as an accompanist for singers from the Metropolitan Opera when they went on concert tours. The singers often included her songs, many of which had been published, in their repertoires. Warren also made a series of piano recordings including a work of her own, *Frolic of the Elves* (reworked in 1950 as *Scherzo* for orchestra), as well as appearing as a soloist with the Los Angeles Philharmonic Orchestra.

In 1925 Warren married doctor Raymond Huntsterger, had a son in 1928 and started divorce proceedings the following year. Based back in Los Angeles she continued to compose and to appear as a pianist and accompanist. By the 1930s her songs were being performed all over the world by singers such as Kirsten Flagstad who obviously appreciated her strong melodic vocal lines and simple, expressive harmonic structures. Although she continued to write songs with piano accompaniments, Warren also began to work at this time on orchestral and choral music. Her first major orchestral work *The Harp Weaver* to words by Edna St Vincent Millay, for baritone solo, women's chorus and orchestra, was published as a vocal score in 1932 and first performed in Los Angeles a few years later. In April 1936 Antonia Brico conducted it with the New York Women's Orchestra in New York.

In 1936 Warren married radio producer Z. Wayne Griffith with whom she had two more children in 1938 and 1940. From 1938 to 1939 she presented a weekly radio programme, discussing music that she played at the piano. By the early 1940s she had stopped performing apart from accompanying her own music, having decided to concentrate on looking after her family and composing. She never taught and rarely lectured on her music, feeling that she would only lose time that could have been spent composing. Warren always stressed the amount of time needed for composition, feeling that it was lack of time that hindered many women composers who had family responsibilities from succeeding.

In March 1940, the Los Angeles Philharmonic Orchestra conducted by Albert Coates gave the first performance of *The Passing of King Arthur*, a work that Warren had been writing since the early 1930s. This is a large, dramatic work for tenor, baritone, chorus and orchestra to a text from Alfred Tennyson's *Idylls of the King*. In 1946 the same orchestra premiered Warren's tone poem *The Crystal Lake.* Like much of her orchestral music, such as *Along the Western Shore* (1954) and *Suite for Orchestra* (1955), this work was inspired by the breathtaking scenery in the High Sierra where Warren and her husband owned a 500-acre ranch. In 1958 Warren was commissioned to write the chime theme to be played at the intervals during concerts at the Hollywood Bowl. She later arranged this *Carillon Theme* for chorus to her own text.

Warren continued to study. In the spring of 1935 she had been to the private lectures given by Arnold Schoenberg when he first arrived in Los Angeles. Of far more importance to Warren's music was her three months' intensive study with Nadia Boulanger in 1959. These lessons made her reconsider the orchestration of her earlier works, many of which underwent extensive revision. In 1960 and again in the late 1970s she revised her Carl Sandburg setting, *Singing Earth,* originally written in the early 1950s. *The Passing of King Arthur* was revised and even retitled *The Legend of King Arthur* for a new edition in 1974. *Abram in Egypt,* a work for baritone and orchestra based on one of the Dead Sea Scrolls and commissioned by singer Louis Sadler in the late 1950s, was later reworked with the addition of a chorus and first performed in this version in 1961.

In her later works Warren moved away from her neo-romantic style to a more angular though still entirely tonal language. Many of these works were commissions, including her *Requiem* (1966) for soprano, baritone, chorus and orchestra commissioned by conductor Roger Wagner; *Symphony in One Movement* (1970) for Stanford University; and *Good Morning America!* (1976), another setting of Carl Sandburg for narrator, chorus and orchestra, commissioned by Occidental College and completed with an NEA grant. Warren's music remained popular in her later years. Her orchestral works were performed more often than those of any other American woman composer during the 1970s. In 1980 Fischer published *Selected Songs by Elinor Remick Warren*, and at the time of her death in 1991 Cambria Records had embarked on a series of recordings of her music.

Judith Weir
b. 1954

Judith Weir is one of the best-known and most successful of the younger composers working in Britain. Although born in Cambridge, she comes from a Scottish family and her interest in traditional Scottish culture and music has played an important part in the development of her distinctive musical language. This is a language that is often witty and concise, with straightforward modal or tonal harmonies and one that has proved popular with audiences, performers and critics.

Weir began writing and arranging music for her school friends to play, using whatever instruments were available, including dustbin lids. While still at school in London, she had composition lessons from John Tavener as well as playing the oboe and percussion in the National Youth Orchestra of Great Britain. After leaving school she spent six months during 1973 studying computer music at the Massachusetts Institute of Technology in the United States. Later that year she returned to Britain where she studied music at King's College, Cambridge, taking composition lessons with Robin Holloway in her final year. While she was still a student at Cambridge, she had an orchestral work, *Where the Shining Trumpets Blow*, performed in London in 1974 and the following year won a Koussevitsky Fellowship from the Boston Symphony Orchestra to study for a few weeks at Tanglewood with Gunther Schuller.

After graduating from Cambridge in 1976, Weir became composer-in-residence for the Southern Arts Board, a job based in local communities that suited her very practical approach to writing music. In 1979 she moved to Glasgow where she taught at the University for three years, holding the Cramb fellowship in composition. Several of her early works grew directly out of her interest in Scottish culture, such as *Black Birdsong* (1977), a setting for baritone and four instruments of two traditional poems, 'The Three Ravens' and 'The Twa Corbies', and *Scotch Minstrelsy* (1982), a cycle of five songs for tenor or soprano and piano.

Another early work shows her growing interest in medieval history and literature. *King Harald's Saga* (1979) is a remarkable 'Grand Opera in Three Acts' for solo soprano that lasts less than 10 minutes and tells the story of an unsuccessful Norwegian invasion of England in 1066. The soprano sings all eight solo roles as well as that of the entire Norwegian army. Weir wrote her own libretto based on a medieval Icelandic saga. She has often returned to medieval texts as the basis for her works, using their flat, deadpan qualities to reach straight to the heart of her subject matter.

In 1983 Weir moved back to Cambridge where she held a Creative Arts Fellowship at Trinity College for three years. Scottish themes continued in works such as *Sketches from a Bagpiper's Album* (1984) for clarinet and piano or *Michael's Strathspey* (1985), a piano piece written for Michael Finnessey which uses rhythmic elements of this traditional Scottish dance. Weir also continued to write dramatic music. *Serbian Cabaret* (1984) is not a music-theatre piece but the four speaking instrumentalists tell the stories of five Serbo-Croat folk songs which are then illustrated with music. Weir was commissioned by Kent Opera in 1984 to write a children's opera, *The Black Spider*.

The following year she wrote the first of her works inspired by early Chinese culture. *The Consolations of Scholarship* (1985) is a music drama in the style of the medieval Chinese Yuan dramas and once again a soprano takes on all the roles in the story, although this time she is accompanied by nine instrumentalists.

Weir first came to widespread public attention with a work that built on the musical style and subject matter of *The Consolations*. This was her first full-length adult opera, the highly successful *A Night at the Chinese Opera*, commissioned by the BBC for Kent Opera and first performed in 1987. Weir wrote her own libretto, based around the Yuan drama 'The Chao Family Orphan', and the work deals with universal themes such as justice as well as exploring Chinese culture through Western eyes. Written for 10 singers and orchestra, the music, based largely around fundamental intervals of the octave and the fifth, has a clear, open sound. The clarity of the vocal writing, using various techniques including rhythmically notated speech, is an example of Weir's constant concern for text to be heard and understood and for her music to be accessible to audiences and performers.

Since the late 1980s Weir has lived in London and earns her living as a freelance composer. Her work has often been broadcast on television and she has written works in collaboration with film-makers such as *Missa del Cid* (1988), composed for the BBC 'Sounds on Film' series. This work for unaccompanied choir and speaker combines a bloodthirsty medieval Spanish epic poem with the liturgy of the Mass. Weir enjoys working with other artists and exploring new areas for her music such as theatre or dance. One of her most striking collaborations has been her work with choreographer Ian Spink and the dance company Second Stride on *Heaven Ablaze in his Breast* (1989), a work based on E.T.A. Hoffmann's story 'The Sandman'. Weir's incidental music for the theatre includes scores for Peter Shaffer's *The Gift of the Gorgon* (1992) and for Caryl Churchill's extraordinary play *The Skriker* (1993), which was also choreographed by Spink.

Weir maintained a connection with Scotland by visiting the Royal Scottish Academy of Music and Drama as composer-in-residence for a few weeks each year between 1988 and 1991, as well as by continuing to incorporate elements of Scottish rhythm, harmony and form into works such as *Airs from Another Planet* (1986) for wind quintet and piano and *Ardnamurchan Point* (1990) for two pianos. One of her most thoroughly Scottish works is her opera *The Vanishing Bridegroom*, commissioned by Scottish Opera and first performed in Glasgow in 1990. Weir's allegorical libretto retells three traditional Scottish tales, 'The Inheritance',

'The Disappearance' and 'The Stranger', all concerned in some way with disappearing husbands as well as bringing elements of the supernatural into everyday matters such as love, sex, money and death. The intimate music uses fragments of traditional Scottish dances and songs. *The Vanishing Bridegroom* uses a chorus and, unlike most of her earlier vocal works, is sung all the way through with no use of speech.

Weir is fascinated by arrangements and reworkings. In 1987 she wrote two works based on the music of the medieval French composer Perotin: *Sederunt Principes* and the humorous *Lovers, Learners and Libations – Scenes from Thirteenth Century Parisian Life*. She has also produced recompositions of Wolfgang Amadeus Mozart, *Scipio's Dream* (1991) for BBC television, and Claudio Monteverdi, *Combattimento II* (1992). In the early 1990s Weir produced two orchestral works. *Music, Untangled* (1991), commissioned by the Boston Symphony Orchestra for the 50th anniversary of the Tanglewood Music Centre, makes use of music from a traditional Scottish weaver's song and builds from a single unison line to denser, more complex textures and then back to a single line again. *Heroic Strokes of the Bow* (*Heroische Bogenstriche*, 1992), written for the Westdeutsche Sinfonia, was named after and inspired by the title of a painting by Paul Klee.

In April 1994 Weir's opera, *Blond Eckbert*, commissioned by English National Opera, was premiered at the Coliseum in London. For this work she wrote her own libretto based on a strange psychological tale of deception and betrayal written in 1796 by Johann Ludwig Tieck. *Blond Eckbert* is an absorbingly lyrical work that retains all the clarity and concision of Weir's earlier operas.

Maude Valérie White
1855–1937

Maude Valérie White was one of the most successful songwriters of the late 19th century. She was a passionate woman who translated her intense love of life and beauty into exquisitely crafted songs, setting an enormous range of poetry in many different languages. She was an energetic and obsessive traveller, often finding inspiration for her own work in the music of other countries.

White was born near Dieppe in Normandy to English parents who had recently arrived in Europe from Chile. The family moved to England before White was a year old. She had a cosmopolitan childhood and education in Heidelburg, Paris and England, which always included studying the piano. In the spring of 1873, at the age of 17, she composed her first song, a setting of Byron's 'Farewell, if ever fondest prayer', which was published the following year. She took some harmony and counterpoint lessons from W.S. Rockstro during a winter spent in Torquay and studied composi-tion with Oliver May in London. Her songs began to be performed in public by her three cousins who were profes-sional singers and by her close friend Mary Wakefield.

In 1876, at the age of 21, White finally persuaded her mother, who was firmly opposed to women taking up public careers, to allow her to study further. She went to the Royal Academy of Music, where she studied composition with George Macfarren and attempted to learn the violin, giving up because of severe muscular pains in her arms. During her years at the Academy she published many songs, settings of English, German and French lyrics, some under the name M. White, an anonymity probably chosen to pacify her mother's fear of public exposure. Her works, including a setting of 'Espoir en Dieu' by Victor Hugo for voice and orchestra, were often sung at student concerts.

In 1879, White became the first woman to win the coveted Mendelssohn scholarship, and her first big success came the following year when she accompanied the famous baritone Charles Santley in two of her songs at the prestigious Monday Popular Concerts. One of these, 'Absent yet present' to lyrics by Lord Lytton, was to become one of her best-selling songs, although she had been told that her accompaniment was too difficult for the general public. The accompaniments that White herself played to her songs were often more complex than those that were eventually published.

White's father had died while she was a child, and her mother, who had been in financial difficulties and suffering from a serious illness, died in 1881. White was devastated, gave up the Mendelssohn scholarship, left the Academy and spent the next 10 months in Chile with her elder sister. She wrote only one song there, a deeply moving setting of Percy Bysshe Shelley's 'To Mary'. She also learned to play the guitar and collected many Chilean folk tunes which she arranged for piano duet and published as *Eight South American Airs* on her return to England in 1882.

In London, White flung herself back into her songwriting and a life as a professional musician. She made many friends with other musicians and with society music lovers such as the Gladstones, the Lytteltons, Frank Schuster and Mrs Henry Gaskell, who frequently asked her to play her music at their soirées. Although she had been left a small legacy, she did not have enough inherited money to support the life that she wanted to lead.

Notoriously bad with her finances, she was nevertheless able to make the money that she needed by teaching her songs, giving piano lessons and playing at musical parties. Later in her life she was also to raise money by giving public concerts and translating books and plays. At musical soirées White frequently performed her songs with Charles Santley's daughter, singer Edith Santley, who was the first singer to perform in public her setting of lines from Shelley's *Prometheus Unbound*, 'My soul is an enchanted boat' (1882). This song was described in the first edition of Grove's *Dictionary of Music and Musicians*, published in 1899, as 'one of the best in our language'.

Towards the end of 1883 White spent six months studying in Vienna with Robert Fuchs, who tried to persuade her to write something other than vocal music. Like so many women of her time, White had obviously internalized the views of the musical establishment about women's abilities and simply did not believe that she was capable of writing instrumental or orchestral music. She felt miserable trying and described her decision to give up such attempts as making her feel like 'a gay and cheerful soufflé'. White rarely wrote anything other than vocal music again, although a piece for cello and piano, *Naissance d'Amour,* and several piano pieces were published in the 1880s and 90s. She is also known to have taken a few orchestration lessons, to have written some incidental music, a ballet, and to have attempted but given up on a Romanian opera. None of this work was published and it has not survived. White's songs from 1883 included her four songs from Alfred Tennyson's *In Memoriam* which she later performed to Tennyson himself. A visit to Sweden in the summer of 1884 resulted in several settings of Swedish and Norwegian lyrics. Other songs from the later 1880s include the hauntingly beautiful Byron setting, 'So we'll go no more a roving', written after her first visit to Italy.

During the 1890s White was at the height of her success. Her songs were sung all over Britain and Europe by the best-known singers of the day such as Raimund von zur Mühlen, Louise Phillips, Clara Butt, Robert Kennerley Rumford and Harry Plunket Greene. Her music was included in prestigious concert series and she also started organizing public concerts of her own works. She wrote a great deal of music in the 1890s, including many German lyrics, in a simple lieder-like style that was quite different from her French or English settings. Other songs written at this time included a setting of Robert Burns' 'John Anderson, my Jo', often sung by the famous Australian diva Nellie Melba, and 'Infinite Love', a

setting of part of a sonnet by Dante Gabriel Rossetti, which was described in *The Musical Times* as ' ... highly-coloured, passionate, sensuous, mystic ...'. In 1898 White was commissioned by Henry Irving to write the incidental music for *The Medicine Man*, a play by her friend Robert Hichens and the journalist H.D. Traill, an experience she did not particularly enjoy or want to repeat.

For much of her life White suffered from very bad health, although she always remained resolutely cheerful in spite of often being in considerable pain. From 1901, when she was 46, she spent a large part of each year living in the warmer climate of Taormina in Sicily. The rest of the year was spent in England or travelling, usually staying with friends and composing wherever she found herself. White was very interested in the music of the many countries she visited. In 1902 she travelled in Algeria with Hichens and became fascinated by Arab music. White especially loved the music of Sicily and used some of it in *From The Ionian Sea*, a collection of piano pieces which has not survived. This was one of the works she played at a concert she gave at Cairo Opera House while visiting Egypt in 1907.

During the early years of the 20th century White's music was falling out of fashion with the critics and the musical establishment, although it was still popular with the public and with

Maude Valérie White

singers such as the famous tenor Gervase Elwes. White continued to compose although her songs were published far less frequently than previously. After the huge Messina earthquake in 1908, she had to abandon her house in Sicily and made her home with her sister Emmie in Florence. She continued to travel and to promote her music, planning a concert tour of the United States for the winter of 1911 to 1912 which then fell through. In the summer of 1912 she travelled to visit friends in southern Russia, a journey which inspired two very different works. One was the ebullient *Trois Chansons Tziganes*, settings of three Russian poems in French translation from one of Leo Tolstoy's plays. The other was a ballet, *The Enchanted Heart*, which White had written after seeing the Russian ballet at Usovska. Various projected performances of this work fell through, including the performance of an orchestral suite that Henry Wood had asked White to arrange for the Proms in 1915.

During the war, White put a great deal of energy into organizing concerts for various war charities. For one of these concerts, in aid of the Serbian Relief Fund, she arranged five Serbian dances for full orchestra with bass clarinet, double bassoon and a vast array of percussion. They were conducted by Henry Wood and the concert also included part of *The Enchanted Heart*.

White also wrote two songs in response to the war, 'Le Depart Du Conscrit' (1917) and 'On the Fields of France' (1919).

After the war White continued to live with Emmie in Italy although the last few years of her life were spent in England. She appears to have written little during the 1920s, but songs such as the *Two Songs* of 1924, 'La Flûte Invisible' (Victor Hugo) and 'Le Foyer' (Paul Verlaine), written when she was nearly 70, show her exploring a decidedly impressionistic language. This atmospheric style of writing had been apparent as early as her 1904 setting of verses from Gabriele d'Annuzio's poem 'Isaotta Blanzemano' which the publisher Signor Ricordi described as like 'un rêve d'opium'.

White translated several books and plays in her final years and followed her first volume of memoirs *Friends and Memories* (1914) with a second, *My Indian Summer* (1932). She continued to organize concerts of her works, often with the help of Roger Quilter and his protegé, singer Mark Raphael, the last in the long line of famous singers to have sung White's songs with the composer herself. Surviving letters from White to Quilter show that she was quite indefatigable, planning endless concerts so that she could afford to winter in Egypt. She died in 1937 at the age of 82.

Margaret Lucy Wilkins
b. 1939

Margaret Lucy Wilkins was born in Surrey in 1939 and taught to play the piano by her mother. In 1952, at the age of 12, she became a Junior Exhibitioner at Trinity College where she spent Saturday mornings studying the piano and the cello. She first started to compose at Trinity and went on to study music at Nottingham University, followed by a year studying for a postgraduate teaching diploma from the Institute of Education in London.

Wilkins' first teaching job was in Nottingham. She then married in 1962 and went with her husband to work for two years in Newfoundland. In 1964 the family moved to Scotland where Wilkins spent the next few years bringing up her two children, born in 1964 and 1967, and giving private piano lessons. In 1969 she was involved in forming the Scottish Early Music Consort and performed with them for the next seven years. A fascination with medieval culture has inspired much of her music.

In the early 1970s, when she was in her early 30s, Wilkins' career as a composer took off. In 1970 her vocal piece *Dieux Est* was broadcast by the BBC, her *Concerto Grosso* for strings was performed at the Wigmore Hall in London and her *musique concrète, Music for an Exhibition,* was written for an outdoor exhibition of sculpture in Scotland. In 1971 her settings of poems by Mary Queen of Scots, *The Silver Casket* for soprano, harp and string trio, won the Cappiani Prize awarded by the Society of Women Musicians during its diamond-jubilee year and was performed and broadcast. In the same year *Witch Music* for mezzo-soprano, clarinet, trumpet and double bass was played at a Society for the Promotion of New Music concert at the South Bank Centre in London. In this mesmerizing work, which sets texts of witches' cures, the singer plays triangles and finger cymbals that hang from a cross six feet high, introducing the element of music theatre and visual imagery that often plays an important part in Wilkins' works.

In 1973, Wilkins had a very productive year. Two works were commissioned for the St Andrews Arts Festival: *Sci-Fi* for electronic tape and the exuberant *Dance Variations* for string orchestra and harpsichord. In the same year, Wilkins wrote the four-movement violin and piano work *Orpheus* which follows an explicit programme telling the story of Orpheus and Eurydice. The violin plays expressive melodic themes with the pianist producing rich harmonies and playing the strings inside the piano with a variety of beaters. Another programmatic work was the orchestral *Hymn to Creation* which follows the act of creation from the percussive, indeterminate opening through to the birth of a lyrical violin melody. The final work of this year was *Struwwelpeter* for soprano, three clarinets, piano and percussion. Wilkins used the 19th-century children's cautionary tales to express some of her concerns about contemporary issues such as racism or nuclear weapons. Her lively music quotes from or refers to a wide range of music, including that of Jacques Offenbach and Luigi Nono.

Wilkins' works often use religious symbolism, perhaps nowhere so much as in the extraordinary *Ave Maria* (1975). This work for mezzo-soprano, flute, clarinet, harp, piano, percussion and string trio explores the two central Biblical women Eve and Mary, and the path from temptation to redemption. Wilkins sets seven texts. The first three come from the Chester Mystery Plays and explore the experience of Eve, ending with her painful lament for her dead son; the central text links the two women; and the last three, from 14th- and 15th-century texts, refer to Mary and her son. There is a refrain between the texts built on the same isorhythmic pattern. During the work the singer moves from an apple tree to a cross, stopping for each text as if at the seven stations. Eve's music, built on a seven-note row, is dark and agonized, while Mary's music, built on a different, six-note row, is full of light, with glowing accompaniment from the piano and the harp.

In 1976 Wilkins joined the staff at the University of Huddersfield where she still teaches composition. Over the next few years she wrote a variety of music including keyboard works such as *A Dance to the Music of Time* (1980) for harpsichord, *Deus ex Machina* (1982) for organ and *Study in Black and White No. 1* (1983) for piano. This last work was followed by a companion piece *Study in Black and White No. 2*, written in 1992 for pianist Ananda Sukarlan who had often performed the earlier work. Both pieces use the pentatonic scale, and the pitches of the second are based on the letters of Sukarlan's name. Wilkins' vocal music from the early 1980s included *Three Skelmanthorpe Carols* (1980) and *Gitanjali,* subtitled 'six song offerings', for choir.

Wilkins took a sabbatical year away from teaching in 1987 to concentrate on composition. During this year she wrote two large-scale works exploring extremes of sound and texture. *Rêve, Réveil, Révelation, Réverbérations* (1988) is an elaborate work for 16 instruments including a DX7 synthesizer using a celeste preset. The instruments are divided into eight groups and each group plays a set of pitches with different equal divisions of the octave. *Revelations of the Seven Angels* (1988) for solo soprano, male choir, boys choir and orchestra is intended for performance in a cathedral. Different groups of instruments at different places in the cathedral represent the seven stations from the 'Book of Revelations' and are visited by a group of brass players representing the seven angels. With music coming from more than one group at a time the overall effect is like that of listening to electronic music from several speakers.

These complex works were followed by *Symphony 1989* and the multimedia work *Kanal* written for students at Huddersfield Polytechnic and intended for outdoor performance. *Kanal* was first performed in 1990 in Huddersfield and repeated for the 1992 International Society for Contemporary Music World Music Days in the town square of Pultusk near Warsaw in Poland. It is a huge work, lasting at least 90 minutes, which uses singers, actors, dancers, brass and percussion, two electronic

music tapes and light. There are four groups of performers at four different locations. Each location uses its own theme and its own text taken from writings by Pablo Neruda, Jorge Luis Borges, Bertold Brecht and William Blake. Each location is self-contained and the order in which things happen is variable, with the players incorporating elements of improvisation. The music created is rich and meditative. Wilkins sees the title as implying a channel, a canal and 'a way through', perhaps to a closer understanding of the infinite.

Since the late 1980s Wilkins has set up the contemporary music group Polyphonia and initiated a project at the University of Huddersfield to ensure that the work of women composers from the 12th century to the present is included in the courses taught throughout the music department. Her own recent works continue to explore a variety of vivid images and sounds. *Musica Angelorum* (1991) for orchestra grew out of medieval pictures of angels playing instruments. First performed at the Huddersfield Contemporary Music Theatre in 1991, this short work creates the music of the angels in shimmering string harmonics and glissandi.

Wilkins is increasingly attracted to the opportunities for the immediate creation of sounds provided by working in an electronic studio. Parts of her electro-acoustic tape *Stringsing*

(1991) were used by choreographer Julie Wilson in the dance project 'Strung Out', performed at the Alhambra Studio in Bradford and at the 1993 Harrogate Festival.

Grace Williams
1906–1977

Grace Williams was a composer renowned for her integrity as a person and as an artist, as well as for her self-criticism and her modesty. She devoted her life to the creation of her powerfully expressive music but refused most of the honours, such as the OBE and a Civil List Pension, that were offered to her. When the Welsh Arts Council funded a recording of her orchestral music in the early 1970s, she simply said that she did not deserve a record to herself.

Williams was born in the port town of Barry in South Wales in 1906. Her parents were both schoolteachers who loved music, owning a large and varied collection of gramophone records and piano scores. Her father was the conductor of the Romilly Boys Choir for whom Williams acted as accompanist as a young girl. She began writing music while she was still at school and claimed that one of her earliest inspirations had been hearing a performance of *Morfa Rhuddlan* by Morfydd Owen at the National Eisteddfod when it was held in Barry in 1920. Three years later, in 1923, she won the newly established Morfydd Owen Musical Scholarship to University College, Cardiff, where one of her professors was the composer David Evans who had also taught Owen.

Williams graduated from Cardiff in 1926 and went straight to London to the Royal College of Music to study composition with Ralph Vaughan Williams. At this time she was a keen Wagnerian but also an enthusiastic explorer of new music. During her time at the College she developed close friendships with the other composers of her generation who were studying there including Dorothy Gow and especially Elizabeth Maconchy. She and Maconchy were friends for the rest of her life. They maintained a close relationship, largely through letters, and their discussion and criticism of each other's works and of music in general was extremely important to both composers. Williams won several prizes at the College, culminating in an Octavia Travelling Scholarship in 1930. She chose to go to Vienna where she studied with Egon Wellesz. Williams loved the musical life in Vienna, and when Maconchy also came over to study, the two friends went as often as they could to the opera. They also enjoyed sitting in cafés, drinking coffee and smoking the occasional cigar.

On her return from Vienna in late 1931, Williams took up two part-time teaching jobs in London: as a visiting lecturer at Southlands College of Education in Wimbledon, and as music teacher at Camden School for Girls, where she was responsible for arranging and producing a variety of school opera performances. Her compositions, some of which had been heard at College concerts, were beginning to be performed and broadcast. In 1932 her *Two Psalms for Contralto, Harp and Strings*, first heard at a student concert five years earlier, were played at a Patron's Fund Concert at the Royal College of Music, a series that gave young composers the opportunity to hear their works professionally performed. This was one of the first of her works that Williams did not later destroy. Three small orchestral pieces and a flute sonatina were given premieres at the early Macnaghten–Lemare concerts, and one of her most successful early works, the overture *Hen Walia* (1930) based on Welsh folk tunes, was broadcast

several times during the 1930s.

Another of Williams' important friendships was with Benjamin Britten. The two composers probably met through the Macnaghten–Lemare concerts and remained close friends throughout the 1930s, commenting on and criticizing each other's works as well as going to the opera and the cinema together. It was through Britten that Williams started working for the Strand Film Company in 1936. Williams continued to draw on Welsh culture and legend as well as Welsh folksong in her music, as can be seen in works such as the *Four Illustrations from the Legend of Rhiannon* (1939) for orchestra, based on a story from the Welsh classic, the *Mabinogion*.

During the war Williams was evacuated out of London with the Camden school, but despite the disruption to musical life caused by the war, her music received several important performances during the early 1940s. The first of these was the BBC Northern Orchestra's premiere of her *Fantasia on Welsh Nursery Tunes* (1940), which was to become one of her most popular works. Another wartime performance, in 1943, was of her virtuosic *Sinfonia Concertante* (1941) for piano and orchestra. Two other wartime works, her First Symphony (later withdrawn) and *Sea Sketches* for string orchestra, were not heard until 1947. *Sea Sketches*, one of several of her works to create vivid pictures of the sea, became very popular and was her first major work to be published when it was issued by Oxford University Press in 1951.

Towards the end of the war Williams returned to London, but the stress of teaching, composing and her other work made her very ill. By 1945 she was thinking about giving up composing, and the following year she took up a full-time job in the BBC Schools department. She soon became ill again, however, and decided to leave London and return to Wales. In February 1947 she moved back to Barry where she was to spend the rest of her life, living in a self-contained flat in her parents' house. Although she had developed a relationship with a Polish man during the war, she never married, claiming it would be unfair of her because music was her first love.

In Barry she established a successful career as a freelance composer. At first she had to spend most of her time on what she called 'jobs', work which bought in money, such as writing scripts for the BBC, making folk-song arrangements for BBC Schools programmes, writing incidental music for radio, television and film, copying other people's music and, for a few years in the early 1950s, teaching composition at the College of Music and Drama in Cardiff. As she became better known in Wales and started receiving more commissions from the BBC, major orchestras and important

festivals, so she was able to cut down on the 'jobs' and concentrate on writing her own music.

There was a change in Williams' music from the mid-1950s onwards as she moved away from the richer, romantic textures of her earlier works towards a more individual musical language. She continued to concentrate almost entirely on vocal and orchestral works, saying that she had no talent for chamber music. At this time Williams stopped using Welsh folk tunes directly in her works although she still drew on some of the forms and structures of Welsh music and literature. One of her best known works, *Penillion* (1955) for orchestra, is based in structure on the old Welsh penillion form of verses of vocal improvisation over a harp melody. Other important orchestral works include her sombre Second Symphony (1957), a Concerto for one of her favourite instruments, the trumpet (1963), and *Carillons* (1965) for oboe and orchestra. In 1969 she wrote an orchestral fanfare, *Castell Caernarfon*, which was played on the ramparts of the castle for the investiture of the Prince of Wales.

Many of Williams' later works were vocal. She had written several solo songs in the 1930s, usually to orchestral accompaniment. One of her first choral works was the entrancing choral suite *The Dancers* (1951) for soprano, women's chorus, string orchestra and harp. Williams set five poems by H.D., Hilaire Belloc, Thomas Chatterton, May Sarton and Kathleen Raine, a collection of texts centring around women dancing, in celebration, to forget pain and, in the final ecstatic setting of Raine's 'To the Wild Hills', to dance away death. Williams' song cycle, *Six Poems by Gerard Manley Hopkins* for contralto and string sextet, was written for the 1958 Cheltenham Festival. This is a passionate work, moving from the lyrical richness of 'Pied Beauty' through a heartfelt, agonized setting of 'No worst there is none' to an exhilarating ending with 'Windhover'.

Although she was not Welsh-speaking, Williams made several settings of Welsh poetry including *Four Medieval Welsh Poems* (1962) for contralto, harp and harpsichord and *Two Ninth-Century Welsh Poems* (1965) for baritone and harp. Williams wrote one stage work, her comic opera *The Parlour,* which was produced to great acclaim by Welsh National Opera in 1966. She wrote her own libretto based on a short story by Guy de Maupassant, 'En famille', about a tyrannical grandmother and her family. One of Williams' largest vocal works was her *Missa Cambrensis,* written for the Llandaff Festival of 1971, in which she added a Welsh carol and the reading of the Beatitudes in Welsh to the usual liturgy.

During the last years of her life, Williams revised many of her earlier works as well as writing some new vocal pieces. These included the beautiful *Ave Maris Stella* (1973), a setting of an anonymous eighth-century hymn for unaccompanied chorus. Her last completed work was *Two Choruses* (1975), settings of Rudyard Kipling's 'Harp Song of the Dane Women' and Thomas Beddoes' 'Mariner's Song' for chorus, harp and two horns, creating a magical evocation of the sea. Williams died in 1977, a few days before her 71st birthday.

Amy Woodforde-Finden
1860–1919

Surprisingly little appears to be known about Amy Woodforde-Finden, although she was the composer of probably the most successful songs of the early 20th century, her set of *Four Indian Love Lyrics*. She was born in Valparaiso in Chile where her father, Alfred Ward, was a British consul. When he died her mother moved the family to London. Woodforde-Finden started composing at nine. She studied music privately and her teachers included Adolph Schloesser and Amy Horrocks, a pianist and composer who had been born in Brazil, studied at the Royal Academy of Music and wrote a wide variety of music including an orchestral piece, *Undine*, which was performed at the Proms in 1897.

Towards the end of the 19th century Woodforde-Finden went to India, travelled in Kashmir and married Lieutenant-Colonel Woodforde-Finden, a medical officer in the Bengal Cavalry. Two early songs survive which she published as Amy Ward, but giving her married name, Mrs

Woodforde-Finden, in brackets afterwards. These are sentimental songs with rich harmonies, setting words by Alfred Austin, 'A Night in June' (1896) with a violin obbligato, and by Gilbert Parker, 'O Flower of all the World' (1897). Both songs were published by Boosey.

After her return to England around the turn of the century, Woodforde-Finden wrote the *Four Indian Love Lyrics*. These songs were initially turned down by all the publishers she approached, so she published them herself in 1902. They were then taken up by the singer Hamilton Earle, and, once the extent of their popularity had been realized, reissued by Boosey in 1903. The *Four Indian Love Lyrics* are settings of four poems from *The Garden of Kama* by Laurence Hope, whom a reviewer in the *St James's Gazette* had described as 'a new and refreshingly virile poet'.

Laurence Hope was actually the pseudonym of Adela Florence Cory

(1865–1904), a poet who married an officer in the Bengal Cavalry. Husband and wife were extremely close and had adventures together all over India, sometimes with Cory disguised as a boy. She killed herself two months after his death. Woodforde-Finden's settings of her poems appealed to the Edwardian British obsession with the East and soon became hugely popular. They were arranged for piano, violin and piano, salon orchestra, military band and a variety of different vocal groups with an arrangement for a trio of women's voices published as late as 1955. Hope's works are quite extraordinary love poems, full of violent and erotic imagery. Woodforde-Finden supplied passionate and exciting music, using harmonic inflections and other rhythmic and melodic touches to create a suitably exotic atmosphere. It has been suggested that the pentatonic opening of the most famous song of the set, 'Kashmiri Song', is actually based on a raga.

Woodforde-Finden followed the success of her *Four Indian Love Lyrics* with many other cycles and collections of songs, mostly using poetry set in the Middle East, Northern Africa, Japan or South America and drawing on elements of the music of these countries, always filtered through the Western ear. The first of these cycles was *A Lover in Damascus* (1904), a set of six songs to poems by Charles Hanson Towne with some evocative melodic lines especially in the opening song 'Far across the Desert Sands'. Woodforde-Finden wrote several cycles setting poems by Towne including *Five Little Japanese Songs* (1906), *A Dream of Egypt* (1910) and *The Myrtles of Damascus* (1918).

Another writer whose lyrics she frequently set was Lieutenant Colonel Frederick John Fraser of the 33rd Punjabis, with works such as *On Jhelum River* (1905), subtitled 'A Kashmiri Love Story', *The Pagoda of Flowers* (1907), subtitled 'A Burmese Story in Song', *Aziza* (1909), subtitled 'Three Oriental Songs', and *The Eyes of Firozée* (1914), subtitled 'Two songs, the words suggested by a Persian Romance'. For her South-American settings she turned to the writer Harold Simpson with *Three Little Mexican Songs* (1912) and *Little Cactus Flower*, subtitled 'A Musical Scene in a Mexican Garden', (1913). None of these later works ever achieved the popularity of the *Four Indian Love Lyrics*. In 1914 Woodforde-Finden gave a concert of her works at the Aeolian Hall in London and five years later, in 1919, she died.

Agnes Zimmermann
1847–1925

Agnes Zimmermann was born in Cologne but came to England with her family as a young child. In June 1857, at the age of nine, she entered the Royal Academy of Music on the recommendation of William Sterndale Bennett. She studied the piano with Cipriani Potter and was twice elected King's Scholar. In 1863, at the age of 16, she made her debut at the Crystal Palace, playing part of Ludwig van Beethoven's *Emperor Concerto*. In the same year her first works were published, three songs to words by Robert Burns, Thomas Moore and William Shakespeare. During 1864, her final year as a student, two sacred part-songs and an orchestral overture were played at Academy concerts. In this year she also appeared at the Gewandhaus Concerts in Leipzig.

From 1865 Zimmermann instituted a regular series of piano recitals and chamber concerts at the Hanover Square Rooms in London, moving to St James's Hall in 1875. She was soon regarded as one of the country's leading pianists, in great demand for series such as the Monday and Saturday Popular Concerts. The programme of one of her early concerts in 1865 included a piano sonata written for her by George Macfarren as well as her usual classical repertoire of composers such as Ludwig van Beethoven and Felix Mendelssohn. Zimmermann also included her own music at these concerts.

The intellectual classicism of her chamber music and piano pieces was greatly praised by critics who were exasperated by the vogue for showy, virtuosic works. A concert she gave in June 1867 included her own *Canon, Sarabande and Gigue* for piano. Many of her piano pieces were in dance forms and later works also used more modern forms such as mazurkas, boleros and barcarolles. She used the more baroque dances again in her Suite for piano, violin and cello in D major, op. 19, which consisted of five movements: Introduction and Allegro, Canon à la 7ième, Gavotte, Air and performed in 1876 and published two years later. It is in four substantial movements: Prelude, Mazurka, Scherzo and March. The Prelude has a dramatic improvisatory opening which recurs throughout the movement. The other three movements are all lively dances in ternary form with strongly contrasting and often lyrical middle sections. Zimmermann followed her first violin sonata with two more, op. 21 in A minor dating from about 1874 and op. 23 in G minor of 1879. They were both performed by Wilma Normann-Neruda (Lady Hallé), one of the leading violinists of the day.

As well as chamber and piano music, Zimmermann continued to write songs and part-songs, although many of her vocal works are early, dating from the 1860s. They never achieved the critical success of her other works. An important part of Zimmermann's output are her many editions and arrangements. She edited the complete piano works of Robert Schumann as well as the piano sonatas of Wolfgang Amadeus Mozart and Ludwig van Beethoven and made piano arrangements of music by J.S. Bach, George Frederic Handel, Joseph Haydn and others. Zimmermann developed friendships and professional relationships with most of the important musicians of the day both in Britain and in Europe where she frequently toured. Her close friends included the violinist Emil Sauret and the cellist Alfredo Piatti.

Agnes Zimmermann

Gigue. This work was first performed in 1872 and published the following year. The critic from the *Athenaeum* was impressed: 'The work is not that of an ordinary mind; there are not only good ideas, but masterly development and treatment.' Earlier chamber music had included a first Violin Sonata, op. 16, dedicated to and performed by Joseph Joachim, and a Cello Sonata, op. 17, 'every movement of which is replete with interest', according to the critic from *The Musical Times*.

One of Zimmermann's most successful works was her Suite for piano, op. 22,

Zimmermann seems to have suffered from bad health. In 1888 *The Musical Times* referred to her recovery from a 'severe illness'. She appears to have more or less stopped performing in the 1890s although she still made occasional appearances, one as late as 1913. She also appears to have stopped composing or at least being published. Without her own promotion at the important concerts at which she had previously performed, her music stopped being played. The only revival of her works appears to have been at the Ernest Fowles' British Chamber Music Concerts in 1896 and 1897 when her Second Violin Sonata and the Suite for piano, violin and cello were heard. When she died in 1925, Zimmermann left all her music and her manuscripts to the Royal Academy of Music.

Ellen Taaffe Zwilich
b. 1939

In 1983 Ellen Taaffe Zwilich was thrust into the media spotlight when she became the first woman to win a Pulitzer Prize in composition, for her Symphony no. 1. Since then she has become one of the most successful composers in the United States with countless commissions from major orchestras and ensembles and great popular acclaim for a prolific series of works in an expressive and accessible idiom. Her music is essentially tonal with lively rhythms and great structural clarity.

Zwilich was born in Miami, Florida, and showed an interest in music from an early age. As a child she played the piano, violin and trumpet, and at about 10 years old began to write down the piano pieces she had been making up for years, feeling that they were better than the inane pieces her piano teacher wanted her to learn. She went on to play, conduct and arrange music for her high-school orchestra and band, and on leaving school went to Florida State University, Tallahassee, to study

music, finally graduating with a master's degree in composition in 1962. While at college, she played a wide variety of music including jazz trumpet and received three prizes from the Florida Composers League.

After graduation she spent a year teaching music in South Carolina before moving to New York where she worked as a freelance violinist. From 1965 she played with the American Symphony Orchestra for seven years, an experience which she found to be extremely useful in her work as an orchestral composer. In 1969 Zwilich married the Hungarian-born violinist Joseph Zwilich for whom she wrote her *Sonata in Three Movements* (1973–4) for violin and piano. In 1970 Zwilich embarked on further composition studies at the Juilliard, studying with Elliott Carter and Roger Sessions and in 1975 becoming the first woman to receive a doctorate in composition from that institution. She then gave up performing in order to concentrate on composing. Her early works achieved considerable success. *Symposium for Orchestra* (1973) was premiered by the New York Philharmonic conducted by Pierre Boulez in 1975, and her String Quartet (1974), a complex, atonal work dedicated to Sessions, was very well received when it was performed at the International Society for Contemporary Music World Music Days in Boston in 1976.

In 1979 Zwilich's husband suddenly died of a heart attack. She was in the middle of a commission for Boston Musica Viva, her *Chamber Symphony*. Her feelings of grief coupled with a new awareness of the value of life led to a significant change in her music. Meaning and communication became of the utmost importance. This stylistic change can be heard in the *Chamber Symphony*, an intensely emotional one-movement work for flute, clarinet, violin, viola, cello and piano. The Pulitzer Prize-winning Symphony no. 1, subtitled 'Three Movements for Orchestra', was commissioned by the American Composers Orchestra who gave the first performance in 1982, conducted by Gunther Schuller. Zwilich builds the entire work on the material of the first 15 bars and on what she has described as her 'obsession' with the interval of a minor third. Drawing on her years as an orchestral musician, Zwilich produces rich, expressive colours from the orchestra, for example, giving the tuba an extended solo in the slow movement.

Orchestral music has continued to be of central importance in Zwilich's output. She has written two more symphonies, Symphony no. 2 (1985), subtitled 'Cello Symphony', which includes a cadenza for the whole cello section and Symphony no. 3 (1992), which was commissioned by the New York Philharmonic for its 150th anniversary. Other orchestral works include *Prologue and Variations* (1983) for string orchestra and *Celebration* (1984). In the five-movement *Concerto Grosso* (1985), Zwilich explores the Baroque world of a Handel violin sonata from which she quotes extensively. Since 1986 Zwilich has written a remarkable number of concertos including Concerto for Piano and Orchestra (1986), *Images* for two pianos and orchestra (1986), Concerto for Violin, Violincello and Orchestra (1991) and concertos for trombone, bass trombone, flute, oboe, bassoon and French horn.

Many critics regard *Symbolon* (1988) as one of her best works. It was commissioned by the New York Philharmonic for their tour of the Soviet Union. The title refers to an ancient Greek practice whereby two people broke a piece of poetry in half and each kept one half as a symbol of friendship. *Symbolon* is a powerful work with dramatic climaxes and moments of quiet reflection. As in so much of her music, the basic material out of which the work will grow is heard at the opening. This includes a violin theme which, again like much of her music, is strongly reminiscent of the music of Dmitri Shostakovich, perhaps particularly appropriate in a work that was premiered in Leningrad.

Although Zwilich has written little mature vocal music and has turned down commissions for opera, she has not abandoned instrumental chamber music and has produced some of her most moving music for smaller ensembles. *Concerto for Trumpet and Five Players* (1984) is an often ebullient work with a virtuosic trumpet part and an important percussion part using vibraphone and marimba. The slow movement contains some wonderfully lyrical writing for the trumpet in its highest register. The four-movement *Double Quartet* (1984), which explores the relationship between two string quartets, contains more dissonance than many of her works.

Chronological List of Composers

Also indicating the country (or countries) with which they are principally associated.

Mary Dering	(1629–1704)	Britain
Maria Barthelemon	(1749–1799)	Britain
Mary Linwood	(1755/6–1845)	Britain
Harriet Abrams	(1760–1822)	Britain
Jane Guest	(*c.* 1765–after 1824)	Britain
Maria Hester Reynolds	(active from 1772)	Britain
Sophia Dussek	(1775–*c.* 1830)	Britain
Maria Parke	(1775–1822)	Britain
Caroline Norton	(1808–1877)	Britain
Ann Mounsey Bartholomew	(1811–1891)	Britain
Caroline Reinagle	(1818–1892)	Britain
Elizabeth Stirling	(1819–1895)	Britain
Augusta Browne	(1821–1882)	United States
Charlotte Sainton-Dolby	(1821–1885)	Britain
Faustina Hasse Hodges	(1822–1895)	United States
Virginia Gabriel	(1825–1877)	Britain
Kate Loder	(1825–1904)	Britain
Claribel	(1830–1869)	Britain
Susan Parkhurst	(1836–1918)	United States
Alice Mary Smith	(1839–1884)	Britain
Oliveria Prescott	(1842–1919)	Britain
Clara Kathleen Rogers	(1844–1931)	Britain/United States
Agnes Zimmermann	(1847–1925)	Britain
Frances Allitsen	(1848–1912)	Britain
Mary Carmichael	(1851–1935)	Britain

Emma Steiner	(1852–1929)	United States
Maude Valérie White	(1855–1937)	Britain
Helen Hopekirk	(1856–1945)	Britain/United States
Rosalind Ellicott	(1857–1924)	Britain
Ethel Smyth	(1858–1944)	Britain
Amy Woodforde-Finden	(1860–1919)	Britain
Carrie Jacobs-Bond	(1861–1946)	United States
Liza Lehmann	(1862–1918)	Britain
Dora Bright	(1863–1951)	Britain
Eleanor Everest Freer	(1864–1942)	United States
Amanda Aldridge	(1866–1956)	Britain
Adela Maddison	(1866–1929)	Britain
Amy Beach	(1867–1944)	United States
Margaret Ruthven Lang	(1867–1972)	United States
Mary Carr Moore	(1873–1957)	United States
Ethel Barns	(1874–1948)	Britain
Mabel Daniels	(1879–1971)	United States
Poldowski	(1879–1932)	Britain
Gena Branscombe	(1881–1977)	United States
Mary Howe	(1882–1964)	United States
Rebecca Clarke	(1886–1979)	Britain
Marion Bauer	(1887–1955)	United States
Florence Price	(1888–1953)	United States
Ina Boyle	(1889–1967)	Ireland
Morfydd Owen	(1891–1918)	Britain
Dorothy Gow	(1893–1982)	Britain
Dorothy Howell	(1898–1982)	Britain
Radie Britain	(b. 1899)	United States
Eleanor Remick Warren	(1900–1991)	United States
Ruth Crawford	(1901–1953)	United States
Priaulx Rainier	(1903–1986)	Britain
Miriam Gideon	(b. 1906)	United States
Elisabeth Lutyens	(1906–1983)	Britain
Louise Talma	(b. 1906)	United States
Grace Williams	(1906–1977)	Britain
Imogen Holst	(1907–1984)	Britain
Elizabeth Maconchy	(b. 1907)	Britain
Minna Keal	(b. 1909)	Britain
Phyllis Tate	(1911–1987)	Britain
Julia Smith	(1911–1989)	United States

Margaret Bonds	(1913–1972)	United States
Vivian Fine	(b. 1913)	United States
Ruth Gipps	(b. 1921)	Britain
Jean Eichelberger Ivey	(b. 1923)	United States
Julia Perry	(1924–1979)	United States
Daphne Oram	(b. 1925)	Britain
Marga Richter	(b. 1926)	United States
Ursula Mamlok	(b. 1928)	United States
Thea Musgrave	(b. 1928)	Britain/United States
Nancy Van de Vate	(b. 1930)	United States
Pauline Oliveros	(b. 1932)	United States
Lucia Dlugoszewski	(b. 1934)	United States
Erika Fox	(b. 1936)	Britain
Janet Beat	(b. 1937)	Britain
Joan Tower	(b. 1938)	United States
Jennifer Fowler	(b. 1939)	Britain
Barbara Kolb	(b. 1939)	United States
Margaret Lucy Wilkins	(b. 1939)	Britain
Ellen Taaffe Zwilich	(b. 1939)	United States
Meredith Monk	(b. 1942)	United States
Tania León	(b. 1943)	United States
Melanie Daiken	(b. 1945)	Britain
Julia Usher	(b. 1945)	Britain
Jane O'Leary	(b. 1946)	United States/Ireland
Daria Semegen	(b. 1946)	United States
Nicola LeFanu	(b. 1947)	Britain
Hilary Tann	(b. 1947)	Britain/United States
Diana Burrell	(b. 1948)	Britain
Eleanor Alberga	(b. 1949)	Britain
Shulamit Ran	(b. 1949)	United States
Beth Anderson	(b. 1950)	United States
Libby Larsen	(b. 1950)	United States
Eibhlis Farrell	(b. 1953)	Ireland
Judith Weir	(b. 1954)	Britain
Helen Roe	(b. 1955)	Britain
Errollyn Wallen	(b. 1958)	Britain
Priti Paintal	(b. 1960)	Britain

Further Reading

GENERAL BOOKS AND ARTICLES

Ammer, Christine. *Unsung: A History of Women in American Music* (Westport, CT: Greenwood Press, 1980)

Barkin, Elaine. 'either/other', *Perspectives of New Music*, 30 (Summer 1992), pp. 206–33 (*see also* McClary, Susan. 'A Response to Elaine Barkin', *Perspectives of New Music*, pp. 234–8)

Barkin, Elaine. 'Questionnaire', *Perspectives of New Music*, 19 (1980–81)

Barkin, Elaine. 'Response', *Perspectives of New Music*, 20 (1981–2)]

Block, Adrienne Fried and Neuls-Bates, Carol. *Women in American Music: A Bibliography of Music and Literature* (Westport, CT: Greenwood Press, 1979)

Boenke, Heidi M. *Flute Music by Women Composers: An Annotated Catalog* (Westport, CT: Greenwood Press, 1988)

Bowers, Jane. 'Feminist scholarship and the field of musicology', *College Music Symposium*, 29 (1989), pp. 81–92

Bowers, Jane and Tick, Judith (eds.). *Women Making Music: The Western Art Tradition, 1150–1950* (London: Macmillan, 1986)

Brett, Philip; Wood, Elizabeth and Thomas, Gary (eds.). *Queering the Pitch: The New Gay and Lesbian Musicology* (New York and London: Routledge, 1994)

Briscoe, James R. (ed.). *Historical Anthology of Music by Women* (Bloomington, IN: Indiana University Press, 1987)

British Journal of Music Education 10:3 (1993), Papers from the Music, Gender and Education Conference (Bristol University, 1993)

Christiansen, Rupert. *Prima Donna. A History* (London: Bodley Head, 1984)

Citron, Marcia. *Gender and the Music Canon* (Cambridge: Cambridge University Press, 1993)

Clement, Catherine. *Opera, or the Undoing of Women* (transl.) (London: Virago, 1989)

Cohen, Aaron. *International Encyclopedia of Women Composers*, 2 vols., 2nd edn. (New York: Books and Music [USA] Inc., 1987)

Cook, Susan C. and Tsou, Judy S. (eds.). *Cecilia Reclaimed: Feminist Perspectives on Gender and Music* (Urbana and Chicago: University of Illinois Press, 1994)

Elson, Arthur. *Women's Work in Music* (Portland, OR: Longwood Press, 1974, repr. of 1903 edn.)

Erickson, Margaret (ed.). *Women and Music 1987–1992. A Selective Bibliography on the Collective Subject of Women, Gender Issues and Music* (Boston, MA: G.K. Hall, forthcoming)

Feldman, Ann E. 'Being Heard: Women Composers and Patrons at the 1893 World's Columbian Exposition', *Notes*, 47:1 (1990), pp. 7–20

Fuller, Sophie. 'British Women Song Composers – Late Nineteenth Century', *Aspects of British Song: A Miscellany of Essays*, Brian Blyth Daubney (ed.) (Essex: British Music Society, 1992)

Green, Mildred Denby. *Black Women Composers: A Genesis* (Boston, MA: Twayne, 1983)

Groh, Jan Bell. *Evening the Score: Women in Music and the Legacy of Frederique Petrides* (Fayetteville, AR: The University of Arkansas Press, 1991)

Handy, D. Antoinette. *Black Women in American Bands and Orchestras* (Metuchen, NJ: Scarecrow Press, 1981)

Heinrich, Adel. *Organ and Harpsichord Music by Women Composers: An Annotated Catalog* (Westport, CT: Greenwood Press, 1991)

Hernden, Marcia and Ziegler, Susanne (eds.). *Music, Gender and Culture*, International Music Studies 1 (Wilhelmshaven: Florian Noetzel Verlag, 1990)

Hyde, Derek. *New Found Voices. Women in Nineteenth Century English Music* (Cornwall: Belverdere Press, 1984)

Jackson, Barbara Garvey. *A Guide to Extant Music by Women Composers in European and American Libraries and Collections from the 16th Century to c.1830* (Fayetteville, AR: University of Arkansas, forthcoming)

Jezic, Diane. *Women Composers. The Lost Tradition Found* (New York: The Feminist Press, 1988)

Johnson, Rose M. *Violin Music by Women Composers: A Biobibligraphical Guide* (Westport, CT: Greenwood Press, 1989)

Keeling, Richard (ed.). *Women in North American Indian Music: Six Essays* (Bloomington, IN: Society for Ethnomusicology, 1989)

Kent, Greta. *A View From the Bandstand* (London: Sheba Feminist Publishers, 1983)

Koskoff, Ellen, (ed.). *Women and Music in Cross-Cultural Perspective* (Westport, CT: Greenwood Press, 1987)

Koza, Julia Eklund. 'Music and the Feminine Sphere: Images of Women as

Musicians in *Godey's Lady's Book*, 1830–1877', *Musical Quarterly*, 75:2 (Summer 1991), pp. 103–29

LeFanu, Nicola. 'Master Musician: an Impregnable Taboo?' *Contact*, 31 (Autumn 1987), pp. 4–8 (see also responses by Diana Burrell ['Accepting Androgyny'] and Rhian Samuel ['Women Composers Today: A Personal View'] in *Contact* 32 [Spring 1988])

LeFanu, Nicola and Fuller, Sophie (eds.). 'Reclaiming The Muse', women composers issue of *Contemporary Music Review*, 11 (1994)

Lepage, Jane Weiner. *Women Composers, Conductors, and Musicians of the Twentieth Century: Selected Biographies;* vol. 1 (Metuchen, NJ: Scarecrow Press, 1980); vol. 2 (1983); vol. 3 (1988)

Leppert, Richard. *Music and image. Domesticity, ideology and socio-cultural formation in eighteenth-century England* (Cambridge: Cambridge University Press, 1988)

MacAuslan, Janna. *A Catalog of Compositions for Guitar by Women Composers* (Portland, OR: DearHorse Publications, 1984)

Marshall, Kimberly (ed.). *Rediscovering the Muses: Women's Musical Traditions* (Boston, MA: Northeastern University Press, 1993)

Martinez, Odaline de la. *Mendelssohn's Sister* (London: Cape, forthcoming)

McClary, Susan. *Feminine Endings: Music, Gender, and Sexuality* (Minneapolis, MN: University of Minnesota Press, 1991)

McClary, Susan. 'Reshaping a Discipline: Musicology and Feminism in the 1990s', *Feminist Studies,* 19:2 (Summer 1993), pp. 399–423

McClary, Susan. 'Of Patriarchs ... And Matriarchs, Too', *Musical Times* (June 1994), pp. 364–9

Myers, Margaret. *Blowing her own trumpet. European Ladies' Orchestras and other women musicians 1870–1950 in Sweden*, Studies from Göteborg University, Dept. of Musicology, No. 30 (Göteborg: Göteborg University, 1993)

Neuls-Bates, Carol (ed.). *Women in Music: An Anthology of Source Readings from the Middle Ages to the Present* (New York: Harper and Row, 1982)

Pendle, Karin (ed.). *Women and Music: A History* (Bloomington, IN: Indiana University Press, 1991)

Rieger, Eva. '*Dolce semplice*? On the Changing Role of Women in Music' in *Feminist Aesthetics,* ed. Gisela Ecker (transl.) (London: The Women's Press, 1985) pp. 135–49

Sadie, Julie Anne and Samuel, Rhian (eds.). *The New Grove Dictionary of Women Composers* (London: Macmillan, 1994)

Schlegel, Ellen Grolman. *Catalogue of Published Works for String Orchestra and Piano Trio by Twentieth-Century American Women Composers* (Alabama: Colonial Press, 1993)

Scott, Derek B. *The Singing Bourgeois. Songs of the Victorian Drawing Room and Parlour* (Milton Keynes: Open University Press, 1989)

Solie, Ruth (ed.). *Musicology and Difference: Gender and Sexuality in Music Scholarship* (Berkeley and Los Angeles: University of California Press, 1993)

Stewart-Green, Miriam. *Women Composers: A Checklist of Works for the Solo Voice* (Boston, MA: G.K. Hall, 1980)

Tick, Judith. *American Women Composers before 1870* (Ann Arbor, MI: UMI Research Press, 1983)

Toorn, Pieter C. van den. 'Politics, Feminism, and Contemporary Music Theory' *The Journal of Musicology,* 9/3 (Summer 1991) pp. 275–99 (see also Solie, Ruth. 'What do feminists want? A Reply to Pieter van den Toorn', *The Journal of Musicology*, 9/4 [Fall 1991] pp. 399–410)

Walker-Hill, Helen. *Piano Music by Black Women Composers: A Catalog of Solo and Ensemble Works* (Westport, CT: Greenwood Press, 1992)

Whitesitt, Linda. 'The Role of Women Impresarios in American concert life, 1871–1933', *American Music*, 7:2 (Summer 1989), pp. 159–80

Women: A Cultural Review, 3:1 (Summer 1992), women and music issue

Zaimont, Judith Lang; Overhauser, Catherine and Gottlieb, Jane (eds.). *The Musical Woman: An International Perspective 1983* (Westport, CT: Greenwood Press, 1984); vol. 2, *1984–1985* (1987); vol. 3, *1986–1990* (1991)

Zaimont, Judith Lang and Famera, Karen. *Contemporary Concert Music by Women* (Westport, CT: Greenwood Press, 1981)

BOOKS AND ARTICLES ON INDIVIDUAL COMPOSERS

Amy Beach

Block, Adrienne Fried. 'Why Amy Beach Succeeded as a Composer: The Early Years', *Current Musicology*, 36 (Spring 1983), pp. 41–59

Block, Adrienne Fried. 'Dvorak, Beach, and American Music' in *A Celebration of American Music: Words and Music in Honor of H. Wiley Hitchcock*, Crawford, Lot and Oja (eds.) (Ann Arbor, MI: University of Michigan Press, 1990)

Block, Adrienne Fried. 'The Child Is Mother of the Woman: Amy Beach's New England Upbringing' in *Cecilia Reclaimed: Feminist Perspectives on Gender and Music*, Cook and Tsou (eds.) (Urbana and Chicago: University of Illinois Press, 1994)

Tuthill, Burnet C. 'Mrs. H.H.A. Beach', *The Musical Quarterly,* 26 (1940), pp. 297–310

Janet Beat

Pearce, N.J. 'Janet Beat: A Renaissance Woman' in 'Reclaiming the Muse',
Contemporary Music Review, 11 (1994)

Margaret Bonds

Bonds, Margaret. 'A Reminiscence' in *The Negro in Music and Art*, Patterson (ed.)
(New York: Publishers Company, Inc., 1967)

Ina Boyle

Maconchy, Elizabeth. *Ina Boyle: An Appreciation with a Select List of her Music*
(Dublin: Library of Trinity College, Dublin, 1974)

Radie Britain

Bailey, Walter B. and Bailey, Nancy Gisbrecht. *Radie Britain: A Bio-Bibliography*
(Westport, CT: Greenwood Press, 1990)

Claribel

Smith, Phyllis. *The Story of Claribel (Charlotte Alington Barnard)* (Lincoln: J.W.
Ruddock, 1965)

Rebecca Clarke

MacDonald, Calum. 'Rebecca Clarke's Chamber Music', *Tempo*, 160 (March 1986)
pp. 15–26

Ponder, Michael. 'Rebecca Clarke', *British Music Society Journal*, 5 (1983), pp. 82–8

Ruth Crawford

Gaume, Matilda. *Ruth Crawford Seeger: Memoirs, Memories, Music* (Metuchen,
NJ: Scarecrow Press, 1986)

Gaume, Matilda. 'Ruth Crawford: A Promising Young Composer in New York,
1920–30', *American Music*, 5 (1987), pp. 74–84

Jepson, Barbara. 'Ruth Crawford Seeger: A Study in Mixed Accents', *Feminist Art
Journal*, 6:1 (Spring 1977), pp. 13–16

Nelson, Mark. 'In Pursuit of Charles Seeger's Heterophonic Ideal: Three
Palindromic Works by Ruth Crawford', *Musical Quarterly*, 72 (1986), pp. 458–74

Tick, Judith. 'Dissonant Counterpoint Revisited: The First Movement of Ruth
Crawford's *String Quartet 1931*' in *A Celebration of American Music: Words
and Music in Honor of H. Wiley Hitchcock,* Crawford, Lot and Oja (eds.) (Ann
Arbor, MI: University of Michigan Press, 1990)

Tick, Judith. 'Ruth Crawford's "Spiritual Concept": The Sound-Ideals of an Early
American Modernist', *Journal of the American Musicological Society*, 44:2
(Summer 1991), pp. 221–61

Mary Dering

Kerr, Jessica. 'Mary Harvey – The Lady Dering', *Music and Letters*, 25 (1944), pp.
23–33

Lucia Dlugoszewski

Gagne, Cole. 'Lucia Dlugoszewski' in *Soundpieces 2: Interviews with American*

Composers (Metuchen, NJ: Scarecrow Press, 1993), pp. 55–83

Vivian Fine

Riegger, Wallingford. 'The Music of Vivian Fine', *Bulletin of the American Composers Alliance*, 8:1 (1958), pp. 2–6

Vercoe, Elizabeth. 'Interview with Composer Vivian Fine', *International League of Women Composers Journal* (June 1992), pp. 18–23

Jennifer Fowler

Fowler, Jennifer. 'Of Smallpipes and Double Basses' in 'Reclaiming the Muse', *Contemporary Music Review*, 11 (1994)

Erika Fox

Losseff, Nicola. 'The Music Theatre of Erika Fox' in 'Reclaiming the Muse', *Contemporary Music Review*, 11 (1994)

Miriam Gideon

Perle, George. 'The Music of Miriam Gideon', *Bulletin of the American Composers Alliance*, 7:4 (1958), pp. 2–9

Petersen, Barbara A. 'The Vocal Chamber Music of Miriam Gideon' in Zaimont, Overhauser and Gottlieb (eds.) *The Musical Woman: An International Perspective, vol. 2, 1984–1985* (Westport, CT: Greenwood Press, 1987)

Ruth Gipps

Gipps, Ruth. 'A Personal Credo', *Composer,* 54 (Spring 1975), pp. 13–14

Wright, David C.F. 'Ruth Gipps', *British Music Society Journal*, 13 (1991), pp. 3–13

Imogen Holst

Cox, Peter and Dobbs, Jack (eds.). *Imogen Holst at Dartington* (Devon: The Dartington Press, 1988)

Strode, Rosamund. 'Imogen Holst', *Royal College of Music Magazine*, 53:2 (Summer 1984), pp. 69–72

Tinker, Christopher, 'Imogen Holst's Music, 1962–84', *Tempo*, 166 (September 1988), pp. 22–7

Helen Hopekirk

Hall, Constance Huntington and Tetlow, Helen Ingersoll. *Helen Hopekirk 1856–1945* (Cambridge, MA: privately printed, 1954)

Dorothy Howell

Mike, Celia. 'Dorothy Howell 1898–1982', *British Music Society Journal*, 14 (1992), pp. 48–58

Carrie Jacobs-Bond

Jacobs-Bond, Carrie. *The Roads of Melody* (New York and London: D. Appleton, 1927)

Libby Larsen

Green, Cynthia. 'Interview with Composer Libby Larsen', *International League of Women Composers Journal* (June 1992), pp. 24–7

Killam, Rosemary N. 'Calamity Jane: Strength, Uncertainty, and Affirmation',
    Women of Note Quarterly, 1:3 (November 1993), pp. 17–25

Liza Lehmann

Lehmann, Liza. *The Life of Liza Lehmann* (London: T. Fisher Unwin, 1919 repr.
    New York: Da Capo Press, 1980)

Mary Linwood

Whitcomb, Norma. *Mary Linwood* (Leicester: City of Leicester Museums, 1951)

Elisabeth Lutyens

Bradshaw, Susan. 'The Music of Elisabeth Lutyens', *The Musical Times*, 112
    (1971), pp. 653–6

Harries, Meirion and Harries, Susie. *A Pilgrim Soul. The Life and Works of
    Elisabeth Lutyens* (London: Michael Joseph, 1989)

Lutyens, Elisabeth. *A Goldfish Bowl* (London: Cassell and Co., 1972)

Elizabeth Maconchy

Macnaghten, Anne. 'Elizabeth Maconchy', *The Musical Times*, 96 (1955), pp.
    298–302

Maconchy, Elizabeth. 'A Composer Speaks', *Composer*, 42 (1971/2), pp. 25–9

Meredith Monk

Sandow, Gregory. 'Invisible Theater: The Music of Meredith Monk' in Zaimont,
    Overhauser and Gottlieb (eds.) *The Musical Woman: An International
    Perspective 1983* (Westport, CT: Greenwood Press, 1984)

Strickland, Edward. 'Voices/Visions: An Interview with Meredith Monk', *Fanfare*
    (Jan/Feb 1988), reprinted in *American Composers: Dialogues on Contemporary
    Music* (Bloomington, IN: Indiana University Press, 1991, pp. 87–104)

Mary Carr Moore

Smith, Catherine Parsons and Richardson, Cynthia. *Mary Carr Moore, American
    Composer* (Ann Arbor, MI: University of Michigan Press, 1986)

Thea Musgrave

Bradshaw, Susan. 'Thea Musgrave', *The Musical Times*, 104 (1963), pp. 866–8

Burton, Anthony. 'A Dramatist in a Seasonal Landscape', *The Musical Times* (July
    1994), pp. 442–5

East, Leslie. 'The Problem of Communication – Two Solutions: Thea Musgrave and
    Gordon Crosse' in Forman (ed.) *British Music Now* (London: P. Elek, 1975), pp.
    19–31

Hixon, Donald L. *Thea Musgrave: A Bio-Bibliography* (Westport, CT: Greenwood
    Press, 1984)

Routh, Francis. 'Thea Musgrave', *Contemporary British Music* (London, 1972), pp.
    120–24

Caroline Norton

Acland, Alice. *Caroline Norton* (London: Constable, 1948)

Chedzoy, Alan. *A Scandalous Woman: The Story of Caroline Norton* (London: Allison and Busby, 1992)

Perkins, Jane Gray. *The Life of Mrs Norton* (London: John Murray, 1909)

Pauline Oliveros

Gunden, Heidi von. *The Music of Pauline Oliveros* (Metuchen, NJ: Scarecrow Press, 1983)

Gunden, Heidi von. 'The Music of Pauline Oliveros: A Model for Feminist Criticism', *International League of Women Composers Journal* (June 1992), pp. 6–8

Oliveros, Pauline. *Software for People: Collected Writings 1963–80* (Baltimore, MD: Smith Publications, 1984)

Oliveros, Pauline. 'Cues', *The Musical Quarterly* (Autumn 1993), pp. 373–83

Taylor, Timothy D. 'The Gendered Construction of the Musical Self: The Music of Pauline Oliveros', *The Musical Quarterly* (Autumn 1993), pp. 385–396

Daphne Oram

Oram, Daphne. *An Individual Note of Music, Sound and Electronics* (London: Galliard, 1972)

Oram, Daphne. 'Looking Back ... To See Ahead' in 'Reclaiming the Muse', *Contemporary Music Review*, 11 (1994)

Morfydd Owen

Crawshay-Williams, Eliot. 'Morfydd Owen', *Wales*, 4 (1958), pp. 50–56

Davies, Rhian. 'Morfydd Owen', *Journal of the British Music Society*, 13 (1991) 38–57

Davies, Rhian. *Morfydd Owen (1891–1918): A Biography* (Llandysul: Gomer Press, 1994)

Jones, Kitty Idwal. 'The Engima of Morfydd Owen', *Welsh Music*, 5:1 (Winter 1975–6), pp. 8–21

Priti Paintal

Paintal, Priti. 'My Journey Through Music' in 'Reclaiming the Muse', *Contemporary Music Review*, 11 (1994)

Poldowski

Anon. *Minature Essay. Poldowski* (London: Chester, 1924)

Florence Price

Jackson, Barbara Garvey. 'Florence Price, Composer', *The Black Perspective in Music*, 5 (Spring 1977), pp. 30–43

Priaulx Rainier

Baxter, Timothy. 'Priaulx Rainier: A Study of her Musical Style', *Composer*, 60 (Spring 1977), pp. 19–26

Baxter, Timothy. 'Priaulx Rainier', *Composer*, 76–7 (Summer-Winter 1982), pp. 21–9

Opie, June. 'Come and Listen to the Stars Singing'. *Priaulx Rainier: A Pictorial Biography* (Cornwall: Alison Hodge, 1988)

Helen Roe

Fuller, Sophie. 'Music and Text in the Works of Helen Roe' in 'Reclaiming the Muse', *Contemporary Music Review*, 11 (1994)

Clara Kathleen Rogers

Rogers, Clara Kathleen. *Memories of a Musical Career* (Norwood, MA: Plimpton Press 1919)

Rogers, Clara Kathleen. *The Story of Two Lives. Home, Friends, and Travels* (Norwood, MA: Plimpton Press 1932)

Daria Semegen

Hinkle-Turner, Elizabeth. 'The Electronic Music of Daria Semegen', *International League of Women Composers Journal* (December 1991), pp. 1–4

Ethel Smyth

Bernstein, Jane A. '"Shout, Shout, Up with Your Song!" Dame Ethel Smyth and the Changing Role of the British Woman Composer' in Bowers and Tick (eds.) *Women Making Music: The Western Art Tradition, 1150–1950* (London: Macmillan, 1986)

Collis, Louise. *Impetuous Heart: The Story of Ethel Smyth* (London: William Kimber, 1984)

Crichton, Ronald (ed.). *The Memoirs of Ethel Smyth* (Harmondsworth and New York: Viking/Penguin, 1987)

Dale, Kathleen. 'Ethel Smyth's Prentice Work', *Music and Letters*, 30 (October 1949), pp. 329–36

Smyth, Ethel. *Impressions That Remained* (2 vols.) (London: Longmans, Green, and Co., 1919)

Smyth, Ethel. *Streaks of Life* (London: Longmans, Green, and Co., 1921)

Smyth, Ethel. *A Three-Legged Tour in Greece* (London: Heinemann, 1927)

Smyth, Ethel. *A Final Burning of Boats Etc.* (London: Longmans, Green, and Co., 1928)

Smyth, Ethel. *Female Pipings in Eden* (Edinburgh: Peter Davies, 1933)

Smyth, Ethel. *Beecham and Pharoah* (London: Chapman and Hall, 1935)

Smyth, Ethel. *As Time Went On ...* (London: Longmans, Green, and Co., 1936)

Smyth, Ethel. *Inordinate (?) Affection* (London: The Cresset Press, 1936)

Smyth, Ethel. *Maurice Baring* (London: Heinemann, 1938)

St. John, Christopher. *Ethel Smyth. A Biography* (London: Longmans, Green and Co., 1959)

Wood, Elizabeth. 'Gender and Genre in Ethel Smyth's Operas' in Zaimont, Overhauser and Gottlieb (eds.) *The Musical Woman: An International Perspective, vol. 2, 1984–1985* (Westport, CT: Greenwood Press, 1987)

Wood, Elizabeth. 'Lesbian Fugue: Ethel Smyth's Contrapuntal Arts' in Ruth Solie (ed.) *Musicology and Difference: Gender and Sexuality in Music Scholarship* (Berkeley and Los Angeles: University of California Press, 1993)

Wood, Elizabeth. 'Sapphonics' in *Queering the Pitch: The New Gay and Lesbian Musicology*, Brett, Wood and Thomas (eds.) (New York and London: Routledge, 1994)

Louise Talma

Barkin, Ellen. 'Louise Talma: The Tolling Bell', *Perspectives of New Music*, 10:2 (Spring/Summer 1972)

Teicher, Susan. 'Louise Talma: Essentials of Her Style As Seen Through the Piano Works' in Zaimont, Overhauser and Gottlieb (eds.) *The Musical Woman: An International Perspective 1983* (Westport, CT: Greenwood Press, 1984)

Hilary Tann

Presslaff, Hilary Tann. 'The Investigation', *Perspectives of New Music,* 20 (1981–2), pp. 525–59

Phyllis Tate

Carner, Mosco. 'The Music of Phyllis Tate', *Music and Letters*, 35 (1954), pp. 128–133

Carner, Mosco. 'Phyllis Tate', *The Musical Times*, 105 (1964), pp. 20–21

Kay, Norman. 'Phyllis Tate', *The Musical Times*, 116 (1975), pp. 429–30

Searle, Humphrey. 'Phyllis Tate', *The Musical Times*, 96 (1955), p. 244

Julia Usher

Usher, Julia. 'Quasi Una Voce Umana' in 'Reclaiming the Muse', *Contemporary Music Review*, 11 (1994)

Errollyn Wallen

Wallen, Errollyn. 'Slave to the Rhythm' in 'Reclaiming the Muse', *Contemporary Music Review*, 11 (1994)

Elinor Remick Warren

Bortin, Virginia. *Elinor Remick Warren: Her Life and Her Music* (Metuchen, NJ: Scarecrow Press, 1987)

Judith Weir

Dreyer, Martin. 'Judith Weir, Composer: A Talent to Amuse', *The Musical Times*, 122 (1981), pp. 593–96

Morgan, Tom. 'Judith Weir' in Wright, Finnissy and Hayes (eds.) *New Music 88* (Oxford: Oxford University Press, 1988)

Wright, David. 'Weir to Now?', *The Musical Times* (1993), pp. 432–7

Maude Valérie White

White, Maude Valérie. *Friends and Memories* (London: Edward Arnold, 1914)

White, Maude Valérie. *My Indian Summer* (London: Grayson & Grayson, 1932)

Margaret Lucy Wilkins

Smith, Geoffrey and Walker Smith, Nicola. 'Sonic Architecture in the Music of Margaret Lucy Wilkins' in 'Reclaiming the Muse', *Contemporary Music Review*, 11 (1994)

Grace Williams

Boyd, Malcolm. *Grace Williams* (University of Wales Press, 1980)

Leighton Thomas, A.F. 'Grace Williams', *The Musical Times*, 97 (1956), pp. 240–43

Various. 'Grace Williams: A Symposium', *Welsh Music*, 5:6 & 7 (1977)

Whittall, Arnold. 'Grace Williams 1906–1977', *Soundings*, 7 (1978)

Ellen Taaffe Zwilich

Duncan, Scott. 'Ellen Taaffe Zwilich: Emerging from the Mythos' in Zaimont, Overhauser and Gottlieb (eds.) *The Musical Woman: An International Perspective, vol. 3, 1986–1990* (Westport, CT: Greenwood Press, 1991)

Organizations and Resource Centres

BRITAIN AND IRELAND

The music information centres of Britain, Ireland, Scotland and Wales hold scores and recordings of music by 20th-century composers and can provide further information about those composers. Many of their materials are unavailable elsewhere.

British Music Information Centre
10 Stratford Place
London W1
tel. (0171) 499 8567

Contemporary Music Centre
95 Lower Baggot Street
Dublin 2
tel. (01) 661 2105

Scottish Music Information Centre
1 Bowmont Gardens
Glasgow G12 9LR
tel. (0141) 334 6393

Welsh Music Information Centre
Music Department
University College
Corbett Road
Cardiff CF1 1XL
tel. (01222) 874000 (ext. 5126)

Women in Music
Battersea Arts Centre
Lavender Hill
London SW11 5TF
tel. (0171) 978 4823; fax (0171) 978 7770
Women in Music was founded in 1987 and aims to celebrate and raise public awareness of women's work in all types of music, from rock and pop to classical and jazz. This national organization has established a resource project which can supply a wide range of information about women composers and details of access to material such as scores and recordings.

UNITED STATES

American Music Center

30 West 26th Street
Suite 1001
New York
NY 10010–2011
tel. (212) 366 5263; fax (212) 366 5265
The American Music Center was
founded in 1939 and aims 'to promote
the creation, performance and appreciation of contemporary American
music'. The Center holds scores and
recordings of music by contemporary
American composers. Approximately
20 per cent of their holdings are by
women composers.

American Women Composers, Inc.

1690 36th Street, NW
Suite 410
Washington, DC 20007
tel. (202) 342 8179
American Women Composers was
founded in 1976. The organization has
an archive, which also functions as a
rental library, of over 3,000 scores of
music by women composers as well as
recordings and information on the
composers. There are also regional
groups such as American Women
Composers, Midwest and American
Women Composers of Massachusetts,
Inc.

The Center for Women in Music

New York University
35 West 26th Street
Suite 1001
New York

NY 10010–2011
tel. (212) 998 5776; fax. (212) 995 4043
This newly opened centre is gathering
information of use 'to all who seek to
support the efforts of women in music
to attain the highest possible professional goals'.

International Institute for the Study of Women in Music

California State University
Northridge
CA 91330
This organization is affiliated to the
International League of Women
Composers (see below). It holds the
extensive collection of books and
recordings gathered by Aaron I. Cohen,
editor of the *International
Encyclopedia of Women Composers*, as
well as many scores and tapes of music
by women composers.

The International League of Women Composers

Abilene Christian University
ACU Box 8274
Abilene
TX 79699
tel. (915) 644 2044
The ILWC was founded in 1975. It is 'a
professional organization devoted to
creating and expanding opportunities
for, and documenting information
about, women composers of serious
music'. In 1990 the ILWC merged with
the International Congress on Women
in Music, an organization founded in
1979 to hold regular conferences and
festivals which are now projects of the

ILWC. The *ILWC Journal* (Coordinating Editor: Sally Reid) is published three times a year.

New York Women Composers
114 Kelburne Ave.
North Tarrytown
NY 10591
tel. (914) 631 4361
Among other activities this organiza-tion publishes a catalogue of members' compositions.

National Women Composers
Resource Center
330 Townsend Street
Suite 318
San Francisco

CA 94107
tel. (415) 543 2297; fax (415) 543 3244
This resource centre has been created by The Women's Philharmonic 'so that today's audiences and future genera-tions will be able to hear works by women composers in any concert hall throughout the country'.

Women's Music Collection
Music Library
University of Michigan
Ann Arbor
MI 48109
This collection consists largely of music by European women composers from the 19th and early 20th centuries with some letters and diaries.

RECORDINGS OF MUSIC BY WOMEN COMPOSERS

Recordings of music by women are being issued (and deleted!) with great frequency. Many of the above organi-zations and resource centres will be able to help with enquiries about what is currently available. Several libraries in both Britain and the United States have invaluable recorded sound archives. Other useful sources for recordings include the following.

Leonarda
PO Box 1736
New York
NY 10025
USA
A record company that specializes in music by women composers, past and present.

Ladyslipper
PO Box 3124
Durham
NC 27715–3124
USA
tel. (919) 683 1570; fax (919) 682 5601
Mail-order distributor with the world's most comprehensive catalogue of CDs, tapes, records and videos of women's music.

WRPM
62 Woodstock Road
Birmingham
B13 9BN
UK
tel. (0121) 449 7041
Mail-order distributor of a wide range of women's music.

Picture Acknowledgements

Eleanor Alberga – photo: Coneyl Jay (p. 34)

Ethel Barns – photo: Lena Connell (p. 45) courtesy of the Royal College of Music

Ann Mounsey Bartholomew – photo: T. Coleman (p. 52) courtesy of the Royal College of Music

Amy Beach – (p. 58) courtesy of the Royal College of Music

Diana Burrell – photo: Eric Richmond (p. 81)

Ruth Crawford – photo: John Henderson (p. 94)

Lucia Dlugoszewski – photo: Peter Kaplan (p.108)

Rosalind Ellicott – photo: Barraud (p. 113) courtesy of the Royal College of Music

Erika Fox – photo: Tim Fox (p. 126)

Imogen Holst – photo: Nigel Luckhurst (p. 149)

Libby Larsen – photo: Ann Marsden (p. 175)

Liza Lehmann – photo: W. & D. Downey (p. 184)

Elizabeth Maconchy and Nicola LeFanu – photo: Malcolm Crowthers (p. 200)

Meredith Monk – photo: Dona Ann McAdams (p. 212)

Pauline Oliveros – photo: Gisela Gamper (p. 228)

Priti Paintal – photo: Judith Hurst (p. 240)

Ethel Smyth – photo: Olive Edis (p. 292)

Errollyn Wallen – photo: Sonia MacAngus (p. 321)

Maude Valérie White – photo: Barraud (p. 333) courtesy of the Royal College of Music